"And Other Neighborly Names"

The Dan Danciger Publication Series

"And Other Neighborly Names"

Social Process and Cultural Image in Texas Folklore

Edited by
Richard Bauman and Roger D. Abrahams

University of Texas Press, Austin and London

Library of Congress Cataloging in Publication Data

Main entry under title:
"And Other Neighborly Names."
Includes bibliographies.
1. Folk-lore—Texas. I. Bauman, Richard. II. Abrahams, Roger D.
GR110.T5A52   398'.09764   80-23697
ISBN 0-292-70352-X

Requests for permission to reproduce material from this work should be
sent to Permissions, University of Texas Press, Box 7819, Austin, Texas
78712.

For Don Américo,
honored teacher, colleague, and friend
"Es un hombre muy valiente"

Contents

Acknowledgments

We would like to thank Mrs. Amelia Paredes for her gracious co-operation in the planning of this collection and Mrs. Frances Terry for her great skill and patience in the typing and preparation of the manuscript. The University of Illinois Press has granted permission for the reprinting of the *corrido* tunes on page 66, from *A Texas-Mexican Cancionero*, by Américo Paredes (Urbana: University of Illinois Press, 1976).

Part I

Introduction

Roger D. Abrahams and Richard Bauman

Doing Folklore Texas-Style

When those of us who have lived and worked in Texas encounter
each other at national meetings, we often find ourselves discussing the special quality of that experience. At one recent meeting
of the American Folklore Society, the informal discussion became
sufficiently pointed and lively that a number of us decided to try
to get a handle on just what "doing folklore Texas-style" means. It
comes not only from living and working in the state, or from having a Texian subject matter (for that is handled very well, annually, in the Publications of the Texas Folklore Society); it comes,
rather, from the special perspective one gets by working in the
humanistic and socially engaged tradition of the Lomaxes, Boatright, Dobie, Brewer, and Paredes. The more we discussed the
matter, the more we individually recalled how these scholars had
affected us personally—not only through their work but also, in
the case of Mody Boatright and especially of Américo Paredes,
through their personal vision and diplomatic prodding. Their
way of looking at living traditions and their talent for sorting out
the important from the merely interesting have enriched us all.
And it is through Paredes that this point of view has been transmitted to the younger members of the corps, for a number of
those represented in this collection entered the profession after
Boatright retired. This book is an unashamed tribute to our pro-
genitors, colleagues, and teachers.

But it is not just a tribute. It is an illustration of a method of
attack, of a critical perspective that insists that, on the one hand,
folklore must be observed in its living place and, on the other, in
terms of its social and even political ramifications. In the first

concern, collecting lore *in situ* and *in vivo*, we Tejanos share much with other schools of thought, especially those represented in the program at the University of Pennsylvania. But in our concern to discover where folklore study and social action come together, with how traditions reveal the points of tension within and between groups and the inequities that arise in any stratified society, we diverge considerably from our brethren. In part, this volume attempts to underscore and document that difference, with a series of essays based on original, largely field-oriented research.

Perhaps folklore is done in a special way in Texas because Texas folklorists have had a special sense of who "the folk" are, and in what relationship the folklorist and the members of the folk stand. The work of people like John Lomax and his children Alan and Bess, of Dorothy Scarborough, J. Frank Dobie, J. Mason Brewer, Mody Boatright, and Américo Paredes, is marked by a deep personal sense of real life that goes through and beyond the nostalgia that tends, in most places, to overwhelm the study of local folklore. In their writings, rooted in their own sense and experience of family, community, and region, we see real people celebrating their own lives and those of their neighbors, even when those lives are hard ones. There is a texture and dimensionality to these scholars' work that grows out of knowing where they came from, if also from knowing where they want to go. In the annals of American folkloristics, they rank among the true pathbreakers, for it was chiefly they who, by their example, helped to show academic folklorists how to get out of the library and out among the singers and storytellers, the cotton choppers and cowboys, the ranchers and roughnecks. Long before there were public movements to foster ethnic pride, these Texas folklorists were exploring how to be both a responsible member of a traditional community and a student of its history and culture. Certainly, each of them had to get some perspective on home and community by going away to school, and by writing about them from the distance of the academy. But this meant, too, that their own folks came to see them as spokespeople to the outside world. They were honored in their own times by their neighbors and friends, even though their "cultural advocacy" often put them in the way of powerful others who had different, more "progressive" ideas.

Another characteristic that sets these Texas folklorists apart from the mainstream of American folklore study (although not from the work of such figures as Zora Neale Hurston and Vance Randolph) is that they have seen themselves not only as scholar-collectors of the lore of their own people or region, or as authors in the purely academic sphere, but as writers for a readership that went far beyond the academy. The books of J. Frank Dobie fit most fully into this popular (as well as populist) tradition, but the work of Lomax and Boatright is also marked by a sure and plain style, short on the adjectives and strong on the active verbs. Just as the major works of the Lomaxes have aimed at the larger audience fascinated by the many voices of America, so Boat-right's vigorous studies of folk humor, tall tales, and the entire range of oil-field and ranching lore have found a wide readership in Texas and elsewhere. And, like Dorothy Scarborough, and William Owens after her, Américo Paredes began as a writer of fiction and poetry (as well as a newspaper reporter). His folklore studies read also like historical adventure (*With His Pistol in His Hand*) or like a sensitive autobiographical homage to his patrimony (*A Texas-Mexican Cancionero*).

When you know your group as an insider, you will also have a clear sense of who the outsiders are. The study of folklore alters its direction considerably when the existence of forces and people outside the group is taken into account. Until relatively recently, folklore was studied as the traditional expressive or material culture of a static, even backwater, community—but this kind of enclave has not existed for some time in the heterogeneous and ever-changing cultural environment of Texas. Perhaps the experience of living on the frontier or the border—cultural and social boundaries that separate "us" from "them" yet mark where we come together—made Texas folklorists more aware than others of how folklore forms can emerge from contact communities and differential identities. Mody Boatright, with his penetrating understanding that frontier humor basically turned Eastern stereotypes of the wild frontier back, in even more exaggerated form, on credulous outsiders, first pointed the way toward transcending strictly within-group conceptions of the province of folklore. In Américo Paredes' work recognition of the generative power of borders and other contact zones assumes really central importance in his lifelong concern with Texas Mexican border ballad ry, with the humor of intercultural contact (a humor that often masks outrage, conflict, and pain), and with the dynamics of cultural stereotypes. In the title of this collection, which is borrowed from his study of the "neighborly names" that are exchanged across the Texas-Mexican cultural boundary, we acknowledge the debt we owe to his seminal work.

It is also from Paredes' work, and from his basic vision of what folklore study might be, that what has come to be known as the Texas brand of "performance-oriented folkloristics" first emerged. This perspective calls attention to the interactional setting of display behavior and to the situated meaning of performance forms. Given the socially engaged position basic to the Texas folklorists, it follows that the reportings of the lore should exhibit a concern with the ways traditions operate within communities, with the settings in which they find expression. Not only are the texts of the songs and stories significant, but also who performs them to whom and for what purposes, and what attitudes and approaches to life, and what cultural universe of meanings, they reflect. Even more than this, Paredes' socially engaged ideology projects the hope that a book of folklore can, through the faithful reporting and interpretation of text and context, lore and life, illuminate, dignify, and even improve the existence of those among whom the folklorist lives and learns. Paredes' much deserved position as the doyen (*don* might be more appropriate) of Chicano studies testifies to the validity of such a program, of the celebration of folk traditions as a means of proclaiming both the dignity of a folk-based counterstatement and the viability and—more important—the continuing creative vitality of folk culture.

The new folklore perspectives spawned in this Texas environment, then, have focused on three dimensions of lore which had been ignored for the most part in traditional field collections: the dialectic of forces (historical, social, and cultural) in the content of the lore; the importance of the community's recurrent situations of performance, play, festivity, and ritual as dramatizations of these forces; and the place of the creative performer in the enactment of these situations. This is the path of development illustrated in the essays collected here—essays on Texas folklore by Texas folklorists (by birth, adoption, or training), all of them recently associated with the University of Texas folklore program. The three dimensions become part of the apparatus of analysis: the performer and his or her place within society and in the performing context; interaction and how it draws on both the traditions of the group and the talents of individuals; and the articulation of real social questions and recurring problems within the context of the items and their performance. It is no coincidence, therefore, that these essays are by colleagues and students of Américo Paredes. We all consider ourselves the heirs of the long and honorable lineage of Texas folklorists, but Américo Paredes is the one who made us what we are. It is in his honor that this book was assembled, and to him it is dedicated, with much respect and affection.

Part II

The Structure and Context of Expressive Forms

Joe Graham

The *Caso*:
An Emic Genre of Folk Narrative

The recent exchange of insights between folkloristics and the ethnography of communication has raised our awareness of a need, in some contexts, to increase the sensitivity of our analytic procedures to the values, attitudes, and creative concerns of the folk groups themselves. The struggle has been to allow the tradition-bearers to define themselves how they organize their expressive lives, and thus how their belief and value systems are embodied and transmitted. In attempting to obtain a more clear-sighted view of specific folk groups, we may find it especially useful to look at the native (or "emic") categories for both composition and belief. Such a procedure is perhaps less important for folklorists who are dealing with matters and materials widely observable in many cultures, such as ballads and *Märchen*. But the closer we get to those stories and explanations that emerge in more casual, everyday talking, the more we need to collect native commentary as well as the texts themselves.

SYSTEMS OF CLASSIFICATION

Classification systems, even the best, are man-made. The best classification system is good only insofar as its elaborations enable the classifiers to give importance or value to those things they consider important. One of the strongest arguments for studying any native system of classification is the insight it provides into what its users consider the most important characteristics of a given domain. In a broader sense, studying native classification systems provides insight into the importance of the alternative, "ground-level" ways of ordering and giving meaning and value to life. This is especially true of folk categories of expressive culture, for in them we can find some of the clearest expressions of the ways in which a group imposes order and value on day-to-day life.

The alternative method of organizing stories has been to impose upon them categories derived from a cross-cultural system of analysis. Such analytic categories of folk narrative have proven valuable in comparative studies and in index preparation; but, if one is concerned with the form, content, and function of folk narratives within a specific cultural context, such cross-cultural categories may prove more confusing than enlightening—as Gossen (1972:145) found among the Chamula. Hence, although the widely accepted "etic" genres of folk narrative—myth, folktale, legend, joke, and memorate—may provide a meaningful way to approach the folk narratives of some groups, they might be like a Procrustean bed for others. The narratives told by Mexican-Americans do not fit neatly into these Western-derived cross-cultural categories.

Obviously, however, large-scale and comparative studies of culture make overarching transcultural categories necessary, and for some types of analysis such etic terminology works fairly well. In his development of an index of Mexican legendry, for example, Robe (1977) has discussed how the terms "*caso*" and "*leyenda*" articulate with other European terms for personal narrative.

The object of the present study is to contrast past uses of the term "*caso*" with the way in which it seems to be used within storytelling traditions in Texas. To fill in the record, I will also briefly examine the *caso*'s form, content, and function, as well as the social contexts in which it has been observed in use.

HISTORY OF THE TERM "*CASO*"

Latin-American folklorists have generally accepted the term "*caso*" as descriptive of a type of folk narrative, without placing it in any native narrative or expressive context. Most of the scholars in the United States who are working with Hispanic materials have preferred the European-manufactured term "memorate."[1] Those who have attempted to define the *caso* have encountered the same types of problems which their colleagues have had in defining the memorate and, more recently, the "personal narrative" or "personal experience narrative." The need for these newer terms arose when folklorists discovered a body of narrative which they found interesting, yet which did not fall into the neat, already established categories of folk prose. In attempting to find order and continuity within the stories and their telling, these folklorists selected or coined names for them—etic terms in the case of "memorate" and "personal narrative"—and then imposed arbitrary definitions which, although they seemingly derived from the data, nevertheless lacked the insights of the folk who tell the stories. Consequently, definers of the *caso* have given us neither a purely native category of folk prose nor a purely artificial term, but rather a mixture of the two.

The term *"caso"* was first adopted by literary scholars and artists who were interested in indigenous folklore—e.g., Samuel Blixen (1909), Juan Carlos Dávalos (1925), and Bernardo Canal Feijóo (1940). They left the word undefined, and it never became widely accepted among literary scholars.[2] The term was later picked up by folklorists who were influenced by these earlier works. What made the word particularly attractive to folklorists was the fact that it was a term known and used by the folk.

One of the earliest attempts at differentiating the *caso* from other types of folk narrative appeared in an article published in Buenos Aires in 1948 (Carrizo, Carrizo, and Jacovella 1948), in which Bruno Jacovella distinguishes *casos supersticiosos* (*casos* of superstition) from *cuentos animistas* (tales of animism) and *cuentos de espanto* (tales of terror).[3] The primary difference, he claims, is that the *caso* is purely local, while the *cuento animista o de espanto* is more universal. While this point may be justified by his data, it is clearly a non-native, etic distinction which would not mean much to the folk who hear and tell these stories.

Susana Chertudi's definition of the *caso* (1958, 1959) is an interesting combination of etic and emic employments, and reveals three forces at work: folklore scholarship in Europe and the United States, earlier Latin-American literary works, and folk usage.[4] The first influence is evident in her reliance on the temporal, spatial, and belief parameters commonly used to distinguish among folktales, legends, and myths: the *caso* is a story, set in the present or immediate past, of a notable event which has happened to a person living in the area where the story is told, and which is believed to be true (Chertudi 1958:123,

1959:132). The *leyenda* tells of an incident which happened only once in a remote time; the *caso* tells of experiences which are repeated—encounters with witches, *duendes*, wolfmen, etc. (Chertudi 1959:150–151).

Chertudi's classification system breaks down when she attempts to incorporate the literary and folk uses[5] of the term. To accommodate the literary use she writes:

Bajo el nombre de casos se relatan tambien cuentos, principalmente chistes de los ciclos de pícaros, tontos o mentirosos; el protagonista es, entonces, alguna persona del lugar. [Under the name *casos* are also told stories, principally cycles of jokes about *pícaros*, stupid ones, or liars; the protagonist is, though, some person from the locale] (ibid.:154).[6]

She does not successfully distinguish this type of *caso* from what she calls *chistes* or *historietas*, a subcategory of *cuentos humanos*, which are "generally short, with humorous endings. . . . These jokes tend to form cycles around a certain person or about notorious habits or defects (*cuentos* of deaf persons, or liars, or *pícaros*, etc.)" (ibid.:134).

The classification system also fails to distinguish clearly between the *caso* and the *tradición*, two apparently native categories. Both are fabulous, and both are believed by teller and hearer; but the people and happenings are truly historic only in the *tradición*. Yet if both are believed to be true, from the emic point of view actual historicity is not a characteristic which differentiates between the two genres. Indeed, the examples of *casos* Chertudi offers seem to fit her definition of *tradiciones* better than her definition of *casos*. Again, much of this confusion can be traced to a lack of differentiation between emic and etic systems.

Paulo de Carvalho-Neto has also worked with the concept of the *caso*, and has noted particularly the great abundance of *casos* in Paraguayan folklore. In *Folklore del Paraguay* (1961:ch. 9) and "Folklore Amazónico" (1963) he simply classifies the *caso* into four groups, without offering a definition of the genre: *casos mitologicos, casos religiosos, casos animisticos*, and *casos mágicos*. But it was not until the publication of his *Historia del Folklore Iberoamericano* (1969a) that he clearly stated a definition of the *caso* and attempted to distinguish it from other narrative types. His approach, too, is clearly etic; for example, in recognizing the similarities of the *caso* and the *leyenda*, he observes that both are classified into the same types—historical, mythological, magical, animistic, and religious (1969a:50–51). But it was he himself who originally proposed these classification systems. The difference between the *caso* and the *leyenda*, he continues, is that the former directly mentions some person, and tells of something that happened to a well-known individual in a given place. He further notes:

In *casos*, then, there is the personal testimony of the narrator because he heard it spoken of or because it happened to him. It is the narration of 'an experience' which he or an acquaintance had (Carvalho-Neto 1969b:64).

Whether Carvalho-Neto derived this defining characteristic from his data or from some other source is unclear, but of the three examples of the *caso* which he offers (1969a), two do not include any "personal experience" or "personal testimony"; and although in one of these two the protagonist is named, there is no indication that he is or was a real person, known to the narrator. The third example is very generalized—the protagonist does not even have a name. It should be noted, though, that most of Carvalho-Neto's sources were literary works rather than collections directly from oral tradition.

Of the many scholars in the United States who have studied and written about Mexican and Mexican-American folk narrative, only Américo Paredes (1968) has made any attempt to define the *caso*. Having grown up in the Mexican-American culture of South Texas, he has essentially an emic perception of the genre, in spite of his scholarly training. His definition and discussion of the form and function of the *caso* were not meant as a thorough study of the genre, but to give perspective to his discussion of a type of joke (a parody of the *caso*) he was examining. The *caso* is, he writes, "a relatively short narrative about miraculous or extraordinary events supposed to have happened to the narrator or to someone he knows" (ibid.:106). While this definition is not complete, it contains two of the elements of the emic definition I shall explore below.

EMIC CATEGORIES OF NARRATIVE AND THE EMIC DEFINITION OF THE *CASO*

Since 1972 I have been doing fieldwork among Mexican-Americans in West Texas. My focus has been primarily on folk medicine and related folk beliefs, as well as on narratives about these beliefs. It became apparent to me that the standard definitions of narrative genres—myth, legend, folktale, memorate, etc.—did not map effectively onto the texts I was encountering. The most common terms used for folk narratives among my informants are *cuento*, *historia*, *leyenda*, *chiste*, and *caso*. I used two techniques to elicit information about these narrative forms: asking for definitions and examples and asking informants to examine and classify printed texts of different narrative types, giving the reasons for their classifications. Although agreement was not complete about all of the genres, there was a very high degree of consistency in my informants' conception of the *caso*. This was true not only in West Texas, but also among informants in South and Central Texas.

Literally translated, "*caso*" means, among other things, "case," "instance," "event," "happening," "occurrence." No dictionary, literary or otherwise, defines "*caso*" as a narrative, yet my informants consistently referred to it as such. It is, with the possible exception of the *chiste* (joke) in some groups, the most common name for folk narrative among my informants. Wherever there is belief, there are *casos*; and the ubiquity of the genre may account for its wide recognition and fairly consistent definition.

In its normal context "*caso*" refers to an experience, incident, or happening (*sucedido*) which has occurred in the recent past. The term "case in point" is an approximate English-language equivalent, although one of far more limited usage. The *caso* and the "case in point" present interesting problems for folklorists, both in their definition and in their collection. For example, when a collector asks an informant, "Do you know any folktales or legends or jokes?" the informant will probably think of these as discrete entities which exist in the same way songs, poems, or books exist. On the other hand, if the collector asks, "Do you know any *casos* or 'cases in point'?" he will probably get a dumbfounded look in response.[7] The informant does not usually dissociate the verbal icon of an experience from the experience itself, particularly if he participated in or observed the experience. Rather than "telling a story" he "relates an experience," and he does so in a social situation where the *caso* or case in point is useful as an illustration of some topic under discussion—not in a yarn-spinning (or *caso*-telling) session or a story-collecting interview.[8] However, when given the text of a *caso* and asked to classify it (e.g., "Is this a *leyenda*, a *cuento*, a *chiste*, an *historia*, or a *caso*?")

he will neither hesitate nor be confused, but recognize it as a *caso*.

Emically, the *caso* is a relatively brief prose narrative, focusing upon a single event, supernatural or natural, in which the protagonist or observer is the narrator or someone the narrator knows and vouches for, and which is normally used as evidence or as an example to illustrate that "this kind of thing happens." Almost without exception, my informants would accept this definition—they gave it to me, if not in these exact words. It is beyond the scope of this paper to attempt an exhaustive emic typology of the folk narratives of West Texas Mexican-Americans, but a brief discussion of the other important emic genres will be necessary here to facilitate comparison later.

"*Cuento*" is a broad category which includes all of the other folk narrative types, including the *caso*. My informants use this term in much the way English speakers use the term "story." A *cuento* can be long or short, true or fictitious. "La Caperucita Roja" ("Little Red Riding Hood") is a *cuento* (when pressed to differentiate, some might refer to it as a "*cuento viejo*" or "*cuentito*"). However, most informants did not think first of *Märchen* or folktales when asked to define "*cuento*" or "*cuento popular*," and did not mention them until specifically asked—a clear indication of the very minor role this narrative type plays in this culture at present. *Leyendas*, too, can be *cuentos*, if they constitute a narrative rather than merely a fragment.

In its broadest, most all-inclusive sense, "*cuento*" has no negative connotation. However, in a narrower sense, to call a story a *cuento* implies that it is thought to be untrue, or at least that there is some question as to its reliability. This *cuento* can be thought of as a subcategory of the broader *cuento*.[9] A *caso*, when it is elaborated upon with seemingly excessive detail, and when the plot structure seems more important than the truthfulness of the story, may be referred to as a "*cuento*" by the hearer to indicate that it may or may not be true. Importantly, stories which are structurally almost identical to the *caso* and which may be used in the same way, but which have happened to persons not known to the narrator, are called "*cuentos*."

The *chiste* is a humorous story, true or false, of any length. The humor may be scatalogical, light, biting, or "sick." My informants mentioned several categories of the *chiste* which are not relevant to this discussion. A *caso* which is humorous may be called a "*chiste*," or a "*caso chistoso*" (humorous *caso*), depending on when and how it is employed. If it is used to illustrate that "this kind of thing happens," it would be considered a *caso*.

While the standard transcultural definition of "legend" includes the element "believed to be true," my informants were almost unanimous in saying that the *leyenda*, while it *may* be based on some historical incident, is not necessarily so. The tendency is to believe that *leyendas*, even when based on actual incidents involving real people, have been exaggerated to the point of being untrustworthy: *"parte es verdad y parte es mentira"* [part is truth and part is a lie]. *Leyendas* may also be fragmentary. As one informant explained:

A *leyenda* can just simply be recalling—a remembrance of something that has happened, sometimes significant, but you don't follow through and tell the entire story, you just—in other words, you're just recalling something specific that has made that person recognizable.

The *leyenda* is most often thought to be about a person or event of the past, usually important to the people, if not in history.

The *historia*[10] is more elaborate than the *caso*, in that it refers to more than one event. Like the *caso*, it is accepted by the narrator and listener as true. The *historia* is more likely to focus on mundane rather than supernatural events, although it may deal with either or both. Several of my informants pointed out that two or more *casos*, tied into a chronological narrative structure, could become an *historia*. But the *historia* is not normally used in the same way as a *caso*—although it usually constitutes the remembering and recounting of some experience of the past, it does so with no intention of illustrating, that "this sort of thing happens." As the name implies, the *historia* is a bit of history. "Reminiscences" or "anecdotes," as defined by Bascom (1964), might be a good English-language equivalent. Certain of the prose narratives ("true tales") which Sandra Stahl (1977) discusses might also fit into this category.

One informant gave the following example in distinguishing between *un caso* and *una historia*. A woman in his hometown had been running around on her husband. They had many arguments over a period of time, until finally the man killed his wife, shooting her several times outside their house, with a number of people watching. My informant went on to explain that if he were to tell the whole story, it would be *una historia*, *"la historia de la güera Fulana"* [the *historia* of the fair-skinned Joan Doe]. On the other hand, several *casos* might be told about different elements of the event, to illustrate any number of beliefs: If you fool around on your husband you could get shot, like *la güera* Fulana; God punishes sin, as in the case of *la güera* Fulana; men have the right to punish unfaithful wives; a good wife and mother is faithful to the family; etc. The whole history of the affair would not be given in the *caso*, only that part which would illustrate the point in question. If the narrative was related as *una historia*, it would probably be told in all of its detail, including not only the shooting and the action leading up to it but also what happened at the trial, and perhaps even what became of the children. The *historia* would probably be told as a reminiscence during a gossip session, where different parts might be told by different participants, each adding further details to the narrative. With the *caso*, the point of the story and the conclusion of the story come together. The *historia* may make several points, there might be different interpretations as to the "meaning" of the described episode, and different narrators or commentators could use it to make different points. The *caso*, on the other hand, is not subject to variant readings because the story, its meaning, and its point, are "in place" within a brief, fixed form.

Let us now examine the different elements of the emic definition of the *caso* given above. To repeat, a *caso* is: a relatively brief prose narrative, focusing upon a single event, supernatural or natural, in which the protagonist or observer is the narrator or someone the narrator knows and vouches for, and which is normally used as evidence or as an example to illustrate that "this kind of thing happens." Importantly, the *caso* can assign meaning and value to the happening either explicitly or by its emplacement within a discussion. It uses past experiences to shed light on the present, and thus can comment in a very personal way on some situation while at the same time giving value to experience as a means of gaining knowledge. To mark, label, or otherwise identify a narrative as a *caso* is to make a statement about its reliability and, therefore, about its value as useful information.

(1) "A relatively brief prose narrative, focusing upon a single event"

Labov and Waletzky (1967), in their analysis of personal experience narratives, find that the most complete narrative types as told by the best narrators consist of an orientation, a complication, an evaluation, a resolution, and a closing. They further claim that the simplest possible narrative consists of a complication without a clear resolution, and that frequently narratives are minimal, having only a complication and a resolution (ibid.:41). Regardless of its length, the personal experience narrative always focuses upon a single event or episode. *Casos* about healing range from the minimal narrative (I got sick; I was cured) to the more complex (I got sick; I was diagnosed; I went to the doctor; I didn't get cured; I tried a folk remedy; I was cured; the cure was verified by the doctor). There may be additional attempts at a cure, followed by failure, before the final healing takes place. But each *caso* deals with only one instance of illness and its cure.

Each element or part of the narrative can be elaborated upon in great detail. Von Sydow (1948) claims that the memorate has no poetic quality but Dégh and Vázsonyi have questioned the validity of this characterization (1974:235–236). Some of my informants point out that the *caso* is often more effective when it is simple, without excess of detail. I shall discuss this point further below.

(2) "Supernatural or natural (event)"

Casos have most frequently been associated with the supernatural, or at least with the very unusual (Paredes 1968; Robe 1977; Chertudi 1958, 1959). All of my informants, when asked, stated that the event cited in the *caso* could be either "natural" or "supernatural." However, they formulated this distinction under direct questioning by me, not spontaneously. Even though, when pressed, my informants would thus distinguish between the natural and the supernatural worlds I suspect that, in the normal process of everyday living, some of them did not always make this distinction—certainly not the way I would. Many events which outsiders would consider supernatural may appear perfectly natural to the insider. For example, the folk name for a sickness, "*susto*," is often glossed in the literature as "magical fright," whereas my informants found nothing magical in it. The outsider notices first those cultural elements which differ the most from his own, and judges them from his own view of what is "natural" and "supernatural."

Américo Paredes recently recalled for me hearing *casos* about incidents observed in nature, such as a coyote stalking a rabbit or a snake "charming" a bird or small animal. This type of *caso* could be used as evidence for any number of beliefs. But it is true that *casos* about the "supernatural" or unusual appear to be more common than *casos* about mundane topics.

Folklorists look for pattern in whatever genre of folklore they study. When they discover a pattern recurring "in different versions" (Brunvand 1968:4), they recognize that they are dealing with folklore. Such patterns can be much more easily recognized in stories involving widely shared folk beliefs, particularly about extraordinary experiences, than in stories which concern only individual beliefs and ordinary experiences. Since exciting and "scary" stories are more interesting to hear and tell than stories about mundane matters, those dealing with extraordinary experiences are more likely to be repeated. Labov and Waletzky found that most personal experience narratives "are so designed as to emphasize the strange and unusual character of the situation— there is an appeal to the element of mystery in most of the narratives" (1967:34).

We should expect a more recognizable patterning in narratives relating shared beliefs and common experiences than in narratives about non-shared, individual experiences. Not everyone observes a coyote stalking a rabbit; but everyone gets sick from time to time, or encounters seemingly strange and even mysterious events, and relies on a shared belief system for an explanation. We have all probably heard stories about experiences similar to our own. Folk belief and stories about folk belief provide us models through which to interpret and to report our own experiences. Thus, because experiences with sickness and healing and with the mysterious are so common, and because narratives about these experiences are apt to be often repeated, it is no wonder that patterning in these *casos* was recognized sooner than in *casos* about mundane experiences. This fact probably accounts for the emphasis on the supernatural found in earlier definitions of the *caso*.

(3) "The protagonist or observer is the narrator or someone the narrator knows and vouches for"

This element has been dealt with in a number of ways by folklorists in the past, but attached to non-emic concept terms. For instance, von Sydow made "personal experience" part of his original definition of the memorate (1948:87), which Reidar Christiansen (1958:5) later expanded to include stories told by someone the narrator knows. Dégh and Vázsonyi have shown from their work that there is no structural difference between first- and third-person narratives (1974:226–229). Pentikäinen found that in one informant's repertoire there could be up to four links in the chain between the narrator and the person who had the experience (discussed in Dégh and Vázsonyi 1974:227).

Pentikäinen notes, however, that in Marina Takalo's repertoire "there regularly are at most two links in the chain between the person who encounters a supernatural being and the narrator" (1978 : 128). Further, "ignorance of the number of links in the chain between the experiencer and the informant proved to be the very criterion for separating memorates from legends" (ibid.). Dégh and Vázsonyi found that a similar principle held for their corpus of materials. They suggest as explanation that a significant but "unwritten folk law of procedure" establishes the reliability of evidence, through the amount and degree of "feasible proofs" in stories purporting to be true and being used as evidence in some degree. Feasibility will often turn on how close the speaker is to the described action: "I have seen it with my own eyes" sounds perfectly convincing. "My father told it, and he never told a lie" is still acceptable. But "My father heard it from my grandfather" leaves a door open for some doubt. . . . The further the message is from its source of perception, the less certain is its truthfulness, according to this unwritten law (Dégh and Vázsonyi 1974 : 231).

This "folk law of procedure" for establishing the reliability of a story provides an insight into how my informants classified and judged the veracity of their stories. According to them, a *caso* is told by the person who had or observed an experience or event, or by someone the narrator knows and will vouch for. The same story, told about someone not known to the narrator, is classified as a *cuento*—which may or may not be true. This, of course, is a statement of the *ideal* situation. By structuring a story as a *cuento*, the narrator frees himself from responsibility for the truth of the experience, even if he does believe it himself. If he reports the experience as a *caso*, he puts his reputation as a truthful person on the line. If someone tells a *caso*, and the hearer knows the narrator has occasionally stretched the truth in the past, the hearer may refer to the story as a *mentira*, a lie. My informants, then, are very aware of the value as evidence of the relative distance between the narrator and the experience, as they are aware of the different means available for telling the story, both on the structural and textual levels.

I should emphasize, of course, that what my informants gave me were the "ideal rules." It is possible, and for some even probable, that they may report stories they have heard about a stranger's experience as the experience of someone they know, or even as their own. Clearly, however, they do distinguish between the *caso* and the *cuento* as genres (cf. Pentikäinen 1978 : 128).

My informants mentioned a number of phrases which they would use to introduce and thus "key" a *caso*: "*a mí me pasó*" [this happened to me]; "*a mí hermano pasó*" [this happened to my brother]; "*en ese ocasión*" [on this occasion]; "*cuando yo estaba [era] chiquito*" [when I was little]; "*cuando yo estaba [era] joven*" [when I was young]. Examination of the two hundred *casos* about healing told to me by my informants indicates that there are numerous ways of introducing a *caso* so that the hearer will know how to interpret the message. A brief sample of these include the following: "*Fíjese, que yo estuve enferma años muy pasados*" [Well, you know, I was sick years back]; "*Yo me lastimé de las caderas levanto una carima así*" [I hurt my hips lifting a (?) thus]; "*Porque a mí me pasó ahora hace como tres semanas*" [Because this happened to me about three weeks ago]; "*Porque yo tuve unos cuatitos, dos niños*" [Because I had little twins, two boys]; "One time, when I, when my parents were here"; "Well, Sally, that girl, she"; "I mean, my uncle that got cured this way"; "Yeah, that one was done to one of my daughters"; "*Una tía mía, ella mató un caballo*" [An aunt of mine, she killed a horse]; "*Un primo de él, un primo de mi esposo*" [A cousin of his, a cousin of my husband]; "*Aquí está un hombre, que tiene familia casada*" [Here is a man who had a family already married]; "Well, this particular little girl had."

To indicate that they are not responsible for the truthfulness of a story, my informants are careful to introduce it as a *cuento*, using any of a number of phrases. Among those suggested by informants are these: "*Me dijo ese*" [This was told to me]; "*Se dicen que*" [It is said that]; "We were told"; "I've heard that"; "*No sé si es verdad o no, pero*" [I don't know if it is true or not, but]; etc. Again, there is no doubt that some narrators may take stories they have heard and structure them as first-person *casos*." Surely a narrator weighs the relative authority of the first person and third-person voices when he is selecting a story to illustrate a folk belief in which he sincerely believes. But a person who considers himself honest and a person of truth may prefer to avoid this type of alteration.

On the other hand, in some social situations the opposite rhetorical strategy may be needed; a first-person *caso* may be told as if the experience had happened to someone else. Using this ploy, the narrator does not have to expose himself to the ridicule of a potentially skeptical listener. By this method he can test the listener's attitude toward the belief in question. Most of us are familiar with such situations: someone who needs advice but does not want to admit he has a problem will say, "A friend of mine has this problem, and I wonder what advice you would give him." My informants have used this ploy, telling their own experiences as though they had happened to someone else.

Mexican-Americans are frequently and often painfully aware of the negative stereotype many Anglos have of them, and in their dealings with Anglos they are often careful not to expose themselves to possible ridicule. Many educated Mexican-Americans recognize the dissonance between what they are supposed to believe (at least what they think they are supposed to believe or not believe) as educated people and their actual belief, validated by their experiences in their culture, in *brujería* (witchcraft), *curanderismo*, or folk illnesses such as *mal de ojo* and *susto*.

Consequently, these individuals adopt various strategies to present or maintain the "proper face" (Goffman's term) in front of a possibly unsympathetic Anglo—the "face" of the non-believer or skeptic. After all, how would it look for a high school teacher to believe in witchcraft? One strategy is simply to deny one accepts a certain folk belief. Another is to relate an experience—a *caso*—and then provide a "rational" or alternative explanation. The most common strategy is simply to establish a "they believe" rather than an "I believe" approach. Accordingly, such narratives will probably be related as *cuentos*, beginning with the words "They say this happened," or "I have heard of this happening," rather than as *casos* about personal experiences. Once such informants feel more comfortable and sense that the collector will not ridicule their beliefs, they find it no longer necessary to maintain this face strictly and will usually tell *casos* in the first person.

One informant, the grandmother of one of my students, steadfastly refused to acknowledge any belief in *brujería* and *curanderismo*. She denied knowing any *casos* about these beliefs, even though her granddaughter informed me that she clearly did believe, and had told numerous *casos* in the young woman's presence. Throughout the interview, the grandmother kept every statement on the "*se dicen que*" [it is said that] or the "some people believe" level. After a lifetime of experience with Anglos, not all of which had been positive, she could hardly be blamed for refusing to expose herself to possible ridicule from an Anglo college professor. Experience with my informants, at least as they talked with me, suggests that more *casos* were changed to *cuen tos* than vice versa—i.e., more first-person narratives became third-person narratives than vice versa.

There is still another factor which the narrator takes into consideration, consciously or unconsciously. Relating a personal experience with the supernatural, such as witchcraft, exposes one to possible ridicule; but, on the other hand, one may also achieve a certain personal power and ego satisfaction from being the protagonist in such an exciting drama (Abrahams 1972). Each informant must judge his hearers and the range of relationships he can establish, maintain, or destroy through his recounting of strange and powerful events.

(4) "Normally used as evidence or as an example to illustrate that 'this kind of thing happens'"

Until I inquired, many of my informants had not thought very seriously about how they used *casos*. Yet, after some consideration, most recognized that they used them as evidence or to illustrate a certain point, often about a given folk belief. *Casos* are used as personal testimony.

In my initial interviews with my informants I was more interested in their beliefs and practices regarding folk medicine than in narrative. Examining these interviews, I became aware that *casos* and *cuentos* about healing and other folk beliefs almost always followed a statement about a belief or practice. When I asked "What is *mal de ojo*?" I would often get a general description of symptoms and causes, followed by a narrative illustrating the stated principle. Sometimes the narrative served as the explanation. It takes only a brief exploration into studies in folk medicine to see that other fieldworkers have had similar experiences. Informants use *casos* as evidence for or to illustrate their beliefs.

One perceptive informant pointed out that the *caso* relates some past experience to a current situation. "A *caso* is intended to have . . . to bear a kind of testimonial—there is a relationship between your *caso* and your listener's situation." He elaborated further:

For example, you say, let's say that you're talking about marriage, just in general. You're talking about family problems, you're talking about unemployment, illnesses. Within that context, within that conversation you think of something that happened to a person at a given time—an instance that you can recall now, it is timely, that relates to whatever you are talking about. That's a *caso*.

Another informant noted that the *caso* is used to communicate true facts.

CONTEXT OF THE *CASO*

Paredes has pointed out that, among Mexican-Americans, different contexts provide the setting for different narrative types:

> There was a marked difference between the way wonder tales and legends were told: in the composition of the groups participating, in the events immediately preceding and following narration, in the emotional tone surrounding the whole performance (1971:98).

He notes further that the factor which distinguishes the legend from the wonder tale is the context (including the attitudes of the narrator and his audience), not the plot content. In an earlier work Paredes (1968) provides a thorough description of the performance context for jokes among his Mexican-American informants.

Unlike folktales and legends, which require a more formal setting for narration, *casos* may appear almost anywhere and anytime where people discuss experiences from everyday life. The *caso* is embedded in the conversation of intimate group situations, where people feel free to share confidences. As noted above, the *caso* is normally used to illustrate that "this kind of thing happens." If "this kind of thing" is a sacred belief, it might be shared only when discussing such things with fellow-believers. The risk of being laughed at by a skeptic would likely prevent a person from using a *caso*, for example, about an encounter with a *bruja* (witch). If "this kind of thing" is a more secular belief, the illustrative *caso* might appear anywhere the subject is brought up. If animal behavior is being discussed—for example, the belief that roadrunners kill rattlesnakes by building a thorn fence around them—a person would readily describe an incident he has witnessed regardless of who is present.

Most *casos* I have collected emerged when there were no more than four or five people, and often only myself and the informant, present. In these situations we were usually discussing folk medicine or other folk beliefs, sometimes in a more formal interview session and sometimes when I was simply a participant observer. I have heard *casos* used in casual conversation between two or three people. But I have never heard them in a storytelling situation, although they can evidently be used on such occasions.

For example, one community center in the area in which I worked is patronized almost exclusively by older Mexican-Americans. A group of elderly women gather there once a week to quilt and talk. Sometimes these conversations turn to folk beliefs of one type or another, such as folk cures. On these occasions, *casos* emerge at first as illustrations of certain beliefs. These sessions usually turn into storytelling events about the supernatural or about unusual experiences with witches, *curanderos*, *lechuzas*, La Llorona, the devil in various forms, etc. However, since as an Anglo outsider my presence inhibits the storytelling, I have had to rely upon an "insider," who works with these ladies, for the information I have about these sessions. Consequently, I do not know the whole range of subjects discussed or the types of narratives related.

Louise Russell (1977) collected a number of *casos* (she refers to them as "memorates") from storytelling sessions among school children in Greeley, Colorado. The *casos* were mixed in with what my informants would call *cuentos* (stories told in third person, protagonist unknown to narrator) and *leyendas*. Many of these *casos* were used to illustrate a point or to answer a question. McDowell (1975) also collected *casos* (called "spooky stories") in storytelling situations. Limón (1978) found *casos* (which he calls "memorates") embedded in the conversations which went on at various types of social gatherings of Chicano students at the University of Texas at Austin. Jordan (1975a) outlines what is probably the most common context for narrating *casos*: informal sessions where the family or a group of intimate friends talk about the subject matter of which *casos* are made. Women frequently make up these informal sessions, during which they may be engaged in any number of activities which occupy their hands while allowing them to think and talk about other things. My informants frequently mentioned that these were the most common occasions for telling a series of *casos*, one after another, intermingled with *cuentos* and reminiscences (perhaps *historias*) about family members and friends, present and past.

FORM OF THE *CASO*

Since the *caso* is about personal experience, and personal experience seems almost infinitely variable, one might suspect that the *caso* would vary widely in form and content. The content, of course, does vary as widely as belief and individual experience, but it always deals with places where belief and experience come together. The *caso* form, however, is highly patterned, particularly in those *casos* about widely shared folk beliefs. The *caso* is in essence a testimony in support of a certain belief—a reported instance of an actual event, told as true. *Casos* are most frequently told some time, perhaps years, after the experience. They are repeated and changed to fit what it seems the experience should have been like—sometimes after others have helped to "interpret" it.

The shape the narrator gives his narrative reflects two forms of experience—cultural and personal. As a child is enculturated during his growth to adulthood in his culture he acquires certain beliefs. These beliefs are communicated, among my Mexican-American informants, not through written means, nor stated in the form "if you do this, that will happen," but rather through a *caso*. When, subsequently, the person has an experience, he interprets it in the light of the folk beliefs he has learned and of others' reports of similar experiences. When the proper situation arises for him to recount the narrative, he relies upon the models his culture has provided him.

As with all genres of traditional verbal or artistic communication, the performer and observer, the teller and listener, of the *caso* must know how properly to code and decode the message. The narrative frame is established in normal conversation when a belief is mentioned in the conversation and one participant chooses to illustrate or provide an example of the belief by recounting an experience he knows of—a *caso*. Other participants could probably provide similar experiences and, indeed, once the narrative frame is established a number of narratives may be told, one after the other.

One important marker of the *caso* is the tone (a facet of what Dundes [1964] calls texture). The genre usually evinces high seriousness and sincere belief. This tone is a crucial element in distinguishing the *caso* from the *chiste* (joke), which parodies the *caso*. The context and tone of the performance prevent any confusion on the part of either teller or hearer, even though the actual structures of the two are often almost identical. This characteristic of the *caso* involves the tone of voice, the literary "tone," and the tone of the whole performance. A mocking or light-hearted tone would be incongruous, particularly when believers

are telling *casos* about *brujería* (witchcraft) and other such
matters.

Once a belief has been introduced into the conversation the
narrative frame may be established a number of ways. The narrator may give an abstract of the story to come and then the orientation, or simply begin with the latter. In one interview, an informant and I were discussing why Mexican-Americans had
relied on herbal remedies in earlier times. I suggested that, in an
earlier interview with her and five other people, the others had
disclaimed any belief in such illnesses as *mal de ojo* only because
I was there. She responded:

Sí, es verdad. No, pos, yo sí lo creo, señor, yo sí lo creo. Porque yo tuve
unos cuatitos, dos niños; no me duraron nomás de quince días. [Yes, it is
true. But I do believe, señor, I do believe. Because I had twins, two boys;
they did not last more than fifteen days.]

She then began a narrative—"*Vino una señora. . . .*" [A lady
came. . . .]—to explain what caused the death of her twins. The
narrative follows here naturally on the brief abstract, beginning
immediately with the orientation.

The orientation of the *caso* may contain four elements: person, place, time, and behavioral situation (Labov and Waletzky
1967:32). Significantly, the orientation often establishes the relationship between the protagonist and the narrator, if they are not
the same individual. This relationship may also be established in
the final coda rather than in the orientation.

A number of opening formulas may begin the abstract or the
orientation, as I noted in discussing the emic definition of the
caso. Structurally, this part of the narrative differentiates the
caso from other narrative forms. The protagonist may be introduced and the time of the event established very briefly: "When I
was little"; "This happened to my brother last year"; "Sally had
el ojo when she was three." The *cuento* about the experience of
someone unknown to the narrator, while otherwise possibly identical to the *caso* in structure, is differentiated from the *caso* in
the orientation. Distance is established between the narrator and
the protagonist; introductory phrases such as "*Se dicen que*" [It is
said that] and "*He oído que*" [I have heard that] clue the hearer in
to the reliability of the testimony to follow.

Since the folktale is more commonly told in formally structured storytelling situations than in conversation, it usually has
little if any orientation (Labov and Waletzky 1967:32). Such

cuentos begin with stereotyped openings such as: *"Éste era"* [This was]; *"Había una vez"* [There was once]; *"Eran dos compadres"* [There were two friends]; and variants. The setting, time, and protagonist (a prince, a woodcutter, a rich man, etc.) are all indefinite—stereotypical characters in a time and place out of real time and space. If the protagonist is named, he is usually some well-known folk character—e.g., Juan sin Miedo or Juan Oso.

Leyendas, also told in more formally structured storytelling situations, begin with openings quite different from those of the *caso*. Unlike the folktale, the *leyenda* may be located in a specific place and time; it may even have a specific date. The time is usually more remote than for the *caso*, but the place is real enough. However, the personae (except for the well-known legendary characters) remain nameless, and not even the giving of a place name to localize the action or of a date to historicize it could cause a Mexican-American to confuse the *leyenda* with the *caso*—primarily because, in the legend, the distance implied between the teller and the protagonist of the story is too great.

Four "legendary narratives," selected at random from Elaine K. Miller's *Mexican Folk Narrative from the Los Angeles Area* (1973) reveal these characteristics of the *leyenda*: *"Éste, éste pasó allí en el rancho de Los Guapos. Éste, era un señor que iba pasando cerca del panteón"* [Well, this happened out there at the Los Guapos ranch. Well, there was a man who was passing by the cemetery] (ibid.:71, no. 19); *"Sabe que ésta . . . es una señorita. Tiene veintiún años de edad. . . ."* [You know, this is . . . is a young girl. She is twenty-one years old. . . .] (ibid.:73, no. 20); *"Pues sabe que, que esta señor . . . era un señor muy pobrecito. Y tenía su familia. . . ."* [Well, you know, there's this man . . . there was a very poor man. And he had his family. . . .] (ibid.:75, no. 21); *"Pos un . . . esposo de una prima un día, un día se fue el esposo a misa, un sábado de gloria"* [Well, a . . . husband of a cousin, one day, one day the husband went to mass, one Holy Saturday] (ibid.:80, no. 22). (The internal ellipses are in the originals.) In each narrative, the protagonist is distant enough from the narrator that someone in the Mexican-American culture (or at least my informants) would likely consider the story possibly true but, since it is based on hearsay, probably at least partly inaccurate.

The complication of the *caso* often puts the protagonist into a threatening, frightening, or extraordinary situation. He (or she) may become ill; or violate a taboo, interdiction, or social norm;

or observe some extraordinary event. The complication may consist of several episodes which lead the protagonist into the situation.

The evaluation, if the *caso* has one, serves to emphasize the apex of the complication. The good narrator uses it to heighten interest. Labov and Waletzky define the evaluation as "that part of the narrative which reveals the attitude of the narrator towards the narrative by emphasizing the relative importance of some narrative units as compared to others" (1967:37). These evaluations may be defined semantically, formally, or culturally (ibid.:37–38). Evaluations in *casos* take many forms: "Boy, was I sick!"; "The doctor couldn't do a thing"; "Boy, was I scared."

The resolution follows the evaluation; it relates the outcome of the experience. The belief—usually the folk belief—is validated. *Curanderismo* works! He *did* have *el ojo*! She *was* a *bruja*! La Llorona *does* appear along waterways! Snakes do charm birds! I got well!

Labov and Waletzky claim that the coda, which serves to return "the verbal perspective to the present moment," may take any number of forms (ibid.:40). This is true of the *caso*. Typical conclusions would be: "And, boy, I can eat anything now"; "He doesn't do that any more"; "He's buried there in Alpine."

Following are fourteen plot summaries of *caso* types which recurred with some frequency among my informants. I do not claim this list is exhaustive; each type could be elaborated upon or expanded vertically (see McDowell 1975), adding a number of events in the complication and resolution sections.

Caso *Type 1*
A Mexican-American becomes ill and is taken to a doctor, who either treats him, with no visible results, or says that the person is not ill. The person is taken to a *curandero* or other folk practitioner, who provides the proper remedy, and the patient gets well.

This type can be greatly elaborated upon, as Paredes has suggested (1968:106–107). The element of the patient's being taken to a doctor may be omitted.

Caso *Type 2*
This is almost the inverse of Type 1. A friend or relative becomes ill, and is taken to a *curandero* for treatment. The narrator is skeptical and ar-

gues against this step, because he thinks the healer is a charlatan. After the visit, the patient's condition becomes worse or at least fails to improve. The narrator convinces the family to take the sick person to a medical doctor or to another healer he has more confidence in. The patient gets well. The story may end without the visit to another healer or doctor, in which case the person either dies or loses a leg (or whatever) as a consequence of the ineptness of the healer.

This type of story may be used not to invalidate *curanderismo* per se but rather to attack a specific healer's reputation, usually one thought to be a charlatan for some reason—perhaps because he charges exorbitant fees, which violates a very important cultural requirement of the *curandero*: the vow of poverty.

Caso *Type 3*
A person gets into trouble with the law or with his friends because of some antisocial behavior. He consults a *curandero*, who claims that the person is hexed and provides him with a means to extricate himself.

Caso *Type 4*
A person is having bad luck in his love life, or in general. He cannot understand why all this is happening to him. A friend, who sees his misery and wants to help, suggests that he may be *embrujado*, and recommends that he go see a certain *curandero* whom the friend knows and trusts. Willing to try anything, the miserable individual goes. The *curandero* verifies that he is hexed and sends him on his way, promising relief. The problem is alleviated. Now the formerly unlucky person believes, too.

Caso *Type 5*
An unbeliever or scoffer goes to a *curandero* pretending illness or similar misfortune in order to expose or to test the healer's powers. The *curandero* exposes the "patient," often punishing him with some embarrassing malady such as diarrhea.

This *caso* type has been identified by Paredes (1968:107); Dodson's collection (1951) contains a number of narratives of this type about Don Pedrito Jaramillo. My informants would probably call these narratives *cuentos*, although Dodson may have heard them as *casos*.

Caso *Type 6*
A person has become afflicted with a certain illness such as *mal de ojo* or *susto*. The evidence as to how those involved knew that this was indeed the illness is presented. The *caso* may not deal with the cure.

Caso *Type 7*
Someone is sick, usually with one of the folk illnesses (*mal de ojo*, etc.).
The person is taken to the doctor, and dies because he is given the wrong
treatment.

Caso *Type 8*
This type is very inclusive; essentially it validates a folk belief. Such a
belief is stated in conversation, usually prior to the *caso*. The *caso* ends
when the folk belief is validated. The story may illustrate the belief that
rattlesnakes charm rabbits (Rubel 1966 : 157). It may illustrate the belief
that witches cannot pass through a door above which a cross is fastened.
A witch or *lechuza* is caught and identified, after being shot or otherwise
incapacitated.

Caso *Type 9*
A person is in trouble, is sick, or is having much bad luck. He (or she)
appeals to a saint, God, the Virgin, etc., and often pledges certain acts or
offerings if healed or if the problem is alleviated. The promised act or
offering is performed. If it is not performed, the person is punished, often
in some embarrassing way.

Caso *Type 10*
A Mexican-American (usually a male) is wrongfully accused of something, and the Anglo law officers come for him. He is mistreated—
beaten, left in jail without food, denied contact with his family. He is
finally freed when the guilty person is found.

Caso *Type 11*
A person is violating the law (e.g., smuggling drugs) and has a narrow
escape from the law (usually Anglo law), often because of some good luck
or because of his own quick wit.

Caso *Type 12*
Someone suspects that treasure is buried in a particular place, because
of strange sounds (a rattling stove, etc.) or a mysterious light. The person
seeks the treasure and either finds it or, for some extraordinary reason,
cannot get it. Someone else may get to the treasure first and leave only
an empty hole. The treasure may be found accidentally, such as when a
person goes into a cave to escape a storm. He cannot find it when he
returns to remove the treasure. (See Granger's [1978] recent index of
treasure-story types.)

Caso *Type 13*
Someone has a terrifying experience with the devil, a witch, or a *lechuza* (Carpenter 1974; Garza 1961). He prays, or holds up a cross, or ties

twelve knots in a string while repeating "the twelve truths." The witch, bird, woman-with-a-horse's-face, or La Llorona disappears, often leaving behind some evidence of its presence—e.g., scratches on the bedpost.

Caso *Type 14*

Someone violates a social norm or taboo (by gambling, drinking, or chasing women). While going home after such activities late at night, he (or she) has a frightening experience with the devil in some form (a beautiful woman who turns out to have a horse's face, a person who turns into a dog, etc.). As a consequence, he doesn't drink/gamble/chase women any more.

FUNCTIONS OF THE *CASO*

The definition of the *caso* proposed in this paper includes the phrase, "which is normally used as evidence or an example to illustrate that 'this kind of thing happens.'" My informants suggested this as the main use (the manifest, as opposed to the latent, function) of the *caso*. The *caso* functions as a testimony to support belief, whether folk belief, individual belief, or orthodox, institutionalized belief. It is convincing evidence for a belief, and therefore important in maintaining it (cf. Mullen 1971; Dégh and Vázsonyi 1973). In some contexts, however, the *caso*'s role of persuading, teaching, or convincing gives way to the sheer pleasure of telling and hearing such narratives.

Jordan (1975a) points to another important use of *casos*: they can be shared as a means of socializing, of demonstrating or reaffirming membership in a group. Folklore materials may be manipulated selectively, as Jordan showed her informant did, "to strengthen [her] position as an insider (and thus her identity as a Mexican-American and as a member of her family), especially when that membership seems threatened" (1975a : 380).

Some scholars have questioned the entertainment or amusement value of narratives such as the *caso*, while others have claimed that they "are of interest mainly as folk prose (i.e., as oral literature)" (Blehr 1967 : 262). Few who have heard *casos* about supernatural experiences would deny their entertainment value, which McDowell (1975) and Russell (1977) have shown in their work with school children. Accounts of experiences with the supernatural, particularly when told as true, add excitement to the lives of both tellers and hearers.

The use of *casos* in storytelling situations—in the community-center quilting events, in family gatherings, in storytelling sessions at school (Russell 1977) or at home (McDowell 1975)—indicates that they are entertaining in themselves. Whiling away one's time telling or listening to narratives of the mysterious, the exciting, and even the macabre, in a setting where one can experience vicariously or relive taboo or potentially hazardous experiences without risk, can be quite entertaining. The great popularity of horror movies would suggest that people enjoy being scared and even terrified in controlled, non-threatening circumstances. Roemer found that, whether they believed the stories to be true or not, her informants liked to hear and tell "scary story legends" because they were scary (1971 : 1–2).

Validation of culture is a particularly important function of the *caso*, dealing as it does with belief. In "Folk Medicine and the Intercultural Jest," Paredes (1968 : 107) comments upon this function:

It helps bolster belief in folk medicine; it encourages acceptance by the younger generation of the old tradition, especially when the group must live among an increasingly skeptical majority. This may be equally true whether the Mexican folk group is living in the United States or across the border in Mexico, since Mexican physicians are at times even more intolerant of folk medicine than their Anglo-American counterparts. But this type of *caso* plays an important role among rural and semirural Mexican groups in the United States, who see their folk culture assailed not only by modern science and technology, but by the belief patterns of rural Anglo-American neighbors who may have their own folk beliefs and tend to be contemptuous of those held by foreigners.

There is no question that the *casos* I have collected, in which my informants often tell of Anglos who have been healed with Mexican-American folk remedies, serve this same purpose. So also do those *casos* which point out that certain illnesses can be cured only by the folk healers in the culture. By their very nature as testimonies, *casos* validate whatever folk beliefs they illustrate. In this sense, *casos* are ego-supporting devices arising in the face of strong pressures from an alien and dominant culture external to that of the storytellers (Paredes 1971).

In a given performance situation a *caso* may serve different functions for different hearers. For some in the audience who are being exposed to a belief for the first time, such as children, the *caso*'s function may well be primarily educational, while for others (those who have long known and accepted the belief and who have felt the intolerance of a skeptical majority), it serves a primarily validating function. Behavioral control may also be an important function of the same *caso* in the same performance situation—it warns that certain actions lead to serious consequences, or it provides a model for behavior in certain situations.

As to education, *casos* are a means of transmitting folk belief from one individual to another and from one generation to another. As children grow up they learn the folk beliefs of their culture, but not necessarily in the form in which fieldworkers often record them: "If *x*, then *y*." My informants would sometimes assert a belief as such a short statement, then illustrate it with a *caso*. Most often, however, the *caso* came spontaneously as an attempt to explain the belief.[12] One informant, when asked if she believed in witchcraft, responded with two *casos*, beginning with the words "This I have seen" and "This I saw." After relating the *casos* she let me draw my own conclusions about whether witchcraft was involved—and, incidentally, about whether or not she believed in witchcraft.

Moreover, a brief statement of a belief does not really explain that belief, at least if it is something as complex as a belief in witchcraft. It would take several lengthy discussions to cover this many-faceted aspect of the Mexican-American belief system. And no adult, parent or otherwise, sits a child down and gives him a lengthy discussion on what causes witchcraft, why it occurs, who is responsible for it, etc. If an adult attempted to do so, more than likely the child would remember only a small part of the lecture. Rather, piece by piece, a *caso* at a time, the belief, in all of its ramifications, is developed as the child grows into adulthood. Adults get constant reinforcement of their beliefs but also gain personal insights into the workings of witchcraft. Consequently, no two people have exactly the same perceptions of any given folk belief, particularly of one so complex as witchcraft.

Studying *casos* can therefore give us important insights into the culture. The literature on memorates in general casts some light on how *casos* in particular work. For instance, Honko (1965:10–11) notes that such stories can reveal, in the study of religion, those "situations in which supernatural tradition was actualized and began directly to influence behavior. On the basis of the memorates we can form a picture of the social context of beliefs, the consideration of which is the fundamental demand of the functionalist approach." Every study of folk medicine made in Mexican-American culture has relied heavily on the *caso*, not only for information but also to substantiate the investigator's report.

Certainly, one of the most important functions of the *caso* is to control social behavior. Many *casos* told to inform also didactically reinforce cultural norms by providing examples of what happens when the norms are violated. The *casos* are used to teach young people how to act, as a model for behavior and a warning against misbehavior. For adults, too, the *casos* serve as warnings of the consequences of violating cultural norms and taboos. In a way, this is just as true of *casos* about medical beliefs as it is of those about norm violations per se. A *caso* about a cured illness certainly offers a model for a person to pattern his own behavior after, should the occasion arise. The information often attached to the *casos* about healing (e.g., that Anglo doctors do not know how to cure certain folk illnesses) certainly may convince someone in that culture not to go to an Anglo doctor if he suffers from one of these illnesses. As Saunders (1954) and others have pointed out, stories about Mexican-Americans' experiences in hospitals (isolation from family and friends, the use of *los fierros* in delivering babies, the attitude that hospitals are where people go to die) are important reasons why many of the more conservative Mexican-Americans do not patronize doctors (who are portrayed in many *casos* as ever eager to operate) and hospitals more readily.

In many instances *casos* are used as warnings not to eat food prepared by strangers because it may contain some hexing agent or a drug such as LSD. I have collected such *casos*, and Jordan reports hearing a similar story (1975a: 380). Children, especially, are warned not to take things from strangers. As others have pointed out, stories of La Llorona can frighten children into obedience, especially to stay away from bodies of water and to stay inside after dark (see, for example, Russell 1977: 275).

One of the most interesting functions of the *caso* is in establishing, or attacking, the reputation of a folk healer. One of the prerequisites for the *curandero*'s ability to heal is that the person to be healed must have faith in the healer (Graham 1976: 183). How does the patient attain such faith? One important way is by hearing *casos* of miraculous cures wrought by the healer; since these stories are told by friends as first-person experiences, the prospective patient believes them. Thus, when he goes to see the healer he is *expecting* to be healed, as his friend was. The *caso* plays an important role in inspiring faith or strong belief in the healer's skill.

The *caso*, then, is the primary means by which the *curandero*'s (or other folk practitioner's) reputation is made, and his reputation is very important to his ability to cure. His fame spreads and, as Romano (1965) has shown, he may become a folk saint like Don Pedrito Jaramillo. Through the medium of these *casos*, people thousands of miles away are inspired to come to be healed. At the *curandero* Don Pancho's "office" in San Sebastian, Texas, I met one patient who said he had come from Chicago to see Don Pancho. A healed patient becomes a most effective advertisement (a true *curandero* in the old tradition never advertises over the radio, on signs, or through handbills).

Some *casos* (see type 2 above) are used to attack the reputations of certain *curanderos*, particularly those who charge for their services and thereby violate the traditional vow of poverty made by true *curanderos*. These *casos* are not necessarily used to invalidate *curanderismo* in general, but rather to discredit a particular healer. There are instances, however, of *casos* being used to discredit the whole concept of folk healing. Jordan, for example, recounts such a story (1975a : 377).

I should note that *casos* also play an important role in the labeling of witches. A number of such narratives in my collection relate experiences which people have had with certain individuals thought to be witches. Some *casos* are structured such that the complication segment tells of someone being hexed, and the resolution consists of the proof that a certain person, a witch, was responsible (see, for example, type 8 above). As with the *curandero*, the witch's reputation is spread via *casos*; and the greater her reputation, the greater her power.

CONCLUSION

With the possible exception of the *chiste* in some groups, the *caso* is the most important single genre of folk narrative in the Mexican-American culture of West Texas. This primacy is evidenced not only by the frequency of their occurrence but also by the fact that the folk have given them a name and a place within their emic classification system. *Casos* are abundant because everyone in the culture has experiences which support his belief system, and assigns value and meaning to these experiences by structuring them into narrative form and placing these narratives into conversations with others. Everyone has *casos* in his repertoire of folk narratives and, given the right social situation, everyone can become an active bearer of tradition, a teller of *casos*. As we have seen, the *caso* has a distinctive form which is readily recognizable by those in the culture, who must be able to differentiate this genre from other emic genres of folk narrative in order successfully to code and decode the messages they contain. Students of traditional culture—particularly those who study folk belief—would be wise, therefore, to gain an understanding of the emic system so that they, too, can properly decode these messages.

This essay has been an argument for the need to understand ethnic genres, not an argument against analytic categories. Ben-Amos tells us that each genre "is characterized by a set of relations between its formal features, thematic domains, and potential social usages" (1969:285). I have attempted here to define the *caso* using these parameters. Perhaps studies among Mexican-Americans in other areas will prove this definition valid beyond West Texas.

NOTES

1. Américo Paredes (1968, 1970, 1971) is the notable exception. An examination of doctoral dissertations dealing with Mexican-American and Latin-American folk narratives revealed that the term "memorate" has been the popular choice (see Miller [1973], McDowell [1975], Jordan [1975b], Russell [1977], Limón [1978], and Blache [1977]). Robe (1977) refers to the memorate, although on at least two occasions he and I have discussed the *caso* by that name.
2. An examination of various literary dictionaries and encyclopedias found no use of the term "*caso*" to designate a narrative genre. Conversations with a number of scholars of Latin-American literature have revealed that they were unaware of the *caso* as a narrative genre.
3. It is apparent from his comments that the *caso* was at the time an accepted type of folk narrative among folklorists (see Carrizo et al., 1948).
4. Greatly influenced by Aarne and Thompson in her definitions of the prose narrative types of Argentina, Chertudi was evidently unaware of von Sydow's work with the memorate.
5. That Chertudi was sensitive to folk nomenclature is evident in that

she notes that her informants did not refer to the stories as *casos* or *sucedidos*, nor did they give the narratives a special name, but referred to them as "*lo que le paso a*" [that which happened to] (1958: 124). This is perhaps the earliest notice of an introductory marker of the *caso*.

6. This concept of the *caso* is borrowed from such author/scholars as Dávalos (1925) and Canal Feijóo (1940).

7. This would be equally true, of course, should the collector ask, "Do you know any memorates or personal experience narratives?"—but for very different reasons. "Memorate" and "personal experience narrative" are etic terms which have become a part of our professional jargon, but "*caso*" and "case in point" are emic terms used by the folk.

8. Labov and Waletzky (1967) asked their informants not for stories but about experiences, which were then told as narratives.

9. A similar situation exists in English. "Story" can either be a broad, neutral, all-inclusive category or it may be used to imply untruth, as when a parent says "Don't tell me a story" or "That sounds like a story to me."

10. Miller's (1973) informants referred to certain narratives as *historias* which my informants identified as *casos*. From her book it is impossible to ascertain how her informants would have distinguished between the two genres, if indeed they did.

11. Dégh and Vázsonyi term such narratives pseudo- or quasi-memorates (1974:228).

12. This supports Abrahams' discovery:

    The most usual way in which superstitions (folk belief) are expressed and transmitted is through memorate legends—stories illustrating the working out of the belief in a specific occurrence. These stories not only illustrate the belief but fill in other important information as to who follows the superstition, in what way, and under what circumstances (1968:45–46).

    Lauri Honko has discovered among his informants the same tendency to relate instances of personal experience rather than just to state a belief. He explains why memorates are so important in establishing or conveying folk beliefs. Through memorates, he claims:

    we grasp the living essence of folk belief, the supernatural experiences of the people. Belief in the existence of spirits is founded not only upon loose speculation, but upon concrete, personal experiences, the reality of which is reinforced by sensory perceptions. In this respect spirits are empirical beings. Although the investigator himself is unable to see the spirits, he must admit that his informant really saw them. In general, informants react critically to supernatural experiences. They want to consider true only that which they themselves saw or which some acquaintance experienced. If, for example, the collector asks: "Are there any spirits in the barn?" then the informant normally keeps away from a generalized presentation in which he would describe what a spirit looks like and what it usually does. Instead he begins to relate: "Last fall when I went to put more wood in the barn's stove, then (such and such happened)." In other words, he reports a memorate (1965:10).

BIBLIOGRAPHY

Abrahams, Roger D. 1968. A rhetoric of everyday life: Traditional conversational genres. *Southern Folklore Quarterly* 32:44–59.
———. 1972. Personal power and social restraint in the definition of folklore. In *Toward new perspectives in folklore*. Américo Paredes and Richard Bauman, eds. Austin: University of Texas Press.
Bascom, William. 1964. Four functions of folklore. In *The study of folklore*. Alan Dundes, ed. Englewood Cliffs, N.J.: Prentice-Hall.
Ben-Amos, Dan. 1969. Analytic categories and ethnic genres. *Genre* 2: 275–301.
Blache, Martha. 1977. Structural analysis of Guraní memorates and anecdotes. Ph.D. dissertation, Indiana University.
Blehr, Otto. 1967. The analysis of folk belief stories and its implications for research on folk belief and folk prose. *Fabula* 9:259–263.
Blixen, Samuel. 1909. *Casos, dichos y anécdotas: Florilegio del ingenio ríoplatense*. Montevideo, Uruguay: Librería Nacional de A. Barreiro y Ramos.
Brunvand, Jan H. 1968. *The study of American folklore*. New York: Norton.
Canal Feijóo, Bernardo. 1940. *Los casos de "Juan": El ciclo popular de la picardía criolla*. Buenos Aires: Compañía Impresora Argentina.
Carpenter, Ann. 1974. Scratches on the bedpost: Vestiges of the lechuza. *Publications of the Texas Folklore Society* 38:75–78.
Carrizo, Alberto, Jesús María Carrizo, and Bruno Jacovella. 1948. Cuentos de la tradición oral argentina. *Revista del Instituto Nacional de la Tradición* 1:209–222.
Carvalho-Neto, Paulo de. 1961. *Folklore del Paraguay*. Quito, Ecuador: Editorial Universitaria.
———. 1963. Folklore amazónico. Systemática sintética. *Perú Indígena* 10, no. 22/23:48–90.
———. 1969a. *Historia del folklore iberoamericano*. Oosterhout, The Netherlands: Anthropological Publications.
———. 1969b. *History of Iberoamerican folklore: Mestizo cultures*. Pollak Neutzer, trans. Oosterhout, The Netherlands: Anthropological Publications.
Chertudi, Susana. 1958. Formas literarias en prosa. In *Folklore puntano*. Instituto de Filología y Folklore.

————. 1959. Las especies literarias en prosa. In *Folklore argentino*. J. Imbelloni, ed. Buenos Aires: Editorial Nova.

Christiansen, Reidar. 1958. *The migratory legends*. Helsinki: Folklore Fellows Communication no. 175.

Dávalos, Juan Carlos. 1925. *Los Casos del zorro: Fábulas campesinas de Salta*. Buenos Aires: El Ateneo.

Dégh, Linda, and Andrew Vázsonyi. 1973. The dialectics of the legend. *Folklore Preprint Series* 1 : 1–65.

————. 1974. The memorate and the proto-memorate. *Journal of American Folklore* 87 : 225–239.

Dodson, Ruth. 1951. Don Pedrito Jaramillo: The *curandero* of Los Olmos. *Publications of the Texas Folklore Society* 24 : 9–70.

Dundes, Alan. 1964. Texture, text, and context. *Southern Folklore Quarterly* 28 : 251–265.

Garza, Humberto. 1961. Owl bewitchment in the Lower Rio Grande Valley. *Publications of the Texas Folklore Society* 30 : 218–225.

Gossen, Gary H. 1972. Chamula genres of verbal behavior. In *Toward New Perspectives in Folklore*. Américo Paredes and Richard Bauman, eds. Austin: University of Texas Press.

Graham, Joe S. 1976. The role of the *curandero* in the Mexican-American folk medicine system of West Texas. In *American Folk Medicine*. Wayland Hand, ed. Los Angeles: University of California Press.

Granger, Byrd Howell. 1978. *A motif index for lost mines and treasures applied to redactions of Arizona legends, and to lost mine and treasure legends exterior to Arizona*. Helsinki: Folklore Fellows Communication no. 218.

Honko, Lauri. 1965. Memorates and the study of folk beliefs. *Journal of the Folklore Institute* 1 : 5–19.

Jordan, Rosan A. 1975a. Ethnic identity and the lore of the supernatural. *Journal of American Folklore* 88 : 370–382.

————. 1975b. The folklore and ethnic identity of a Mexican-American woman. Ph.D. dissertation, Indiana University.

Labov, William, and Joshua Waletzky. 1967. Narrative analysis: Oral versions of personal experience. In *Essays on the verbal and visual arts*. June Helm, ed. Seattle: University of Washington Press.

Limón, José E. 1978. The expressive culture of a Chicano student group at the University of Texas at Austin 1967–1975. Ph.D. dissertation, University of Texas at Austin.

McDowell, John H. 1975. The speech play and verbal art of Chicano children. Ph.D. dissertation, University of Texas at Austin.

Miller, Elaine K. 1973. *Mexican folk narrative from the Los Angeles area*. Austin: University of Texas Press.

Mullen, Patrick B. 1971. The relationship of legend and folk belief. *Journal of American Folklore* 84 : 406–413.

Paredes, Américo. 1968. Folk medicine and the intercultural jest. In

Spanish-speaking people in the United States. June Helm, ed. Seattle: University of Washington Press.
———. 1970. *Folktales of Mexico.* Chicago: University of Chicago Press.
———. 1971. Mexican legendry and the rise of the Mestizo: A survey. In *American folk legend.* Wayland Hand, ed. Los Angeles: University of California Press.
Pentikäinen, Juha. 1978. *Oral repertoire and world view: An anthropological study of Marina Takalo's life history.* Helsinki: Folklore Fellows Communication no. 219.
Robe, Stanley. 1977. Problems of a Mexican legend index. *Journal of the Folklore Institute* 14:159–167.
Roemer, Danielle. 1971. Scary story legends. *Folklore Annual of the Center for Intercultural Studies in Folklore and Ethnomusicology* 3:1–16. Austin: University of Texas.
Romano, Victor O. I. 1965. Charismatic medicine, folk-healing, and folk sainthood. *American Anthropologist* 67:1151–1173.
Rubel, Arthur J. 1966. *Across the tracks: Mexican-Americans in a Texas city.* Austin: University of Texas Press.
Russell, Louise. 1977. Legendary narratives inherited by children of Mexican-American ancestry: Cultural pluralism and the persistence of tradition. Ph.D. dissertation, Indiana University.
Saunders, Lyle. 1954. *Cultural difference and medical care.* New York: Russell Sage Foundation.
Stahl, Sandra K. D. 1977. The personal narrative as folklore. *Journal of the Folklore Institute* 14:9–30.
von Sydow, C. W. 1948. *Selected papers on folklore.* Copenhagen: Rosenkilde and Bagger.

John Holmes McDowell

The *Corrido* of Greater Mexico as Discourse, Music, and Event

The *corrido*, a ballad genre cultivated throughout most of Greater Mexico, enjoys today a notable presence in folklore scholarship, due largely to the efforts of Américo Paredes, himself an insider to the *corrido* tradition of the Texas-Mexican border area. In this paper I wish to direct attention to what I consider the three essential facets of the *corrido*: the *corrido* as discourse, that is, as an artistic, verbal message exploiting given linguistic and conceptual codes and styles; the *corrido* as music, that is, as an esthetic product occupying acoustic space; and the *corrido* as event, that is, as a moment of performance articulating a range of social structures and cultural norms. Thorough exploration of these three perspectives (the latter two are only briefly addressed here) would allow the precise specification of the *corrido*'s unique position within the universe of human expressive behavior. Material supportive of the argument I will develop below comes from two sources: *A Texas-Mexican Cancionero* (1976) by Américo Paredes; and my own field collection of *corridos* from the state of Guerrero, Mexico, made in the summer of 1972.[1]

I should warn the reader at the outset that I shall be indulging in two serviceable fictions: first, in assuming that there is such a thing as "the" *corrido*; and, second, in positing the existence of "ballad communities." There are, of course, many *corridos*, not just "the" *corrido*. A great deal of formal, thematic, and stylistic variation occurs within the *corrido* tradition—variation which should itself be studied, as an index to the productivity of the folk imagination working through a particular expressive genre. But, for the purposes of lean argumentation, I am assuming here a general *corrido* type, which evinces the features most commonly associated with the genre. The *corrido* I have in mind is most nearly akin to the *corrido trágico* or heroic *corrido* reported in Greater Mexico and, of course, particularly along the Texas-Mexican border (Mendoza 1964; Paredes 1958a).

As for my second "fiction," it may well be that ballad communities have existed and continue to exist, although it seems peculiar to characterize a necessarily diverse group of people on the basis of one genre in their expressive repertoire. Américo Paredes (1963:231) provides a useful concept when he speaks of a ballad tradition as a "crystallization" of traditional ballads "at one particular time and place into a whole ballad corpus, which by its very weight impresses itself on the consciousness of the people." Such a ballad tradition, we surmise, existed along the lower Rio Grande border into the early decades of the present century. But the conceptual leap from ballad tradition to ballad community is difficult to justify from concrete ethnographic data. In this paper the term "ballad community" refers to a hypothesized human community which supports an active ballad tradition while providing the cosmological orientation represented in those ballads. Whether ballad communities may be located in time and space, or must be assigned a more tenuous ontological status, I leave open for treatment elsewhere.

THE *CORRIDO* AS DISCOURSE

As a unit of discourse, the *corrido* has certain properties which allow us to locate it within the larger discourse system of the ballad community or of any human community. Specifically, the *corrido* is *narrative*, *reflexive*, and *propositional* in semantic intent and *poetic* in technique.

Narrative
Labov and Waletzky (1967) argue that narrative, at a minimum, encodes one instance of temporal disjunction. In other words, narrative must place at least one pair of events in some necessary temporal relation to each other. Narrative, we could go on to say, is potentially iconic, in that a chronological sequence native to someone's experience is reproduced in a verbal icon which con-

serves the original chronology. The narrative need not present events in the same order as they occurred; but any departure in narrative exposition from the original temporal ordering must be keyed in such a manner as to allow a faithful reconstruction of the experiential substratum.

The *corrido*, then, is in part a narrative form of discourse, reproducing in verbal icons a sequence of events drawn from someone's experience. The *corrido* is not typically a form of personal narrative. A personal narrative reproduces in the first-person pronominal mode, a sequence of events idiosyncratically experienced. The *corrido* tends towards the literary fiction of an understood observer, who encases his observations in the impersonal third-person—although some *corridos* may identify the voice of the *corridista* (the *corrido* singer/composer) with the *corrido's* protagonist, as I shall discuss below. But the typical case involves an impersonal authorial voice, present but not implicated in the events it depicts.

The *corrido* as narrative may be further characterized as historical in content. *Corridos* focus on events of particular consequence to the *corrido* community, events of immediate significance to it and productive of heightened awareness of mutual values and orientations. The *corrido* is thus a form of historical narrative, selecting events for narration which have instrumental and symbolic value in the *corrido* community. In this respect the *corrido* can be distinguished from other forms of narrative, in which essentially idiosyncratic perceptions are cast in the third-person guise of impersonal narrative. Merle Simmons (1957) has shown how the *corridos* of Mexico provide a fascinating folk counterpoint to the "official" history of the *corrido* period, and Américo Paredes (1958b, 1961, 1972) has explored in a number of publications the intricate relationship between *corrido* discourse and history.

The *corrido* as narrative discourse is a verbal icon, in manner impersonal and in content historical. But the *corrido* is a very incomplete icon; it reproduces only casually the full sequence of events on which it is based. The *corrido* tells a tale, but it is at no pains to present all of the information pertinent to that tale. In fact, most *corridos* (except broadside ballads based on newspaper accounts) are somewhat inscrutable as narratives. It is not that they tamper with chronology: *corridos* follow the ordering of events inherent in the experiential substratum, thereby preserving intact the iconic relation between art and experience. The inscrutability of *corridos* derives rather from the omission of vital elements requisite to the proper decoding of the verbal icon. The famous leaping and lingering technique of the ballad insures that we enter *in medias res*, and skip unpredictably through insufficiently glossed narrative details to an often mysterious conclusion.

This remarkable feature of *corrido* narration derives from the community orientation of the genre, a factor I will treat in greater detail below. The *corrido* as a form of narration supplements and complements other information available to the *corrido* community. In short, it presupposes an informed audience. Américo Paredes (1976:xxi) has pointed out that *corridos* and legends dealing with the same sequence of events can interact, and this kind of symbiotic relationship between the *corrido* and other forms of narration seems typical. Therefore, the purpose of the *corrido* is not, as some scholars have supposed, to convey news. News travels readily enough through less formal channels such as gossip, anecdote, etc. Generally speaking, the *corrido* depends on a prior transmission of news; its purpose is to interpret, celebrate, and ultimately dignify events already thoroughly familiar to the *corrido* audience.

Narrowing our focus slightly, we might inquire: What narrative mechanisms are utilized in the *corrido*? One of the most central is reported speech and dialogue. The emotional kernel of the *corrido* is the clever and defiant use of speech reported by the *corridista*. These focal incidents dramatize that most dramatic of human involvements, the face-to-face interaction. The *corrido* hastens to set the scene, alerting us to the time, place, and participants in the event, so that it may expend the greater portion of its energy in presenting dialogue. Several of the border *corridos*—for example "Jacinto Treviño," "Los Sediciosos," and "Pablo González"—devote the body of their narratives to incidents of reported speech.

When a *corrido* presents reported speech it transcends the iconicity we have attributed to narrative, in that a relation of identity is presumed to obtain between the words spoken in the experiential substratum and the words sung by the *corridista*. These episodes exploit the conversational frame of quotation, whereby "the words spoken are to be interpreted as the words of someone other than the speaker" (Bauman 1975:293)—in this in-

stance as the words of the *corrido* protagonists. Perhaps this tran-
scendence of iconicity accounts for the peculiar power of these
scenarios in the *corrido*: by a convention of our communicative
system, we are transported beyond the narrative frame into the
experiential substratum itself. The narrative discourse is thus
punctuated by flashes of identification between the narrative
frame and the experiential substratum. Since the *corrido* is not
obliged to give every pertinent narrative detail, it concentrates
instead on these striking verbal interactions. We shall note below
that the content of these altercations is particularly suited to the
propositional drift of *corrido* discourse.

The narrative portion of the *corrido* exhibits the following
pattern of interaction between the planes of iconicity and
identification:

narrative .... dialogue .... narrative
1   2   1
iconicity   *identity*   *iconicity*

The preservation in verbal form of an experiential sequence
yields to a dramatization of narrative units within that sequence,
which in turn yields to the presentation of the experiential sequence. The typical *corrido* frequently repeats the pattern dia-
grammed above, though not all *corridos* evince such an intense
focus on episodes of dialogue.

Reflexivity

The *corrido* as discourse is not confined to the narrative mode. It
also employs two other discourse types: the reflexive and the
propositional. *Corrido* reflexivity abides in the metanarrative segments which conventionally frame the narrative, and occasionally surface elsewhere as well in the narrative structure. These
metanarrative segments draw attention to the occasion of performance rather than to the occasion of narrative action. In other
words, the *corrido* presents two contrasting referential frames,
one firmly grounded in an experiential sequence prior to the singing of the *corrido* (the narrative frame), and the other reaching
out to the moment of performance itself, with its cast of singer,
audience, and song.

Metanarrative segments are reflexive in that they enable the
song to refer to itself. They may be quite short, as in the opening
stanza of "Gregorio Cortez":

En el condado de El Carmen
miren lo que ha sucedido. . . .
In the county of El Carmen, look what has happened. . . .

Here it is only the imperative form of the verb that signals metanarrative reference. Other instances are more elaborate. For
example:

Pónganle bien la atención
les voy a correr la lista,
el que compuso el corrido
no digan que es un buen artista,
se llama Memencio López
le dicen la gallinita.

Pay close attention, I'll run through the list;
the one who composed the *corrido*, don't say he's a great artist;
his name is Memencio López, they call him the *gallinita*.
"La Gallinita"

The reflexive segments appear most regularly at the edges of the
corrido. They thus establish a metanarrative frame within which
the narration is embedded, producing the following pattern:

metanarrative	narrative . . . . narrative	metanarrative
1	2	1
(opening formulas)		(the *despedida*)

The *corrido* as a form of discourse presents narrative material
moving from iconicity to identification, lodged within a metanarrative frame which verbally reflects the moment of performance.

Propositionality
The third discourse mode employed in the *corrido* is the proposition. A proposition is a speech act which affirms or denies, thereby making a statement concerning some state of affairs. The *corrido* is both overtly and covertly propositional. In *corridos* the
authorial voice occasionally introduces editorial commentary
into the narrative, generally to formulate explicitly concepts already abundantly evident in the selection and presentation of the
narrative material. The customary observation that ballads
maintain a stance of objectivity toward the events they narrate
has some application to the *corrido*. *Corridos* are primarily con-

cerned to tell a story, not to pass moral or partisan judgments on the actors or events in the story. In this sense, most *corridos* are fundamentally non-propagandistic, although important exceptions to this rule can easily be found. However, even the most objective of *corridos* is propositional to some extent, and the propositional character of the *corrido* can be readily turned to partisan ends.

In one important sense the *corrido* is intensely subjective, in that it is securely planted in the collective world view of the *corrido* community. While the *corrido* may strive to present events in an unbiased fashion, it shows no comparable effort to transcend its own ethnocentricity. On the contrary, this ethnocentricity figures prominently in the *corrido* ethos, rendering each *corrido* a powerful statement of community values and orientations. In the term suggested by Roger Abrahams (1978 : 80), the *corrido* is an "enactment"—that is, a:

cultural event in which community members come together to participate, employ the deepest and most complex multivocal and polyvalent signs and symbols of their repertoire of expression, thus entering into a potentially significant experience.

More particularly, the *corrido* may be characterized as an enactment of the serious sort, departing from the everyday through intensification of conventional codes and orders.

The *corrido* is propositional in this broadest sense, asserting a collective sense of identity by incorporating signs and symbols which have special resonance in the *corrido* community. The propositional character of the *corrido* is implemented through several devices, all of which interact to reinforce a common cosmological orientation. To begin with, the *corrido*'s very selection of events worthy of narration proceeds from a notably ethnocentric bias. The *corrido* seeks out moments of active, violent confrontation, in which death to either or both parties is a distinct and immediate possibility. It is in these tense moments that individuals show their true nature, whether heroic or cowardly.

So pervasive is the *corrido*'s orientation to violent action that it may pass over other striking aspects of an event without mention. An example is "Gregorio Cortez," which Américo Paredes (1976 : 31) calls "without doubt the epitome of the border *corrido*." The song concentrates on vignettes of mortal struggle with the hero's life in the balance. Totally absent is any mention of this man's remarkable pilgrimage through the Anglo-American legal system, from which he emerged relatively unscathed (he was actually acquitted, on appeal, of the charge of killing a sheriff and a constable). The omission of these intriguing details clearly reveals the *corridista's* selectivity: confrontations in the mesquite are in, confrontations in the courtroom are out. The events selected for narration in the *corrido* answer to community values and orientations.

Moreover, the force of a collective outlook can actually overpower historical reality in some cases. Américo Paredes (1972, 1976) develops one very instructive case, "José Mosqueda." This *corrido* treats of a train robbery in which all the principals were Mexicans, Texas-Mexicans, or Spaniards. Nonetheless, the *corrido* explicitly locates the event on American soil ("en terreno americano") and depicts the gringos complaining about it. As Paredes observes:

The patterns of folk literature and the stresses of intercultural conflict triumph over historical fact in "José Mosqueda." Some minor historical data (a train robbery) are superseded by an overriding historical fact (the clash of cultures) (1976:30).

Incidentally, this tendency does not mean that *corridos* are useless as historical documents. Rather, like all such documents, the *corrido* is partly opaque and requires careful decoding.

The *corrido's* selectivity ensures that it will be laden with references to objects and emblems expressive of the community's orientation to experience. Thus "Gregorio Cortez" mentions items such as the *pistola, corral, balazo,* etc. Since the *corrido* ends its narration with the capture of Cortez, it makes no reference to bailiffs, judges, courtrooms, pardons, and the like. But this is entirely appropriate: the Anglo legal system is foreign to the *corrido* ambience just as it is foreign to the significant world of the border population. A *corrido* can deal with imprisonment, as does "Cananea," for example, but it must use terms familiar to the community. This focus on significant action as defined by the community world view populates *corridos* with numerous references evocative of life within the community.

One element which makes a crucial contribution to the propositional character of the *corrido* is the content of the kernel episodes of reported speech. The words of men and women in conflict reflect the same value system implicit in the selection of events to narrate and the modification of history to suit folk orientations. Let us consider some of the postures conveyed in these scenarios of verbal exchange. A prevalent attitude is that of (often haughty) defiance on the part of an individual facing probable or certain death:

a) "Gregorio Cortez"
Decía Gregorio Cortez
con su pistola en la mano:
—No corran, rinches cobardes,
con un solo mexicano.

Then said Gregorio Cortez with his pistol in his hand, "Don't run, you cowardly *rinches*, from a single Mexican."

b) "Jacinto Treviño"
—Entrenle, rinches cobardes
que el pleito no es con un niño,
querían conocer su padre
yo soy Jacinto Treviño.

"Come on, you cowardly *rinches*, you're not playing games with a child. You wanted to meet your father? I am Jacinto Treviño."

c) "Arnulfo"
Pero ¡ay! le dice el teniente,
ya casi pa' agonizar:
—Oiga amigo, no se vaya,
acábeme de matar.

But oh, the lieutenant says, almost with his last breath, "Listen, friend, don't go away. Come back and finish me off."

d) "Felipe Angeles"
—El reloj marca sus horas,
se acerca mi ejecución;
preparan muy bien sus armas,
apuntenme el corazón.

—Yo no soy de los cobardes
que le temen a la muerte,
la muerte no mata a nadie,
la matadora es la suerte.

"The clock ticks off the hours, my execution draws near; prepare well your weapons, and aim at my heart.

"I am not one of those cowards who are afraid of death. Death does not kill anyone; it is our fortune that kills."

These examples could be multiplied endlessly, since the great majority of *corridos* provides one or several examples of defiant speech at the prospect of death. But let me introduce one final instance which approaches the macabre:

Fue cayendo poco a poco
con el sombrero en la cara,
dice—Está bueno, muchachos
y soltó una carcajada.

He was falling little by little with his hat in his face; he says, "That's fine, boys," and let out a guffaw.

"Villarreal"

These instances of defiance are clearly exemplary. The fearless man of action, the capacity to die honorably—these are themes characteristic of a heroic world view, and the world view of the *corrido* is decidedly heroic. Part of the propositional intent of the *corrido* is to stipulate that a man *should* die honorably, *should* confront death fearlessly.

The honorable course of action is highlighted by presentation of its opposite, the man who disgraces himself by flinching at impending death. The border *corrido* often depicts this contrasting behavior among the *americanos*:

a) "Gregorio Cortez"
Decían los americanos:
—Si lo alcanzamos, que hacemos?
Si le entramos por derecho
muy poquitos volveremos.

Then said the Americans, "If we catch up with him, what should we do? If we fight him man to man, very few of us will return."

b) "Gregorio Cortez"
Decía el Cherife Mayor
como queriendo llorar:
—Cortez, entrega tus armas,
no te vamos a matar.

Then said the Major Sheriff, as if he were going to cry, "Cortez, hand over your weapons; we do not want to kill you."

One important contributing element of the *corrido* statement is thus the exemplary attitude (and its opposite) expressed in the words of men confronting death.

At certain points in the *corrido*, we encounter material which is explicitly propositional, material that summarizes in so many words the conceptions which are conveyed less directly in the other propositional elements discussed above. Here the *corridista* departs from his normal role of narrator to introduce editorial commentary concerning the events being narrated. A notable example occurs in "Arnulfo":

Que bonitos son los hombres
que se matan pecho a pecho,
cada uno con su pistola,
defendiendo su derecho.

How admirable are men who fight to the death face to face, each one of
them with his pistol, defending his right.

Here we have an especially complete editorial statement inserted
into the narrative. The *corrido* tells of a duel, fatal to both parties, provoked by a seemingly trivial instance of excessive eye
contact between strangers. From one point of view, the two
deaths might appear quite unnecessary, but the *corridista* hastens
to shape our interpretation of these events in another fashion: the
two men were defending their rights. The principle of defending
one's honor through armed combat, repeatedly illustrated in *corrido* narrative, is here stated in overt propositional form. The
same proposition is enunciated in a *corrido* from Guerrero, "Juan
Colón":

Bonitos hombres se rajan
cuando les llegue la hora. . . .

Fine men are undone when their hour comes. . . .

In some cases, the editorial commentary may reflect a partisan bias, rather than simply articulating values common to the
corrido community:

a) "Los Tequileros"
Los rinches serán muy hombres
no se les puede negar,
nos cazan como venados
para podernos matar.

Si los rinches fueran hombres
y sus caras presentaran,
entonce' a los tequileros
otro gallo nos cantara.

The *rinches* are very brave, there is no doubt of that; the only way they
can kill us is by hunting us like deer.

If the *rinches* were really brave, and met us face to face, then things
would be quite different for us tequila runners.

b) "La Toma de Ciudad Juarez"
¡Ah, qué valor de Madero
bonitas son sus acciones!
Que mandó a sus cabecillas

a echar fuera las prisiones.
¡La Virgen de Guadalupe
lo colme de bendiciones!

Ah, how brave was Madero, how admirable were his acts! For he sent his chieftains to empty out the prisons. May the Virgin of Guadalupe heap benedictions upon him!

c) "Ramón Romero"

El señor Perez y Perez
como señor ingeniero
hacía lo que el quería
como gozaba de un cuero,
pero allí se lo olvidó
que tenía blandito el cuero.

Mr. Perez y Perez being an engineer
always did what he wanted, since he enjoyed a certificate;
but there he forgot that his skin was soft.

As these three examples demonstrate, the *corridista* can editorialize in a most partisan fashion, reflecting his support of an underground gang, a political faction, or a class interest. The prevailing ethnocentric bias of the *corrido* can easily yield a partisan bias of the kind illustrated here, depending on the affiliations of its audience. As noted above, there are definite limits to the objectivity of the *corrido*. It is worthy of notice that, in *corridos* biased in this fashion, the voice of the *corridista* tends to merge with the voices of the protagonists, as shown in example a above. Even in partisan *corridos*, however, the primary emphasis is on the straightforward narration of events, and editorial commentary is kept in the background.

In these indirect and direct ways the *corridista* expresses an attitude toward the events he narrates, thus conferring on the *corrido* a propositional dimension. In the selection of material and emphasis, in the alteration of historical fact to conform to community patterns of thought, in the context of dialogue inserted into the narrative, and in direct editorial commentary, the *corridista* asserts a range of propositions lodged in the ethos of the community. The *corrido* does indeed make a statement, one which always reflects the world view and value system of the *corrido* community and, sometimes, includes still finer calibrations of ethnic, political, and class affiliation.

To summarize our progress so far, we have established the following points about the *corrido* as a form of discourse:

a) The *corrido* is a multifaceted discourse, with reflexive, narrative, and propositional elements;
b) *Corrido* narrative is generally embedded within a metanarrative frame;
c) *Corrido* narrative is iconic, but in occasional segments transcends iconicity to produce identification with the presumed experiential substratum;
d) *Corrido* narrative tends to be impersonal, historical, and inscrutable; and
e) The *corrido* is indirectly and directly propositional, making assertions which derive from the collective outlook and experience of the *corrido* community.

These perspectives identify the *corrido* as a particular form of discourse, and isolate the basic conceptual moves entailed in *corrido* discourse. However, to complete the discussion we must consider the poetic character of *corrido* discourse, whose distinctive texture and structure mark *corridos* off from other forms of discourse.

The Poetics of Corrido *Discourse*

We conceive of the poetic dimension in verbal art as the patterning of the medium of expression above and beyond the requirements of referential communication. Roman Jakobson (1960:356) characterizes the poetic function of language as the focus on message form, thereby "promoting the palpability of signs." Expressive genres exhibit varying degrees of saturation with regard to the poetic function. Some prose narratives reveal only slight, intermittent patterning of the medium of expression beyond the level requisite to grammatical encoding of the message. The *corrido* obviously belongs at the opposite end of this spectrum, as in it we find the poetic function highly marked. The *corrido* is a demanding poetic form, which requires unflinching attention not only to the content but equally to the manner of expression.

Preeminent among the *corrido*'s poetic effects are those which derive from the recurring structural unit, the stanza. The typical *corrido* evinces a discourse structure composed of a chain of these units, each unit containing four or six lines of octosyllabic verse. Typically, the *corrido* lacks a refrain: the content of each successive stanza is new. The final word or words in each even-numbered line must be controlled for rhyme or assonance. The constitutive unit of *corrido* discourse, the stanza, displays the following features:

a) A series of four or six lines (depending on the number of phrases in the melody);
b) Each line contains eight syllables (note the convention of eliding certain unstressed syllables and counting a final stressed syllable as two); and
c) The last word or two of even-numbered lines is controlled for purposes of rhyme or assonance.

This kernel structure is illustrated below:

1) En el condado de El Carmen
   1   2 3 4 5   6   7   8

2) miren lo que ha sucedido, (i-o)
   1 2   3 4   5 6 7 8

3) murió el Cherife Mayor,
   1 2   3   45 6 7/8

4) quedando Roman herido (i-o)
   1   2   3   4   5   6 78

As I have mentioned, these constitutive units are strung together into a chain without verbatim repetition from one another. That is to say that, while the form of each stanza remains constant, the content is novel, except for occasional repeated bits found in some *corridos*.

From the composer's point of view, the critical moments in this structural unit are those key words at the end of lines 2 and 4 which must display either the same final two vowels (assonance) or the same final vowels and consonants (rhyme). Sound correspondences are fortuitous in languages: linguistic codes are not specifically designed, that is, to produce phonological coincidence within the lexicon. But the construction of lexicons from extremely sparse phonological inventories insures that some such fortuitous sound correspondences will occur in all natural languages. Spanish, with its tendency to alternate vowels and consonants and even to delete certain unstressed consonants, contains many words which fortuitously end with the same pair of final vowels. It is the task of the *corridista* to exploit these congruences in tailoring his stanzas, while maintaining the semantic integrity of the *corrido*.

The need to control these pivotal words tends to divide the *corrido* into smaller units of two lines. Thus the constitutive unit, the stanza, is in turn composed of a pair or trio of nuclear elements, the verse dyad which meets all stipulations of meter and rhyme or assonance. The compositional primacy of the verse dyad is indicated by its detachable character, which allows it to float freely in a *corrido* tradition (see McDowell 1972). Consider the following examples from Paredes' *cancionero*:

Decía [insert name]
como queriendo llorar
Then said [insert name], as if he were going to cry

a) "Ignacio Treviño"
   Decía Pedro Saldaña
   como queriendo llorar
   Decía José Calderón
   como queriendo llorar

b) "Gregorio Cortez"
   Decía el Cherife Mayor
   como queriendo llorar

c) "José Mosqueda"
   Decía don Esteban Salas
   como queriendo llorar

These handy, detachable units allow the *corridista* to begin the stanza. They must be complemented by a second dyad which completes the thought they initiated, and which contains the final word with appropriate vowels or consonants.

But these building blocks are themselves constructed from smaller, stable units: the individual lines. Many of the formulaic dyads are themselves composed of relatively free-floating units. For example:

a) Decía [insert name]
   como queriendo llorar
   Then said [insert name], as if he were going to cry

b) Decía [insert name]
   con su pistola en la mano
   Then said [insert name], with his pistol in his hand

c) Decía [insert name]
   con su alma muy encendida
   Then said [insert name], with his soul aflame

d) Decía [insert name]
   en su caballo melado
   Then said [insert name], on his honey-colored horse

Here I have given only the more productive instances. Innumerable more specialized cases and variations on these patterns occur in the *corridos*. Thus, if his protagonist were named Cortez, the *corridista* might find it useful to incorporate the following variation:

Decían los americanos
decían con timidez
Then the Americans said, and they said it fearfully

These formulaic systems facilitate composition in a demanding form, by supplying the given essential idea in a manner which permits maximum flexibility for the creation of the sound correspondence demanded by the *corrido*'s stanzaic structure. Thus the insertion of the name is phonologically inconsequential, and the introductory gambit ("decía") uses up only two of the eight syllables allowed per line. The remaining six syllables may be partitioned out among some version of the name—either the entire name, the last name only, or some other modification such as "don Esteban Salas." The set of lines capable of completing the dyad provides the *corridista* with a range of phonological choices. The four common types I cited above yield these possibilities:
a) llorar (ar)
b) mano (a-o)
c) encendida (i-a)
d) melado (a-o)
Also, the formula may be adapted to the particular phonological resources of specific *corridos*; "decían con timidez," for example, would suit a *corrido* about a man named Cortez (the -ez is common to both words). The *corridista* may thus look ahead to the information the second dyad of the stanza will convey, and anticipate the coordination of pivotal words in lines 2 and 4 (and possibly 6).

I do not mean to imply that *corridos* are composed in any mechanistic fashion. I have selected here the most conspicuous stanzaic patterns in order to illustrate a compositional process which operates in a multiplicity of forms throughout a corpus of *corridos*. Within *corrido* traditions there is much room for composition during performance (cf. Lord 1960), although the general format of a given *corrido* may be fixed in the singer's memory. The compositional process I have described above enables the composer/performer to attend simultaneously to the sense and the sound of his discourse.

The poetic character of *corrido* discourse thus has many
structural consequences. The need to control the phonological
make-up of the final words in even-numbered lines determines a
major substanzaic unit, the dyad. Dyads in turn are built with
more basic units, individual octosyllabic lines. There is a semantic correlate to these units. The stanza retains a semantic integrity, expressing a complete idea which can be readily disjoined
from the surrounding discourse context. Within the stanza, the
dyads tend to express complementary ideas. Ordinarily each dyad takes the syntactic form of a complete sentence, although exceptions to this rule can be found. Even the individual line has
some syntactic integrity, often in the form of an immediate constituent to the sentence. Rarely is enjambment so radical as to
break off the verse line within a more local constituent of the
phrase marker.

Let us turn now to the question of imagery in the *corrido*.
Imagery results from the operation of the poetic function at the
level of the signified in language (cf. de Saussure 1959). Lexemes
are, fortuitously, capable of polysemic reference—that is, reference to more than one object—and verbal artistry incorporates
this fortuitous capacity above and beyond the needs of simple referential communication. By means of polysemic lexemes, referents not usually associated with one another can be brought into
momentary association. *Corrido* imagery presents a split distribution. The narrative segments tend to be literal, or mono-
semic, models of clear and economic narrative exposition. Often
in their simplicity these segments are quite elegant, as the following stanza from "Jacinto Treviño" illustrates:

Y en la cantina de Bekar
se agarraron a balazos,
por dondequiera saltaban
botellas hechas pedazos.
They had a shootout at Bekar's saloon;
broken bottles were popping all over the place.

Another example is the exquisite stanza from "Chicharrón":

Cuando lo iban a enterrar
su caballo iba de luto,
a las arenas del mar
fueron a hacer el sepulto.

When they went to bury him his horse went in mourning;
they went to the sands of the sea to make the grave.

As these passages indicate, narrative exposition in the *corrido* can
attain high levels of grace and beauty, in descriptive verse devoid
of any imagery.

The *corrido* does not favor poetic conceit in its presentation
of narrative detail. The portions of reported speech, on the other
hand, provide the *corridista* with ample scope to wax poetic (although always, of course, within the constraints imposed by the
esthetic canons of the ballad community). An important message
is conveyed in the process: the *corrido* hero is not only a man
of decisive action, but a man of words as well, able to formulate colorful verbal interpretations of the events at hand. In fact,
corrido heroes seem irresistibly drawn to the use of figurative
language; their speeches often invoke "the deepest and most com
plex multivocal and polyvalent signs and symbols" of the community's expressive system (Abrahams 1978:80; cf. Turner 1969).

Two speech acts predominate in *corrido* dialogue: the boast
and the insult. In the former the hero employs figurative language to signal metaphorically the nature and extent of his ac-
complishment, in the latter to impugn the character of his adversary through unsavory comparisons. While these two speech acts
in no way exhaust the *corrido* hero's repertoire, they are the
forms most amenable to the display of his verbal artistry. This
skill is especially evident in the telling application of tropes. We
will consider three examples of each speech act, beginning with
three boasts:

a) "Alonso"

Margarito se murió
Alonso está en las espumas:
—Ya les maté el gallo fino
nomás quedaron las plumas.

Margarito is dead, Alonso is riding high;
"I killed you the fighting cock; nothing was left but his feathers."

b) "Alonso"

Un domingo por la mañana
Alonso salió pa' Texas:
—Ya les tumbé el panal
Ahi les dejo las abejas.

On a Sunday morning, Alonso left for Texas:
"I knocked down the hive for you, but I'm leaving you the bees."

c) "Gregorio Cortez"

Decía Gregorio Cortez
echando muchos balazos;
—Me he escapado de aguaceros
contimás de nublinazos.

Then said Gregorio Cortez, shooting out a lot of bullets: "I have weathered thunderstorms; this little mist doesn't bother me."

The underlying conceptual move is the same in these three cases. It can be identified as the rhetorical figure known variously as the diagram or analogy, wherein a relation between two or more items is designated by means of another relation (cf. Todorov 1973; Sapir and Crocker 1977). This figure is especially complex because it sets up two forms of relationship among the referents: metonymy between the adjacent items, and metaphor across the two referential domains. The hive and its bees are terms drawn from a single semantic or perceptual domain, and therefore exhibit the relationship of metonymy. But these terms are meant to implicate referents pertinent to the *corrido* narrative—the fortress of the adversaries or the main adversary (the hive), perhaps, and the minor adversaries associated with that fortress or main adversary (the bees). The relationship between the bees and the minor adversaries is metaphoric. These relationships may best be understood in schematic form:

$$\text{A:B :: X:Y}$$

metonymy

hive:bees :: fortress:minor adversaries

metaphor

The other two figures may be depicted similarly:

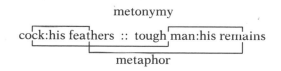

metonymy

cock:his feathers :: tough man:his remains

metaphor

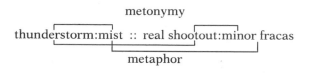

metonymy

thunderstorm:mist :: real shootout:minor fracas

metaphor

It would be a mistake to assume that the *corridista* gives full vent to his poetic instincts in these passages, that he indulges in an uninhibited display of poetic conceit. Two obvious constraints affect the imagery of the *corrido*. First, the objects enshrined in these tropes must come from the common experience of the ballad community. The *corridista* must confine his imagination to the relevant ecological foundation of the people of whom and for whom he sings. The hive, the cock, and the thunderstorm all derive from the agrarian roots of the community; the *gallo*, in particular, is an especially resonant figure within the community world view. The second constraint on poetic license in *corrido* imagery stems from the oral tradition of the community. The figures themselves are most often traditional; they recur not only within the *corrido* corpus but in other forms of oral poetry as well. To cite only one example, "a slightly bawdy *son veracruzano*" (quoted in Paredes 1977 : 30) uses an image analogous to that of the hive and its bees:

Me picaron las abejas
pero me comí el panal.

The bees stung me
but I ate the comb.

Of course one would not have to look very far in Greater Mexican oral poetry to find many variations on the comparison of a tough man to a *gallo bien jugado*, a game cock. The imagery of these boasts is thus highly complex conceptually while thoroughly grounded in the oral tradition and world view of the ballad community.

Insults in the *corrido* are loaded with figurative speech, but we confine ourselves here to three examples, all from "Jacinto Treviño":

a) —Entrenle, rinches cobardes,
   que el pleito no es con un niño,
   querían conocer su padre
   yo soy Jacinto Treviño.

   "Come on, you cowardly *rinches*, you're not playing games with a child. You wanted to meet your father? I am Jacinto Treviño."

b) —Entrenle, rinches cobardes,
   validos de la ocasión,
   no van a comer pan blanco
   con tajadas de jamón.

"Come on, you cowardly *rinches*, you always like to take the advantage; this is not like eating white bread with slices of ham."

c) Decía Jacinto Treviño
que se moría de la risa:
—A mi me hacen los ojales
los puños de la camisa.

Then said Jacinto Treviño, who was dying of laughter, "All you're good for is to make the buttonholes and cuffs on my shirt."

Each of these insults is lodged against the *rinche*, or Texas Ranger, a deservedly unloved character to the Texas-Mexican. In the first example, the rangers are compared to children, and more specifically to the children of Jacinto Treviño himself. The insult here is double-barreled: the *rinches* are children, thus not mature adults; and the *rinches* are the product of presumably illicit relations between Jacinto Treviño and their mothers. Thus the *corrido* manages to work in one of the most traditional forms of insult within the Greater Mexican repertoire (cf. Paredes 1977).

The second example of the insult makes fun of the eating habits of the *rinches* and their people: their taste for ham sandwiches. Before the arrival of the Anglo, border cuisine had no knowledge of that delicacy, and reference to it is thus in itself a form of derision. The third example implicitly compares the *rinches* to women, by assigning to them the work traditionally associated in the ballad community with females. As with the first example, this insult has an underlying sexual intent. In comparing the *rinches* to women, Treviño is insulting them as less or other than manly; but, at the same time, he is implying that they are, as women, sexually available to someone like himself.

Like the boasts discussed above, these insults are both clever and traditional. They operate on more than one level (in the case of the first and third examples) and invariably connect with the world view of the ballad community. The implicit sexual allegations of examples a and c above bring to mind some of the most standard devices of insult in Greater Mexican oral tradition. They are typical of the *albur*, a form of sly ritual insulting, and are present in a great deal of casual banter among males of Mexican descent. Our analysis of imagery in the *corrido* suggests that, in these passages of reported speech, the *corridista* incorporates complex and subtle poetic conceits native to the oral tradition of his community, employing them to portray the *corrido* hero as an accomplished man of words.

The *corrido* as poetic discourse exhibits at least these two interesting facets: the patterning of sound according to the stipulations of meter and rhyme, with consequent structural effects; and contrasting literal and figurative languages which are largely segregated into their respective niches in the discourse. These aspects of the *corrido* draw attention to it as a system of signs by illustrating that certain features of the code can be exploited and patterned without regard to the referential function of language. The *corrido* is, as we observed at the outset, a highly determined and markedly poetic form of discourse.

THE *CORRIDO* AS MUSIC

The *corrido* is also a unit of musical sound. While a complete treatment of the *corrido* as music would be desirable, I confine myself here to a few preliminary comments derived from the discussion of *corrido* poetics. In particular, I am concerned with how the two autonomous systems, music and discourse, are brought into synchrony in the *corrido*. As we proceed, however, it will be convenient to record some observations on the *corrido* as a musical form.

The first point is that the *corrido* is strophic. The same music, or essentially the same music, returns with each successive stanza of poetry. The poetic stanza, then, has a musical counterpart, the musical strophe, presenting one full statement of the melody with its harmonic underpinnings. (An occasional *corrido* is in rondo form, with a second melodic element periodically inserted, but the typical *corrido* is, as described above, strophic.) The melody generally consists of four or six musical phrases, each phrase corresponding to one line of poetic verse. Minor adjustments are possible when the number of musical and verse phrases is not identical: thus, if there are four verse lines for six musical phrases, the last two verse lines of each stanza may be repeated to fill out the musical structure.

The musical strophe enjoys the same completeness and detachability as the verse stanza. Likewise, the musical structure may be subdivided into units comparable to the verse dyad and the individual verse line. The complete melody (the strophe) is composed of a pair or trio of phrase dyads, each displaying, at the same time, some degree of musical integrity and mutual interdependence. The dyad is made of individual musical phrases, the building blocks of the *corrido*'s musical structure. Musical and poetic structures in the *corrido* are thus similarly designed. We will explore this relationship with reference to two *corridos,* "Jacinto Treviño" and "Gregorio Cortez":

a) "Jacinto Treviño"

b) "Gregorio Cortez"

En el condado de El Carmen
miren lo que ha sucedido,
murió el Cherife Mayor,
quedando Román herido.

En el condado de El Carmen
tal desgracia sucedió,
murió el Cherife Mayor,
no saben quién lo mató.

As these examples demonstrate, the *corrido* undertakes a harmonic journey which is completed with each full statement of the total melodic line. The *corrido* strophe begins and ends in the tonic key. The intervening steps for each example are:

a) "Jacinto Treviño"
phrase 1   D   tonic
phrase 2   D to A⁷   tonic to dominant
phrase 3   A⁷   dominant
phrase 4   A⁷ to D   dominant to tonic

b) "Gregorio Cortez"
phrase 1   G   tonic
phrase 2   G to C   tonic to subdominant
phrase 3   D⁷ to G   dominant to tonic
phrase 4   G to D⁷ to G   tonic to dominant to tonic

The simpler of the two structures is that of "Jacinto Treviño."
Here the two musical dyads are parallel and complement one another. The first dyad opens in the tonic and moves to the dominant; the second dyad reverses this progression. The musical
integrity of the single musical phrase is evident in the harmonic
implication of each (staying within a single key or moving from
one key to one other key) and in the pauses inserted between
phrases 1 and 2. The musical structure of "Jacinto Treviño" is
thus simple and lucid.

The musical structure of "Gregorio Cortez" offers a little
more challenge to the analyst, and in fact here it could be argued
that, instead of two dyads, the musical structure is composed of
one triad and one single musical phrase. The triad undertakes a
harmonic journey from tonic to subdominant to dominant and
back to tonic, while the final musical phrase partially recapitu-
lates by moving from tonic to dominant and back to tonic. This
movement in the last musical phrase insures a strong impression
of harmonic closure, which the more adventurous harmonic character of this musical structure makes necessary.

The harmonic structure of "Gregorio Cortez" may challenge
the prevalence of the dyadic structure in the *corrido*, but other
aspects of this song point toward the presence of dyads there as
in other *corridos*. Consider the contour of its melodic line:
phrase 1   g
phrase 2   b to c
phrase 3   b to a to g
phrase 4   b to a to g
The melodic contour of the first dyad leads from the tonic triad to
the highest pitch encountered in the melody, and, moreover, the
melody comes to rest momentarily on this high pitch, the c of
beats 7 and 8 in the second measure. The task of the melody in
the second dyad is to descend from this high point and thoroughly ground itself in the tonic triad, coming to rest on g in the final
measure. Therefore, in the melodic contour of "Gregorio Cortez"
the dyads evidently retain their structural significance.

The musical structure of the *corrido* articulates units comparable to the units of the poetic structure of *corrido* discourse.

To the poetic stanza corresponds the complete melodic statement; to the lyric dyad, the dyad of musical phrases; to the verse
line, the musical phrase. Each of these units is consequential
within its own universe of discourse; and at each level we find a
congruent equation of completeness, detachability, and interdependence. The interaction of words and music in the *corrido* is
thus far from casual. What we find, in fact, are two complex
structures, music and discourse, each defined in its own terms yet
each maintaining a structural identity with one another. The *corrido* as a unit of music is structurally identical to the *corrido* as a
unit of poetic discourse.

Having made this bold proposition, I must now introduce
some qualifications. I have already noted that not all *corridos* exhibit the neat structural affinity of poetry and music visible in the
two examples given here. A more serious problem, however, is the
relationship of verse line to musical phrase. The verse line has
eight syllables in the standard *corrido trágico*; one might expect
the musical phrase to contain eight melodic moments, each moment in the melody corresponding to one of the eight syllables in
the text. However, our sample *corridos* present no such handy
correlation. "Gregorio Cortez" has nine melodic moments per
musical phrase. In "Jacinto Treviño" the situation is more complicated, as shown below:

phrase 1: 12 pulses
phrase 2: 12 pulses
phrase 3: 8 pulses
phrase 4: 10 pulses

Since the poetic line invariably contains eight syllables in these
corridos, the musical beats would appear to be unmotivated by
the constitution of the poetic text. How are we to explain this dis-
crepancy between syllables in the text and pulses in the musical
phrase?

Let us first note the means of adjustment which brings the
two systems into synchrony. In "Gregorio Cortez" a single syllable of text is held for two musical pulses at the beginning of
each musical measure. Thus a musical emphasis or prolongation
is attached to the poetic text, as follows (prolonged syllables are
italicized):

En *el* condado de El Carmen
mi*ren* lo que ha sucedido,
mu*rió el* Cherife Ma*yor*,
que*dando* Román herido.

With the single exception of "Ma*yor*" (which is stressed and counts as two syllables) the musical prolongation here bears no relation to either semantic or syntactic properties of the text. There is no likely poetic logic which would emphasize these particular syllables. But we can locate a musical logic that accounts for these prolongations. Each musical phrase in "Gregorio Cortez" begins with a quick upbeat, followed by a prolonged downbeat. It is this opening gambit that gives the melody its distinctive jauntiness, and clearly defines the boundaries of the musical phrases within this *corrido*.

In "Jacinto Treviño" we find a more elaborate adjustment of verse line to musical phrase, with longer and less regular prolongations of linguistically inconsequential syllables.

Ya con ésta van tres ve*ces*
que se ha visto lo boni*to*,
la primera fue en Macalen,
en Brónsvil *y en* San Benito.

The prolongations in the first dyad are for three pulses, in each instance, while the prolongation in the last line is for two pulses only. The third line in the stanza allots one syllable to one musical pulse, with no prolongations. The controlling logic here is that of the melodic line. In the first dyad of musical phrases, the melodic line pauses on its final pitch, the f♯ of measure 2 and the c♯ of measure 4, thereby creating a musical parallelism which tends toward a momentary stabilization at the end of each of these phrases. The second musical dyad establishes quite another pattern, tending toward a one-to-one correspondence between poetic syllable and musical pulse which is violated at two points: first, that striking moment of syncopation spanning the border between the two final measures; and second, the final pitch of the melody at the end of the last measure. The syncopation on the d of the last two measures is striking because it is unheralded in the earlier behavior of this melody. Coming as it does toward the end of the melody, it signifies the move to closure. With the prolongation of the final pitch in the melody, the *corrido* announces its firm reversion to the tonic triad.

Both "Gregorio Cortez" and "Jacinto Treviño" provide evidence of a verse line tailored to meet the specifications of a musical phrase. The prolongation of random syllables within the verse line answers to musical rather than poetic considerations. It brings the verse line and the musical phrase into synchrony, so that the larger structural units, the dyad and the stanza, can promote a parity between the musical and poetic systems operative in the *corrido*. Are we then to conclude that the poetic text is dependent on the musical structure? I would suggest instead that in the *corrido* two autonomous systems, the poetic and the musical, are brought into parity through minor adjustments of the verse line to the musical phrase. In this manner the higher-level correlations of the two systems are allowed to proceed unhampered.

THE *CORRIDO* AS EVENT

Finally, we may consider the *corrido* as social event. It is in social interaction, with its attendant social structures and rules of etiquette, that the systems of discourse and music operative in the genre are actualized. The *corrido* presupposes a performance setting lodged within a larger framework of interactional roles and strategies, social occasions, and cultural norms and values. In these pages I cannot attempt a thorough coverage of this vast domain; I will only mention some of the larger systems which are implicated in *corrido* performances.

Américo Paredes (1976) has isolated two main singing occasions among the border folk: those involving a casual audience, perhaps only the singer himself (termed "lonesome singing"); and those involving an organized audience, either within the family sphere (*de familia*) or in a cantina or other male-group setting. Some *corridos* are performed in the casual-audience situation but, for the most part, they belong to the organized-audience situation. A *corrido* performed in the family sphere would be somewhat subdued, and would be supplemented by commentary on the events told in the song. A *corrido* sung in a cantina or on a *parranda* (defined by Paredes [ibid.:xxii] as "an ambulatory version of the cantina situation") would tend to be more raucous. It would involve loud singing, punctuated by *gritos* (shouts from the audience), and little in the way of supplementary narrative.

Paredes observes that the *corrido* is primarily a male performance genre, although women may occasionally perform them. They are commonly sung either by a solo voice (in the casual-audience situation) or by two voices in harmony with a guitar or more extensive instrumental accompaniment. In former days, *corridos* were regularly accompanied by the *bajo*, a twelve-string bass guitar which permitted few frills and thus was suited to "the straightforward pattern of the *corrido*" (Paredes 1976:xxiv). Paredes also notes a variety of overlappings between the *corrido* and other musical forms known in the border community, such as *décimas* (ibid.:116) and *coplas* (ibid.:40).

The *corrido*, then, is a particular class of event—a performance event. As performances, *corridos* entail: performers, embarked on a display of communicative competence (see Bauman 1975); audiences, attending to these displays with a critical ear; and a set of rules or expectations regulating the proper fulfillment of these interdependent roles. For the border *corrido*, Paredes cites three performance occasions: the solitary setting, in which singer and audience may well be one; the family setting, in which the singer is most likely male although the audience may be composed of men, women, and children; and the cantina or *parranda*, an all-male setting. Social roles clearly affect *corrido* performance: women may be described as essentially marginal to these performance occasions among the border folk. The *corrido*, with its propositional content drawn from the heroic world view, belongs primarily to men. Thus it reflects the large-scale allocation of men and women to separate material and symbolic spheres maintained within this community (see Paredes 1976; Madsen 1964).

The proper fulfillment of performer and audience roles in *corrido* performance entails a complex set of esthetic rules. Prominent among these, and most readily seized on by ballad students, are the global factors of vocal style, instrumentation, audience response patterns, and the like. But of equal importance are the minute details of paraphonology, proxemics, and kinesics, which give performances much of their palpable fidelity to community patterns of expressivity. The esthetics of *corrido* performance rests upon an "expressive ecology," which is present in the everyday articulation of sound, space, time, and motion but comes into focus through the genres of artistic expression recognized within the community. The *corrido*, as one art form among others, selectively and uniquely taps this reservoir of indigenous expressive motives. Proper fulfillment of performance roles depends on an intimate acquaintance with the entire expressive ecology.

The *grito*, a necessary companion to *corrido* performance in its more robust settings, offers a good illustration. The *grito* is a shout carefully timed and contoured, and equally carefully inserted into the musical fabric by a member of the audience (see Limón 1972). Even though a good deal of leeway is allowed in the performance of *gritos*, it is difficult for non-natives of the community to produce them correctly—evidently because they lack the necessary intimacy with the native expressive ecology. To perform properly as a member of the audience in a cantina setting, one must be able to launch *gritos* appropriately as the *corrido* unfolds. This skill requires a knowledge of the intonational patterns of conversational Norteño Spanish and of the *ranchero* musical corpus, to name only the most obvious prerequisites. In a similar fashion, every detail of *corrido* performance ultimately presupposes the entire edifice of communicative resources.

Moreover, subcultures within Greater Mexico may cultivate different *corrido* performance styles. The present essay has focused on two *corrido* traditions, one located around the Texas-Mexican border and the other in the Mexican states of Guerrero and Oaxaca. While each region assuredly cultivates the *corrido*, their local styles have important differences, which perhaps derive from differences in their expressive ecologies. One salient distinction is that *corridos* are sometimes sung and played in the minor key in Guerrero and Oaxaca, but not in the border region. Significantly, in Guerrero and Oaxaca the musical form known as the *chilena* is of great importance; and the *chilena* is invariably sung and played in the minor key. The expressive ecology of the border area evidently provides no comparable stimulus. As Paredes observes, in that region the interaction has been between the *corrido* and the *décima* and *copla*, neither of which exerts any pronounced impulsion toward the minor modality.

Regions which are notably endowed with a lively *corrido* tradition may reflect the intervention of other global considerations. Those regions of Greater Mexico which have been longest and most intensively exposed to the national culture tend to nourish the singing of a finite set of traditional ballads rather than an active ballad tradition (Paredes 1963). Here we are dealing with yet another sort of expressive ecology, one drawn from the older subcultures but blended into a new phenomenon in the electronic crucible of the mass media. One obvious result of this process, visible (or audible) in the *corrido*, is the trimming of *corrido* discourse down to a small number of stanzas (to fill a three- or four-minute period), and the introduction of instrumental virtuosity in the musical accompaniment. Thus the gradual incorporation of the scattered regions into the national economy, and the attendant introduction of the national culture into these regions, affects the status of the *corrido* as an event.

Finally, in complex social environments such as Mexico City, the *corrido* exhibits a remarkable adaptation to the variety of expressive ecologies characteristic of a diversified society. Thus, in barrios composed of migrants from the north, or from the coast of Oaxaca, one might encounter a living ballad tradition somewhat like the traditions in the immigrants' home territories; among the general working population, a set of traditional ballads derived mostly from the mass media; among some upwardly mobile strata, a reluctance to acknowledge the *corrido* on any terms; and, in artistic circles, a cultivation of literary *corridos* which owe more to the influence of García Lorca than of Emiliano Zapata. Our investigation of the *corrido* as performance event has led to the very socioeconomic foundations of the society of Greater Mexico.

Although much more could be said on the subject, we can summarize our insights into the *corrido* as event in the following terms: the *corrido* is a performance event which calls into play a wide range of communicative resources belonging to the native expressive ecology, articulating them by means of an impressive inventory of esthetic, social, economic, and political variables. The study of the *corrido* as performance event offers a fascinating entrée into the cultural configuration of modern Greater Mexico, as well as a glimpse of a Mexico that was and perhaps, in certain remote areas, continues to be. We have plotted the intersection of *corrido* performance with several cultural codes:

a) The codes which determine the native expressive ecology—in particular the linguistic, sociolinguistic, kinesic, and proxemic codes;

b) The code allocating men and women to separate material and symbolic domains;

c) The code of subregional development, with its variable levels of integration into the national economy and culture; and

d) The code of socioeconomic diversity.

In conjunction, these and other factors condition the set of local expressive ecologies, and from these realms of communicative potential emerge situated *corrido* performances, each performance a unique dramatization of the possibilities of the genre.

NOTE

1. Five *corridos* from my Guerrero collection are cited: "Villarreal," "Juan Colón," "La Gallinita," "Ramón Romero," and "Chicharrón." All other *corridos* come from Dr. Paredes' *cancionero*.

BIBLIOGRAPHY

Abrahams, Roger D. 1978. Toward an enactment theory of folklore. In *Frontiers of folklore*. William Bascom, ed. Boulder: Westview Press.

Bauman, Richard. 1975. Verbal art as performance. *American Anthropologist* 77:290–311.

de Saussure, Ferdinand. 1959. *Course in general linguistics*. New York: McGraw-Hill.

Jakobson, Roman. 1960. Linguistics and poetics. In *Style in language*. Thomas Sebeok, ed. Cambridge: MIT Press.

Labov, William, and Joshua Waletzky. 1967. Narrative analysis: Oral versions of personal experience. In *Essays on the verbal and visual arts*. June Helm, ed. Seattle: University of Washington Press.

Limón, José. 1972. *El grito mexicano* as folkloric performance. Unpublished MS.

Lord, Albert. 1960. *The singer of tales*. Cambridge: Harvard University Press.

Madsen, William. 1964. *The Mexican-Americans of South Texas*. New York: Holt, Rinehart, and Winston.

McDowell, John. 1972. The Mexican *corrido*: Formula and theme in a ballad tradition. *Journal of American Folklore* 85:205–220.

Mendoza, Vicente. 1964. *Lírica narrativa de México: El corrido*. Mexico: UNAM Instituto de Investigaciones Esteticas.

Paredes, Américo. 1958a. The Mexican *corrido*: Its rise and fall. In *Madstones and Twisters*. Mody Boatright et al., eds. Dallas: SMU Press.

———. 1958b. *With his pistol in his hand*. Austin: University of Texas Press.

———. 1961. Folklore and history. In *Singers and storytellers*. Mody Boatright, Wilson Hudson, and Allen Maxwell, eds. Dallas: SMU Press.

———. 1963. The ancestry of Mexico's *corridos*: A matter of definition. *Journal of American Folklore* 76:231–235.

———. 1972. José Mosqueda and the folklorization of actual events. *Aztlán* 4:1–30.

———. 1976. *A Texas-Mexican* cancionero. Urbana: University of Illinois Press.

————. 1977. On ethnographic work among minority groups: A folklorist's perspective. *New Scholar* 6:1–32.

Sapir, J. David, and Christopher Crocker. 1977. *The social use of metaphor.* Philadelphia: University of Pennsylvania Press.

Simmons, Merle. 1957. *The Mexican* corrido *as a source for the interpretive study of modern Mexico.* Bloomington: Indiana University Press.

Todorov, Tzvetan. 1973. Analyse du discours: L'Example des devinettes. *Journal de Psychologie Normale et Pathologique* 1/2:135–155.

Turner, Victor. 1969. Forms of symbolic action: Introduction. In *Forms of symbolic action.* Robert Spencer, ed. Seattle: University of Washington Press.

Part III

Social Types and Stereotypes

Richard Bauman

"Any Man Who Keeps More'n One Hound'll Lie to You": Dog Trading and Storytelling at Canton, Texas

The coon hunter and the trader, like their compatriots elsewhere in the American expressive landscape, have constituted a presence in Texas folk tradition, and their tales and exploits have captured the attention of Texas folklorists from J. Frank Dobie to Américo Paredes. Dobie (1946) for example, adapted two tall tales of coon hunting in his sketch, "The Cold-Nosed Hounds," while Mody Boatright (1965:96) recorded a coon-dog story attached to Gib Morgan, the legendary oil driller. One of the core episodes in the saga of Gregorio Cortez, which Américo Paredes has chronicled, is a crooked horse trade carried off by Gregorio's brother, Román (Paredes 1958:37–39). In contemporary Texas the horse trader may have been pushed off the scene by the tractor, and the coon hunter may ride around in an $8,000 pickup, but the traditions of the sharp trader and the hound-dog man have lost none of their vigor in the East Texas area around Canton.

Canton, Texas is a small town of approximately three thousand people, located about sixty miles east and a little south of Dallas. Its principal claim to fame is that, on the Sunday preceding the first Monday of every month, Canton becomes the scene of a large and very popular trading fair. The average attendance is about twenty thousand—perhaps double that on Labor Day. The fair draws traders and dealers from as far away as New York, California, Oregon, and Minnesota.

First Monday at Canton—for so it is still called, though the action has shifted to Sunday in accommodation to the modern work week—fits into a long tradition of American trade days.

These seem to have originated in this country, before the middle of the seventeenth century, in conjunction with the sitting of the county courts (Craven 1949:167). These courts met as often as once a month in some convenient spot, corresponding to the shire town of England or New England. Court day was a holiday, an occasion on which county residents came into town not only in connection with court functions, but to transact all kinds of business: to discuss public affairs, hold auctions, trade, and visit on the courthouse green (Carson 1965:195–196; Fiske 1904:62–66; Verhoeff 1911:7n). County courts usually met on the first Monday of the month—hence the term "First Monday." Though the sitting of the court was the nucleus around which the court days first developed, the occasion became a social institution in its own right; Sydnor (1948:34) calls it one of the most important in the antebellum South. As political organization changed, however, and county courts developed other schedules, trade days often disengaged from court sessions to become autonomous occasions; they continued to be economically and socially important to the people of the regions in which they were held.

From the beginning, an important commodity in the trading that went on during First Mondays was horses and mules. Professional horse and mule traders were called "jockies"; hence, "Jockey Day" and "Hoss Monday" are other names for the occasion, and "jockey ground" or "jockey yard" designate the area in which the trading was conducted (Sartain 1932:253). Numerous local histories and personal documents testify to the high degree of interest and excitement generated by the action on the jockey ground during the height of the trade days in the nineteenth and early twentieth centuries. But, as horses and mules declined in importance with the mechanization of Southern agriculture, First Monday trade days declined as well, to the point that very few now remain. Still, some trade days have been in continuous existence since they began, while other have been revived, reincarnated as flea markets.

First Monday in Canton, like most others, began in conjunction with a county court day; Canton is the county seat of Van Zandt County. The event developed in the years following the Civil War, probably in the early 1870s (Mills 1950:191–192). Like most others, too, this trade day became as much or more an occasion for coming to Canton as for attending to court business. Until 1965 the trading took place in the courthouse square, but by the mid-sixties the crowds simply got too big, and separate grounds were set aside. At present, there are more than one thousand lots available on the trading ground, and more are being added all the time. The entire event is now sponsored by the Canton Chamber of Commerce.

Though an occasional mule or two is still hauled to Canton for trade, and a considerable amount of domestic poultry is sold there as well, where animals are concerned, coon dogs are the real focus of interest during First Monday. This dog trading was an early feature of Canton First Monday. No one seems to know precisely when it began but my oldest informants, who are past eighty, remember it from their earliest visits to Canton. In 1960, a few years before the general trading left the courthouse square for separate grounds, the dog trading was moved to its own site across the highway from the main area, down on the river bottom. The dog grounds and dog trading are not part of the Chamber of Commerce operation. The grounds are privately owned, and the dog trading generally has a very different tone from the flea-market atmosphere across the road.

First, whereas many of the flea-market dealers and public are women, the people on the dog grounds are almost exclusively men. Again, the flea market attracts many urban types—as well as townspeople from surrounding towns. On the dog grounds one sees mostly rural people: farmers, hunters, more blacks, more people of lower socioeconomic status generally. The activity on the dog grounds begins in earnest on Friday night, when people begin to gather, set up tents and campers, stake out their dogs, drink, play cards, shoot dice, talk dogs, go off into the surrounding countryside to hunt, and generally have a good time.

At the peak of the trading there are hundreds of hunting dogs of all kinds on the dog grounds, though coon-hounds are clearly predominant. Some coon-dog men are as serious as other dog fanciers about breeding, standards, registration, papers, and the other trappings of "improving the breed." Most dealing in dogs at this level involves fancy stud fees, careful records, big money—into the thousands of dollars for a top dog. Many hound-dog men, however, are far more pragmatic. They just want good, working hunting dogs, and cannot afford to pay a great deal of money for them. These men tend to be less careful about the niceties of breeding, record keeping, and so on; they are satisfied with whichever dogs get together behind the shed, breeding old Handy to old Ready. This is the group of dog traders that comes to Canton, and as a group they tend not to be highly regarded by the serious coon-dog breeders or by the townspeople in general. One citizen of Canton described dog traders to me as people for whom "making a living gets in the way." Some are professional dog jockies; most are amateurs. Their motivations for coming to Canton are various and often mixed. Some come to get "using dogs," while others just like to "move their dogs around" or "change faces." The professionals come to make some money, but many traders just want the activity to pay for itself—i.e., to pay for the trip and for the dogs' feed.

The dominant reasons for coming to Canton, though, are to get together with other hound-dog men to talk about dogs and hunting, and to trade for its own sake, as recreation. For the majority of traders at Canton the economic motive is far from the top of the list; dog trading for them is a form of play, a contest of wits and words. Some men actually keep one or two dogs around at any given time just to trade, and, not surprisingly, these are usually rather "sorry" dogs, "old trashy dogs that ain't worth a quarter for nothin'." One trader put it this way: "My experience is, I'll be in Canton in the morning, be there Sunday all day, I've got a dog trade always. Reason I want to go because a man's gonna meet me there and demonstrate his dog and I'm gonna take mine. Course the one I'm gonna take ain't much of a dog. . . . Now and then I get a good dog, then I get one that ain't worth bringin' home, but still it's trade that I like to do."

In other words, Canton is "where the action is" (see Goffman 1967). Of course, no dog trader is averse to making some money, and one of the stated goals of any swap is to "draw boot"—i.e., to get a dog and some cash for your dog. One man told me that his fellow traders would "trade with you for ten when ten's all they got in their dog, then they'll make five on your dog." These are small sums, though. In most cases cash profit stands as a token of having played the game well; it is a sweetener that enhances the encounter. It is also true that many of the transactions at Canton are straight cash sales; but the dynamic of these transactions is the same in all essentials as trading, and they are considered to be and labeled trades.

When I asked what brought him to Canton, one old trader, who has been coming to First Monday for more than seventy years, replied, "Well, I enjoy trading and enjoy seeing my old friends." For him, as for most others on the dog grounds, the essence of First Monday is trading and sociability. I propose in the remainder of this paper to explore some of the interrelationships between the two activities. In the course of the analysis I hope to demonstrate how traditional narratives of the kind studied primarily by folklorists and the personal narratives of special interest to linguists and sociologists can be productively studied within a unified framework, based on these genres' coexistence in the repertoires and performances of those who tell them. The formal and functional interrelationships among these stories within the institution of dog trading can best be uncovered by an analytical perspective that merges the concerns of folklore and sociolinguistics, to the enrichment of both.

As a point of departure, let us consider the following two excerpts from dog-trading encounters at Canton. The first involves two participants: John Moore,[1] a black man in his early forties, and Mr. Byers, a white man in his early fifties. John Moore has the dogs, and Byers has just walked up to look them over.

BYERS: He strike 'is own fox? [I.e., can he pick up the fox's trail by himself?]

MOORE: He strike 'is own fox. Strike 'is own fox. Clean as a pin, strike 'is own fox. [Pause.] And he'll stand to be hunted, he'll stand to be hunted [Byers interrupts—unintelligible]. What is that?

BYERS: He run with a pack good?

MOORE: Oh yes, oh yes. And he'll stand . . . he'll stand three nights out a week. He has did that and took off—ain't seen 'im waitin' behind that. [Unintelligible.] He'll stand three nights out a week. I've known that to happen to 'im. [Pause.] I try to be fair with a man 'bout a dog. Tell the truth about a dog, tell you what he'll do. If there's any fault to 'im, I wanna tell the man. If I get a dog from a man, if there's any fault to 'im, I want 'im to tell me. I bought . . . we bought some puppies from a man, we asked 'im, said, "They been vaccinated?" Said, "Now we gonna buy the puppies," say, "Now if they been vaccinated, we wanta know if they ain't." Say, "Now, what we's gettin' at, if they ain't been vaccinated distemper's all around." We wanted 'a vaccinate 'em. And he swore they was vaccinated and after we bought 'em they died, took distemper and died. Then he tol' a friend o' ours, he say he hate that he didn't tell us that the dogs, the puppies, wasn't vaccinated. See, and I begged 'im, "I tell you somethin' man, we gonna buy the puppies, gonna give you a price for 'em," I said, "but there's one thing we just wanta know if they been vaccinated." And then turned right around . . . then turned right around and told the man that they hadn't been vaccinated. And here I begged him, "I'm beggin' you, gonna buy the dogs, puppies, at your price."

BYERS: I traded two good coon dogs for two Walker dogs [a breed of hounds] [Moore: Mmm hmm] supposed to be good fox dogs.

MOORE: Mmm hmm.

BYERS: Sumbitches wouldn't run a *rabbit*.

MOORE: You see that?

BYERS: Boy, I mean they wouldn't run nothin'.

MOORE: I tell you for . . . what is your name?

BYERS: Byers.

MOORE: Mr. Byers, this here is John Moore, everybody know me here. I can take you to some people in here any day—I'm talkin' about some rich, up-to-date people—I have sold dogs to, and they'll tell you. . . . I'm talkin' 'bout for hunnerd dollars, sold some hunnerd-dollar dogs, seventy five–dollar dogs, fifty–dollar. . . . I haven't got a dog over there for fifty dollars. You can't raise one for that, 'cause a sack o' feed down there where we live cost you four fifty for fifty pounds, what we feed the hounds on, we feed the hounds on, and then we get scraps from that slaughter pen to put in. And if I tell you somep'n 'bout a dog I'm not gon' misrepresent 'im. Not gonna misrepresent 'im. You see that little ol' ugly gyp [bitch] there? She'll git in the thicket. . . . We was runnin' the Fourth o' July, I think it was, runnin' a big grey fox. Across the road runnin' right down 'side this culvert, oh, 'bout like that [unintelligible] you've seen it where, that's what, briar, you know, you know briar up under there, you know, know what I'm talkin' 'bout, these ol' . . . where . . . got them stickers on, 'bout like that [holds up his finger], 'bout that size, got that runner, big runner to them. And jus' had the place solid. And we had a fox under there, and got 'im under there 'bout three o'clock, and he stayed there till it got daylight, he stayed under there to daylight. The road on east side o' that place. And daylight come and them ol' feet comin' out from under round there drove her all buggy. He just walked in them briars. Place he could get in, you'd just see 'im every while just walkin', just walkin'. You could hear that gyp now smell that fox. He got 'im hot, he just walk in them briars, that little gyp come up in now, and she come up, man, there, like this fox, far like to the middle o' dis pickup, quite that far, come out, shot out from under there, wasn't long before she come out just sprawled on her belly. There she is, right there. There she is right there. [To dog:] Yeah, come over here.

(Recorded Canton, Texas, July 31, 1971)

In the second encounter there are three participants, only two of whom are heard in this excerpt: Homer Townsend and

Herman Smith. Townsend's son is interested in Smith's dogs, but his father does the talking.

TOWNSEND: Will them ol' dogs you got catch a rabbit?
SMITH: Yeah.
TOWNSEND: Really get up there and catch one?
SMITH: Yessir, I'd buy another one that'll outrun 'em.
TOWNSEND: Well, a man told me 'while ago they wouldn't hardly *run* a rabbit.
SMITH: I tell you what I'll do. I'll take the man out here and *show* him. That's all I can do . . . that's the *best* way, is to take 'im out and show 'im. I'll buy another 'un that can run with 'em . . . uh, keep them or sell them or buy another 'un that could run with 'em, see. . . .
TOWNSEND: [Interrupts:] He's interested in some dogs, some greyhounds, an', uh, that man says they wouldn't hardly run a rabbit.
SMITH: [Angrily:] I'll *show* you! That's all I can do. You know me. I don't lie about these dogs. I tried 'em out, see, I tried them dogs out before I ever bought 'em, see. And I do the *coon* dogs thataway. I wouldn't give a dime for nary a dog I didn't know on this ground until I hunted 'im. I sold one last . . . uh . . . summer and the man asked me what I'd take. I said, "I won't even price him 'til you go huntin'." I said, "I sell mine in the *woods!*" An' when we went huntin', he treed three coons. Come out, and he said, "Whatcha want for that dog?" I said two fifty. An' he went countin' out them twenty-dollar bills.

    I got a lit'l ol' gyp out there I've had three years. An' she's three years old—she's been treein' coons ever since she was a year old! And she's still in mah pen! An' I got one o' her puppies mated to that 'un yonder . . . that's the one over there. Took him out the other day, just started trainin' him, ya' know. That's the reason I got them greyhounds, 'cause I can see them, see? I cain't hear a thing outta this ear. I gotta go with somebody an' they got a bunch of trash an'. . . . No, somebody got one to run with them, I'll buy 'em this morning.
TOWNSEND: [Leaving:] Well, we'll talk to you a little bit . . . after a while. . . .
SMITH: [Loudly:] I'll take 'em out here and *show* you! That's the way I am. I don't lie about these dogs. I ain't . . . I don't believe in it. I bought a dog here about three or four months ago down here from an old man and ended high nigh walkin' him! And he was tellin' me about that dog, trainin' young dogs and this and that, and I give him thirty dollars for it, an' I *give* him to that little boy down there. That

hound don't tree. I *give* 'im to him! I wouldn't lie to him, I
give it to him! I don't lie about it. I'll buy 'em on the tree or
sell 'em on the tree, I don't care about the money. I don't lie
about these dogs. Ya' hear anything very long and you'll say
it's all right, ya' know what I mean?
(Recorded by Donna West, Canton, Texas, November 1, 1970)

For our purposes, two features stand out from these excerpts.
First, the participants clearly devote a considerable amount of
interactional attention to the issue of truthfulness and lying; and,
second, one of the devices they resort to in addressing this issue
is telling stories. Anyone who is at all familiar with hound-dog
men, coon hunters or otherwise, will feel no surprise at hearing
they have some involvement in lying and storytelling. Georg Simmel suggests that "sociological structures differ profoundly according to the measure of lying which operates in them"
(1950:312), and coon hunting certainly ranks fairly high on this
scale.

To an audience familiar with coon hunters, the association
between lying and coon hunting is so well-established that it constitutes an expressive resource for performance. The humorous
monologue of the featured speaker at a Fourth of July celebration
in Pekin, Indiana—an area near the Indiana-Kentucky border
which is full of coon hunters—included the following introduction to a series of hunting stories:

You know, now, somebody's accused me of lying, and I told somebody one
time how bad it hurt me to lie, and they said, "You must be in awful
pain, then, buddy." But I have had to lie some just to get by, you understand? I didn't want to lie, I was pushed into it. I done a lot of coon
hunting, and when you go out with a bunch of coon hunters you got to lie
just to stay with 'em.

I can see by looking that there's no coon hunters in this audience today. I'm glad I did, I didn't want to insult anybody. But when you get out
there in the field with a bunch of coon hunters, and get you a chew of to-
bacco in your mouth, and the dogs start running, you better start telling
some lies, or you won't be out there long.
(Byron Crawford, recorded Pekin, Indiana, July 4, 1978)

Or, as summed up for me with artful succinctness by a Texas coon
hunter, "any man who keeps more'n one hound'll lie to you."

One type of lying associated with coon hunting, and of long-
standing interest to folklorists, is the tall tale, the traditional tale
of lying and exaggeration. Hunting has always been a privileged

domain for tall tales: *The Types of the Folktale* (Thompson 1961) established the hunting tale as a special subgroup of tales of lying (types 1890–1909), and the standard American tall-tale collections are full of hunting windies (see Baughman 1966: types 1890–1909 and motifs X1100–1199, with the references therein).

Traditional tall tales are told at Canton, but not often. Since the regulars have heard them over and over again, they tend largely to save them for newcomers not yet fully integrated into the coon-hunting fraternity (cf. Toelken 1979:112). The following tale, widely recorded, was addressed by a veteran hunter to a nineteen-year-old novice in the group:

This old boy, he had him a coon dog. He had him a little coon [hide-] stretcher, looked like a piece of wire, V-shaped. He'd bring it out of the house, he had that coon dog, and it'd go out in the woods, kill him a coon, bring it back to the house, and all that boy had to do was just skin that coon out, put on that stretcher and skin. He was doing that for about two or three years, and was plum proud of his dog, and everything, and was telling everybody in town how good that dog was. One day his mama told him to take the ironing board outside to fix it; there was something wrong with it. That dog seen that ironing board and that dog hadn't showed up yet.[2]
(Recorded Canton, Texas, June 2, 1973)

Tall tales such as this one play upon the generic expectations of another type of story which is ubiquitous among hound-dog men: narratives of personal experience about the special qualities and hunting prowess of particular dogs. The story of the dog and the ironing board/hide-stretcher followed closely on the heels of this one:

A: I run a coon down the creek back down home at Fred's a couple weeks ago. . . .
B: Yeah?
A: An' I couldn't get 'im out, couldn't get in there to 'im, so Speck and I got . . . I caught Speck to lead 'im off now: "Let's go, Speck." Went on down there, struck another coon and treed it. He jumped it out, and old Speck just whirled and left there, and I didn't know where in hell that sumbitch went. First time I heard 'im opened up back down on the tree. He went back there and checked the hole, that coon had come out and he treed that sumbitch down there [laughing].
C: Yeah.
D: Sure did. Dog's smart.
A: That durn coon come outa that hole. He went and treed that coon.

c: That's what me and Bud done one night. Treed one down there. . . .
a: [Interrupting:] He was thinkin' about that coon, wasn't 'e?
(Recorded Canton, Texas, August 1, 1971)

Stories like this one dominate the sociable encounters of coon hunters wherever they come together, including the dog-trading grounds at Canton. These accounts stick close to the actual world of coon hunting and to the range of the possible—though not, in the best of them, to the ordinary. The extraordinary, the "reportable" in Labov's terms, is necessary if a personal narrative is to hold the listener's attention (Labov and Fanshel 1977 : 105). A dog like old Speck that can remind itself of a piece of unfinished business and go back to finish it off after treeing another coon is special, though believable; why not, then, a dog that will catch a coon on order, to fit his master's hide-stretcher? The more common story of personal experience, told straightforwardly as truth, contextualizes the tall tale; it contributes to the latter's humorous effect by establishing a set of generic expectations that the tall tale can bend exaggeratedly out of shape. The effect is reciprocal, of course: the obvious exaggeration of the tall tale creates an aura of lying that colors the "true" stories as well.

When we juxtapose the personal narrative and the tall tale, there are actually two dimensions of "lying" that become apparent. First, the unusual but not impossible events of the former are transformed into the exaggeratedly implausible events of the latter. Thus tall tales are lies, insofar as what they report as having happened did not happen, nor could have happened.

There is more, though. The tall tale presented above is told in the third person, which distances it somewhat from the narrator, and contrasts with the characteristic use of the first-person voice in the personal narrative. A common feature of tall-tale style, however, is also the use of the first person (Brunvand 1978 : 136–137), either directly ("I had an old coon dog that would go out in the woods. . . .") or as a link between the narrator and the third-person protagonist ("I knew an old boy, he had him a coon dog. . . ."). This device occurs in the second traditional tale we will consider below. When the first-person voice is employed a second dimension of "lying" comes into play. The use of the first person brings the tall tale closer to personal narrative; it allows the story to masquerade for a while as a "true" personal narrative, until the realization that what is being reported is impossible shatters the illusion. In other words, these first-person tall tales are what

Goffman calls "fabrications," "the intentional effort of one or more individuals to manage activity so that a party of one or more others will be induced to have a false belief about what it is that is going on" (1974:83). What appears to be going on is an account of actual events; what is really going on is a lie masquerading as such an account—hence, a double lie. The man who tells such a tale in the third person is a liar; the man who tells it in the first person is a tricky liar, a con man. Thus two potential dimensions of "lying" enter into the expressive ambience of coon hunters: outright lies and fabrications.

As I have noted, however, traditional tall tales are not very common at Canton. Even without them, though, the aura of lying persists around the personal dog stories because, although recounted as true, they are susceptible to creative exaggeration, another dimension of "lying," for at least two major reasons. First, like all natural sociable interaction, the encounters of coon hunters are at base about the construction and negotiation of personal identity. In them sociable narratives are a vehicle for the encoding and presentation of information about oneself in order to construct a personal and social image (Bauman 1972). In Watson and Potter's apt formulation, "social interaction gives form to the image of self and the image of the other; it gives validity and continuity to the identifications which are the source of an individual's self-esteem" (1962:246). The way to establish that you are a good coon hunter is to show that you have good hounds, and are thus knowledgeable about quality dogs—even more so if you have trained them yourself. Thus, because hunting stories are instruments for identity building, for self-aggrandizement (Labov and Waletzky 1967:34), there is a built-in impulse to exaggerate the prowess of one's dogs with hyperbole ("When he trees, hell, if you ain't give out, you're plum gonna get 'im of starvation before he comes away from there"), or by selection (omitting mention of the faults of a dog you're bragging on) as a means of enhancing one's own image (cf. Gilsenan 1976:191). This tendency toward "stretching the truth," as it is often called, has been widely reported in men's sociable encounters (see, e.g., Bauman 1972; Bethke 1976; Biebuyck-Goetz 1977; Cothran 1974; Tallman 1975). It is one more factor that gives hound-dog men the reputation of being liars.

The other factor which promotes the expressive elaboration of the hound and hunting story is that, whatever its referential and rhetorical functions, it also constitutes a form of verbal art.

That is, it is characteristically *performed*, subject to evaluation, both as truth and as art for the skill and effectiveness with which it is told (Bauman 1977 : 11). The esthetic considerations of artistic performance may demand the embellishment or manipulation—if not the sacrifice—of the literal truth in the interests of greater dynamic tension, formal elegance, surprise value, contrast, or other elements which contribute to excellence in performance in this subculture. "Stretching the truth," of course, which chiefly exaggerates and selects, is not exactly the same as the outright lying of the tall tale. Nevertheless, although the two activities can be terminologically distinguished to point up the contrast between them, they are usually merged; and the term "lying," in an unmarked sense, is used to label both (see the figure below). Fabrication, our third analytically distinguished type of lying, has no folk label.

lying

[outright] lying   stretching the truth

For these reasons, then, some expectation of lying attends the telling of these stories about special dogs and memorable hunts. Realizing this, the tellers frequently resort to various means of validating their accounts. These range from verbal formulas like "I guarantee," to the testimony of witnesses (as in the above story), to offers to demonstrate the dog in action. One man concluded a lengthy story about the hunting prowess of his hound with:

You don't believe it, take and let your dogs run a coon loose, and I'll lead 'er, anybody tonight, anybody got their damn good cold-nose dogs [i.e., dogs able to follow a cold trail], and if she don't run that coon and tree that coon, it's gonna be somethin' that ain't never happened. She'll run that sumbitch till by God, she'll tree that sumbitch.
(Recorded Canton, Texas, August 1, 1971)

Even such emphatic attempts at validation, however, often contain elements that subtly undermine the intended effect. In the statement just quoted, the owner backs up his previous claim about his dog's ability to follow a cold trail to the tree by stating that it has *never* failed to do so. While the dog in question did in fact have a far higher success rate than most others, both the owner and several of the onlookers knew of times when it had failed, as any dog must once in a while. So, despite these attempts at validation, the expectation persists that hound-dog men will lie when talking about their dogs.

Occasionally, among intimates, someone may make a playful thrust at discrediting a story. To cite one example from Canton, a man, spotting an old friend who was giving an account of a recent hunt to a circle of fellow hunters, called out as he approached, "What you doin', lyin' to these people?" This is joking, however. The interesting and noteworthy thing about the sociable storytelling of hound-dog men is that, although it is strongly recognized as susceptible to lying, the lying is overwhelmingly licensed as part of the fundamental ethos of sociability. That is, by not challenging the truthfulness of another's stories, one may reasonably expect to be accorded the same license in presenting one's own image-building narratives and crafting one's own artful performances. Then too, it is only susceptibility we are talking about; not every personal narrative about dogs and hunting involves lying, nor is it always clear or consciously recognized which do and which do not. There is merely a persistent sense that every story might. To call another man a liar in this context, then, is to threaten his "face," with some risk and no possible advantage to oneself; whereas to give apparent acceptance to his accounts is to store up interactional credit toward the unchallenged acceptance of one's own tales.

Hunting tall tales and ordinary dog stories do not exhaust the repertoire of storytelling at Canton. The special character of First Monday for the hunters who attend is that it is an occasion for dog trading; not surprisingly, then, trading itself constitutes an important conversational resource for those who gather there. Like the hunting tall tales, some of the trading stories are traditional fictions, part of the national—even international—treasury of lore about shrewd trades, deceptive bargains, gullibility, and guile. To underscore his observations about a smart fellow trader, a dog jockey from Oklahoma who almost never misses a First Monday at Canton told the following story:

An' they're smart, too. I know an ol' boy, by God, he fell on a damn scheme to make some money, you know? Got hisself a bunch o' damn dog pills. 'Stead o' them damn . . . he called 'em "smart pills," you know, an' by God, he'd sell them damn things, an' an ol' boy'd come along, an' he'd sell 'em a little to 'em, an' tell 'em how smart they'd make 'em, you know, an' he'd get a *dollar* apiece for 'em. An ol' boy come along, an' he sold him one. He said, "Hell, I don't feel any smarter than I did." He said,

"I found sometimes when you're pretty dumb it takes several of 'em, by God, to get you smartened up." He bought another one, took it, stood around there a few minutes, and said, "Now, I ain't no smarter than I was." "Boy," he says, "you're somethin', you're just pretty dumb. You . . . you've got to take four or five for you." Well, he bought another one, took it, so he stood around, and he said, "Man, them things ain't helping me a damn bit." He said, "I told you, you was pretty dumb." He said, "By God, you're gonna have to take another one." So he bought another one, by God, and he took that son of a bitch and rolled it around in his damn hand, an' he reached up to taste it, and he said, "That tastes just like dog shit." He said, "Boy, now you smartenin' up."[3]
(Recorded Canton, Texas, June 5, 1977)

Let us examine this story in the light of our discussion thus far. Linked to the conversation that precedes it, and opened in the first person ("I know an ol' boy. . . ."), the story appears at first to be a conventional personal narrative of the kind that is told as true. Ultimately, of course, it is revealed as a humorous fiction. Like the traditional tall tale told in the first person, then, this story is both a lie and a fabrication. Its content, however, endows it with an additional dimension of deception. The trader here has clearly swindled the dupe by playing on his expectation that the "smart pills" would make him wiser by virtue of their medicinal powers. That, after all, is how pills work. But the trader, of course, has made no such explicit claim. He has merely advertised his wares as "smart pills," and they do in fact make the dupe smarter—he wises up to the fact that he has been paying a dollar each for pellets of dog dung.

This story is one of a type of traditional tale in which the shrewd trader, while not actually telling an untruth—and thus not lying in a limited, literal sense—lies in effect nevertheless, at least in the sense set forth by Charles Morris (1946:261): "lying is the deliberate use of signs to misinform someone, that is, to produce in someone the belief that certain signs are true which the producer himself believes to be false." In the story above, the trader's ploy is actually a kind of fabrication, insofar as he induces the dupe to believe that he is taking pills that will affect him medicinally while in fact such effect as they have is the result of his realization that this belief is false. The tale thus underscores in expressive form the semi-paradoxical fact that traders can lie by telling the truth. The "smart pills" deception is at least arguably a "benign fabrication," in Goffman's terms (1974:87), leading as it does to the enlightenment of the dupe. However, "ex-

ploitive fabrications" (ibid.:103) also abound in this body of folklore and, as we shall see, in actual trading as well.

My impression, unverified by conclusive data, is that traditional tales about trading, like the one I have just presented, are
less generally familiar to the population on the dog grounds at
Canton than are the traditional tall tales about dogs and hunting.
The latter are appropriate, in a general sense, whenever coon
hunters come together sociably, whereas the former are more
likely to be familiar to those with a regular involvement in trading, a much smaller group. In the setting of a First Monday,
though, trading tales are highly appropriate, and I have heard
more traditional stories about trading than traditional tall tales
about hunting on the dog grounds.

Still more common, though, are personal narratives about
trades in which the teller himself was involved. Some of these,
interestingly, are about being taken. Dog trading is, after all, a
contest, and even the canny trader can be bested occasionally, as
in the following account:

A: That's that little Trigg [a breed of hound] I's tellin' you about.
B: I bought one o' them one time, Cal, was the funniest thing I got in.
       When I swapped for 'er, and give some money, in Texarkana, old
       boy said, "I guarantee 'er." Said, "She's one of the finest coon dogs
       I've ever had in the woods in my life." I carried that dog home, I
       pitched 'er out, first thing she hit was a deer. I think a day or two
       later, I finally found 'er. And I mean she wouldn't run *one* thing on
       Earth but a deer, not anything. So I carried 'er back to Texarkana
       and just give 'er away. Yessir, and *five* minutes after the boy drove
       off with that dog, a guy drove up and said, "Do you know where I
       can find a deer dog anywhere for sale?"
C & D: [laugh.]
B: I'll bet he hadn't got two mile outa town, when. . . .
D: [interrupting:] Outa town, dog and all?
B: Yeah. Ain't no tellin' what he'd give for the dog, and she was per-
       fect. I mean she was a straight deer dog. Wouldn't run nothin'
       else. But that's my luck.
(Recorded Canton, Texas, August 1, 1971)

In this story the teller loses out not once, but twice. He is
victimized by being lied to outright by another trader—note the
inevitable preoccupation with lying—and then compounds the
problem by giving away the deer dog, worthless to a coon hunter,
moments before he is presented with a golden opportunity to sell
it at a handsome profit. Still, he is philosophical about it; he in-

troduces the story as the *funniest* experience he has had with Trigg hounds, and chalks up the whole experience to luck.

While admitting that one has been taken in a trade might seem to expose one to some risk of losing face, the risk is apparently offset by the reportability and performance value of a good story. And, after all, it did take an outright lie on the trader's part to accomplish the deception. Moreover, any trader worth his salt has plenty of stories about how he bested someone else in a trade by the exercise of wit, cleverness, or deception. The same man who lost out twice on the deer dog told the following story, recounting a classic example of the short con, a fabrication *par excellence*.

Last time I went over to Canton, I had a dog I called Blackjack. He was just about as sorry a dog as I ever had owned. He wouldn't do nothin' but eat. Take him huntin' and he lay out under the pickup. So I decided I'd take 'im over to Canton, and I did, and I met a friend of mine over there, named Ted Haskell, out o' Corsicana. I told Ted, I said, "Now, you go up that alley up yonder and meet me 'bout half way where they's tradin' dogs yonder, and then we'll introduce ourselves. You . . . we'll . . . sell this dog, and I'll give you half what I get outa it." I met ol' Ted, and he says, "Well, ol' Blackjack," he says, "I haven't had a coon race since I sold him," he says. "Where'd you get him?" "I got him over to Palestine." "Well, I declare, I wisht I had him back," he says. "What are you askin' for 'im?" I said, "I'll take thirty dollars." Well, they began to gather 'round and listen and listen. We kept talkin' 'bout him. He'd brag on Blackjack. And finally, an ol' boy eased up and called me off and says, "I'll give twenty dollars for 'im." And I said, "Well, pay me." Well, he paid me; course I told Mr. Haskell mighty glad I'd met 'im, an' he turned and went one way, an' I went the other way, and we met at the pickup and divided the money. I come home, and he come back to Corsicana. So I'm sure that man felt about like I did when I bought 'im, 'cause he wasn't worth carryin' a-huntin'.
(Recorded by Thomas A. Green, Blooming Grove, Texas, May 31, 1968)

Stories like this one manifest a significant ambivalence about lying and other swindles, especially about lying—whether outright lying, stretching the truth, or fabrication—in conducting the trading itself. As I have noted, dog trading is viewed by the confirmed traders as a game of strategy in which, like many other games of strategy, deception occupies a central and accepted place. There is a long tradition in American folklore and popular literature of admiration for the shrewd trader, from the Yankee peddler to the Southern horse trader, who makes his way through the world by wit and words (Dorson 1959:47–48; Ferris 1977; Green 1968, 1972). The numerous entries in Baughman's *Type and Motif-Index of the Folktales of England and North America* (1966) under K134, Deceptive horse sale (or trade), as well as such literary pieces as the horse trade in Longstreet's *Georgia Scenes* or the recent popular collections of horse-trading tales by Ben Green (1968, 1972), suggest that Americans enjoy hearing about shrewd traders and therefore, at some level at least, accept their crooked dealings (cf. Boatright 1973:146). The interplay between the trader's verbal skill in trading and his verbal skill as a storyteller is probably significant here; the two are complementary aspects of his overall image as quick-witted and shrewd, one who manipulates men and situations—whether trading encounters or social gatherings—to his own advantage. Good traders are not reluctant self-publicists; one Canton regular told me with obvious pride: "I'll tell you what you can do. You can put me right out there on that road, barefooted, if it wasn't too hot, and before I get home, I'll have a pair of shoes, I want to tell you."

Nevertheless, whereas chess, for example, is unequivocally and only a game, in which such strategic deception as may occur is completely contained within the play frame, dog trading is not so unambiguous. While trading is certainly engaged in as play by many of the participants at Canton, the play frame is almost never overtly acknowledged. The only instances I observed that were openly marked as play were framed by such obviously inappropriate offers as five dollars plus a toothless old dog for a proven hound in prime condition. Otherwise, the public construction placed upon the trading encounter depicts it as a serious business transaction, and it is *always* susceptible to being understood as such by one or both participants. Here is the crux of the matter. The traditional American ideal demands, if not absolute honesty in business transactions, at least the maintenance of the public fiction that the participants are telling the truth (cf. Simmel 1950:314). Thus lying does not accord with the public construction of a dog-trading transaction, nor is it consistent with the actual understanding of those who consider a dog trade straight business, not a game. The trader who lies about a dog during the conduct of a trade may see himself and be seen by some other traders as a master player, gulling the marks as they deserve; but he may also be despised as a swindler who cheats honest people. No harm is done by telling stories about shrewd or crooked trades—indeed, such accounts may be relished for their performance value—but actually hoodwinking someone is a different matter. It makes the difference between Goffman's benign and exploitive fabrications (1974:87, 103).

At the same time, therefore, that a trader is telling a well-formed and entertaining story in which he beats someone by a classic confidence trick, he may also be at pains to disavow any dishonesty. The veteran trader who unloaded Blackjack by trickery and obviously relished telling about it had just a few minutes before beginning his story made a gesture at resolving the moral dilemma by framing his trading swindles as the excesses of youth: "Most men my age won't lie about a dog; but just before you get to my age, they'll lie and tell you any kinda tale just to get to sell you a dog."

Having explored the relationship between lying and storytelling among the dog traders at Canton to this point, we can now return to the excerpts from the trading encounters with which we began our exploration. The strong preoccupation with lying and storytelling that characterizes both encounters should be relatively more comprehensible in light of the preceding discussion.

The rich expressive tradition of storytelling associated with hound-dog men and dog traders—the tales of hunting and trading and the personal narratives about both activities—as well as the conception of dog trading as a game of strategy in which the goal is often to get rid of a worthless dog at a profit, help to endow dog trading at Canton with a considerable aura of lying and deception. These expressive forms both reflect and sustain the sense that misrepresentation of one sort or another permeates the institution, and many participants can confirm from first-hand experience that lying is indeed a factor to be reckoned with. It is not at all surprising, therefore, that parties on both sides of a dog trade should enter the transaction anticipating that the opposite party might lie about a dog and expect to be lied to in return. At the same time, either man (both parties if a trade is involved, only the seller if it is to be a cash sale) might in fact be ready and willing to lie to unload a dog. Yet even if one is ready to lie, to acknowledge as much is impossible; it would violate the public construction that dog trading is an honest business transaction, and very likely undermine the interactional foundation of the trading relationship itself.

The strategy that thus emerges from the expectations and conventions of dog trading is that one should take pains during an actual transaction to *dispel* the aura of lying that surrounds it. The most direct means of doing so is by explicit insistence on one's truthfulness and by disavowal of lying. In the encounters under examination, both John Moore and Herman Smith employ this means of establishing their trustworthiness. John Moore volunteers early in the encounter: "I try to be fair with a man 'bout a dog. Tell the truth about a dog, tell you what he'll do. If there's any fault to 'im, I wanna tell the man." And then, employing the powerful rhetorical device of identification (Burke 1969:20–23), Moore puts himself in Byers' position: "If I get a dog from a man, if there's any fault to 'im, I want 'im to tell me." A little later, to validate the information he is providing about his dogs, he insists: "If I tell you somep'n 'bout a dog, I'm not gon' misrepresent 'im. Not gonna misrepresent 'im." In the second encounter, Herman Smith is rather seriously challenged by Homer Townsend; he reiterates with some vehemence throughout the encounter, "I don't lie about these dogs!" These are all disclaimers of outright lying or of stretching the truth by selection or distortion. I have not recorded or observed any instances in which a participant disavowed pulling off a fabrication, though it is conceivable that such disavowals might occur.

Another means of establishing one's veracity in a trading encounter is to offer to let the dogs prove the claims made for them, just as the tellers of dog stories do in sociable encounters. This is Herman Smith's main thrust; he offers repeatedly to "take 'em out here and show you." He also resorts to the identificational strategy of putting himself in the place of the buyer. When he is buying dogs, he tries them out: "I wouldn't give a dime for nary a dog I didn't know on this ground until I hunted 'im." By trying out the dogs he is offering before he bought them Smith has, in effect, already acted on Townsend's behalf, and Townsend is safe in buying them now.

For our purposes, perhaps the most interesting means by which the dog traders seek to establish and substantiate their identities as honest men is in telling stories. If we examine these stories, we see that they are closely related to the sociable narratives discussed at length earlier in this paper—specifically, to personal narratives about the performance of particular dogs and to personal narratives about trading experiences.

Three narratives appear in the excerpt from the first trading encounter, two told by John Moore and one very minimal one told by Mr. Byers. Moore clearly tells his first story, about being victimized in a trade by buying some puppies which the seller falsely assures him had had their shots, as a rhetorical strategy to convey his negative attitudes toward a trader who would tell an outright lie about a dog. By implication he emphasizes his own trustworthiness in a context where trickery and deceit are widespread. Moore's central rhetorical purpose is to distance himself from dog traders who lie, and his story is obviously and strongly adapted to that purpose. Much of his narrative is given over to establishing this polarization (Labov 1979) between the dishonest trader and Moore himself, as customer. The trader's lie is doubly destructive because it was both unnecessary, since Moore was going to buy the dogs whether or not they had had their shots, and cruel, since it resulted in the death of the dogs. The evaluative dimension of the narrative is heavily elaborated, both through repetition (both the query to the trader about whether the puppies were vaccinated and the narrative report of those queries are repeated) and lexical intensifiers (emotion-laden words like "swore," "hate," "begged") (Labov and Waletzky 1967:37–38). The point is that Moore gave the trader ample and repeated opportunity to tell the truth, but he remained firm in his lie; and everyone suffered as a result, even the liar himself, since the death of the puppies brought him remorse ("he hate that he didn't tell us. . . .").

Byers too has been taken in a trade. He comes back with his account of having traded once for two dogs that were supposed to be good fox dogs and then discovering that the "sumbitches wouldn't run a *rabbit*." This story establishes that he has already been victimized at least once in a trade and, by implication, that he does not intend to let it happen again. Since he is not the one whose honesty is on the line, however, having no dog to trade, his story is rather minimal—just long enough to make his point, without attempting to be strongly persuasive. Still, there is not a clause in his narrative that lacks a clearly evaluative element.

Moore goes on to reaffirm his *bona fides* by mentioning his satisfied customers, including "some rich, up-to-date people." Then, picking up on Byers' apparent interest in fox dogs, Moore points out a fox dog among his own string, and proceeds to tell an extended story about her prowess in a recent hunt in order to build up her credentials—a sales pitch in narrative form. Stories of this kind are especially motivated during trading transactions because one cannot tell from merely looking at a dog what its hunting abilities are. Straightforward enumeration of the dog's qualities could also get the information across, but corroborating narratives, convincingly told, may add verisimilitude to the seller's claims. Skill in storytelling may thus enhance the overall rhetorical power of the sales pitch. One must maintain a delicate balance, however, because stories are also felt to be vehicles for creative or duplicitous misrepresentation. Hence the usefulness of combining such narratives with additional claims to honesty, as Moore does both directly and by telling his story about a dishonest dog trader in order to distance himself from such practices. As the one offering the dogs, Moore has to tell stories that are persuasive enough to establish both his honesty, as in the first story, and the dog's quality, persistence, toughness, etc., as in the second. In sociable interaction there is no immediate negative consequence if your audience does not accept the truth of your story; in trading encounters, others must accept your story sufficiently to be persuaded to *act* on it, hopefully by trading for or buying your dog.

The second excerpt contains two stories, both told by Herman Smith, the man with the dogs. Townsend has rather seriously challenged him with offering dogs that won't perform. Smith accordingly counters with a story to demonstrate that, far from being willing to risk a customer's dissatisfaction or skepticism, he would actually *refuse* to conclude a sale until the dog has proven itself in the woods. This is not just honesty, it's superhonesty. Smith's second story is in the same vein: having been taken in by an unscrupulous trader who lied about the treeing ability of a dog, Smith would not himself stoop to selling the worthless hound, but gave it away to a little boy. Any man who gives dogs to little boys can't be all bad. Here is another instance of extreme polarization between the dishonest trader and the honest man: the unscrupulous trader places profit over honesty, while Smith values honesty over profit ("I don't care about the money. I don't lie about these dogs"). Just so there is no question about his own honorable values, he repeats the relevant points again and again.

Honesty	—over Profit
I wouldn't lie to him.	I *give* him to that little boy down there.
I don't lie about it.	I *give* 'im to him!
I don't lie about these dogs.	I *give* it to him!

Interestingly, however, this story compromises one of Smith's earlier claims to Townsend—that he himself tries out all the dogs he acquires before buying them. If he had done so in this case, he would not have had a worthless dog fobbed off on him. But it is more important to tell an emphatic story for its rhetorical effect than to worry about a minor inconsistency like this. Should Townsend pick up on it, however, this inconsistency could undermine Smith's claims to scrupulous honesty.

Close formal comparison of the stories told during trading with their counterparts in sociable interaction must be reserved for a later paper. However, this second story of Smith's is so closely parallel to the story of the deer dog, discussed earlier in the paper, that even a brief comparison highlights certain significant differences generated by the differing contexts in which they occur and their respective functions in these contexts.

In both stories the narrator acquires a dog from someone who lies to get rid of it and then, discovering that the dog does not perform as expected, gives it away. The story of the deer dog, told for entertainment in sociable interaction, is connected to the discourse that precedes it solely by the fact that the dog in question was a Trigg hound, and the previous speaker had pointed out a Trigg in his own string of dogs. No more is needed for the story to be appropriate in this sociable context. The extra twist at the end of the story, in which a customer appears for the dog immediately after it has been given away, makes the tale unusual and endows it with entertainment value; there is credit to be gained, as a performer, in telling it. The event sequence consists of six principal episodes, most of which have subepisodes: (1) trading for the dog in the expectation that it was a coon dog; (2) taking it home; (3) taking it on a disastrous trial hunt, in which it turns out to be a deer dog; (4) having to search for the now apparently worthless dog; (5) returning to Texarkana to give it away; and (6) being approached by someone looking for a deer hound exactly like the one just given away. The evaluative dimension of the story serves to highlight the reportability of the experience, the humor and irony of the situation.

Herman Smith's story, however, is more strongly motivated and rooted in its conversational context. Smith's prospective customers are leaving, apparently because they don't believe his dogs are any good, and he is very concerned to establish his trustworthiness as a dog trader. The narrative line of the story is minimal: (1) trading for the dog; (2) discovering that it won't perform as promised; and (3) giving it away. More important by far is the rhetorical impact. The rhetorical power of the story resides in the fact that, unlike the unscrupulous trader, Smith spurned the opportunity to swindle someone else with a worthless dog; instead, he gave it away to the little boy. This is the point that he emphasizes most strongly in his story. Most of the work of the narrative, the thrust of its heavy evaluative dimension, aims at a polarization between the dishonest trader and the honorable narrator. Note, however, that this story, like those of John Moore and Mr. Byers, does also involve a trader who is not as honest as Smith presents himself to be, one who lies outright about a dog. Thus we come full circle: the very story that is told in the course of a trading encounter to dispel any suspicion of the trader's dishonesty reinforces the aura of lying that surrounds trading in general. Any man who keeps more'n one hound'll lie to you.

Dog trading at Canton First Monday brings together and merges two important figures in American tradition, the hunter and the trader. Both are strongly associated with storytelling as subjects and performers, and both are major exponents of the widely noted American predilection for expressive lying. Since at least the time when a distinctive body of American folk humor first emerged in the early years of the American republic, the hunter and the trader have occupied a privileged place in American folklore. Dog trading at Canton is a thriving contemporary incarnation of this American folk tradition; the tall tales and personal narratives of its participants place them in unbroken continuity with the generations of hunters, traders, and storytellers that have given American folklore some of its most distinctive characteristics.

NOTES

Except where noted, the data on which this paper is based were recorded by the author in and around Canton, Texas, between July 1971 and June 1977. I owe special thanks to Thomas A. Green for introducing me to the world of the Canton dog traders and for allowing me to use some of his own field materials. I am also grateful to Richard Hulan for important and useful historical references on First Monday trade days; to Mr. T. E. Curry, owner of the dog-trading grounds at Canton, for introductions to several valued informants; to Debora Kodish for bibliographical assistance; and to Patricia Jasper for aid in the transcription of field recordings. Thanks too to Keith Basso, Erving Goffman, Michael Herzfeld, Joel Sherzer, and Beverly Stoeltje for their valuable comments on an earlier draft of this paper; the final product is much the better for their critical insights.

1. Pseudonyms are employed throughout this paper to protect the privacy of individuals.
2. Baughman 1966, motif X1215.8 (aa): Master shows dog a skin stretching board; the dog brings in a raccoon just the size of the board. Master's mother puts ironing board outside one day. The dog never returns.
3. Thompson 1955–1958, motif K114.3.1: *Virtue of oracular pill proved.* The dupe takes it. "It is dog's dung," he says and spits it out. The trickster says that he is telling the truth and demands pay.

BIBLIOGRAPHY

Baughman, Ernest W. 1966. *Type and motif-index of the folktales of England and North America.* The Hague: Mouton.
Bauman, Richard. 1972. The La Have Island general store: Sociability and verbal art in a Nova Scotia community. *Journal of American Folklore* 85:330–343.
———. 1977. *Verbal art as performance.* Rowley, Mass.: Newbury House.
Bethke, Robert D. 1976. Storytelling at an Adirondack inn. *Western Folklore* 35:123–139.
Biebuyck-Goetz, Brunhilde. 1977. "This is the dyin' truth": Mechanisms of lying. *Journal of the Folklore Institute* 14:73–95.
Boatright, Mody C. 1965. *Gib Morgan, minstrel of the oil fields.* Dallas: SMU Press. (Orig. pub. 1945.)
———. 1973. The oil promoter as trickster. In *Mody Boatright, folklorist.* Ernest Speck, ed. Austin: University of Texas Press. (Orig. pub. 1961.)
Brunvand, Jan. 1978. *The study of American folklore,* 2nd ed. New York: Norton.
Burke, Kenneth. 1969. *A rhetoric of motives.* Berkeley and Los Angeles: University of California Press. (Orig. pub. 1950.)
Carson, Jane. 1965. *Colonial Virginians at play.* Williamsburg, Va.: Colonial Williamsburg.
Cothran, Kay L. 1974. Talking trash on the Okefenokee Swamp rim, Georgia. *Journal of American Folklore* 87:340–356.
Craven, Wesley Frank. 1949. *The Southern colonies in the seventeenth century, 1607–1689.* Baton Rouge: Louisiana State University Press.
Dobie, J. Frank. 1946. The cold-nosed hounds. In *The pocket* Atlantic. New York: Pocket Books.
Dorson, Richard M. 1959. *American folklore.* Chicago: University of Chicago Press.

Ferris, Bill. 1977. *Ray Lum: Mule trader, an essay.* Memphis: Center for Southern Folklore.

Fiske, John. 1904. *Civil government in the United States.* Boston: Houghton Mifflin.

Gilsenan, Michael. 1976. Lying, honor, and contradiction. In *Transaction and meaning: Directions in the anthropology of exchange and symbolic behavior.* Bruce Kapferer, ed. Philadelphia: Institute for the Study of Human Issues.

Goffman, Erving. 1967. Where the action is. In *Interaction ritual.* New York: Doubleday-Anchor.

————. 1974. *Frame analysis.* New York: Harper Colophon.

Green, Ben K. 1968. *Horse tradin'.* New York: Knopf.

————. 1972. *Some more horse tradin'.* New York: Knopf.

Labov, William. 1979. A grammar of narrative. Lecture presented at the University of Texas at Austin, October 10, 1979.

————, and David Fanshel. 1977. *Therapeutic discourse.* New York: Academic Press.

————, and Joshua Walctzky. 1967. Narrative analysis: Oral versions of personal experience. In *Essays on the verbal and visual arts.* June Helm, ed. Seattle: University of Washington Press.

Mills, W. S. 1950. *History of Van Zandt County.* Canton, Texas.

Morris, Charles. 1946. *Signs, language and behavior.* New York: Braziller.

Paredes, Américo. 1958. *With his pistol in his hand.* Austin: University of Texas Press.

Sartain, James Alfred. 1932. *History of Walker County, Georgia,* vol. 1. Dalton, Ga.: A. J. Showalter Co.

Simmel, Georg. 1950. *The sociology of Georg Simmel.* Kurt Wolff, trans. and ed. Glencoe: Free Press.

Sydnor, Charles S. 1948. *The development of Southern sectionalism, 1819–1848.* Baton Rouge: Louisiana State University Press.

Tallman, Richard. 1975. Where stories are told: A Nova Scotia storyteller's milieu. *American Review of Canadian Studies* 5:17–41.

Thompson, Stith. 1955–1958. *Motif-index of folk-literature,* 6 vols. Bloomington: Indiana University Press.

————. 1961. *The types of the folktale,* 2nd rev. ed. Helsinki: Folklore Fellows Communication no. 184.

Toelken, Barre. 1979. *The dynamics of folklore.* Boston: Houghton Mifflin.

Verhoeff, Mary. 1911. *The Kentucky mountains,* vol. 1. Louisville: John P. Morton.

Watson, Jeanne, and Robert J. Potter. 1962. An analytic unit for the study of interaction. *Human Relations* 12:245–263.

Alicia María González

"Guess How Doughnuts Are Made": Verbal and Nonverbal Aspects of the *Panadero* and His Stereotype

From the first nineteenth-century *vaqueros* of South Texas who drove their cattle north to "Kiansis" (Paredes 1976:53–55), to the contemporary migrant farm workers who follow the harvest north from the Rio Grande Valley to the Canadian border, being on the move has been part of the economic life of many Mexican workers in Texas and elsewhere in the United States. One type of itinerant worker, however, has altogether escaped the notice of the historians, folklorists, sociologists, and anthropologists who have attempted to document the life of his fellow migrants: the *panadero*, the itinerant Mexican baker. The *panadero* is a figure known throughout Greater Mexico—north and south of the border and indeed wherever people of Mexican descent have settled (ibid.: xiv).

Despite technological advances in the production of bread, the *panadero* continues to use traditional methods, which have allowed him[1] to turn bread making into an art form. The *panadero* may be seen as a traditional artist who uses dough as a sculptural medium, creating breads he associates with the various animals, objects, or people he has encountered in his lifetime of experience as an itinerant baker. An index of the *panaderos'* creativity is the over three hundred different bread types they can create—the types varying according to the individual styles of each baker and the geographical region in which he finds himself. However, the *panadero* does not confine himself to one medium. In his performance as a traditional artist he often incorporates other expressive media, such as gesture, speech play, and song. In each medium he may play on the attributes, such as promiscuity,

drunkenness, and transiency, with which *panaderos* are stereotyp-
ically associated. This paper is a preliminary exploration of the
role of the *panadero*, his art, and his place in Greater Mexican
society and culture.[2]

The data to be presented were collected in interviews conducted in three areas: Los Angeles, California (December 1976);
Austin, Texas (March 1978–April 1979); and Xiutepec, Morelos,
Mexico (April 1978). Of those interviewed, the people from Los
Angeles and Austin have traveled back and forth across the border several times. The others have traveled within Mexico. Only
one man from the bakery in Xiutepec has traveled as far as the
United States. It is important to note the *panadero's* mobility,
since it has an effect on every aspect of his life.

My informants were bakery owners and their families and
employees. For example, my first source was a woman from Los
Angeles. She is the daughter of a baker who has been practicing
for over sixty years. Her father is from Mascota, Jalisco, geo-
graphically in the center of the Mexican republic. His children,
two sons and the daughter, all learned the traditional way of
making Mexican bread and all work at the family bakery. My informant considers herself a Mexican-American, since she immi-
grated at a very early age to the United States. The name of the
bakery, "La Mascota" (The Mascot), comes from the family's
hometown in Mexico. In Austin, Texas, one informant, who is
in his early forties, is from Saltillo, Mexico. He learned how to
make bread from the *maestros* (master bakers) at a corner bakery
in his hometown when he was about fifteen years old. The bakery
where he apprenticed in Saltillo was called "La Reyna" (The
Queen), and this is the name he has given to his own bakery in
Austin. The bakers whom he employs there come from various
parts of Mexico, mostly the central and northern regions: Guada-
lajara, Jalisco; Guanajuato; and Saltillo and Villa Acuna, Coa-
huila. They are from seventeen to fifty years old. In Xiutepec,
Morelos, I interviewed and observed a woman who had learned
how to make bread at the age of eight. Her father, brother, husband, and eight children are all *panaderos* as well. All of my informants felt that each *panadero* had something specific to contribute toward the continuation of the traditions associated with
Mexican bread making.

In Mexico and the United States the *panadero* caters to a segment of society which prefers traditional breads to *pan de caja*, or
the packaged bread loaves which may be purchased at any gro-

cery store or supermarket. This clientele usually buys directly from the baker in his home or at his bakery, where he makes the bread fresh for specific meals, rituals, and festive occasions. The customers who are responsible for the *panadero's* economic liveli-hood may also be responsible for perpetuating the folklore about him, since through their close rapport with the *panadero* they confront often the various expressive forms he utilizes.

Because of this relationship between the *panadero* and his clientele, the *panadero* may follow his customers if they move to other areas. For example, an informant from California told me how he and other *panaderos* had followed the Mexican miners because they felt any new job site would eventually develop into a boom town where the *panadero's* services would be needed and welcomed. In such ways the Mexican *panadero* can alleviate eco-nomic pressure in one area by tapping the economic resource cre-ated by new outpost settlements of Mexican workers and their families (Barth 1969:21). Other itinerants, such as the enter-tainers of Magadi theater (Baghban 1977) and Irish tinkers (Gmelch 1977), are also known to travel where there is a new market for their work. Stereotypes develop about these people as about the *panadero*, linking mobility to abnormal powers, un-clean activity, and (especially) untrustworthiness.

Having explored a new area, a *panadero* may decide to return to his hometown. There, by telling others of the places to which he has traveled and the adventures he has had, he may attempt to reenter the social order of his community. But the *panadero* always remains on the periphery. If nothing else, the late hours his work requires alienate him further from his family and friends and create fear in those who see him as a stranger. The mobility of the itinerant *panadero*, who is known to work in one place for a couple of days, at the most several weeks, and then leave, separates him even more from the norms of the conven-tional social structures into and out of which he moves. In a sense, the *panadero* is constantly on the margin of society, in that area which Mary Douglas defines as polluting because "all margins, the edge of all boundaries which are used in ordering the social experience, are treated as dangerous and polluting" (1972:200).

From the time of his apprenticeship, which often begins at a very early age, the *panadero* is introduced to a way of life which deviates from the normative behavior to which his non-*panadero* family and friends will more than likely adhere. As an apprentice he learns the procedures which he must follow to be accepted fully into the trade. He begins his apprenticeship with such menial tasks as sweeping the floors of the bakery and running errands for the full-fledged bakers. Older *panaderos* and his *maestro* (master baker and teacher) observe his conduct, as well as his interaction with them and with the bakery's customers. The novice's sharpness, cleanliness, and orderliness are tested at every moment. The *maestros* and older bakers then decide if the apprentice is ready for the more important jobs, which will acquaint him with every aspect of the bakery. It is important that the apprentice be observant and quick-witted, since this is a testing period and the bakers may playfully ridicule him about his incapacity to perform in specific areas. His mentors judge the apprentice's motivation to be a good baker by the enthusiasm and attitude that he displays, even in his most menial assignments. Some *panaderos* may be jealous of their knowledge and will not offer advice to an apprentice. My informant from "La Reyna" bakery in Austin felt that when he was learning his trade the more intelligent *panaderos* would teach him what they knew, whereas others would keep their recipes and other secrets to themselves. Usually, he said, the selfish *panaderos* really didn't have much to offer. In either case, it was the more unselfish who acted as teachers or *maestros*.

In time, the apprentice baker may decide to go elsewhere to get more experience. He may transfer to another bakery within the same town or in a different area. By the time he leaves his first job, his peers will have given him a name which will differentiate him from any other *panadero*. This nickname, or *apodo*, pinpoints an attribute peculiar to the individual. The actual assigning of a name involves a certain amount of play and has a symbolic meaning. Victoria Bricker's study (1973) of Zinacantan society discusses nicknaming and other name assigning. She finds there certain "diagnostic criteria" for symbolic representations which she associates with the literary term "kenning," "through which an object or an idea may be implied by mentioning several of its qualities or attributes" (ibid.:153). The *apodo* serves the same purpose. The attributes associated with a particular person are incorporated into the name assigned. Often the association implies defamation and ridicule.

An apprentice in a Xiutepec bakery had an *apodo* which played on several of his characteristics. The little boy was quite plain and his straight, unkempt hair stuck out in different directions. My informant would refer to the boy as "Chulo," which in Mexico means "good-looking," "cute," or "pretty," but which may also suggest pretentiousness, laziness, or a person of leisure. The boy was the first apprentice at that particular bakery to slip away from work and head for the upstairs room where the television was located. In this case the name assigned to the apprentice reflected a characteristic of his personality (that he was lazy) and ridiculed his untidiness and plainness.

According to my informant in Los Angeles, a baker is assigned a name which suits his character. The name may mock a certain personality trait or physical attribute (as I witnessed in Xiutepec), or it may be complimentary. For example, "El Pato" (The Duck) was the nickname given to one *panadero* in Los Angeles because of his gait and oversized feet. "El Payaso" (The Clown) designated a man who was considered too serious; he always walked around with a straight face and rarely smiled. "El Professor" (The Professor) was the *apodo* of a man who had been a teacher but became a baker in order to come to the U.S. He apprenticed himself when he found out that as a baker he would be guaranteed a job on this side of the border.

Each *apodo* serves as an identity marker because, once he is given a name, the *panadero* has been initiated; other *panaderos* are now his peers. This initiation means he knows or has been told about his obligation to help any *panadero* who needs help. The *estable*, or stable, baker, who stays in one location for a long period or for his lifetime, usually feels obliged to provide a job for the *caminante*, the itinerant *panadero*. The *caminante*, on the other hand, offers his creative expertise. Both acknowledge their obligations to one another.

According to my informants, there is a bakers' society somewhat like an informal Masonic Society. It is characterized by the sense of responsibility shared by all bakers. They told me that, in conversations among *panaderos*, whether north or south of the U.S./Mexican border, their camaraderie is always emphasized. Jobs are just as readily available to a *caminante* in the United States as in Mexico. No *panadero* need be idle for long in the U.S. There is always a demand for his product in areas where other migrant workers have newly settled and besides, he is guaranteed a job as a member of the bakers' society.

This cooperation among *panaderos* also works to the advantage of the stable baker, especially the one who owns the bakery. According to my informants, the *caminante* is responsible for the

regional variations of bread styles and is usually the most innovative or creative baker. He will often experiment, molding
dough into different animals and shapes which represent various
people and objects. He assigns names to these breads and, later,
other *panaderos* may copy them. The *caminante* in Xiutepec, for
example, came from Michoacán, Mexico. He could make anything requested of him, including amphibious creatures and fantastic dragons which he experimented with during the night. A
caminante at the Austin bakery was also considered the most creative *panadero* who worked there. He too experimented most at
night. Unfortunately, he had left "La Reyna" a couple of days before I began interviewing there. No one knew which way he was
headed—possibly back to Mexico to see his family. The *panaderos*
spoke admiringly of him. The owner of the bakery had saved two
alligator-like creatures that the *caminante* had made.

All the bakers with whom I spoke felt that they were creating
obras (works of art). The woman in Xiutepec mentioned that the
most interesting aspect of bread making was the way in which
flour or wheat became meaningful once it took on certain characteristics. She kept referring to the powder that became transformed into a significant piece which she knew would have as
much meaning for her customers as for her once she explained its
significance to them.

A new locality may inhibit the *panadero*'s bread making, especially if he cannot locate other *panaderos*. This was the case of
the founder of "La Reyna" when he first arrived in the U.S. fifteen
years ago. He got a job as a baker at Butter Krust, a large Texas
bread company, producing manufactured bread. The loaves came
down the assembly line, one right after the other, all the same
shape and color. He felt very frustrated but continued to work dil-
igently. Eventually he was assigned a better position mixing the
ingredients. During his breaks he began again to bake Mexican
bread, forming dough into the traditional bread varieties that he
remembered. He distributed these to his fellow workers. He constantly reminded himself that he was a *real* baker and an artist.
His friends suggested that he should work some place where he
could practice this art. By this time he had contacted another
baker from his hometown who was working in Dallas; he would
visit this man and bake with him on his days off. After a while
he found an old oven in Austin and started making bread at
home, discontinuing his trips to Dallas. He would come home after work to experiment with new bread styles and try to remem-

ber old ones. Eventually he founded his own successful Mexican bakery. The experience this man had is not unique. A machine cannot satisfy an artist's creative urge to make something with his hands. The *panadero* feels his hands are the proper tools for creating bread. Bread making is more than just a job to many *panaderos*; it is the medium through which they interpret life.

The *panadero* is open to ideas from others. In his travels the *panadero caminante* has the opportunity to learn from many different people. A stable baker will pick up as many ideas as he can from the *caminante*, since he knows that the latter may only stay for a short while. The stable baker may try to coax a particularly talented *caminante* to stay by offering him higher wages. But once he refuses, the stable baker can only accept the *caminante*'s decision and keep the door open for his return. The bakery may suffer because of this loss—but only for a short while, because it is more than likely that another *caminante* will soon come along.

On the United States side of the border, some *panaderos* became more settled after 1962 because they joined the American bakers' unions. Union regulations required that *panaderos* stay in one area if they wanted to secure the benefits offered to them. This trend has particularly affected Los Angeles. My informant there mentioned that the majority of the *panaderos* working for her have been there for several years; only one or two still come and go.

No matter how stable or settled a *panadero* may be, the notion persists that the baker is a *borracho* (drunkard) and a promiscuous man who fathers children in every town he visits. Popular song and folklore also depict the *panadero* as an *hombre perdido* (a man without a home), who drinks too much and is promiscuous and elusive. My informants were concerned that this stereotype made them the subject of speculation in their hometowns. Both the stable and the itinerant bakers, according to all my sources, remain on the threshold of their community because the characteristics of the stereotypical *panadero* are attributed to all. This view of the *panadero* contributes to his marginality.

The *panadero*'s marginality is ambiguous. He brings a threat of contamination to any person who comes in contact with him. A mother might hide her daughter from the *panadero*'s polluting advances, while at the same time she must seek him out because he provides daily nutritional sustenance. The *panadero* is looked upon with contempt, yet he is admired for his talent as a baker. He is considered very clean and responsible as a worker and it is understood that his job is a difficult one. The *panadero* must be up at all hours of the night so that the bread will be fresh and still warm when his customers come for it early in the morning. The *panadero* is accepted as a worker and provider; but at the same time he is stigmatized because he does not completely fit into the social structure of the community where he works (see Goffman 1963). The *panadero* consistently remains on the periphery, in a "liminal" state.

Victor Turner notes:

Liminality is, of course, an ambiguous state, for social structure, while it inhibits full social satisfaction, gives a measure of finiteness and security; liminality may be for many the acme of insecurity, the breakthrough of chaos into cosmos, or disorder into order (1974:77).

Turner's definition of liminality as a state or phase excludes the possibility of its being a constant feature of a certain personality. Turner discusses liminality in terms of ritual, but the trait is a persistent feature of the lifestyle peculiar to the itinerant *panadero*. Abrahams and Bauman (1978) claim that adequate account has yet to be taken of the persistence of expressions of disorder and license or of ludic behavior (which is usually associated with liminality) in cultures. They note a need for further analysis of symbolic classifiers and expressions of the opposition between order and disorder. The dichotomy of order and disorder underlies the creation of negative and positive stereotypes. The person who maintains the orderly patterned behavior of a particular society is usually stereotyped positively. The disordered person who constantly breaks the norms created by the society is seen in a negative way. The *panadero* is viewed by his peers and customers in a positive way because they consider him a hard worker and very clean. At the same time, the members of his community also view him as a deviant, immoral but humorous in his interactions with them. Moreover, he is often the subject of ridicule because he cannot take part in the everyday activities of other members of his community (cf. Bricker 1973), since he never stays long in one place and works at odd hours.

Some of the bakers I interviewed, concerned that I may have been biased by stories about *panaderos*, emphasized the positive aspects of their work (their creative talent, hard working schedule, etc.) at the beginning of our talks. As the interviews gained momentum and rapport was established, they would mention the negative stereotypic traits in jest. For example, my informant from Austin first discussed his apprenticeship and his experiences in the United States. Later he distinguished between himself and the *caminante*. Finally he asked if I had heard various narratives and puns about *panaderos* that the baker uses in talking to his customers. He made it clear that he himself was quite stable, even though he found it difficult at times to partake in family activities. My informant in Los Angeles mentioned that she could not attend regular church services even if she wanted to because of the time her work demanded.

A *panadero*'s marginality affects how he perceives life and how he interprets it artistically through the various media he learns to manipulate as early as his apprenticeship: physical artifacts as well as verbal and nonlinguistic art forms. The most important of these art forms, of course, is bread.

The *panadero* makes some breads by shaping a ball of dough into a bun. These are usually egg breads, or *pan de huevo*. *Pan de huevo* is what most people identify as Mexican sweet bread; it comes in the most varieties. Many of these breads are sprinkled with lumps of sugar on top of a doughy sugar paste. The *panadero* shapes most of the breads he makes by hand, using coils, strips, and other techniques also found in pottery making and sculpture. In the coil technique a portion of dough is separated and rolled back and forth with the palm of the hand. The coils are then formed into such shapes as the *estribo* (the stirrup), the *trenza* (the pigtail or braid), and others whose names are assigned by the *panadero* who creates them. The nomenclature attached to the breads is another dimension of bread making.

In some cases the breads are concrete metaphors of the name assigned, so that dough functions as a sculptural medium as well as a form of nonverbal, symbolic communication. One classic example is the *chilindrina*. I heard its story from two *panaderos*, one in Mexico and the other in Los Angeles. La Chilindrina was supposed to have been a very beautiful, flirtatious prostitute. She was being pursued by a certain *panadero*. The woman, although beautiful, had one defect which could not be ignored: her face was scarred and acned. But this flaw did not matter to the *panadero* who so desired La Chilindrina's attention. In spite of all his persistence, however, she completely ignored his advances. In his frustration the *panadero* returned to his bakery and went to work immediately to create a new bread. A *pan de huevo*, the bread was browned and covered with large lumps of yellow doughy sugar to represent the beautiful prostitute's blemished face. This story not only demonstrates how bread is made symbolic but also reinforces the stereotype of the *panadero* as a sexual profligate.

The cake breads, such as the *niño envuelto* (or jelly roll), the *quequecito* (cupcake), and the *borracho* (drunkard), are not unique to Mexican bakeries. Nonetheless, they have different names (such as those listed) and some characteristics may be changed. For example, the *borracho* is an upside-down cupcake soaked in tequila or rum. This inversion gives it a "drunken" character.

The name of a bread may change in a new environment. For example, the *alamar* is a pretzel-shaped sweet bread. In Los Angeles, where this bread is quite popular, it is now often called a "freeway." The change is not surprising, considering the number of freeways traversing the city, particularly in the area where my informant's bakery is located. The name is arbitrary, and can alter if its context alters (Leach 1976:20).

The baker may use the verbal art forms that are part of the *panadero* tradition of Mexico for play, to break away from his daily routine by manipulating language. Barbara Kirshenblatt-Gimblett and Joel Sherzer discuss just this type of manipulation, which to them is a key concept for discussing play:

speech play can be conceived as any local manipulation of elements and relations of language, creative of a specialized genre, code-variety, and/or style. . . . "manipulation" . . . implies a degree of selection and consciousness beyond that of ordinary language use (1976:1).

The *panaderos'* use of nomenclature illustrated here is a good example of this conscious manipulation of verbal forms. Their naming, as can be seen, is not confined to people, and may be purposely intended to have a double meaning. The idea of speaking to other *panaderos* or to customers with *doble sentido* is very prevalent. Usually it is the names themselves that carry the underlying meanings the customer is attempting to communicate to the shopkeeper or vice versa.

According to the baker in Los Angeles, a popular story about the interaction of customer and *marchante*/baker shows the *panadero* using the names of two breads to tease a female customer. A woman walks into the store and asks for several types of breads, including *calzones*, a bread shaped like pants. After asking for some other breads the woman changes her mind about the *calzones* and tells the *panadero*, "*No, mejor quíteme los calzones y deme dos besos*" [Better yet, remove the "panties" and give me two "kisses"] (a "beso" is "a kiss" and, also, another type of bread). The *panadero* takes advantage of the woman's slip of the tongue to tell her he is too busy at that particular moment. The embarrassed woman cannot look the *panadero* in the eye. This story comes up time and time again when *panaderos* talk about their interactions with female customers. Each one of my sources asked if I had heard this narrative before, as it is one of the most widespread. Another baker, in Austin, said that a male customer would often ask a female clerk if he could have some *besitos* (a diminutive for "besos") that day. The clerk would reply that there were no *besitos* but there were plenty of *trompadas*, (another bread—literally, "blows with a fist").

Panaderos sometimes incorporate gesture into their speech play, particularly when they discuss the ways in which certain breads were invented. For example, the *bisquete* is a round biscuit with a small protruding button shape on the top center of the bread. The *panadero* may ask, "*¿Sabes como se hacen los bisquetes?*" [Do you know how biscuits are made?], and answer by flattening out an imaginary ball of dough with his hands. Then, pressing the "dough" to his belly he leaves you to imagine the biscuit being molded by his navel. He then asks, with unmistakable *doble sentido*, "*Adivina como se hacen las donas*" [Guess how doughnuts are made].

Some of the bakers mentioned that among the night workers one *panadero*'s verbal repertoire usually surpasses all the others'. This person usually gets the other *panaderos* to participate in his games, whether singing, verbal dueling, or any of the other forms of speech play which have been presented, including nonlinguistic activities such as gesture. Much of what is said in the bakery finds its way out to the general populace. In *Picardía mexicana*, an anthology of mischievous lore taken from traditional culture, for example, A. Jiménez (1958) depicts a conversation between a man and his guest. The guest is discussing the significance of the names assigned to breads and how they have been applied to certain types of people. He gives the example of the *bolillo*, a yeast bread resembling the French roll which is a staple throughout Greater Mexico. The guest says that "*bolillo*" may also refer to someone who is fair-complected and blond. These characteristics are often associated with foreigners—originally with Frenchmen and later with American tourists. "*Bolillo*" can also mean "something of little value or importance," as in "*una cosa que vale bolillo*" [something that's worth a *bolillo*]. The analogy is apt because

the most inexpensive bread in a traditional bakery is the *bolillo*.
The guest explains the significance of various sayings such as "*Le
madrugo con el pan a zutanito*" [He got the jump on someone],
which implies that someone went off with another's wife or got
ahead of someone else. Literally, the phrase means he got the
bread ahead of others. It is easy to see how this saying might originate in a bakery, especially since bakers have a reputation as
heart breakers or lady killers.

Two songs popular throughout Greater Mexico offer further
examples of the *panadero's* influence on his culture. The first is
more often recited than sung. The following is a common version:

¡Aye, cocol!
¿Ya no te acuerdas cuando eras chimisclán?
Hoy porque tienes tú ajonjolí
ya no te quieres acordar de mí.
My, *cocol*!
Don't you remember when you were a *chimisclán*?
Now that you have your sesame,
you no longer remember me.

The *cocol* and the *chimisclán* are basically the same bread, except that the former is decorated and glossed with egg and sesame seeds. The *cocol* here thus represents a person who has risen
from a formerly low status and now acts as though he or she no
longer remembers having been a person of more modest means,
shunning his or her old acquaintances. One can imagine the
panadero flirtatiously addressing this song to a female customer
who enters the bakery dressed in fancy clothes.

The second song, "El Panadero"[3] by Ventura Romero, is often
played on Mexican-American radio stations. The first part is
whistled and, on the recording, a horn honks in imitation of the
panaderos who deliver bread on their bicycles, balancing the
bread basket on their heads and tooting their horn as they ride
along. The song goes as follows:

Tu, tu, tu, tu.
[Chiflando, se repite dos veces
"el panadero con el pan."]
El panadero con el pan, tu tu,
el panadero con el pan, tu,
el panadero con el pan, tu tu,
el panadero con el pan, tu.

Tempranito va y lo saca,
calientito en su petaca,
pa' salir con su clientela,
por las calles principales,
y también la Ciudadela,
y despues a los Portales,
y el que no sale se queda,
sin su pan para comer.

—Digan si van pronto a salir,
porque si no,
para seguir
repartiendo el pan,
repartiendo el pan,
repartiendo el pan para comer.

—Traigo bolillos, y teleras,
también gendarmes, besos, conchas a montón,
y traigo faldas, novias, cuernos!
— ¿Qué pasó marchantita? ¿Va usted
a salir? ¿Sí o nó?

—¡Allí voy que me estoy peinando!

—Andile pues marchantita,
tómele, traigo corbatas, volcanes,
piedras, monjas, viudas, rejas,
y un abrazo, ¡nó?

—¿Y los cuernos? ¿Qué pasó?

—¡Aye! ¡No se va poder marchantita!
[Cantando]
Panadero se va,
panadero se va,
panadero se va.

El panadero con el pan, tu tu,
el panadero con el pan,
el panadero con el pan, tu tu,
el panadero con el pan

Tempranito va y lo saca,
calientito en su petaca,
pa' salir con su clientela,
por las calles principales,
y también la Ciudadela,
y despues a los Portales,
y el que no sale se queda,
sin su pan para comer.

Toot, toot, toot, toot.

[The verse "the baker with the
bread" is whistled twice.]

The baker with the bread, toot, toot,
the baker with the bread, toot,
the baker with the bread, toot, toot,
the baker with the bread, toot.

Early, he takes it out,
puts it warm into his basket,
so as to take it to his customers,
through the main streets,
and to "la Ciudadela,"
and then to "los Portales" [old districts of Mexico City],
and those who don't come out,
will have no bread to eat.

"Tell me if you will soon be out,
for if you won't,
I shall be on,
distributing the bread,
distributing the bread,
distributing the bread for others to eat.

"I have 'spindles' and 'rolls',
also 'gendarmes', 'kisses', and 'shells' in great abundance,
and I have 'skirts', 'brides', and 'horns'!

"Where are you little client?
Are you coming out? Yes or no?"

"There I go, I'm combing my hair!"

"Well, all right little client.
Here, I've got 'bow ties', 'volcanos',
'rocks', 'nuns', 'widows', 'grills';
and a warm 'hug', yes?"

"And the horns, where are those?"

"Oh little client, that's not possible right now!"

[Singing]
The baker goes on,
the baker goes on,
the baker goes, on his way.

(The first and second stanzas are repeated.)

This song demonstrates, once again, the *panadero*'s interaction
with his clientele, and with one female customer in particular.
("*Marchantita*" is a term of endearment for a female customer.) It
reflects the stereotype of the *panadero* which persists among the
populace. The song begins with a description of the *panadero* as a

third person. Then the *panadero* speaks to his clients, and one of his clients (the *marchantita*) answers. This conversation implies more than the normal flirtation between a woman client and a baker; but the *marchantita* has spent too much time prettying herself for the *panadero* only to be disappointed by what he could offer her that day. In the recording the woman's tone is quite coquettish, while the *panadero's* is very insinuating, especially as he manipulates the names of the breads to suit his needs.

As can be seen, the verbal folklore related to the *panadero* tradition enhances his artistic character as well as contributes to his reputation. The *panadero* is shown manipulating media, not only by making breads but also in verbal performances. The *panadero* and his customers have different social identities but share an appreciation for the Mexican bread tradition—the first as the creator/performer and the others as the consumer/audience. Bread and speech play are two important mechanisms that bring together these groups (Bauman 1972:35), even if only across a counter. However, what happens when the tradition is challenged by nontraditional or other consumers in the United States?

The nontraditional consumer, such as the *agringado* Mexican-American (see Limón 1977:38) (who considers himself of a different status than the *panaderos* and traditional consumers) and the Anglo, may purchase Mexican bread—but usually as a delicacy rather than a staple. In the interaction between the *panadero* and these clients, much of the verbal play he customarily uses with his traditional consumers is foregone, or not understood. The *doble sentido* is lost. The *agringado* tries to dissociate himself from the Mexican and will not usually frequent a *panadería*. If he does, he will more than likely not know the names of the breads (or pretend not to know them) and will merely point to those he desires to purchase.

Thus far I have discussed how the *panadero* assigns names to breads and people. The customers also assign names—to the *panadero*. Besides "*borracho*" and "*hombre perdido*" he may be called "*gorgojo*" along the Texas-Mexican border, according to one of my sources, the owner of "Joe's Bakery" in Austin. He translates the word as "boll weevil," although the literal translation is merely "weevil." He explained laughingly, "They used to call the *panaderos* in those days '*gorgojos*,' or boll weevils of the wheat because they [the panaderos] were always covered with flour; always all white."

The weevil is a pest which destroys many different grains and crops, including wheat and cotton, which grow plentifully in Texas and northern Mexico. It seems more than accidental that the *panadero*, who is considered a social pest because of his liminal character, and the boll weevil both come:

F'um Mexico, dey say,
He come to try dis Texas soil
En thought he better stay,
A-lookin' for a home,
Jes a-lookin' for a home (Lomax and Lomax 1934:113).

This folksong has had various interpretations, including one by Carl Sandburg in *The American Songbag* (1927:8). It has also been recorded by popular artists. Still, the relationship between "The Boll Weevil" and the *panadero* (or any itinerant Mexican laborer) is curiously exact. The black narrator of the song has the protagonist, a farmer, ask the boll weevil:

Where is your native home?
"Way down in the bottom
Among the cot'n an' corn" (Lomax 1960:535).

From the lines of this folksong, one can draw a strong suggestion that the "boll weevil" designates any Mexican farm worker or laborer. (Lomax [ibid.] suggests that the "bottom" of the verse above is the "river-bottom land," or the Rio Grande Valley.) Black laborers may have felt threatened by the number of Mexicans who were coming into Texas to work in the fields.

"The Boll Weevil" is believed to have come from the same general region as the term "*gorgojo*." One baker mentioned that her father, who was a *panadero*, also worked in the cotton fields at one time. It is possible that the wheat weevil and the cotton weevil were confused in the translation from English to Spanish and vice versa. Both weevils are pests and the characteristics of the boll weevil in the song fit the stereotype of the *panadero*. For instance, the *panadero*'s reputed sexual prowess and supposed penchant to leave children in every town he visits are reflected in this stanza from the "Boll Weevil" ballad:

De fus' time I saw de Boll Weevil
He wuz settin' on de square,
De nex' time I saw de Boll Weevil
He had all his family der—

Dey's lookin' for a home
Jes a-lookin' for a home (Lomax and Lomax 1934:114).

The relationship that I have drawn between "The Boll Weevil" and the *panadero* is purely a conjecture. Moreover, the term "boll weevil" was at one time also used by "roughnecks" (seasoned laborers on an oil rig). "The 'boll weevil' is supposed to be a greenhorn about his business, and the name is often used derisively by roughnecks to characterize fellow workmen who show unfamiliarity with their work" (McTee 1964:64). The term has thus been used in more than one way. The *panadero* may be considered a social pest or *gorgojo* by his community because the folklore about his drunkenness as well as his flirtatiousness and promiscuous dealings with women depicts him as such.

Often the only time the *panadero* has to socialize with others is at night. Other people who are usually out at night tend to be social outcasts such as drunkards and prostitutes—who have a specific status and a limited domain. The *panadero*, on the other hand, may enter any sphere he pleases in his dealings as a provider of bread. He may work during day or night. He has his own home and family, but enters other domains such as the public streets and the homes of his customers when he is delivering bread; the bakery where he works; the bars where he plays on his off hours; and other areas, including remote towns and cities. As a "*gorgojo*," he is considered "vermin"—which Leach (1965:206) describes as pests which are ambiguous because they have no direct relation to man: they are found in the house, farm, field, and remote areas, and do not kill or serve as food. As social pests, then, the *panaderos* are neither strangers nor kin. They may be seen daily at the bakery, but may have no relations in a particular town. At the same time they are tabooed as sex partners.

In the folklore about the *panadero* as a woman chaser and lady killer the *panadero* somewhat resembles a *macho*, because he flaunts his sexuality. He leaves poor women broken-hearted; and his artistic verbal and nonverbal metaphors have sexual overtones. However, in the story about La Chilindrina, the *panadero* does not conquer even a prostitute. Similarly, in the song "El Panadero" the *panadero* insinuates certain sexual passes at his client but ends up by riding away. The *panadero*'s supposed *machismo* may be symptomatic of a lack of sexual activity due to his odd working schedule and itinerancy. His sexual identity may be threatened in reality while the folklore is an outlet for his frustration. By working until all hours and traveling to find better economic conditions, the *panadero* is trying to realize himself (Paredes 1971:36); but sometimes he becomes a victim of the stereotypes attributed to him.

A woman baker is not negatively stereotyped like the male *panadero*. She is held in respect by male bakers and by society. The *panadera* is stationary unless she travels with her husband or male members of her family. All the women I spoke with asked me if I had heard stories about the *panaderos* or male bakers. They joked about their stereotype. In Xiutepec and Los Angeles these women had very important roles in their bakeries as the co-owners. Yet in Xiutepec, the woman baker talked first about her husband as the *panadero* and artist. Later she admitted that in his absence (which was frequent) she and her sons made the bread, then slept a little and woke up early to deliver it. At last she revealed that she had been a baker longer than her husband. A male baker from Austin mentioned that he was considering hiring female bakers because they joked around less often and got more work done. Nevertheless, all of my informants felt the male *panadero* was the key figure of the folklore about the Mexican baking tradition. What, after all, could be the reaction if a woman asked, "*Adivina como se hacen las donas*"?

NOTES

1. The use of the masculine pronoun throughout this essay is not meant to imply that there are no female bakers, or *panaderas*; it merely reflects the fact that male bakers are traditionally perceived as more itinerant than their female counterparts. Therefore, reference to the male baker incorporates the perspectives of both the male and female bakers I interviewed.
2. My study of the *panadero* developed originally under the stimulus of Américo Paredes. I would like also to express my thanks to Roger Abrahams for helping me to formulate my ideas about the stereotypes attached to the *panadero*.
3. The song "El Panadero" was transcribed from Américo Paredes' tape collection.

BIBLIOGRAPHY

Abrahams, Roger, and Richard Bauman. 1978. Ranges of festival behavior. In *The reversible world*. Barbara Babcock, ed. Ithaca: Cornell University Press.

Baghban, Hafiz. 1977. *The context and concept of humor in Magadi theater*. Ann Arbor: University Microfilms International.

Barth, Fredrik. 1969. *Ethnic groups and boundaries*. Boston: Little, Brown.

Bauman, Richard. 1972. Differential identity and the social base of folklore. In *Toward new perspectives in folklore*. Américo Paredes and Richard Bauman, eds. Austin: University of Texas Press.

Bricker, Victoria. 1973. *Ritual humor in Highland Chiapas*. Austin: University of Texas Press.

Douglas, Mary. 1972. Pollution. In *Reader in comparative religion*, 3rd ed. William Lessa and Evon Vogt, eds. New York: Harper, Row.

Gmelch, George. 1977. Economic strategies and migrant adaptation: The case of Irish tinkers. *Ethnos* 42:23–37.

Goffman, Erving. 1963. *Stigma*. Englewood Cliffs, N.J.: Prentice-Hall.

Jiménez, A. 1958. *Picardía mexicana*. Mexico: Editorial B. Costa-Amic.

Kirshenblatt-Gimblett, Barbara, and Joel Sherzer. 1976. Introduction. In *Speech play*. Barbara Kirshenblatt-Gimblett, ed. Philadelphia: University of Pennsylvania Press.

Leach, Edmund R. 1965. Anthropological aspects of language: Animal categories and verbal abuse. In *Reader in comparative religion*. William Lessa and Evon Vogt, eds. New York: Harper, Row.

———. 1976. *Culture and communication*. New York: Cambridge University Press.

Limón, José. 1977. *Agringado* joking in Texas-Mexican society: Folklore and differential identity. *New Scholar* 6:33–50.

Lomax, Alan. 1960. *The folksongs of North America*. New York: Doubleday.

Lomax, John, and Alan Lomax. 1934. *American ballads and folk songs*. New York: Macmillan.

McTee, A.R. 1964. Oil field diction. In *Happy hunting ground*. J. Frank Dobie, ed. Hatboro, Pa.: Folklore Associates.

Paredes, Américo. 1971. The United States, Mexico, and machismo. *Journal of the Folklore Institute* 8:17–37.

———. 1976. *A Texas-Mexican cancionero*. Urbana: University of Illinois Press.

Sandburg, Carl. 1927. *The American songbag*. New York: Harcourt, Brace.

Turner, Victor. 1974. Liminal to liminoid, in play, flow, and ritual: An essay in comparative symbology. *Rice University Studies* 60:53–92.

Beverly J. Stoeltje

Cowboys and Clowns: Rodeo Specialists and the Ideology of Work and Play

One of the most neglected areas of folklore scholarship is the large-scale public event: festivals and fairs, concerts, and other celebrations. This is a notable lack precisely because in such events, specifically those rooted in a certain locale, the performing community enacts its traditions for itself and outsiders, selecting features from the past but incorporating change as well so that the interpretation also reflects the present. Moreover, social and symbolic structures function to organize participation and performance in dance, drama, meals, contest, music, and costume. The heroes, the fools, the devils, and the officials are strategically positioned in these festivities, permitting the articulation of values, themes, and social history. Such is the case with many rodeos throughout the United States, especially where these shows arose out of the actual social and cultural conditions of the cattle trade.

In these settings the rodeo often functions as the major attraction in a celebration of several days' duration that also features a parade, barbecues, fiddle contests, dancing, and multiple opportunities for socializing. In this paper I will look closely at one of these cowboy celebrations: the Texas Cowboy Reunion, held annually from July 2 through 4 in Stamford, Texas.[1] Of central concern will be the roles available, within the rodeo performance itself, for communicating the defining features of the cowboy as perceived in this locale. Through the enactment of these roles the performance embodies the tensions as well as the accomplishments of the cattle-raising enterprise, drawing from them the dominant symbolic images and actions that give form to the rodeo.

A study of this celebration, as of other large festivities, faces the challenge presented by its complexity and ephemerality. Activities go on simultaneously, varied social groups participate, and performance governs activity such that the occasion is fleeting and cannot be reproduced for the sake of research. Furthermore, participants' interpretations of the event may vary widely. A comprehensive approach must be applied to such ocasions in order to relate the constituent parts to a whole system; for rarely does the stated purpose of an event capture its broader meanings. Discrete events such as these, which embody and exhibit the culture of a people, have been labeled "cultural performances" by Milton Singer (1972). These cultural performances bring into focus the elementary constituents of the culture; the most productive way to study a complex society, then, is through observation of such units of performance. Useful here as well is Robert Redfield's notion of "cultural specialists": "kinds of role-occupiers in characteristic relations to one another and to lay people . . . performing characteristic functions concerned with the transmission of traditions" (1956:58). This label identifies individuals who enact specific traditional practices and performances. Singer (1972:75) distinguishes two such roles: the urban specialist, more specialized and involved in more full-time professional activity; and the village specialist who is more of a generalist, and may perform several special expressive functions.

Central to the American cultural performance of rodeo, as well as to many other American entertainments relating to our frontier history, is, of course, the figure of the cowboy. Since the cowboy first emerged as a Western frontier hero in the nineteenth century, American popular culture has drawn heavily on his image, transforming the adventuresome horseman of the frontier into a national symbol of radical individualism (Boatright 1964). Notable among those who have explored this evolution are Américo Paredes and Mody Boatright, Texas folklorists who knew the cowboy from first-hand acquaintance as well as from literature. Boatright notes that the public exhibitions of cowboy skills in the rodeo were among the most effective means by which a positive public image began to countervail the obvious antisocial tendencies of these tramps of the saddle. In the twentieth century the cowboy became the popular symbol of the frontier through his representation in the mass media. Boatright predicted that rodeo would survive as a ritual of the American frontier: "the last frontiersman, the cowboy, or, more accurately, a man in ceremonial garb representing him, re-enacts the conquest of the West, and on a deeper level symbolizes man's conquest of nature" (1964:202).

Paredes (1963), in examining this symbolic process in the literature and folklore of the late nineteenth and early twentieth centuries, emphasizes the historical conditions and commercial interests which influenced both forms. The image of the cowboy which appeared in these popular sources expressed something fundamental to North American life. He observes that a similar process has affected the Argentine gaucho. These two occupational figures became national symbols for their respective countries because they represented, through a heroic character, the period of greatest importance in the development of national identity: when the young nations were dissociating from their colonial ancestors at the same time as they were trying to impose civilization (including social forms) onto the natural environment (Paredes 1963:240).

In their rich and suggestive studies Boatright and Paredes provide a solid understanding of the process by which America turned the Western cowhand into a national hero who embodied the pioneer dimensions of its ideology: the American cowboy. Today, almost twenty years since these articles appeared, the rodeo has become one of America's most popular entertainments, in rural and urban communities alike. Certainly, then, it seems that rodeo does reenact the Western frontier experience by presenting the popular hero of that experience, the cowboy, in a live performance.

Therefore, acknowledging that a broad range of experience and ideology enter into the cultural performances of a complex society, and considering the widespread popularity of rodeo in modern America, we may legitimately explore the question. what, specifically, does rodeo communicate that qualifies it as a cultural performance and distinguishes it from the formulaic mass-media genres which also feature the cowboy?

Toward this end I will employ the construct "cultural specialist" to identify the communicative performance roles in the rodeo held as the feature event of the Texas Cowboy Reunion. I posit here that these roles, derived from the cowboy experience and shaped by historical conditions, serve as a vehicle to express am-

biguities in America's value system. It should be no surprise that
the cowboy image expresses national ideology since, as Paredes
has pointed out, the heroic cowboy developed along with the national identity. Close study of the rodeo specialists, however, suggests that together these roles articulate a characteristic opposition in that ideology: work versus play (cf. Rodgers 1978).
Further, the opposition between regional and national cultures,
common in America as well as other modern countries, also finds
expression in the rodeo specialists: they come from both the local
area and the general rodeo circuit, thus paralleling Singer's
(1972) village and urban specialists.

The performance roles of each of the three major specialists—the traditional cowboy, the clown, and the announcer—
communicate these general oppositions. Moreover, each individual rodeo expresses its particular interpretation of them through
the selection and combination of these communicative roles.

Modern rodeo varies little in its essential components; it follows a basic form, with some slight variations, and features the
same categories of performers throughout the United States. Historically, the form developed from the popular entertainments
of the late nineteenth and early twentieth centuries: Wild West
shows, vaudeville, the circus, medicine shows, county fairs, and,
of course, early rodeos. The cowboy rodeo as we know it today
combines elements from these earlier shows with unique features
derived from actual cowboy life. The rodeo has syncretized the
elements borrowed from non-cowboy entertainments into the
rodeo environment so that they are consistent with the cowboy
tradition. Like other art forms, then, rodeo does not reflect literally the experience it depicts. Rather it gives expression to some
of the dominant themes of that experience.

The rodeo program itself divides the action into two categories—"contest events" and "special acts." Both the social structure of the event as well as its organic principles can be comprehended through the arrangement of these expressive units.
Contest events include bronc riding, bull riding, wild-mare racing, cowgirl barrel racing, and roping. The special acts are circus-
like and feature a clown or trick riders who perform humorous
entertainment or unusual stunts, frequently in conjunction with
a trained animal. A ceremonial Grand Entry opens the rodeo, and
it concludes with bull riding, a contest event incorporating the
clown in a dual role.

Performers like the activities, tend to be divided into two classes: contestants and contract entertainers. Contestants must pay an entry fee for each event they enter; they receive no payment for appearing in the rodeo. Winners in each event do receive prizes, usually up to the third place. Roping and barrel racing may be specially marked with prizes of saddles, buckles, or spurs and hats, as well as money. Bucking-event winners receive buckles and cash. No invitations are issued, and no contestants are under contract. Any individual may enter the event who pays the entry fee and has the required equipment.[2] Responsibility for lodging, transportation, and care of their horses rests with these cowgirls and cowboys themselves.

Cowboys and the bucking animals they will ride are "matched" by a drawing, and the rodeo organizers determine in what order all the contestants will appear. Most of the contest events present one individual contestant at a time. A few events are organized for teams, but in most of these one individual is the contestant and the other a helper. The one exception is the wild-mare race. In this event four teams, of three cowboys each, compete simultaneously in the arena to catch, saddle, and ride a wild mare. Though the event requires an entry fee it is a small amount only, as is the prize. Interest lies largely in the excitement and entertainment the race provides. No other rodeo event has simultaneous competition. The rodeo's focus then, is on the individual performer who pays a fee to compete in hopes of winning the prize.

Clowns and trick riders belong to the category of "contract performers," as does the announcer. (Also included among those whose services are contracted is the producer and those who work with him. The producer provides the bucking stock to be ridden and the calves to be roped.) These performers advertise their acts and build reputations by performing. The rodeo sponsors or producer select several for each rodeo, and pay them for their services. They do not compete, and receive no prizes.

The category of special entertainment includes three kinds of performance specializations. In the "dress-up" or "fancy" acts the actors wear fitted, glamorous costumes which glitter and shine under the arena lights. They perform trick acts which involve both themselves and their trained animals in difficult or unusual action—most commonly trick riding, though other circus-type acts may also be performed. These acts emphasize physical feats and fancy dress. The actors do not speak though the announcer provides a running commentary while they perform.

Clown acts emphasize humor in both speech and action. The clowns dress in loose-fitting clothes of clashing colors; they present a motley image, often that of the tramp. They make up their faces with a large red nose and some combination of black and white, and usually wear a wig and a hat. Trained animals are also included in most clown acts—usually horses, monkeys, dogs, bulls, or donkeys. The clown's humor draws heavily upon risqué and otherwise taboo subjects such as sex and bodily functions. In addition, the clown characteristically plays with cultural categories, confusing and rearranging the normal behavior of men and animals. The clown, like clowns in other cultural contexts, often enacts the role of fool, while the animal in his act may seem to be clever and to outsmart him or the announcer—thus upsetting our usual expectations about animal behavior. This inversion seems particularly significant in the rodeo, where other, more central animals are made to appear wild.

The third act which features a special entertainer places the clown in the bull-riding event; in this role he is called a "bull-fighter." A cowboy enters riding a bucking bull. To protect the cowboy from being stomped or gored when he lands on the ground, the clown distracts the bull, like a cape man in a bull-fight. As the clown must also be amusing and appear foolish, he has to attract the attention of the bull, and often engage it in a dangerous chase around the arena while simultaneously providing the audience with excitement and humor. In addition, between bull rides, the clown tells jokes from the arena. The announcer responds to the clown for the audience but also repeats each line, often functioning as the dupe of the joke. The following example illustrates this genre. (Each sentence or phrase was spoken by the clown, standing in the arena, to the announcer, in the judges' stand, who repeated the line over the microphone.) Responding to a wave for attention from the clown, the announcer said, "What's this, you've got to tell me something?" He then repeated after the clown:

There were two old maids that lived out in the country. They walked down the road a mile and a half to church every time the church doors opened. One Wednesday night they went to church and they were gonna walk home. They got outta church and were walking home, and two hippies attacked them. Jerked them right over to the side of the road. Were attacking them right there. One old maid looked up to heaven, said, "Father forgive him, he knows not what he's doing." Other old maid said, "This one over here does." [Audience laughs.]

The announcer directs the performance, interacting with the performers in the arena and explaining their action to the audience; he functions much like the master of ceremonies in any of a number of cognate "shows." His specialty is interpretation—presenting the action and suggesting its meaning—through speaking. Throughout the rodeo he remains at the microphone in the judges' stand. The stand is a two-level platform over the alley (the fenced space which serves as the formal entrance and exit for the arena). Though the announcer is visible, he is not actually in the arena where the action is. Thus he is identified by his voice alone, amplified over a public-address system. His functions are several: announcing the names and hometowns of the contestants, entertaining the audience when there is a pause in the arena action, interacting verbally with the clowns, and interpreting the action to the audience. He is thus the intermediary between the performers and the audience.

Rodeo thus patterns relations among the performers through the use of two categories: contestants (cowgirls and cowboys) and contract entertainers (the actors—clowns and trick riders—and the announcer). Because this pattern characterizes American rodeo generally, contestants and contract performers can enact their roles in rodeos throughout the country.

Within particular communities and regions, rodeos can develop a social organization representative of the specific groups which participate in their production and performance. It is to this social organization that we will look now to see how the meaning of a specific rodeo is constituted and communicated.

The Texas Cowboy Reunion is held in the heart of a cattle-raising region which is dominated by some of the largest ranches in Texas and where many cowboys have worked since the late nineteenth century. The central purpose of the Reunion, since its origin in 1930, has been to honor the old-time cowboy and to celebrate the cowboy heritage as the inhabitants perceive it. Over the years several techniques have been used to give this public recognition to the old-time cowboy, techniques which serve simultaneously to define the cowboy and the regional heritage.

Thus the star of the Reunion is not the cowboy specialist, but rather an old-time cowboy who embodies both formally and informally the cowboy heritage valued in the region. This role depends on the personal identity developed by the individual in the routines of his everyday life, and formal recognition during the Reunion acknowledges this role by incorporating its most salient features in public display. The Reunion's announcer needs more than the basic knowledge of rodeo and a facility for public speaking. The role must be assumed by an individual steeped in local tradition who can articulate the values of the tradition in his commentary on the performance. Certain individuals have filled these two roles year after year, but the clown changes each year. Anyone who wears the appropriate costume and make-up will be recognized immediately as a clown, but the more successful ones are good athletes, understand certain principles of mime and acting, and can dramatize traditional humorous cowboy conventions.

CULTURAL SPECIALISTS

The Traditional Cowboy

As the major symbol of the Reunion, the old-time cowboy links the past and the present; in him, too, the local ranching tradition and the larger rodeo circuit meet. Even more important, perhaps, the cowboy specialist reflects the vitality of tradition, demonstrating adaptability to change as well as loyalty to old styles and values. Three individuals of three generations have served as the cowboy specialists *par excellence* of this rodeo reunion since the time of its inception. These men have all resided in the local region and been active in the rodeo community throughout the year. Their position within this social group is widely known, established at many levels and through a variety of activities. They are "the village specialists," those who live in the community and fill a larger number of local roles than do urban specialists. In contrast to the clown and the announcer, their status, more than any specialized performance, gives them distinction.

The first of these specialists was regarded as an example of the true old-time cowboy, one who spent his life working on large ranches. He perfected the role, transmitted the tradition to others, participated in the organization of the Reunion, and was a prominent figure in it for forty years until his death. The memory of this man continues to shape the Reunion in several ways.

"Scandalous John" Selmon started punching cattle when he was fourteen years old. In 1915 he began working for the SMS Ranches because he had married, and the ranch where he had formerly worked would not employ married cowboys. The manager of the SMS, a native of Kansas, described Selmon at that time as follows:

He is a very picturesque character and would do for a model cowboy in one of the moving picture shows. He has a reputation of being the best rider in the whole country. It may be that he is a trifle "windy," but he carries a whole lot of good humor with it, and I think he will prove to be one of our most valued men. He is true blue in every way (Hastings in Clarke 1976:286).

By 1919 Selmon had become foreman of the SMS Flat Top Ranch, a position he held until his retirement in 1968. Legend claims that he acquired his nickname when he was bucked off by a very rough horse which he referred to as "scandalous." The cowboys applied the term to him and began calling him "Scandalous John." Not only was he an exemplary cowboy himself, but he taught other young men to rope and ride and encouraged them to perform their skills in rodeo as well as on the range.

Active in organizing the Reunion, he was Arena Director of the rodeo for more than thirty-five years. In 1932 he was named the most typical cowboy under fifty-five years of age at the Reunion, and in 1958 he was featured on the cover of the Reunion program as "typifying the cowboy, past and present, which the Reunion honors."

The respect accorded Selmon by both cowboys and ranch owners and managers continues today. Large photographs of him hang in the office of the SMS Ranch in Stamford and in the ranch headquarters in New York City. Members of the rodeo community still speak of him as exemplifying all that the Reunion signifies. The prize saddle which is awarded to the winner of the old-time cowboy calf-roping contest has been designated the John Selmon Memorial Saddle, and the Western art gallery located in the entrance building to the rodeo grounds is named the John Selmon Memorial Art Gallery. Stories which he told and stories about him still circulate, and his daughter-in-law based a musical on his stories that was performed by the community.

One of the most comprehensive statements about this man comes from a preacher who knew him personally and directed

his funeral—and who also acts as the rodeo announcer. The pallbearers at Selmon's funeral, he says, illustrate the broad social
range of Selmon's friends and admirers:

at this funeral the church was packed. I got to lookin' while I was sittin'
there waiting to get up. Bunch of pallbearers was a millionaire truck
owner, a couple of Mexican ranch hands, and another ranch hand, a retired Texas Ranger, and a rancher. Just really cut across this whole
section.

John Selmon, then, possessed what his community considered the
ideal cowboy qualities, both technical and social. He has thus acquired legendary status since his death. Not only did he have outstanding cowboy skills, but he was constantly engaged in the
transmission of tradition through teaching these skills and nur-
turing the Reunion.

With Selmon's death in 1971, his good friend George Humphreys succeeded to the position of ideal cowboy. Also widely
known and respected for both his technical skills and his social
activities, he had been foreman on a large ranch, the 6666, for
most of his adult life. Yet there were differences in the ways Selmon and Humphreys enacted the role of ideal cowboy, which the
difference in generations accounts for. Selmon left his home in
central Texas at the age of fourteen to work in West Texas as a
cowboy on a large ranch. Humphreys was born in this West Texas
region, in Stonewall County in 1899, and spent his entire life
there and in neighboring King County. In 1919 he was hired by
S. B. "Burk" Burnett, owner of the 6666 Ranch, to work as a
bronc buster, and in 1932 he became foreman and manager of the
ranch, one of the ten largest in the state, with its headquarters in
King County. Humphreys held this position until his retirement
in 1970, when he moved back to his own small ranch in Stonewall County and managed his cattle until he died in March 1979.

Humphreys proved himself an outstanding cowboy and cowman and earned the respect of the entire region for his expertise
in handling cattle and horses; but he also assumed several other,
related roles. He was not only the foreman of the 6666 but the
manager, a job with more authority and financial responsibility
than that of foreman. Further, he held the office of sheriff of King
County for twenty years, simultaneously with that of ranch manager, and was as fully respected as a lawman as he was as a cow-
boy/cowman. The Texas Rangers named him an honorary mem-

ber, and Midwestern University in Wichita Falls bestowed an honorary degree upon him. Further, he was a member of the Board of Trustees for the Stamford Art Foundation, the organization which sponsors the Western Art Exhibit and Sale at the John Selmon Memorial Art Gallery during the Reunion, and he always attended their annual opening function on the evening preceding the first day of the Reunion. His one daughter and several granddaughters were active barrel racers at the Reunion and continued to attend after they moved away, bringing his great-grandchildren to ride with Humphreys in the rodeo's Grand Entry.

Humphreys did not win his prestige through the position of authority which he held, however, but as a result of his social relations. People of all levels of society, throughout the region, considered him the ideal man; he demonstrated the qualities which all individuals should aspire to possess. He has been described as a "cowboy's cowboy," a "good man," and "a man who loved and would help everybody."

The major newspaper of the region carried lengthy articles for several days following Humphreys' death in 1979, quoting extensively from people who had known him well. Fred Dalby, his successor as cowboy specialist and his close personal friend, described him as a person who was always ready to help anyone else, a man who liked to visit with people and a man who loved his family. An old-time veterinarian considered him "the best cowman we ever had in this county . . . no better judge of cattle than George—and he was just as good with horses." The noted Texas and Western historian, Rupert Richardson, professor emeritus of Hardin-Simmons University, felt that Humphreys represented "the genuine qualities of the western cattleman . . . friendly, very loyal to his friends," and that he was a man who loved the ranching and cattle industry.

Like Selmon and other cowboy specialists, Humphreys possessed the ability to tell a good story, a quality still described at times as "windy." At his funeral the preacher stated: "I don't suppose there's a person in this church who hasn't got a story they could tell about him; or have[n't], themselves, listened to one of his 'corny' stories . . . for the third time . . . and, all the while, loved every minute of it." The preacher then told a story which illustrated Humphreys' generosity.

At Humphrey's death thousands of West Texans came to his hometown of Aspermont to pay their final respects; the largest church in town was filled at the funeral and large crowds stood outside. The music included "Home on the Range," "Rock of Ages," "Beyond the Sunset," and "The Last Roundup." The preacher wrote a poem for George using the familiar metaphors of the cowboy; it began "Each life is like a cattle drive" and ended "Where God owns all the pastures and cattle on a thousand hills."

As a man whose social network included the entire population of cattle people within his region, Humphreys transcended the limitations of one particular cultural role. He functioned in several roles simultaneously, roles both literal and symbolic. He represented not only the cowboy, but the large rancher and the lawman; not only the man of honesty and integrity, but the storyteller and joker; not only the cowman but the supporter of the arts. It is not surprising, then, that he functioned as the major cultural specialist for the Reunion in the 1970s, a period long after that of the early-day cowboy who came West in his youth. In the mid-twentieth century the ideal cowboy was also a family man who could assume the responsibility of enforcing the law. Yet Humphreys' style was heavily laced with humor and generosity, and he maintained strong bonds with both the past and the future.

In the third generation we see again both change and continuity in how the role of cowboy specialist is played. Fred Dalby, Jr., the present incumbent, is approximately twenty years younger than Humphreys was at his death. Dalby learned to rope from John Selmon, and was a lifetime friend and neighbor of Humphreys. Unlike Humphreys or Selmon, however, he has never been a foreman. He raises cattle on the small ranch he shares with his father and mother, and concentrates heavily on roping at rodeos in the local area.

As a young man Dalby earned a degree at Texas A&M. After serving in the Army he returned to his native area and married a ranch cowgirl who was an active barrel racer at the Reunion. She had grown up on one of the SMS ranches in the area, where her father was a cowboy. He was also a fiddler and participated in the Reunion, winning the saddle in the old-timers' roping during the 1950s. The Dalbys' two daughters have been dedicated barrel racers, competing at the Reunion as well as in collegiate and local rodeos. Both are married now and live in the region, and they attend the Reunion regularly with their husbands and young children.

Dalby has competed in the roping events for many years at the Reunion, and in 1979 he won the John Selmon Memorial Saddle for the old-timers' roping event. That saddle completed his collection of Reunion prize saddles.

In addition to raising cattle, Dalby also fills several other roles in the cattle trade, especially training horses and teaching children to rope. He also acted for many years as general organizer and trouble shooter at a local cattle auction. The community of auction-goers relied heavily on him for advice and for assurance of making a fair deal.

As with the other cowboy specialists, a major part of Dalby's qualification for his role is his sociability. He and his wife know not only every resident of the region, but all their family histories, their children, and their major interests. Visiting and joking and the sharing of food and drink are prominent features of their everyday life, and dominate their time at the Reunion as well. When this author was searching for an ideal cowboy roper to represent Texas at the Bicentennial Smithsonian Festival of American Folklife in 1976, everyone I consulted in the region, from both managerial and cowboy social groups, agreed that Dalby fit the description.

A local event held in February of each year demonstrates the recognition of Dalby's position as successor to Humphreys. In the Annual Haskell Trail Drive about twenty-five cowboys and one hundred head of cattle reenact the old-time trail drive. Honored cowboys called "trail bosses," representing the old-time cowboys, lead the short drive to the Auction Barn. There a barbecue and sale are staged. A large crowd attends the event, and the trail bosses are among its main attractions. George Humphreys was one of the three trail bosses until 1979, when illness prevented his participation. His place was assumed by Dalby who, though only sixty-two, clearly qualified as the man for the position.

In the lives of these three specialists, then— John Selmon, George Humphreys, and Fred Dalby—the cowboy tradition is defined, represented, and transmitted to others. Each reflects changes in both how the cowboy works and lives and how the ideal image is projected: the early-day cowboy who left home to spend his life cowboying; the native who rose to success as lawman and cowboy; and the contemporary college-educated cowboy who works primarily for himself, and concentrates on performing in amateur rodeos in his region. Their social abilities, coupled with their proven cowboy expertise, won them the accolade, "good cowboy, good man." Each of them earned respect for his knowledge of cattle and horses, and, equally important, for his concern for and interaction with other people in the roles of teacher, trainer, performer, friend, and humorist. Furthermore, all three have possessed the quality of wide social access, they have been at home in all levels of local society and, at the Reunion itself, have moved with ease from one social scene to another.

The Announcer

Above all else, the announcer must be able to speak fluently and spontaneously and to communicate an intimate knowledge of local traditions through speaking. He is the representative of the audience and of community values, charged with maintaining the sense of common effort even while assuring the flow of the event. This role was successfully performed by the Reverend Jerry Boles for more than twenty years. He came to the community as a preacher in 1953, and he and his family lived there and participated in the civic life for approximately eighteen years. Now a minister in another community, he still returns each year to announce the rodeo, for both he and the rodeo participants consider his presence necessary for a successful Reunion. A native of the region, he grew up around cowboys and rodeo; thus he understands that to those who anticipate it and participate in it this occasion is the major social event of the year. And, finally, he is aware that the announcer's specialty is speaking:

I've been a sports fan always, and hung around rodeos. Grew up in West Texas and it's pretty hard not to. Dad was a minister also. Got on a bronc once and tore my pants and Momma got mad at me, so I never was a bronc rider. But I do like these kinda folks. As a matter of fact, when I was a boy my father was preaching up in Tulia on the plains, and that was during the Depression, during the thirties, and local merchants would do anything to stimulate a little trade and get people to come to town; didn't have many and so they staged a rodeo on the corner of the square every Saturday. My father got to announcin' that, and that was before they even had PA systems. Lotta times on Sunday he could hardly preach for tryin' to holler over the crowd.

Boles has spent his life in this rugged region of northwest Texas, and is devoted to the place and its way of life. "I love this part of the world. I told somebody that if the Lord ever called me any place else he sure would have an argument. I just feel sure if the Kingdom of God ever comes, it'll be someplace between the Brazos and Rio Grande rivers." As dedicated as any cowboy to this "cow country," as it is often called, the preacher is equally dedicated to the people. He explains how the rodeo and Reunion serve a revitalizing function, stressing the place of the old-time cowboy:

It changes all the time, and yet it's just basically the same. The reason for its existence is the same. It's just the visiting. The rodeo's incidental. If you'll look at these ole-timers, the rodeo is fun, it's important, it's why they say they come, but they really come. . . . You know you see these old rascals meet, and they'll say, "Are you still alive?" And you can tell that they're really glad that they are, and that he's still alive and that they can be together one more time, and lie to each other and whatever the case may be. But that's the reason for it. That's really it.

Describing an old-time cowboy who entered the old-timers' roping event, Boles captures the essence of the experience:

You know that ole man out there this morning. We had an old man out there, he's seventy-one years old and had a wooden leg. He roped and tied a calf, and it took him a long time, over a minute, but he'll live on, he'll live all winter on saying, "I caught my calf at Stamford." That keeps 'em goin'.

Thus Boles has been a self-conscious participant in the regional cultural tradition since his youth. Throughout his adult life he has been immersed in the lives of the tradition bearers of the area. Further, he acknowledges the importance of the Reunion, that the town is his own home and that he himself is an active part of the religious tradition of the region.

Rev. Boles is equally conscious of the importance of local standards of good talking. He points out that preaching and announcing are related genres of public speech in this social group:

'Course you work to try to keep the show moving. Rodeo is by nature slow. They lag. Cowboys want everything just right and I don't blame 'em, and so fillin' time and just bull, gift of gab, I think, is important, and that also works good in the other business I have; not to make light of it, but you generally do think on your feet.

Even possessing this talent, the announcer must stay alert to nuances of language. Each generation has its idiom:

The language, of course, of rodeo, changes. Not doing but just this one I need to get here a day or two ahead and kinda hang around and get the feel for it. They've got new sayings, like kids in any walk of life, and new ways of saying the same thing. You wanna speak the language. Of course, this one, the old ways of saying things are important too.

In addition, the announcer recognizes a delicate relationship between rodeo and humor:

Rodeo humor with clowns and whatnot tends to be a little earthy, and sometimes I'm sure that people who are a little more straight-laced, or who go around with a face long enough to eat oatmeal out of a churn and call that religion, they'd take offense at the thought, for example, of a minister saying some of the things I do, but I hope they're taken in the spirit in which they are said, and that's a part of rodeo. You can't be around livestock and not talk about life and things rather earthy. That's a part of rodeo. Humor. But the tension and knowing just how far to go. . . .

In the careful manipulation of this tension, of course, lies the excitement of the rodeo. When the cowboys and animals are in action, tension between the two dominates the arena, and the announcer simply emphasizes with language what is happening at the moment. He notes that an animal was particularly tough to ride or that a cowboy had hard luck and receives "no time" or a "goose egg," clarifying the nuances of rules for the audience. He points out that a contestant may have placed among the winners in past years or that the father or mother may have been a prize winner.

However, when contestants are not actually performing—between events, for example—or when a complication arises, the attention of the audience must be captured in order to sustain the tension and hold their interest. At such times, talk takes the place of action in the flow of the event. "Earthy" things—especially uncontrolled animal behaviors—are often the subject of both practical and verbal jokes. The announcer will direct comments at the band, at individuals in the stands, at those working in and around the chutes, or at the clown. The boundaries between the arena and the audience are temporarily dissolved by joking. The band members usually respond with noises from their instruments, particularly the trombone or trumpet, and other individuals on the ground will engage in verbal byplay with the announcer. The purpose of this play is "to try to keep the show moving."

that's just filler. I hurrah them, the band, pick on 'em, and pick on the clown, but it's mainly filler. Crowds seem to enjoy it. Keep something going with him. And this clown is a pro, of course. He's an excellent clown, and he senses when you're dragging and he'll stir up something. Usually I'll pick out somebody in the stands, or something, that I know. . . . mainly you just have to make noise.

As in all elements of the event, the success of this brief and unexpected byplay requires that the community be familiar enough with its nature to appreciate the interaction and respond accordingly. Finally, when an animal or contestant is injured or temporarily immobilized, the announcer must interpret the situation for the audience.

As a specialist, then, the announcer must not only provide running commentary on the action, but amuse the audience and respond to unusual and critical situations—all the while transmitting the humor, values, and styles of this performance tradition to contestants and audience alike.

The Clown

The "special entertainers" category includes both clowns and trick riders. However, only the clown is essential to the rodeo. Some rodeos use trick riders as a special act, some do not. The clown is always present: in brief appearances before his acts; in the special acts when the slot is not filled by trick riders; and as mock bullfighter, an essential element of the bull-riding event.

The clown must be adept in speaking, especially joke telling and narrative. Equally important, he must be skilled in managing animals, in training animals for his own act, if he uses them, and in manipulating the bulls. Two traits are essential simply to qualify a clown to enter the arena: familiarity with the cowboy tradition, specifically rodeo; and a speaking ability much the same as what the preacher called "bull" or "the gift of gab." For the clown, knowing the cowboy tradition involves not only familiarity with the events of rodeo and with what cowboys do and how they talk, but also having particular skills with animals. To train animals to do tricks requires concentrated work, and protecting the cowboy from the bull demands both courage and familiarity with bulls. The clown, then, of all the cultural specialists, practices the most specific and focused specialization. As in Singer's study (1972), the urban, mobile performers are the most professional and specialized. Unlike cowboys and announcers, the clowns featured in community amateur rodeos are mobile; they travel from show to show, building a reputation which allows them to work full-time as professionals.

One successful rodeo clown who has worked in rodeos all over the United States, in Canada, and even in South Africa, is Nocona George. He now prefers the smaller community rodeos because he has a family, and he especially likes working at the Reunion rodeo. Nocona George was not raised around rodeo. When he was seven years old his father, a preacher, took him to a rodeo in Oklahoma; he decided then that he wanted to be a rodeo performer. In his words, "I never did get out of the idea of it." Like many other young clowns, he participated as a contestant for many years while developing his clown acts. For ten years he rode bareback broncs and performed trick roping. He has achieved success with every kind of contract act and with several of the contest events.

At the present time, George is concentrating on his special acts, in which he includes his wife and eight-year-old daughter. Though he has worked as the bullfighter and can still do so, he prefers to form part of a team in the bullfighting, telling the jokes himself while one or two other clowns handle the bullfighting. He and his wife are also raising quarter horses and he is establishing a booking agency for contract acts. His wife had never performed before they met, but now they have developed a bulldog act of which she is the star; their daughter participates in the trick-roping act.

Rodeo clowns learn their trade through informal means. Most of them begin as cowboy contestants and slowly develop their special acts as Nocona George did. He stresses that there are no books of jokes and that no one teaches the tricks of the trade. They are learned through practice and observation, and each clown must rearrange the jokes or acts to fit his own needs.

Being a rodeo clown is very hard work if one hopes to be a success, according to Nocona George:

It's harder work than it looks like, and everybody's looking for a easy ride and they won't put the work out, and if a fella is lookin' for a easy gig, he's in the wrong field in this business; it's double tough to be a contestant and make a living. I've done 'em both.

You learn whether an act is good largely by trial and error:

You just have to fall out there with it and take your chances. You git all hipped on it yourself. You gotta be to get it done, and then when you go out there, if it works right and the people like it, and they brag on it, and they keep hiring you, then you figger it's good. . . . Now if an animal just don't work right, you can figger, well, time. Cause you have to get an animal used to that arena. . . .

You can go to some farmer's house and he's got an ole horse that'll kneel, crawl, bow, kiss you, lay down on you, and haul him out there in that arena amongst them lights and them people, and he won't do it. They ain't none of 'em will. It's easier to train 'em back here. I can train 'em back here at home. Gettin' 'em out there and gettin' them to workin' is a different deal, and it takes a lotta time. . . . I can cheat one and give him cues and make him work halfway and cover it up with some of my ability, and you'll never know the difference until I get him workin'. But this I couldn't do when I was young. I didn't know, and nobody will tell you their secrets. You just gotta learn it. . . . Clowns don't teach others much. There's not very many clowns that stay in the business long.

Besides training the animal, the clown actor carefully rehearses details of his acts to create specific effects—in contrast to the contest events of rodeo, which depend on unpredictable actions. One especially important matter is timing:

Well, just like the fiddle act. Everything was in timing. When it was over with, we start to leave the arena; we tip our hat; we start to walk off, and it [the music] starts back up again, and we start giving the announcer this you know and run back. Timing. You don't just walk out there. You get out there a certain way, and in an act, it's the way you get in the arena and the way you get out. You gotta get in there with a bang; you can do a lotta little things in the middle of it. The last thing you do, make it big. People always remember that last thing.

Surprise is also necessary for success. The audience is led to expect one thing and is then surprised with another. George's wife, Kathy, performs an act in which she is introduced by the announcer as a female matador from Spain, Catalina Rodriguez, who is going to fight a bull. She enters the arena dressed in a cape, red satin shorts, and high boots. Then two little bulldogs with horns attached to their heads enter the arena and chase her cape. The "fight" concludes with release of balloons which the dogs attack. Kathy says of this act:

When I come out there they look at me. Well, they think, is she really gonna fight a bull? They think, I guess she will. Then when the little dogs come out. . . . it's just the surprise, you know. It's just like the carnival. The nightmare ride—you know there's not gonna be anything there to get you but. . . . it's the element of surprise. Everything that's a winner has just the right little nick.

These performance principles apply to all of the special acts, but the acts differ in content and means of communication. Comedy acts use narrative and are based on humor, usually about risqué or taboo subjects. Entertainment or dress-up acts may be humorous but, as with the dog act, the humor may rest on a surprise element rather than a joke or narrative. The clown's skills in speaking accompany the performance of the trained animal in comedy acts; and during the bull riding joke telling is interspersed between rides, balancing the intense danger and excitement of the contest between bull and cowboy with light-hearted verbal play which rearranges the norms of society.

Although the cowboy is the main performer associated with rodeo, it is the clown who must possess the most specialized skills. He generally learns the tradition as a participating competitive cowboy; and, if he is dedicated, he gradually develops his acts with animals, projecting humor and skill in his multiple roles.

PERFORMANCE

In addition to the complete rodeo performance held each day of the Reunion in this community, and twice on July 4, a special calf-roping contest is organized on one morning for "old-timers"—those fifty-five years of age and older. A small crowd of very enthusiastic viewers gathers to see relatives and close friends rope their calves. The setting is casual and intimate, there is no formal opening or closing, but the intensity is greater around the arena at this time than at any other. Almost everyone present knows a majority of the others, their ages, the condition of their health, and their children and grandchildren, many of whom are present. There is no charge for viewing the roping, and a small entry fee permits an old-timer to participate. Those cowboys with the fastest times rope as finalists in the rodeo performance held on the afternoon of July 4. The two roping times are added together, and the man with the fastest combined time is the first-place winner. This winner is awarded the John Selmon Memorial Old-Timer's Saddle during the final performance in the evening.

Although the time which the old-timers spend roping in the arena is relatively short compared to the overall length of the combined performances, the event contributes heavily to the definition of the Reunion because it allows the older cowboys to participate. Further, the event is symbolically brought into the main performance when the finalists rope and when the prize saddle is awarded, thus reminding all present of the heritage represented by the old-timers.

This special roping event, then, both creates a meaningful sphere of action for the older cowboys of the community and provides a means by which the regional community of traditional cowboy people is honored. For example, George Humphreys was always present at the old-timers' roping as at the other performances, and Fred Dalby participates as one of the most important ropers. Thus, whatever the make-up of the general rodeo population, a strong link connects the performance to the regional cowboys.

Other techniques are also used to link the older cowboys to the rodeo. For example, before the calf-roping in the performance, the announcer directs a ritual action in the arena that honors the memory of deceased old-timers:

We're sentimental about those on whose shoulders we stand in this part of the world. We're sentimental about the alumni of this rodeo and particularly those who have gone on to other arenas, and are no longer in our sight. Several years ago we began a tradition here—sometime during the rodeo to run a calf through with no one after him, just run a lonely calf through for those who are through chasing over here. There are too many to name so we won't try. In the morning at eight o'clock if you really want to see what this rodeo is all about, the old-timers' roping will begin. The man who won the old-timers' saddle last year is now numbered among those who are a memory at the Texas Cowboy Reunion. He is not back here with us. But to him and Rusty Bradley who is sick and couldn't be here and for whom we're all praying that he will get well and be back next year, for them and a host of others, we're gonna run one through. Let's turn him out if you will, please. And all of us, let's observe a moment of silence for those who are not with us but who would be. [The announcer takes off his hat, and the calf is released into the arena.] If Rusty were here, he'd say, "Somebody rope him. He needs it." Now then, let's rope one.

And the calf-roping contest begins. Prefaced in this way, the performance communicates the relationship between the present contest among young ropers and those old-timers who lived their lives as working cowboys and as participants in the rodeo.

In addition to scenes where the cowboy specialist is featured, the performance honors one cowboy specialist in its opening ceremony. To lead the Grand Entry is the highest honor in this community, and the leader holds the position until death. Only two cowboys have led the Grand Entry since the beginning: John Selmon and George Humphreys. Selmon led it every year until his death in 1971, and Humphreys until his death in 1979. The honoree is selected by the organizers of the rodeo. The Grand Entry opens each rodeo performance with a serpentine procession through the arena. Moving single-file, the riders follow the honored cowboy, who in the case of George Humphreys was also a judge of the roping events. Humphreys was followed by his granddaughters and then by the other judges. The cowgirl barrel racers form the second group in the procession and next in line are the Sheriff's Posses, riding groups organized by county that are invited to ride and be judged in the parade. The largest category of riders comes last—individual cowboys and cowgirls and anyone else who wishes to ride. The ceremony displays all of the segments of frontier cowboy society as perceived by the rodeo organization. To ride at the head of this procession is to hold the highest honor of the Reunion and to be presented publicly as the recipient of that honor.

The cowboy specialist also holds a special position within the actual rodeo itself. John Selmon not only led the Grand Entry but was Arena Director for many years. George Humphreys was active as a judge of the calf-roping events almost from the beginning. Unlike these two, Fred Dalby has been an active competitor in the rodeo for many years. Until recently he competed in all of the roping events in the regular performances and has won saddles in each. In 1977, 1978, and 1979, he limited his participation to the old-timers' roping; in 1979 he won that championship saddle also, much to the pleasure of the entire community. Indeed, the preacher/announcer even informed him that he had "prayed loops off of several of those other calves." Thus the third-generation specialist participates more generally than the first two and in that capacity serves as a link between the younger performers and the retired specialists.

In addition to these regular features in honor of the traditional cowboy, other special scenes are presented when appropriate. In 1978 a special ceremony was planned after the Grand Entry to dedicate the entire Reunion to George Humphreys, who rode into the arena to be honored. By Reunion time in 1979 both "Uncle George" Humphreys and "Mr. Bill" Swenson, who was one of "the daddies" of the event, had died. Therefore, in a special scene in the first rodeo performance of 1979 Humphreys' and

Swenson's horses, saddled and riderless, were released to run through the arena; and the descendants of these two specialists were presented plaques in the arena in honor of their fathers.

In the rodeo itself, then, what is now a regional, even a national, tradition is given local interpretation through the presentation of the general category of old-timers to the public: honoring one of them as leader of the Grand Entry; drawing on them as judges and as old-timer ropers; and memorializing deceased specialists. In the special acts the clown and the announcer work as a team to provide alternative entertainment for the crowd, based on the humor and the stereotypes of the tradition.

RODEO AND THE IDEOLOGY OF WORK AND PLAY

The rodeo specialists have widely varying tasks—working cowboy, preacher-announcer, and professional clown—and occupy a small percentage of the rodeo performance time in comparison to the cowboy contestants. Nevertheless, they are responsible for the articulation of complex meanings in this cultural performance. James Peacock (1967) has effectively demonstrated the dynamic relationship between performance roles and cultural classifications systems in his study of specific singer/actors in "communicative events" (Hymes 1964). In relating ideological categories of the culture to the song performances of clowns and transvestites in Javanese popular theater Peacock identifies traditional popular performance as a means of communicating relevant concepts in a complex and changing society.

Extending the construct of "cultural specialist" to include the task of communicating ideological categories through performance contributes significantly to an understanding of the rodeo specialists as performers in American society. Specifically, the rodeo specialists encapsulate the experience of the range cowboy, enacting dramatically the essential features of the cowboy role as it was defined at the end of the developmental period of the cattle trade. Subsequent economic and technological conditions radically altered cattle raising and cowboying, resulting in a need for fewer cowboys and in a new role more accurately reflected in the term "ranch hand." The ranch hand's duties can include fencing, milking, windmill repair, management, and other jobs for which groups of cowboys are not required and which cannot be accomplished on horseback. The last stages of evolution on the Western frontier were completed; the open range was fenced, crossed with railroads, and dotted with windmills.

Challenges to the social role of the cowboy appeared, however, before technology arrived to mark the final changes. With the extension of the Eastern American value system of the nineteenth century to the Western frontier, the cowboy role assumed a dual character, reflecting the differing goals and values of the two social environments. Prior to this large-scale expansion, cowboy life had been characterized by a rhythmical movement between periods of intense cattle work and periods of leisure, both on and off the range. Though popular images of the cowboy tend to distort certain features, the nineteenth-century cowboy did indeed rope and ride, laboring in difficult but adventuresome conditions for little pay. Those same cowhands, however, many of whom were young boys, regularly engaged in the telling of tales, verbal and practical jokes, card games and mumbledypeg, music and dancing, drinking whiskey, horse racing, and showing off their skills when herding cattle did not demand their attention. The routines of cattle work and the social organization of the range frontier both contributed to these activities. (Though it is obvious, it should be stressed here that cowboys generally lived and worked together in all-male groups.) Thus, the role assigned the traditional cowboy recognized both his occupational skills, his work, and entertainment, his play.

With the establishment of the corporate ranch on the frontier, a tension developed between the labor and the recreation of the cowboy. Some large ranches in the twentieth century established formal rules dictating when various recreations were permitted and strictly forbidding some forms of entertainment. This tension paralleled and reflected the opposition between work and play which occupied such an important position in nineteenth- and early twentieth-century American ideology. The work of the cowboy became publicly identified with riding, especially bucking broncs, and roping—his most dramatic occupational skills.

Simultaneously with the expansion of corporate interests into cattle ranching, the American traveling show expanded to include frontier enactments, among them cowboy displays. Buffalo Bill's Wild West Show, begun in 1882, was the prototype for and the best-known example of these popular forms (Russell 1970). Thus, while American industry, representing the ideology of work, incorporated cattle ranching, American popular entertainment, representing the ideology of play, integrated the cowboy into its show. The corporations literally transformed the frontier range into the cattle industry, defining the cowboy as a laborer; the traveling show dramatically transformed the frontier range into a performance, defining the cowboy as player. Due to the radical effects of such historical events as World War I, within a short period the corporate ranch and the traveling show were modified, and in some cases abolished. The public discussion of the work/play opposition also abated, though the tension had not been resolved.

During this period of intense and rapid change, the ideological schism between work and play affected the cowboy, leading to a double image—the shiftless, irresponsible, disrespectful cowboy who engaged in "rough" or uncivilized play; and the serious, responsible, polite cowboy who was dedicated only to work. Meanwhile the traveling show had brought the cowboy and the clown together in the same milieu. When the rodeo emerged after World War I as a popular entertainment independent of the traveling show and representing the range of the frontier, the cowboy and the clown split this dual image between them into two separate performance roles.

Today's rodeo cowboy and clown share common experiences and common values. Participants in the same tradition, one may become the other and often does, even within one rodeo. Yet in performing the cowboy demonstrates his working skills—riding and roping—while the clown entertains in rehearsed acts. The worker dresses and acts like a cowboy, while the player has become idealized in the clown. This distinction is clearly articulated in the Reunion. Traditional old-time cowboys, representing the hard-working, law-abiding, loyal workers, occupy an honored and visible position. Yet it is widely acknowledged informally that the specialist's prestige derives from his social, playing, character as much as from his working skills. (All three cowboy specialists have been characterized as "windy" at one time or another, meaning that they are good and frequent storytellers.)

Furthermore, the expression of this ideological opposition has not remained static in a nineteenth-century model. Though the early-day cowboy honored at the Reunion in the person of John Selmon has acquired legendary status, each of the two subsequent specialists reflect modern changes. An adventuresome young boy of the nineteenth century, the first specialist remained a working cowboy and foreman all of his life. The second-generation cowboy specialist expanded the role of cowboy and foreman to include manager, lawman, and cattleman. And the current specialist has a college education, works for himself, and concentrates on roping in community rodeos as his major interest. Yet each of them represents the local working tradition in the performance, for they are all considered old-timers on the basis of their age, lifework, and social identity.

These rather significant changes in the cowboy specialist redefine the traditional ideal cowboy from the lifetime worker on a large ranch to an independent cowboy who uses his roping skills primarily in the rodeo arena. The actual occupation of the specialist has assumed secondary importance, and effective identification with and transmission of the tradition serves as the primary defining feature of the specialist. In this general role as "working cowboy," a term frequently used at the Reunion to refer to the possession of skills relevant to the raising and handling of cattle and horses, the cowboy specialist represents the ideology of work.

The role of the rodeo clown also demonstrates adaptations to current interests. Though many rodeo clown acts appear to differ only slightly from circus acts, an effective rodeo clown selects acts and jokes which deal with values, topics, and experiences relevant to cowboy people. These reflect modern themes, as when Nocona George modified his trained horse act, replacing an automobile (the Oatsmobile) with a hippie motorcycle. Rodeo audiences and participants find this humorous as most of them regard the contemporary phenomena, hippies and their motorcycles, with antagonism. Equally significant in his enactment of cowboy play is the clown's role in the bull-riding event, which especially distinguishes rodeo clowns from other clowns. Roping and riding contest events are supposed to display the cowboy's working skills, while it is said that bull riding developed as a rodeo event "just for fun." Bull riding never played a part in cowboy work; moreover, the clown provides protection for the cowboy bull rider, in contrast to the pick-up men on horseback who assist the bronc riders.

In his role as bullfighter, the clown not only distracts the bull from the cowboy once he has hit the ground, but antagonizes the bull and engages him in a chase around the arena or in a game of hide and seek using a barrel. All of this requires the clown to place himself in a position of vulnerability to the bull. He must use his wits and fleetness of foot to avoid contact with the bull, but the entire act must also be humorous. Between bull rides, he entertains the crowd with risqué jokes, told in cooperation with the announcer. For this event-act then, the clown needs courage and athletic ability in addition to humor and performance skills. The combination of humor and danger suggest that this "fun" is related to the concept identified by Clifford Geertz (1973) as "deep play." Originally used by Jeremy Bentham, the term refers to "play in which the stakes are so high that it is, from his [Bentham's] utilitarian standpoint, irrational for men to engage in it at all" (ibid.:432). However, according to Geertz, what is really at stake is esteem, honor, dignity, respect, and status (ibid.:432–433).

That these qualities relate directly to the bullfighter/clown is obvious from any discussion with clowns or cowboy bull riders. Only in this event does one human have such influence over the fate of another. Therefore, both in and out of the arena, cowboys treat clowns with great respect; their safety will depend on the clown during their performance. A clown's status, however, depends on his effectiveness in protecting each cowboy; moreover, to maintain his honor as a clown he cannot abuse his power by allowing personal prejudices to affect his role in the arena. Further, the material gains for the cowboy (possible prize money) and for the clown (his contractual payment) are certainly disproportionate to the risks to life and limb incurred. As player then, the clown is the most highly specialized, functioning as a special entertainer in his acts and also as bullfighter, a role which combines humorous entertainment of the crowd and protection of the bull rider with such facility that the effort is indistinguishable to the viewer.

Considering the obvious risks associated with this event, there seems to be no inherent reason why it should be defined as play; yet this interpretation is not only stressed in the rodeo program and by the announcer, but is clearly communicated in the choice of the clown to play the role of bullfighter, whose convincing antics and jokes intensify the action by focusing attention alternately on a dangerous encounter with a bull and on humorous expression of socially taboo subjects, or verbal "bull." This event provides a stark contrast to the riding and roping events, which display the cowboys' working skills and utilize no humor or clowns. In this event, then, the clown pushes the boundaries of play well beyond the domain of the safe and the rational into the domain of uncertainty, where behind the costume and make-up of the clown/fool he gambles with danger to win status.

In these performance roles the clown, a traveling specialist with particular skills who is identified with play, is juxtaposed with the traditional cowboy, a local specialist with more general skills who is identified with the ideology of work. Of particular significance, however, is the rearrangement of these roles when the clown assumes a dangerous role in the final event. Play becomes high risk and the player's performance is not only evaluated by the audience, as in his acts, but by the cowboys as well.

This cluster of performance conditions places the play specialist in a position of high status as the one who can wield power in the dangerous arena yet still present himself as a clown. Such a specialized role of player combines features of risk with clowning, suggesting that cowboy courage and cowboy humor are inseparable, a condition consistent with the social life of early cowboys but in conflict with the dominant social system of America which incorporated the ranch and still insists on opposing work and play.

Essential to both specialists, the announcer mediates between performer and audience, interpreting the action. His commentaries repeatedly remind us of the cowboy heritage, defined in terms of the traditional working cowboy and represented in the performance by the cowboy specialists. However, through his voice the clown's acts and jokes reach the audience, and he is actually the verbal partner in the jokes. Using his authority as spokesman he articulates the values of both work and play, but makes no judgment. This impartiality is of particular interest since Rev. Boles' social role of preacher could cause him to have some reluctance to express "earthy cowboy humor," as he himself describes it. But his awareness that his specialty is speaking, and his understanding of and dedication to the tradition, supersede any limitation of his enactment of the role of interpreter.

Through the specialists of cowboy culture—the native announcer, the local traditional cowboy, and the traveling clown—rodeo replays cowboy history, reflecting contemporary influences and communicating an opposition between work and play characteristic of American ideology. Yet the performance achieves a momentary balance in the opposition when the specialist of play integrates his rehearsed acting techniques with athletic skills in the unrehearsed and dangerous action of the bull-riding event. The rodeo thus seems to resolve the ideological conflict by an act of redefinition. Bull riding represents deep play: the risks are great and the major rewards are measured in status for both bull rider and clown. These conditions characterized both the work and play of the cowboy on the frontier range before the dual image emerged and altered his role. The clown specialist, then, whose unique performance introduces deep play into the cowboy context, momentarily restores play to the domain of the cowboy.

NOTES

1. The fieldwork on which this article is based was conducted in Stamford, Texas, and neighboring communities between 1972 and 1979.
2. Many rodeo organizations have developed, such as the professional, collegiate, all-girl, junior, or other associations. To enter a rodeo sponsored by one of these organizations one must be a member of the group. Membership requirements are based on dues, age, and sex, and one must agree to follow the rules and regulations. The membership requirements do not include any criteria based on abilities.

BIBLIOGRAPHY

Boatright, Mody. 1964. The American rodeo. *American Quarterly* 16: 195–202.
Clarke, Mary Whatley. 1976. *The Swenson saga and the SMS Ranches.* Austin: Jenkins.
Geertz, Clifford. 1973. *The interpretation of cultures.* New York: Basic Books.
Hymes, Dell. 1964. Introduction: Toward ethnographies of communication. *American Anthropologist* 66: 1–34.
Paredes, Américo. 1963. El Cowboy norteamericano en el folklore y la literatura. *Cuadernos* 4: 227–240.
Peacock, James L. 1967. Javanese clown and transvestite songs: Some relations between 'primitive classification' and 'communicative events.' In *Essays on the verbal and visual arts.* June Helm, ed. Seattle: University of Washington Press.
Redfield, Robert. 1956. *Peasant society and culture.* Chicago: University of Chicago Press.
Rodgers, Daniel T. 1978. *The work ethic in industrial America, 1850–1920.* Chicago: University of Chicago Press.
Russell, Don. 1970. *The Wild West.* Fort Worth: Amon Carter Museum of Western Art.
Singer, Milton. 1972. *When a great tradition modernizes: An anthropological approach to Indian civilization.* New York: Praeger.

Archie Green

Austin's Cosmic Cowboys: Words in Collision

Having reached the eighties, we are conscious that much of the new vocabulary of the sixties and seventies, psychedelic or apocalyptic, is already dated. The very technology which extends language into space through computerized rocket travel also renders many neologisms obsolete before they take hold widely. Nonce words have a partial life, fluid and catchy; they live furtively, grasping at substance. The combination "cosmic cowboy" surfaced during the seventies, caught on to describe a new stylistic synthesis within the ferment of American music, and fell from favor by the decade's end. Words hardly receive formal burial or marble headstones; they merely fade out of usage, unlamented except by lexicographers. When *Newsweek* featured Willie Nelson in a cover photo as "King of Country Music," reporter Pete Axthelm (1978) managed a concise article without once using "cosmic." As this qualifier descended, others arose. At the end of 1979, Robert Redford and Jane Fonda appeared in a call-to-the-wild film about a wasted cowboy, *The Electric Horseman*; today, we use a related cinematic phrase, "urban cowboy" (Latham 1978:21).[1]

These references put me at the end, not the beginning, of an etymological study. The American cowboy's name has long been potent throughout the world. Responding to and reflecting upon cowboy imagery, many folklorists—among them John Lomax, J. Frank Dobie, Mody Boatright, and Américo Paredes—have helped explicate his language and lore. Following their trail, I focus on a short-lived term, tangential to cowboy reality, used to describe country rock music and its audience in Austin, Texas, during the seventies.

Austin's eclectic composer/performers, in the past decade, drew upon folk or popular expression to mark contemporary social collision and convergence. Some conflict is endemic within any community—ethnic, regional, occupational, or social. Even as loosely defined a coterie as the fans of "low-brow" music (folk/country/blues/rock) includes individuals of different esthetic preference and linguistic behavior. Musical enthusiasts can mark such dissonance, or consonance, in arenas from honkytonk to recording studio, by their use of certain words. "Cosmic cowboy" reveals such tension and resolution; it commented upon the considerable degree of interaction among vernacular and popular forms—musical, graphic, and literary. Moreover, like other discrete verbal tags, it demonstrated the clash of large values in American life.

COWBOYS OLD AND NEW

It has taken "cowboy" three centuries to draw to itself a rainbow of meaning, supplanting the earlier terms "herder" and "drover."[2] Jonathan Swift used the new word in 1725, in a poem for Stella, to refer to Irish lads who tended cattle. During our Revolutionary War, however, the then-novel "cowboy" developed a pejorative connotation. It was used to describe Tory guerrillas who, by tinkling cowbells, beguiled patriotic Americans into the brush. Such King George loyalists—bushwackers and cattle skinners—also ambushed and savaged George Washington's men.

After the Texas Revolution, this villainous connotation appeared along the Rio Grande, where *vaquero* met cowboy. The former had little use for the latter, who rustled Mexican longhorns. In 1847, Mirabeau Lamar—soldier, poet, historian, and second president of the Texas Republic—noted in his papers (1978:99) that Anglo "Cow-Boys" were marauders, thieves who rounded up "wild cattle" between the Nueces and the Colorado. In this predatory border region (*El Desierto Muerto*), a "cow driver" was often a robber and, at times, a murderer (Nance 1963:45–67).

It was not until the Civil War's close that "cowboy" again changed in value. When Texas cattle started to be driven north to market, the word lost its opprobrious color. Cowboys at the Chisholm Trail's end did raise Cain, but there was little need to stigmatize them as violent raiders. The food needs of a growing industrial nation thus established a social setting in which "cowboy" gained a positive connotation. In economic terms, cowboys were the cousins of all other food handlers, earlier and later: of dusty millers, sweaty butchers, wheat threshers, fruit tramps, salmon fishermen, airplane-flying crop-dusters, bracero crop-pickers, and supermarket stackers. Glenn Ohrlin (1974), an Ozark rancher and traditional singer, has tagged cowboy workers neither tough nor mean but rather plain and regular. To labor endlessly at hard, rough, unglamorous jobs precludes being a cruel gunslinger or mythic hero.

In short, "cowboy" is a semantically elastic marker. It has denoted variously a Tory guerrilla, a Western outlaw, a skilled rider, or a puritanical worker. To this array we can add the cowboy as a carouser, a prankster, a man full of raw vitality, a brother of Puck and Falstaff. Two early humorous images are found in Joseph G. McCoy's *Historic Sketches of the Cattle Trade of the West and Southwest* (1874). This classic, illustrated by Henry Worrall, offers an important eye-witness account of the Texas drives to Kansas boomtowns, where herds were held for rail shipment to Chicago. Worrall's engravings include the earliest visual portrait I have found of the shoot-'em-up, hell-raising cowboy—the figurative ancestor of many recent country and rock singers (fig. 1). McCoy highlighted this character at play in a "vortex of dissipation" at an Abilene dance hall (fig. 2):

A more odd, not to say comical, sight is not often seen than the dancing cow-boy; with the front of his sombrero lifted at an angle of fully forty-five degrees, his huge spurs jingling at every step or motion; his revolvers flapping up and down like a retreating sheep's tail; his eyes lit up with excitement, liquor and lust; he plunges in and "hoes it down" at a terrible rate, in the most approved yet awkward country style; often swinging "his partner" clear off of the floor for an entire circle, "then balance all" with an occasional demoniacal yell, near akin to the war whoop of the savage Indian (1874:139).

Cowboy literature includes autobiographies, histories, critical essays, picture books, and fiction. Such reports make it clear that the cowboy remained both a working and a comic figure through the closing decades of the last century. He also became a legendary figure, courageous and formidable, who could ride even under the weight of distorted rhetorical comparisons such as "Pegasus of the Plains."

1. *Drunken Cow-Boy on the "War-Path"* by Henry Worrall

2. *Dance-House* by Henry Worrall

Although folklorists generally distinguish legend from myth, most writers on the West treat these genres as interchange. While old trail drivers and ranchers romanticized their callings in memoirs, others—dime novelists, pulp journalists, tent show-men—also sought to create a new folk hero, a Rousseauian nobleman. The legend makers often borrowed attributes from predecessors of the cowboy: mountain trappers, Indian scouts, explorers of the prairie and plain. Retrospectively, one does not marvel that some workers in the cattle trade were enshrined both in folk imagination and in popular literature, only that this process began so early. John Baumann, a British traveler, wrote:

The cowboy has at the present time become a personage; nay, more, he is rapidly becoming a mythical one. Distance is doing for him what lapse of time did for the heroes of antiquity. His admirers are investing him with all manner of romantic qualities; they descant upon his manifold virtues and his pardonable weaknesses as if he were a demi-god, and I have no doubt that before long there will be ample material for any phil-osophic inquirer who may wish to enlighten the world as to the cause and meaning of the cowboy myth (1887:516).

After the turn of the century, movie producers joined the myth makers. *The Great Train Robbery*'s Western outlaw sequence was made in 1903; a three-reel presentation of Buffalo Bill's tour-ing Wild West Show was released in 1910. Also, in this year, the Essanay Company began a long series of Broncho Billy miracle plays for Saturday matinees. These formulaic productions, based on countless dime-novel and tent-show predecessors, set cinema-tic patterns still visible on television. During the twenties Tom Mix replaced Billy, but Mix, too, was frozen in contrived and ro-mantic plots. Many adults reacted ambivalently to film hokum: it was trash to spoil youthful minds, harmless escape, or dangerous fantasy. Because the cowboy as an American exemplar emerged dually as a normal worker and a mythical hero, he simultaneous-ly attracted defenders and detractors. While pulp writers and screen directors featured guns, guitars, and bravado, realistic ethnographers stressed thorns, fleas, and grit. Often it proved dif-ficult to judge the symbolic role of either gun or grit.

Popular images of the cowboy engendered criticism. Al-though some riders embellished their own lives, modeling them-selves after their fictional incarnation, most wranglers objected to such theatrical portraits. Meanwhile, writers sympathetic to reality noted or ridiculed the (self-) caricatures. For example, Isabelle Randall, traveling from England to Montana, wrote of her train trip on the Plains: "In swaggered two men, dressed to the highest pitch of cowboy dandyism" (1887:6). Humorist George Ade depicted Teddy Roosevelt's Rough Riders as players "cavort-in' around town here in their cowboy hats and gassin' in front of every store" (1903:251).

During the twenties the swaggering dandy cavorted in a very specific place—the drugstore. By definition, the "drugstore cowboy" was a braggart, loafer, or good-for-nothing poseur dressed like a Westerner. Credit for bringing him to life artistically be-longs to Thomas Aloysius Dorgan ("Tad"), cartoonist, sports writer, and shaper of much American slang. His "Indoor Sports" cartoon for *The San Francisco Call and Post* (July 5, 1923) first presented three drugstore cowboys in the saddle, dressed sharply but not in cowpoke costume. Tad saw them as ladies' men, flap-pers' foils, or collegiate sheiks, and equated the sexual euphe-mism "cake eater" with "drugstore cowboy" (fig. 3).

In February 1925, *College Humor* used the new term gener-ically, and soon John Held, Jr., and his many imitators, began to draw Jazz Age cowboys in exaggerated bell-bottoms, with or without chaps, lounging at soda counters and ice-cream parlors. Youngsters kidded them: "A drugstore cowboy is quick on the straw!" One target was Will Rogers. Corey Ford wrote the follow-ing uncomplimentary caption for Miguel Covarrubias' caricature of Rogers (fig. 4):

In his familiar chaps and two-gallon hat, America's Drug Store Cowboy loiters as usual at the corner of Main Street and Park Avenue, his long lariat mouth uncoiling slowly as he drawls a few homely observations for the *Times* (each in a little worse taste than the last), calls all the pass-ing celebrities by their first names, offers his advice to every one free for what it is worth, and pursues his daily racket of "jes' bein' common folks" (1930:84).

The mocking term lives. Pat Frank described a character in *Seven Days to Never* as marrying "a marijuana-smoking drugstore cowboy" (1957:102). Frank's novel added a new dimension to the locution. In Tad's America the drugstore had been the milieu for adolescent bravado—an innocent place for hanging-out. Now, adult drug hangups have intensified the overtones of "drugstore cowboy."

Hollywood, Nashville, and Austin have combined to deline-ate a new breed of "cowboy"—neither ordinary worker with cat-

3. "Indoor Sports" by Tad, *San Francisco Call and Post*, July 5, 1923

tle, wild renegade, nor national mythic figure, but rather a bitter-sweet antihero. The movie *Midnight Cowboy*, released in May 1969, centered not on a brave rider but on a callow bus rider, one who reversed Horace Greeley's dictum by going East to hustle fame and fortune. From a small-town café in Texas ranch country, the dishwashing cowboy plunged into a surrealistic Manhattan of perversion and poverty. The film resonated powerfully in a cosmos populated by Tim Leary, Ken Kesey, and their camp followers; it also managed to invert the time-tested message of writers like Ned Buntline, Owen Wister, and Zane Grey, and of painters like Frederic Remington, Charles Russell, and Will James.

Subsequent to this film, the midnight cowboy's many buddies within song texts became mysterious, rebellious, nostalgic, lonely, gypsy, hip, or cosmic. The noun "cowboy," when used to describe country rock musicians, functions as a badge of distinction. In a sense, these latter-day buckaroos have recycled "cowboy" to hitch themselves to a romantic past, as well as to explain to each other something of their troubled present.

4. Will Rogers by Miguel Covarrubias in Ford's *The John Riddell Murder Case*, 1930

One contemporary nuance surfaced in Peter Rowan's composition "Lonesome L.A. Cowboy." The song appeared on *The Adventures of Panama Red* (1973), an LP by the New Riders of the Purple Sage. Rowan's hero proclaims: "I been smokin' dope, snortin' coke, tryin' to write a song, forgettin' everything I know 'til the next line comes along." This passage is striking not because of the reference to drugs, but rather because the cowboy has been removed completely from his traditional range. Neither rescuing a companion nor trailing cattle, he is transformed into a writer trailing an elusive refrain. Not only is this Angeleno lonely and frightened, but he finds himself an alienated intellectual distanced from life. Pens and guitars may or may not be superior as tools to lariats and saddles, but the accoutrements of the muses are the only tools available to modern musical cowboys.

How did the cowboy emerge, within scores of country songs, as a tattered hippy under a Stetson? Record liner notes, as well as interviews and concert reviews, offer widespread answers. Waylon Jennings, a "bad boy in leather," talking with *Rolling Stone* reporter Chet Flippo, used "cowboy" to signify oppositions: an El Paso honkytonk, where Jennings had performed, housed "some pretty wild old cowboys. . . . You walk in there, like last night, and they say, 'He's a cowboy singer, let's whup his ass'" (1973b:28). In this tightly compressed statement the El Paso beer drinkers (old cowboys) are booted hellions, died-in-the-wool conservatives ready to pounce on any alienated, long-haired stud (cowboy singer), who, seemingly, represents creative freedom. Thus, the cowboy becomes a Janus figure, for he is at once redneck audience and isolated artist, straight and freak, hunter and hunted.

A drugs-drugstore connection underlies the country music establishment's first emotional reactions in the sixties to "turned on" or "hippy" songwriters such as John Hartford. Does it not now seem strange to recall that in 1967 "Gentle on My Mind" was perceived by many country stalwarts as a "far out" or "high" composition? When Glen Campbell first presented "Gentle" to television audiences he made it an instant hit. In Nashville at that time, I can recall no critic who equated the word "hippy" with "cowboy"; but only a few years later, enthusiasts were using the latter to describe country music's rebellious fringe. On October 14, 1970, the Country Music Association presented an annual award to Kris Kristofferson for "Sunday Morning Coming Down," a somber drugs song. The composer, appearing on prime-time

television, offended his hosts by his offbeat conduct. Symbolically, Kris helped transform the road-weary musician into a trail-
weary cowhand. It was after the CMA broadcast that I first heard
Nashville people class Kris as a "cowboy"—light years removed
from Gene Autry and Roy Rogers.

While Kristofferson's conduct nettled Nashville's brass, Paul
Hemphill commented on the CMA awards program for the *New
York Times*:

You could sense Tex Ritter and Roy Acuff and all the rest hunkering
down in their seats as [Kris] floated to the stage of the Grand Ole Opry
House to accept the award: suede bell-bottoms, shoulder length hair,
strange deep-set Jack Palance eyes; weaving back and forth with his back
to the audience for nearly 10 seconds like a cowboy who had lost his
way. . . . Nashville's Music Row is still seething. "I mean, hell, he didn't
even wear a tux" (1970:54).

Hemphill, a superb reporter, grasped at once the irony of a tux-
less cowboy, who nonetheless was not so wasted that he could not
rope a Nashville prize.

Kristofferson's appearance has become an oft-told anecdote
in the shop-talk which clusters around the country music industry. David Allan Coe, self-billed as the "Mysterious Rhinestone
Cowboy," in *Picking Up the Tempo* paid tribute to Kris as a leader
who opened Nashville's doors to other underground artists:

[Kris] snuck right by 'em. And the next thing you know he was being
nominated for awards and worse, he was winning them. Then the truth
came out when he appeared at the awards show wearing levis (heaven
forbid). Nashville was in a tizzy. . . . Here was this goddam hippy, right
in front for the world to see, staggering around, drunk as shit, insulting
dignitaries with his uncouth mouth and setting a bad example for national television (1975:1).

These vivid accounts of cowboys in suedes or hippies in levis
shrewdly prodded at the industry's real weakness—its inability to accept the talented outsiders who were forging new country sounds. Dave Hickey, a Texan from Fort Worth and a former
graduate student at Austin, reported scornfully from Tennessee
that his "favorite low riders, lonesome pickers, and telecaster
cowboys" were "just about the only folks in Nashville who will
walk into a room where there's a guitar and a *Wall Street Journal*
and pick up the guitar" (1974:90).

By the mid-seventies, "cowboy" for an outsider or outlaw
had assimilated into country music language. The word that had

previously connoted romance in group names such as Hank Williams and the Drifting Cowboys or Pee Wee King and his Golden West Cowboys now bespoke marginality. Country fans during the early seventies also used "cowboy" for performers like Waylon Jennings and Willie Nelson. These two stars had earned their spurs by being Texans; more importantly, they were willing to flaunt openly their break with Nashville's sounds and codes. Their music also earned the sobriquet "outlaw." Michael Bane, in his book, *The Outlaws: Revolution in Country Music*, relates how the term arose. Hazel Smith at the Glaser Studios ("Hillbilly Central") received a phone call "one day in 1973" from a disc jockey in Ashboro, North Carolina, who wanted to feature the then-new music of Kris, Waylon, and Willie and "needed a hook, something to give the show an image." Hazel obliged: "Call it 'Outlaw Music.'" Later she explained that she had been influenced in her choice by Lee Clayton's "Ladies Love Outlaws," the title song of a Jennings LP released in 1972 (Bane 1978:4–10).

Significantly, Dave Hickey called his report for *Country Music* on the new trend in Nashville "In Defense of the Telecaster Cowboy Outlaws." The words "cowboy" and "outlaw" couple naturally. But the latter term had built-in limitations. How can "outlaw" be applied to popular culture heroes who decorate their dens with platinum records and jet around the world for lucrative concert tours? An irreverent reporter for the *Village Voice*, Nick Tosches, made fun of such "outlaws," picturing them as "oligarchs" who hung high only in the hit charts, not the gallows tree (1976:142).

AUSTIN IN THE SEVENTIES

"Cowboy," the recent generic term for country music's tricksters and gypsies, achieved currency not only in Nashville but also in Austin, Texas, during the early seventies. It served to describe many writer/performers: for example, Waylon Jennings, Doug Sahm, Jerry Jeff Walker, Guy Clark, David Allan Coe, Ray Wylie Hubbard, Michael Murphey, Kinky Friedman, and Willie Nelson—not all of whom were comfortable thus linked with each other. The music they played was variously labeled "redneck rock," "outlaw music," "progressive country," and "country rock."

Jan Reid coined the first term for his book, *The Improbable Rise of Redneck Rock* (1974), a report on Austin's bizarre cowboy musicians. Coming from a blue-collar family in Wichita Falls, Texas, Reid was familiar with Southern vernacular speech and had seen country customs carried to city centers. He picked "redneck," a two-century old synonym for "clod" to describe Austin's exciting fusion of orthodox country and high-energy rock music. Reid, with Don Roth (1973), had employed the accurate but less dramatic "country rock" in their earlier article "The Coming of Redneck Hip." Also seeking a catchy name, Austin radio station KOKE-FM introduced "progressive country," which achieved a limited currency beyond Texas (Carr 1973:D9).

A dynamic process of change, not yet fully explained by musicologist or historian, has driven many American country musicians to reach to blues, jazz, and rock expression. Conversely, "uptown" musicians have turned "down" and "back" to rural or folk roots. This reach "across the tracks" has moved some individual creators from mainstream to marginal life, and others in the reverse direction. Country rock did not originate in any single community nor with a special set of creators. In 1968 audiences from Sunset Strip to Harvard Square enthusiastically received The Byrds' *Sweetheart of the Rodeo*, an LP which anticipated Bob Dylan's *Nashville Skyline*. Gram Parsons from Waycross, Georgia, sought to play white soul music and pioneered in fusing genres before his untimely death in 1973. Emmylou Harris and Linda Ronstadt, both from urban settings, are present-day country-music queens. The Allman Brothers, beginning in a Muscle Shoals, Alabama, studio in 1969, pulled country blues and hard rock together and, incidentally, used the new music to raise funds for Jimmy Carter in 1976.

Despite this spread in site, style, personality, and nomenclature, the richest single setting for musical convergence was Austin. A puzzling combination of influences fused not only the styles of country music and rock, but also the social identities of "hippy" and "cowboy." It became hip to be a hick. Why did this happen initially not in Nashville, San Francisco, or Manhattan, but deep in the heart of Texas?

I will not compress Austin music into a history capsule, but rather will describe the setting in which both rednecks and rockers began to portray themselves in dress and song as cowboys. The common conflict between those from opposite sides of the track—rich/poor, worldly/parochial, mainstream/minority, "straight"/"freak"—received a special expression in Austin. "Cowboy" or "kicker" were synonyms for "straight" and essential-

ly designated a youth from a poor, rural, and outspokenly patriotic family. By contrast, "freak," "long-hair" and "head" suggested
a well-to-do or urban background. Throughout this century, parents of Austin "cowboys in blue jeans" were locally called "cedar
choppers." This term identified hill folk who cleared timber for
ranchers, burned charcoal for city dwellers, and hacked ties for
railroad construction crews. With Austin's urbanization, "cedar
chopper" was carried to the schoolyard, along with a similarly
derogatory ruralism, "goat roper."

Many members of Austin's music audience were students directly out of rural homes, or only a generation removed. The ambivalence they felt about their origins was not a new phenomenon. John Avery Lomax had labored in Austin itself long ago to
help Texans appreciate their frontier roots. J. Frank Dobie, the
"Cowboy Professor," while teaching Southwestern life and literature, had opened the eyes of students to previously overlooked regional values. Kris Kristofferson had found fans among Austinites
ready for a rock philosopher in shaggy denim. And long before
any hippies rocked in Austin's black bars, Jimmie Rodgers, a
white Mississippi railroad boomer, had pulled together Anglo and
Afro expressions. In his Kerrville mansion near Austin, the singing breakman had also donned a Stetson and play-acted the cowboy. The crossbreeding of music in Texas (black and white, rural
and urban) moved ahead after World War II in Buddy Holly's and
Roy Orbison's rockabilly innovations. We sense the pained pleasure of the response of young Texans to their rural roots in Roxy
Gordon's *Some Things I Did* (1971) as well as in his literate criticism of "new music" in *Picking Up the Tempo*, a "half-savage"
country Western tabloid published from 1974 to 1978.

References to certain musical styles or movies frequently reflect youthful tension. For example, reporter Pat Lewis in Prince
Georges County, Maryland, noted that student "dropouts" or
"grits" borrowed Kung Fu film techniques to fight "niggers" and
"freaks." What is important about Austin—indeed, almost mysterious—is that the early seventies seemed to bring a local inversion in style. Young cedar choppers/cowboys/goat ropers had regularly enjoyed country music and Western swing, often blaring it
from pickup truck radios. Their antagonists had lived on rock
and roll and revival folksong. Yet, in time, some Austin rock
freaks borrowed elements of kicker style and perceived themselves as cowboys.

In breaking these identity barriers or, more properly, internalizing these dual artistic forms, young Austinites were commenting upon a complicated dialectic between Southern and national norms as well as between black and white expressions. In a time of civil-rights strife, dissent about Vietnam, and altered moral codes, all played out against the backdrop of an unrelenting industrialization of the South, it proved impossible for musical or social taste and style to remain compartmentalized.

The meeting of partisans from Austin's two separate sectors created new performers and audiences. Native Texans and strangers drawn to the open Austin community experimented by integrating the sounds of Bob Wills and Mick Jagger. This mix crossed lines of race, residence, and status. In their patter, musicians asserted that "small-town" Austin was "laid-back," or relaxed. The pressure of conforming to business demands was less rigid in Austin than in Nashville or Hollywood. To depart these "hype" and "jive" centers asserted freedom. Also, students in great numbers, touched by Haight-Ashbury's and Berkeley's liberating breezes, formed ready and paying audiences. Finally, Texas regionalism (and chauvinism) shored up moves toward independent creativity. It was as much fun to trumpet musical experimentation as it was to flaunt that Texas could go it alone with gas and oil: Let them freeze in the dark listening to moldy fig music!

New sounds and styles demand new locutions. Austin's young rednecks and schoolyard goat ropers extended their names and dress to Texas rock musicians returning home from both coasts, as well as to thousands of college students who grooved and boogied to post-Beatles rhythm-and-blues tunes. Hip musicians were drawn to the image of the cowboy-as-rebel breaking with Nashville and other established institutions. The genuine rangerider was seen as a loner—perhaps he could double as a cultural radical or displaced intellectual. These musicians, strong enough to feel comfortable with psychedelic light shows as well as with screen cowpokes down the canyon, helped Austinites bridge past and present. A University of Texas student at a Willie Nelson picnic could be loyal to parents and peers simultaneously. In collegiate terms, it was fun to seek the traditional highs of beer and the innovative highs of dope, while listening to music that spoke to both pleasures.

Attractive as it was to Nashville expatriates, Austin had little need to import musical talent. Local performers and club owners had prepared well the way for cultural synthesis in the early seventies. While the Kingston Trio defined folksong for most American students, a handful of Austin dissidents turned to mountain ballads and frolics or to bluegrass, often hootenanny flavored. Local folk buffs performed in off-campus pads, at the University of Texas Union, and at the now legendary gas station/hillbilly beer joint, Threadgill's. The Waller Creek Boys—Janis Joplin, Lanny Wiggins, Powell St. John—played there, meeting uncompromising country musicians out of blue-collar life. In the din of a Wednesday-night picking session at Threadgill's bar, St. John (1974) recalled later he met Bill Neely in "tailored Western shirt, starched jeans, and gleaming Tony Lamas," playing "a big red Gibson Hummingbird guitar." Powell liked Bill and his personal country songs which reflected farm, Depression, and work experience. The two played together for several years at barbecues, parties, and rallies until St. John went on to rock with Austin's Conqueroo and San Francisco's Mother Earth.[3]

Marcia Mouton Ball, a young pianist and sure-voiced singer from a Vinton, Louisiana, Cajun family, had tried her hand in a "folk trio" while attending LSU in 1968. After college she turned to "Joplin-screaming" in Baton Rouge rock clubs. In Austin, in February 1972, she and Bobby Earl Smith formed Freda and the Firedogs, one of the first long-haired country bands to meet rural fans on their own turf. At the Split Rail, Austin's downhome honkytonk, Marcia handled with ease blues, boogie, and soul, winning short-haired "ultra-conservative" audiences by her infectious "Cotton-Eyed Joe" and her yodeling "Cowboy's Sweetheart."

Janis Joplin had been drawn to folksong while she was attending the University of Texas during 1962 (fig. 5), but forged success a few years later in San Francisco's cauldron. She and Haight-Ashbury rapidly drew Austin musicians; in this new setting, Texas blues and rockabilly fed into California electronic music. Like a compelling light show, rock turned off and on, bathing its victors in gold and punishing its failures with base colors. A few Austin musicians resisted San Francisco and remained at home; some, broken there, returned to form and reform local bands; others tripped back and forth unscathed. Three of the best Austin rock bands were the Thirteenth Floor Elevators, Conqueroo, and Shiva's Headband.

Bob Brown recalled for Jan Reid the Conqueroo's performance at the IL, a run-down Negro bar in Austin's East Side: "It was the kind of place where older black people gathered in the afternoon to play dominoes. But here a bunch of cracker hippies marches down and starts playing so loud that food is flying off

5. John Clay, Janis Joplin, and beer drinker by Hal Normand, *Texas Ranger*, December 1962

forks all over the neighborhood" (1974:34). Brown's account is highly significant, for it catches the double incongruity of white youngsters performing unconventionally in a Southern black setting and of collegiate rock-and-rollers ("acid heads") marching under the old poor-white trash banner, "cracker." Brown bridged the linguistic polarity built into the then-discrete categories, separated by color or esthetic taste. Both "cracker" and "hippy" were pejorative terms, but they were seldom joined in ordinary speech in 1967. Interestingly, proprietor Ira Littlefield advertised the IL as featuring Austin's "best beatnik bands." The claim shows a wry sense of humor—for the word "beatnik" was already dated—or else a keen prescience in anticipating the cultural explosion on the horizon.

I read considerable meaning into the act of a black owner renting his Austin bar to a white college-based rock group in the sixties. Before random behavior can become situated or patterned to symbolize large social events, it must begin in time and place and be repeated. The participants in any new cultural enactment must sense both the fragility of their debut and the possibility for reward in repetition. The usual term in musical vocabularies to mark black/white (as well as folk/pop) hybridization is "crossover," which resembles "creole" as used of speech or cooking. No two Texans agree on what single act marked the crossover in Austin, although all agree that it denoted a musical and communal ambience alike. The IL Club happening is a tiny, now obscure, chip in a panoramic mosaic—one that shows starry cosmic cowboys, some riding ethereal broncos and others mounted on mystical little armadillos.

Some of the young Texan musicians in the Elevators and Conqueroo knew and played country music, but none was ready to go beyond exciting and liberating rock to country. However, a few members of Shiva's Headband helped nudge Austin toward recognizing its own crossover music. In 1969 this band had performed in the Vulcan Gas Company—a "hippy spot," tolerant of dope—which closed down after conservative criticism. Homeless, Eddie Wilson and Spencer Perskin, both associated with the Vulcan and Shiva, opened the Armadillo World Headquarters in August 1970. Originally conceived as a rock club, the 'Dillo soon turned to other musics and community arts. In one of the first attempts to explain the Armadillo to a political audience, *Texas Observer* reporter Henry Staten noted that Wilson wished to avoid the Vulcan's insularity and consciously sought to "break down some of the barriers between hip and straight in Austin" (1971: 19).

Wilson had seen this process in action when he accompanied artist Jim Franklin to the Cactus Club. Wilson recalled for Chet Flippo in a report to *Rolling Stone*: "It was a smoky little joint that had discovered what hippie music could do for beer sales. Hippies and rednecks were forced into the same bar—the hippies because the music [rock] was there and the rednecks because the beer was there" (1972: 18). The Cactus Club no longer exists, but it served to link the Vulcan's followers to the Armadillo's dreams. There is a logical progression from cracker hippies at the IL, to hippies and rednecks sharing at the Cactus, to large new audiences at the Armadillo hearing the best of America's musicians—Willie Nelson, Bill Monroe, Earl Scruggs, Gram Parsons, Ry Cooder, Commander Cody, Mance Lipscomb, Lightning Hopkins, Clifton Chenier, Jimmy Cliff, Randy Newman, and countless others.

In covering the anomalous reach across social barriers, as well as the emotional shift from hostility to accommodation, nearly all Austin reporters remarked on the amazingly disparate types who gathered to hear the music. Wayne Oakes, a sponsor of the Kenneth Threadgill Jubilee (July 10, 1970) wrote that this "most improbable social event to occur in a decade" brought together "thousands of Texans ranging from insurance salesmen to hippies to cedar choppers." Janis Joplin flew in from Honolulu to honor patriarch Threadgill, who had befriended her in her college days. She was cheered by "women in beehive hairdos and gold lamé western pants [who] mingled congenially with long haired hippie chicks in Mexican blouses and bluejeans" (Oakes 1970: 17–19). Janis' death three months later inspired pundits to explain the role of her Austin "mentor." Threadgill, they said, had the power to suspend generational and class distrust because listeners from all backgrounds recognized his country ballads and Nazarene hymns as real.

An attempt by Austin's liberated community to stage an out-of-town rock festival in Bastrop during 1970, on the heels of the Threadgill Jubilee, fell flat when "straight" citizens expressed displeasure. The rumor that Bastrop dwellers had set up a new firing range within gunshot of the festival site discouraged participation. Two years later, however, the Dripping Springs Reunion dissipated considerable tension. This festival, billed as both a "Country-Western Woodstock" and a "Redneck Olympiad," was simultaneously an esthetic success and a commercial washout. Commentator Dean Rindy, who had made the hegira from a Houston John Birch Society journal to campaigning in Austin for George McGovern, was present at Dripping Springs and understood its dichotomy: "The Reunion was an amiable encounter between two rival civilizations—Middle America meets the Freaks. About 30 percent of the audience was Austin hippies . . . barefoot, long-haired, dangerous radical ideas, the slavering mad dogs of Wallace and Agnew's fantasies. But everybody got along fine." Rindy also witnessed some sartorial crossover: "There were lots of flunkies and Dallas PR smoothies affecting a kind of mountebank chic (double-knit suits and silk ties, cowboy boots and velvet pants)" (1972: 17–19). After Dripping Springs in 1972, only a very obtuse reporter in or near Austin could fail to see the dramatic juxtaposition within audiences, as well as the glaring examples of mountebank chic displayed by urban saddlebums and ersatz cowboys.

One of the Nashville performers at Dripping Springs was Willie Nelson, who sensed considerable potential in his then-new barefoot audience. A year later he returned to this site to stage his first Texas Fourth of July picnic. Building Austin pride, Nelson moved there from Nashville shortly after the original Reunion. Townsend Miller, country commentator in the *Austin American-Statesman*, had been a keen fan since Nelson used to sing on road tours to small "cowboy" audiences at local Austin dance clubs like the Broken Spoke and the Big G's. On August 12, 1972, the born-again Nelson played at the Armadillo World Headquarters. Miller was struck particularly by the incongruity of seeing Willie on psychedelic posters, possibly the first such depiction of a country star. Knowing that students and street people—regulars at the 'Dillo—would surely turn out, Miller appealed to "conservative, traditional fans" to join the "young liberal fans" at the concert. Miller decried self-segregated audiences for country music, and used his column deliberately to narrow such esthetic and generational gaps (1972a : 37).

ADVENT OF THE COSMIC COWBOY

Out of all the names and descriptions applied to Austin's fusion of contradictory cultural modes, one phrase caught on as the symbol of the style and the era. Michael Murphey supplied it with the release in the summer of 1973 of his LP *Cosmic Cowboy Souvenir* (see fig. 6). The lyrics of the title song are, like those of much rock composition, rather vapid. We have come to expect strong patterns and familiar structures when reading traditional folksong as poetry. Because "Cosmic Cowboy" is not cast in a conventional ballad mold it is diffuse. Nostalgically, it projects open-ended images away from New York and California toward Texas—the land of cattle-in-mesquite and home-on-the-range. The text follows:

Burial grounds and merry-go-rounds
Are all the same to me;
Horses on posts and kids and ghosts
Are spirits we ought to set free.
Them city slicker pickers got a lot of slicker licks than you and me—
But riding the range and acting strange
Is where I want to be—
At.

6. *Cosmic Cowboy Souvenir* jacket cover by Bill Holloway

I just want to be a Cosmic Cowboy;
I just want to ride and rope and hoot.
I just want to be a Cosmic Cowboy;
A supernatural country rockin' galoot.

Lone Star sippin' and skinny dippin' and steel guitars and stars
Are just as good as Hollywood and them boogie-woogie bars.
Gonna buy me a vest and head out West
my little woman and my Self;
When they come to town they're gonna gather round
And marvel at my little baby's health.

Now big raccoons and harvest moons keep rollin' through my mind.
Home on the range where the antelope play is very hard to find.
Don't bury me on the lone prairie; I'd rather play there live.
I'm doin' my best to keep my little pony in overdrive.

Murphey composed "Cosmic Cowboy" while he was singing at the Bitter End in New York's Greenwich Village in August 1972. Born in Dallas, Murphey had turned from Baptist orthodoxy to Albert Schweitzer, and from a job as a Hollywood Screen Gems tunesmith to the free life of a composer/performer of rock poetry. Although some of his material, recorded by the Monkees and other pop figures, was highly successful, Murphey became dissatisfied with glitter. Raising his flag high, he set out to emulate the poetry recitals of Vachel Lindsay and the folksong concerts of Carl Sandburg. He left California for Texas in 1971 and took the hard road of cross-country performance.

Murphey's 1972 LP *Geronimo's Cadillac*, whose title song criticized the white exploitation of Indian life and land, had been well received by folk and rock fans alike. Hence, Nashville producer Bob Johnston, aware of Music City's grudging but accommodating acceptance of the cowboy/outlaw figure, selected "Cosmic Cowboy" as the title number for Murphey's 1973 LP *Cosmic Cowboy Souvenir*. Murphey had wanted the name "Souvenir," to suggest the variety of his compositions. However, Johnston, and his associates, sensed the potential of "Cosmic Cowboy" and added it to the LP title after the jacket's art work had been prepared by Bill Holloway in Austin.

One can never satisfactorily explain what makes a song a hit—provocative title, simple melody, instant humor, haunting sadness, memorable poetry, ready symbolism. "Cosmic Cowboy" was for a brief period a country rock favorite, yet when it dropped from the charts its title still remained in public consciousness as a generic label, both positive and pejorative. Its value as a naming term exceeded its worth as a song, for no better label surfaced in the seventies to encompass cracker hippies, beer-drinking or dope-smoking rednecks, collegiate faddists, and folk-like musicians in levis.

The chronology of Murphey's song reveals the movement of his catchy title into general Austin speech. After its composition in New York, he recorded "Cosmic Cowboy" on January 17, 1973, for Herb Alpert's A&M label, during a four-day session in Ray Steven's Nashville studio. Murphey premiered the song for Austin audiences on February 23–24 at the Armadillo World Headquarters, a setting of great exuberance. On March 16 the new song was copyrighted, and on May 1 the LP on which it appeared was also copyrighted. Murphey displayed the album in a concert at the Armadillo on June 29–30, and on August 30 *Rolling Stone* reviewed it favorably. A year later the Nashville-based Nitty Gritty Dirt Band recorded "Cosmic Cowboy" on their album *Stars and Stripes Forever*.

Austin's provocative blend of country and rock music found no sign more striking than "cosmic cowboy," and even this term was never appreciated unequivocally. No artist—musical, literary, or graphic—working within a cultural greenhouse can arbitrarily select a name for an era. Words like "jazz," "blues," "funk," and "rock" emerged slowly from Afro-American experience to identify musics and periods. A similarly lengthy process extended the Anglo-American words "hillbilly," "country," "Western," and "bluegrass" to musical forms. No Austin neologism ever underwent such a basic evolution.

Early in 1972 Ray Wylie Hubbard, a young Dallas performer who had moved from folk rock to honkytonk music, introduced a tongue-in-cheek piece both at Austin's Castle Creek and the Saxon Pub. "Up against the Wall, Redneck Mother" was at once irreverent, perverse, and vulgar. It put down kickers and ropers, yet with enough raucous humor to appeal to a few of them. Hubbard had composed "Redneck Mother" in 1969 after a "real American mother" had hassled him about his long hair in Red River, New Mexico. Eventually, Jerry Jeff Walker brought this "albatross song" to national audiences with his *Viva Terlingua* LP—yet neither Hubbard nor Walker could pin the word "redneck" to Austin's vigorous music. Neither was it in Eddie Wilson's power to label Austin's music "dillo."

In Austin's honkytonks I heard "cowboy" constantly, both as a derisive and appreciative tag, but I never heard "outlaw" in ordinary speech in any musical setting. During the mid-seventies Austin fans tied "cowboy" directly to long hair, dope, revival folksong, cliché-laden poetry, and pop astrology. Yet Michael Murphey's phrase "cosmic cowboy" finally caught Austin's imagination. It helped pull country musicians and rock fans into one milieu by giving them at last a label both could use.

"Cosmic" has its antecedents, too. Steve Miller's composition "Space Cowboy" (1969) and Sly and the Family Stone's "Spaced Cowboy" (1971), formed part of the referential frame for Murphey's catchy title. Sly, Miller, and Murphey, of course, all performed for audiences who had grown up in post-Sputnik America. Some saw cosmic life as a series of *Star Trek* dramas, while others related cosmic creeds to the revival of astrological belief by counter-culture converts. *Hooka*, a Dallas underground paper, appeared briefly to trumpet the Human Order of Kosmic Consciousness. Before and after Murphey wrote his piece, dozens of other songs had joined the word "cosmic" to "boy," "Charlie," "chicken," "dancer," "debris," "funk," "overload," "ray," "street," "vortex," and "wheels." None was as influential as "cosmic cowboy"; none served to specify a wide social need.

The first printing known to me of "cosmic cowboy" as a discrete word combination was on Michael Priest's Armadillo World Headquarters poster (February 23–24, 1973). The shift from poster to naming device was immediate. That March Al Reinert's "So Long, Cosmic Cowboys," which dealt not with music but with the Houston-based space program, appeared in *Texas Monthly*. Reinert's prose was colorful: "Astronauts, tight-lipped, square-jawed and blue-eyed, dedicated patriots . . . a species of Cosmic Cowboy storing up energy to blaze a trail to the Moon" (1973:39).

Reinert's borrowing was complimentary to Murphey's coinage, but when "Cosmic Cowboy" began to bother some listeners, satiric versions materialized. David Hisbrook and Gary Wilcox offered "Too Much Cosmic (Not Enough Cowboy)" (United Recording Artists 921) on a 45-rpm disc. Before this record was issued, John Clay, a dedicated performer of old-time music, composed and sang another parody. From Stamford, Texas, Clay had come to Austin in 1960 and had turned to the campus "folksong revival" at its beginning. He has experienced a variety of Austin's musical scenes and has observed closely most of the city's musicians—famous or obscure, original or derivative. The text of his "Plastic Plowboy" appeared in *The Rag*, Austin's radical tabloid (on September 4, 1973), and more recently on the 1980 LP *Drifting through the Seventies*. Two stanzas follow:

And where has Psychedelic America gone?
All those swinging days and nights of yesteryear,
When we'd trip out for hours on dreams of fruit and flowers,
But the kids nowadays are drinking wine and beer.

Where have my psychedelic posters gone?
Did the landlord burn 'em where we used to live?

My memory has lapsed, and it used to be a steel trap,
But nowadays it's much more like a sieve.

So I wanna be a plastic plowboy. . . .

Three typical deprecatory uses of "cosmic cowboy" appeared in *Texas Monthly*. Larry King, Texas-born novelist and political essayist who abhors romanticized rurality, stated in "Redneck":

Now, the Rednecks I'm talking are not those counterfeit numbers who hang around Austin digging the Cosmic Cowboy scene, sucking up to Jerry Jeff Walker and Willie Nelson, wearing bleached color-patched overalls and rolling their own dope, saying how they hanker to go live off the land and then stay six weeks in a Taos commune before flying back on daddy's credit card (1974:50).

William Martin, Rice University sociologist, also reported sourly on thirty-six hours of progressive country music in "Growing Old at Willie Nelson's Picnic":

I had expected thousands of cosmic cowboys and assorted freaks, but I had also expected fairly large numbers of authentic rednecks, and I knew if I got uncomfortable with the freaks I could go sit with the kickers. . . . There were some kickers there, all right. About six. The other 25,000 were freaks or freakish, all under 25 (1974:94).

Finally, Bill Porterfield, Texas newspaperman and radio commentator, took a swipe at cosmic brethren riding "In Search of the Modern Cowboy":

The new musical romanticism has [the cowboy as] a gentle knight, repulsed by arms and armor and aggression and refinery air, returning to a pastoral West. . . . It is a curious hallucination. Cosmic cowboys around counterfeit campfires, breathing burning grass and drinking longnecks, listening to the lowing of Darrell Royal's Longhorns (1975:59).

Although, I feel, Murphey had composed "Cosmic Cowboy" seriously, intending it to be relevant to a wide audience, and recorded it without a hint at parody, he backed away once the song became a subject of ridicule. In hindsight, Murphey averred that "he had written the song tongue-in-cheek, never intending it to be taken seriously." Further, he came to despise his Austin fans as "hooting hippies who fancied themselves goat roping cosmic cowboys" (quoted in Reid 1974:264). When Jan Reid's publisher put a color photo of Murphey on the dust wrapper of *Redneck Rock*, Murphey was distressed at being associated with this alliterative book title. Partly he was sensitive to the gimmickry of the title and partly he questioned Reid's credentials.

In an interview with Chet Flippo for *Texas Parade*, Murphey distanced himself from "Cosmic Cowboy," asserting that he had been misunderstood:

I never intended that it be taken seriously. I wrote that one night at the Bitter End in New York. Jerry Jeff and I were there, playing cowboy . . . and I just kinda made it up and sang it that night as a joke. We cracked up—look at us, we're the cosmic cowboys. . . . It gets under my skin a little bit. Somehow that phrase caught on and people said, yeah, that's what we are and they started wearing boots and huge cowboy hats. It went too far. It's fun to have fun but we came off as Clint Eastwood all the time, Clint Eastwood with hair (1974a:20).

It is futile to dispute, retrospectively, whether or not "Cosmic Cowboy" arose as a joke. Murphey perceived himself as a poet/philosopher for the seventies, and his songs were too precious to him to let others reinterpret them. He was not the first composer to be made uneasy by success. Ironically, his hit was anchored to the very ambivalence felt by so many Americans about the shift from rural to urban society. Whether he liked it or not, Murphey's song title took hold in speech and helped label a cultural amalgam that had been building for decades. Cedar-chopping/goat-roping youngsters in the Texas hill country were born into Western life codes. They may have been pained when hippy school rivals took up their levis and downhome music, but it was also a conquest for the rural life, a vindication of good horse-sense in clothes and musical taste.

In retrospect, the counter-culture of the sixties was almost as much sartorial as it was moral or political. A. R. Gunter, in the University of Texas' student newspaper, the *Daily Texan*, saw country rock as bringing together "two social factions . . . flower children and cowboys" (1972:14). Gunter stressed the disappearance of visual and aural barriers as these factions came together, and lauded Murphey as a boundary-breaker—who pulled the barbed wire down instead of keeping it taut. Austin fans liked the euphony of "cosmic cowboy." More significantly, the semantic overlap of "cosmetic" and "cosmic" helped the former word cover the incongruity of well-to-do youngsters dressing down in cowboy make-up—urban dudes for the seventies.

Interestingly, Murphey's sidemen give a more detailed account of the song's composition than does the composer himself.

Herb Steiner and Craig Hillis were playing in Murphey's band when he composed "Cosmic Cowboy" in New York and when he recorded it in Nashville. Steiner had studied anthropology at UCLA, and had been influenced by the folksong boom before he turned to rock in Hollywood clubs. Hillis, an "Air Force brat," had attended the University of Texas, when acid rock surfaced, and had made the pilgrimage to California, where he met and played with Steiner. Both toured with Murphey: Herb on steel pedal guitar, Craig on lead guitar.

Steiner and Hillis recalled for me the specific circumstance of Murphey's composition of "Cosmic Cowboy," literally at the edge of a Manhattan Holiday Inn's roof swimming pool (above 57th Street). (The notes on the album give this credit to the Bitter End's dressing room.) From Steiner and Hillis, I learned that the song was inspired directly by the antics of Bob Livingston, a Texan musician from Lubbock. While at the Bitter End, Livingston had met Cosmic Suzanne, a lost Austinite in Manhattan. Livingston served as the butt for much band humor, and Suzanne, temporarily on the scene, brought the word "cosmic," connoting drugs, into constant group usage by the band members. Livingston's special contribution was eventually credited in the liner notes for *Cosmic Cowboy Souvenir*, where he was identified with background vocals, electric rhythm guitar, bass, and "funky energy."

Murphey literally taught the new song to his sidemen at the pool's edge; it helped them trip back from the skyscrapers rimming the Holiday Inn to the open range. Hillis immediately sensed the contradiction in the song's title: cowboys then were not usually expected to experience altered states of consciousness. However, Steiner liked very much the alliteration of the title. Both sidemen, of course, caught the phrase's verbal charge; they saw themselves as participants in a high drama of musical linkage.

Not all country rock stars enjoyed this drama or proved prophetic of its power. Doug Sahm, an eclectic San Antonio musician, sourly told Chet Flippo that the cowboy music era had ended: "This cosmic cowboy shit has had it" (1973a:30). What had gone wrong? A rather mild and opaque portrait of a spaced-out cowboy, a dopey rider from outer space, had become for Sahm a dubious symbol. Why? Part of the answer lies within Murphey's song, and part in the Austin scene. On first hearing the lyric, I was uncertain whether Murphey thought his cowboy was a hero or antihero, redneck kicker or liberated philosopher. He, too, may have been uncertain. Yet, despite the song's fuzzy nature, the word "cowboy," whether linked with "cosmic" or standing alone, has fantastic strength. It holds always in bond the multiple images of guerrilla, buckaroo, wrangler, stoic, dude, braggart, hustler, rebel, mystic.

Not all of Austin's actors on the stage of convergence performed music; the cultural meld also released other artistic energies. An early visual image of the new order emerged when Austin's KOKE-FM settled into a progressive-country format. The station released a magazine ad by Kerry Awn (Kerry Fitzgerald) featuring a super-roper cowgirl lassoing an out-of-date radio. Next, a bumper sticker (and an ad) appeared showing a lean cowboy, his rope taut around the neck of a reluctant goat. In 1975, KOKE sold mail-order "Super Roper T-Shirts" with the goat logo (fig. 7). Perhaps the most succinct application of "goat roper" to musical expression occurred in the summer of 1974 when the entertainment guide *Free & Easy* featured a full-page bar-club guide called "Austin Bands from Dopers to Ropers." These incongruous twins, dissolute satyr and spirited dude, have been depicted endlessly in Austin graphics; Kerry Awn's series of monthly calendars for the Soap Creek Saloon has, over the years, been especially abundant in dopers and ropers (often indistinguishable from each other).

Michael Priest's wonderful graphics best extended the meaning of Professor Worrall's carousing cowboys (1874), Tad Dorgan's cake eating cowboys (1923), and Miguel Covarrubias' drugstore cowboy (1930). Priest, a self-taught artist, came to Austin in 1969 and was caught up immediately by the laid-back community. By 1971 he was trying his hand at commercial work for the Armadillo World Headquarters and other musical clubs. The major artist associated with the Armadillo is Jim Franklin, but it was Priest's sardonic cowboys rather than Franklin's droll armadillos which gave a visual dimension to cosmic cowboy music.

For a concert on September 15–16, 1972, shortly after "Cosmic Cowboy" was composed but before it was sung in Austin, Priest portrayed Willie Nelson and Michael Murphey as two relaxed cowboy musicians (fig. 8). In this commentary, I have not detailed Nelson's fabulous story, for it has been well told by others. By any measure, he is a giant in country music, at once soulful and oracular. His travels from Texas to Tennessee and back to

7. Super Roper logo, used as KOKE FM ad in 1975

Texas form a rich saga appropriate to a Dos Passos trilogy. Priest's
first linkage of Murphey and Nelson as tipsy comrades, arm-in-
arm, was itself a visual emblem which said that straights and
freaks were ready to ramble together. Significantly, Murphey, the
college-educated citybilly, is shaggy and bearded, while Nelson,
the Texas country boy, is cleanshaven. This contrast reflects very
accurately the "pre-cosmic" notion that country musicians were
straight while city folksingers were freakish.

Priest has told me that he chose cowboy costume as a symbol
to bridge town and country. Alabama-born, he had come to Austin by way of small-town Texas, and had known the word "cowboy" as a derogatory equivalent for "cedar chopper" and "goat
roper." Because he liked kicker music but lived mainly within the
open Austin community, he desired to bring his dual worlds to-

8. Willie Nelson and Michael Murphey concert, Armadillo World Head-quarters poster by Michael Priest, September 15–16, 1972

gether. In short, Priest had not foreseen Murphey's specific song, but had already observed and welcomed the mixing of styles. Priest was ready to draw a mustang rider in space lassoing a comet (fig. 9) as soon as Murphey was ready to sing "Cosmic Cowboy" in Austin. One detail in this poster (February 23–24, 1973) is important historically, for it credits Stan Alexander as "The Original Cosmic Cowboy." Professor Alexander, now at Stephen F. Austin State University, Nacogdoches, had first introduced Murphey to folksong in the early sixties, when Murphey was a student at North Texas State University, Denton. Alexander, while himself a student in Austin, had been a regular at Threadgill's, and was a pioneer in bringing Texas country music and urban folksong into conjunction.

Priest also helped advertise "A Tribute to the Cosmic Cowboy," a benefit concert for Houston's non-commercial FM station, KPFT (February 10, 1974) (fig. 10). For this occasion Priest outdid himself with a poster cowboy, stars on chaps and fat joint in hand. This little imp was later reincarnated when Lone Star beer emblazoned him on Texas T-shirts. Chet Flippo reported on the Houston event for *Rolling Stone* in "The Day the Kickers Ruled," noting that the concert included, among others, Michael Murphey and some eight thousand fans in cowboy hats and boots: "Big doggin'-heel jobs caked with the remains of dusty trails and cowflop-clearings. Between the headgear and footwear, a snappy parade of cowboy shirts and pants floated by" (1974b:24).

One of the fascinating aspects of Murphey's composition was that it helped many Austinites deal with plasticity and reality, with long hair and country roots. His song touched liminal existence itself—did one live at home, away from home, or perhaps in the doorway? *The Rag* raised these concerns in a reflective story on KPFT's benefit concert. In "The Kosmic Kowboys," reviewer "Danny" (1974) confessed that he had previously been unimpressed by cosmic cowboys' time-wasting and bullshit. But he came over at the crazy concert when everybody joined Murphey in his chorus line. Danny noted: "Everyone onstage was swapping hats. Doug Sahm had come back out and was dancing around Jim Franklin, who wore possibly the biggest white Stetson this side of the moon. I must've sung along too, the whole thing felt that good. The image finally made sense."

The Rag's iconoclastic reporter was conscious that the new portrait of hip Texans held contradictions (long hair and long-

9. Cosmic Cowboy concert, Armadillo World Headquarters poster by
Michael Priest, February 23–24, 1973

horns)—that the country rock colony did not include Negroes or Chicanos and flaunted its male machismo. Critically, he could reject the false values in Murphey's construct, but at the concert Danny, too, was caught up in the song and dance. Intellectuals and radicals who live outside also need to come inside, to swap hats, to sing along, to savor communitas.

Cowboys never were given to bunking entirely in one place; they have moved from home ranch to town flophouse to rodeo motel to neon honkytonk. Precisely because we Americans wanted a folk hero who could express our hidden liminality, who could live in many doorways, who could be orderly lawman and disorderly brawler, we stretched the elastic word "cowboy" to its limits. It is easy to find cowboy portraits in sketches and songs frozen within ethical frames, positive or negative; it is difficult to find them poised between sets of values. Murphey's "Cosmic Cowboy," at best, struggles to carry loads we all share.

To close my comments on the negative valence engendered by Murphey's song, I offer two views. *Cosmic Cowboy Souvenir* evoked from a *Creem* reviewer this squib: "Lobotomy music, one cliche after another" (1973:71). By far the most thoughtful criticism of the composition as a symbol was penned by editor Jeff Nightbyrd (1975) for the *Austin Sun*, an alternative community newspaper. In "Cosmo Cowboys" he distinguished Murphey, the sensitive composer, from his song, which had come to personify collegiate "nerds" (who wore embroidered cowboy shirts and simulated-alligator boots). Nightbyrd despised Austin's fake cowboys (dopers) for their cosmetic finery as well as straight cowboys (ropers) for their previous trashing of hippies. Taking a dim view of these two groups, even when they coexisted at Willie Nelson's picnics, the writer pointed out that such celebrations had spread stench and trash over the Texas countryside. Nightbyrd, a veteran of SDS activism in the sixties, felt that the cosmic cowboy phenomenon not only masked political realities, but, worse, held back people in their need to remove masks.[4]

Jack Jaxon offers the last picture of the "Cosmic Cowboy"—a cartoon with running text published in the *Austin Sun* (March 11, 1976) as a "handy guide for out-of-staters" (fig. 11). A "genuine bad-ass redneck Texas cowpoke" stares down a hairy, "austin-tatious," jewelry-bedecked dude, while the artist explains their sartorial contrast. A two-page comic-strip sequence on pickups, dancehalls, and other earthy pleasures elaborated the differences.

10. Benefit concert for KPFT, poster by Michael Priest, February 10, 1974

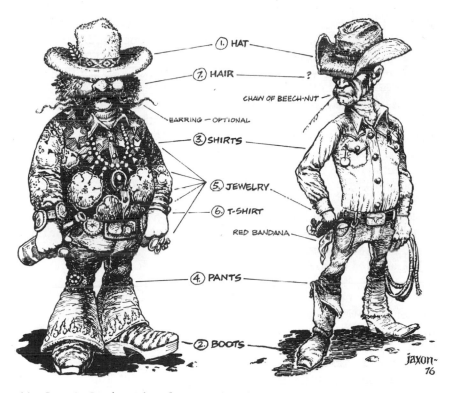

The following labels appear in the chart:

1. HAT
7. HAIR — ?
CHAW OF BEECH-NUT
EARRING — OPTIONAL
3. SHIRTS
5. JEWELRY
6. T-SHIRT
RED BANDANA
4. PANTS
2. BOOTS

jaxon-76

11. *Cozmic Cowboy Identification Chart* by Jack Jaxon in the *Austin Sun,*
March 11, 1976, and the *National Lampoon,* December 1977

National Lampoon reprinted Jaxon's cowboy pair at year's end
1977 in an "Identification Chart" (without the accompanying
comic strip). Depending on one's point of view, one can either say
that the *Lampoon's* use marked the cosmic cowboy's coming of
age in national consciousness or else the end of the phrase's
utility.

PERSPECTIVE

I have shaped this study largely in terms of dated references to a
song title, some contextual background, and the reproduction of
several graphics. A brief discussion of two Texas musicians, Kinky Friedman (the "Texas Jewboy") and Guy Clark ("Old No. 1"),

who used new cowboy music to explicate ethical issues, can add perspective. Kinky has gone to great pains to reject labels, but he has deliberately juxtaposed cedar-chopper and freak values in his compositions. Dressed in Western garb he is an irreverent practitioner of guerrilla theater. His painful social commentaries ("They Don't Make Jews Like Jesus Anymore") invoke the searing moral conflict of modern times, while his flamboyant choreography recalls the high drama of cowboys on an end-of-the-trail spree. To see him use his stage-prop Star of David as a hat rack for a Stetson is to be outraged.

Nashville, in the mid-seventies, adapted to some Austin country music, but Kinky pushed beyond both sites to extraordinary limits. His "Sold American" delineates a faded cowboy star whose sequins have fallen from his jeans. He is not just a country music has-been; he is Everyman—fleeced, flawed, fallen. "Ride 'Em Jewboy" employs the waltz-like lilt of a traditional night-herding song, but its biting message attacks the scourge of fascism. At a concert at the Armadillo World Headquarters (September 20, 1975), I observed that this song moved some of its auditors to dreamy dancing and others to troubled introspection. Yet Kinky, in bold chaps, held the divergent audience together.

Guy Clark soaked up cowboy and oil-field lore during his childhood at Monahans, West Texas. Like a magnet, this flat and arid land drew boomers and roustabouts, many bringing tales of work in fields as far as Venezuela or Saudi Arabia. When Guy took to wandering as a minstrel he fell back on his early memories to compose a set of fine songs. One is "Desperados Waiting for a Train," the story of a driller whose wells have run dry. Guy recalled Jack Prigg playing dominoes in his grandmother's kitchen and was pained that his friend had grown old. Using poetry to transcend age, he transformed old Prigg into the archetypal outsider, a desperado.

My favorite Clark song is "L.A. Freeway," recorded initially by Jerry Jeff Walker in 1973. Guy used to commute from a straight job in Long Beach to Hollywood to try to sell his pieces. His anxiety about surviving the freeway, a steel and concrete spider web, spilled over into "L.A. Freeway." It is nominally a song about a nostalgic trip back home to Texas. When I heard Guy sing it at Castle Creek (January 15, 1976), his sidemen literally stood aside to let him spin the ballad of travel and death alone. Clark posed for his auditors a set of metaphoric questions: Is the open road still the symbol of freedom, or the site of deathly wrecks? Shall we ever escape modernity's steel and concrete? Guy in concert is flashy in neither dress nor mannerism; his denim shirt is more appropriate to a drilling platform than to a collegiate bar. But his powerful songs span seminar room and rotary rig, while his que rics are central to our times.

For many years, Nashville composers have inflicted countless cloying songs upon America's blue-collar workers and rural poor. Understandably, a Tom Joad or a Flem Snopes became a social object for Tin Pan Valley—recipients of packaged country banality. But Kinky Friedman, an Austin misfit, and Guy Clark, a young West Texas good ol' boy, have been able to make old workers and fallen cowboys sympathetic subjects in song. This is a real achievement within an industry geared to unraveling emotion on sanitized discs.

Not all Austin fans in the seventies perceived Guy or Kinky as filling their musical cornucopia. Nashville patriots, jazz buffs, rock diehards, reggae cultists, and new wave pioneers all rejected the cosmic cowboy as an unadulterated disaster. We need to document the views of these naysayers as well as those of the "holdout" performers. We must also explore the tense relationship which young Western swing performers such as Alvin Crow and his Pleasant Valley Boys established with the progressive scene. In the thirties Bob Wills had been truly progressive—an exponent of heady cultural syncretism. An exemplary Wills stylist, Crow, based in Austin, had been influenced deeply by rock and boogie, yet he found it most difficult to describe his music as convergent in style.

In exploring the various responses to cosmic cowboy music, we need to look at one of its early influences, the "folksong revival" at the University of Texas. Pete Seeger, Joan Baez, Bob Dylan, and their companions inspired many campus followers. Some sought out local old-time musicians in order to learn their traditional styles, and some used folksong as grist for the popular mill. Many other paths opened. For example, Segle Fry, after a Kingston Trio concert (December 17, 1958), was caught up by folksong. He went on to perform, to manage the Chequered Flag coffee house, and to help aspiring stars move to the cactus circuit. Looking back to Austin days, Fry's fellow student Bill Malone recalls encountering esoteric "folksingers" who knew militant Spanish Civil War ballads but none of his beloved country music classics (1976:243–257). Ultimately, participants and audience members together must detail Austin's full musical history.[5]

Hopefully, in treating the rise and fall of a seventies phrase I have enlarged our understanding of the cowboy as hero and anti-hero, as dweller in bunkhouse and honkytonk. However, no word study really ends until its referent has vanished from speech. Looking back at his hit from the vantage point of a half-decade, Michael Murphey stated: "the cosmic cowboy myth is dead" (Zibart 1978:D15). But even for Murphey the mythic figure is not really dead, for his Epic album, *Peaks Valleys Honky-Tonks & Alleys* (1979) includes a reborn "Cosmic Cowboy," recorded live at Hollywood's Palomino Club and still questing for the Texas range. The term "cosmic cowboy" caught on because it helped us understand crossover music—music that meant not only tunes listed on folk, country, or rock charts, but also texts signifying deep social change. We need a language able to describe those expressions which comment on the constant meeting of rural and urban, black and white, and innovative and conservative forces in America. A pluralistic society, with or without a transcendent national ethos, must find words to mark a people's travel across borders of class, ethnicity, and region.

Finally, when "cosmic cowboy" vanishes, other terms will arise to describe hyphenated music growing from folk and pop roots. In the twenties, "hillbilly" was extended from the name of a rural bumpkin to a music which bridged mountain sounds and city performance. The progression of the phrase "rhythm and blues" to "rock and roll" comments not only on musical styles, but on processes of synthesis in Anglo- and Afro-American cultures alike. The combination "Western swing" holds white and black tension in balance. In Texas, parallels occur as performers from French- and Spanish-language communities play "zydeco" and "norteño"—adding blues to Cajun music or polkas to Mexican music. Many words like "rockabilly" developed from the fifties term "rock." Other words such as "folk," "hard," "acid," "raga," "swamp," "glitter," and "punk" have all joined "rock" to mark special musical forms. The pairing "country rock," ultimately, seems best to cover Austin's cosmic cowboys and their lore; its emergence deserves a discrete study.

Austin's creators, and their fellow composer/performers throughout America, have been superb artists. They have balanced extremes of cloying sentiment and frightening dissonance, mediated much of the polarity built into modern life, and articulated the need to get off the freeway. I treasure the union in companionship of goat ropers and liberated freaks, of superkickers and isolated intellectuals, much more than I fret about the sham of romantic rednecks or their myopia. In short, I lack any anxiety over rhinestone-decorated, cosmic cowboys—Austin's centaurs. Sensitive to cosmetic portraits and plastic packaging, I am chiefly concerned about our fragmented polity, about Americans in collision with each other. Is there any way to pull our society together into a sane future if disparate cultural expressions cannot be respected and shared?°

NOTES

1. I include in my bibliography all items which are cited by page within my article, select items which are referred to without page citation, and some general background material. However, the bibliography does not list every song, book, film, sound recording, review, and lexicographical allusion mentioned in my article.
2. I have in progress a study on the cowboy in English-language dictionaries.
3. Neely's story is forthcoming in a monograph by Nicholas Spitzer. The many articles on Threadgill form a source for anecdotes and photos of Austin music. See M. Dreyer (1972), B. King (1972), Langham (1973), Mays (1973), Miller (1972b), Oakes (1970), Olds (1970), Smith (1979).
4. For additional evaluations and reconsiderations see Burnett and Titley (1978), Flippo (1979), Frink et al. (1974), Johnson and Lightfoot (1973), Morton and Conway (1977), Perry (1979), Reid (1976a, 1976b), Tucker (1976), E. Ward (1979).
5. University of Texas students wrote papers which hold rich details on Austin music. For example, Cecil Jordan has made available to me a typescript on his experiences as a Soap Creek Saloon bartender (1977). Some needed papers are: (1) an interview with Burton Wilson to supplement his *Book of the Blues* (1971, 1977), a superb collection of photographs; (2) a study of radio station KOKE-FM's introduction of the phrase "progressive country music"; (3) a report on public television station KLRN's show "Austin City Limits," which beamed such music to national viewers; (4) an account of the filming in Austin of the movie *Outlaw Blues* (1976).
6. I owe thanks to Austin performers, commentators, and enthusiasts who have made vibrant for me their music. Special thanks go to Roger Abrahams, Richard Bauman, and Nicholas Spitzer for reading drafts of this paper. Peter Tamony prepared me to listen to words about music; Michael Priest helped me to see Austin music. I am grateful to staff members in three libraries: the Travis County Collec-

tion of the Austin Public Library; the University of Texas Writings Collection; and the Barker Texas History Center of the University of Texas. Finally, I want to thank Michael Murphey for permission to quote "Cosmic Cowboy" and A&M Records, Inc., for permission to reproduce the cover of *Cosmic Cowboy Souvenir*.

BIBLIOGRAPHY

Ade, George. 1903. Mr. Lindsay on "San Jewan." In *In Babel: Stories of Chicago*. New York: McClure, Phillips.
Adkins, Lieuen. 1962. What to do til the cops arrive. *Texas Ranger* 77 (December):19–22.
Allen, Bob. 1979. *Waylon & Willie*. New York: Quick Fox.
Allen, Nelson. 1975. KOKE-FM. *Picking Up the Tempo* 6:7–8.
Anonymous. 1973a. "Cosmic Cowboy" orbits Murphey. *Dallas Iconoclast* (June 15):8.
———. 1973b. Review of *Cosmic Cowboy Souvenir*. *Creem* (September):71.
———. 1976. Ray Wylie Hubbard haunted by his hit "Redneck Mother." *Country Style* (October):31.
Axthelm, Pete. 1978. King of Country Music. *Newsweek* (August 14): 52–57.
Bane, Michael. 1978. *The outlaws: Revolution in country music*. New York: Country Music Magazine Press.
Baumann, John. 1887. On a Western ranche. *Fortnightly Review* 47: 516–533.
Bentley, Bill. 1976. Austin's favorite honky-tonk songstress, Marcia Ball. *Austin Sun* (March 11):13, 17.
Brammer, Bill. 1974. Review of *The improbable rise of redneck rock*. *Austin Sun* (October 17):18–19.
Burnett, John, and Bob Titley. 1978. Putting up a front: The truth about Austin's music scene. *Austin Sun* (January 20):12–13.
Carr, Patrick. 1973. It's so "progressive" in Texas. *New York Times* (July 22):D9, D16.
Clay, John. 1962. The folkmusic revival. *Texas Ranger* 77 (October): 30–31.
Coe, David Allan. 1975. Kountry Muzak. *Picking Up the Tempo* 9:1–2.
Cusic, Don. 1976. Neil Reshen: Riding herd on the new breed. *Record World* (March 6):6ff.
"Danny". 1974. The kosmic kowboys. *The Rag* (February 18):10–11.
Dreyer, Martin. 1972. In the shadow of greatness. *Houston Chronicle, Texas Magazine* (August 13):18–23.
Dreyer, Thorne. 1975. Who are we to say the boy's insane? *Austin Sun* (May 1):13, 20–22.

Endres, Clifford. 1974. Jaxon returns: The long road back to Austin. *Austin Sun* (November 7):13, 20–23.

Flippo, Chet. 1972. Uncle Zeke's rock emporium. *Rolling Stone* (October 12):18.

———. 1973a. Random notes: Doug Sahm. *Rolling Stone* (December 6):30.

———. 1973b. Waylon Jennings gets off the grind-'em-out circuit. *Rolling Stone* (December 6):28.

———. 1974a. Hill country sound. *Texas Parade* 34:16–23.

———. 1974b. The day the kickers ruled. *Rolling Stone* (April 11):24.

———. 1978. The saga of Willie Nelson. *Rolling Stone* (July 13):45–49.

———. 1979. The Austin scene and Willie Nelson: A reconsideration. *Popular Music and Society* 6:280–283.

Ford, Corey. 1930. *The John Riddell murder case*. New York: Scribner's.

Frank, Pat. 1957. *Seven days to never*. London: Constable.

Frink, Clayton, et al. 1974. Austin music: Progressive country. *Austin American-Statesman, Show World* (July 14), 1–28.

Gordon, Roxy. 1971. *Some things I did*. Austin: Encino Press.

———. 1975. Stars. *Picking Up the Tempo* 8:1–7.

Greco, Mike. 1979. "Honeysuckle Rose": Somethin' 'bout a cowboy. *Los Angeles Times, Calendar* (December 23):47–48.

Green, Archie. 1965. Hillbilly music: Source and symbol. *Journal of American Folklore* 78:204–228.

———. 1975. Midnight and other cowboys. *JEMF Quarterly* 11:137–152.

Green, Douglas B. 1978. The singing cowboy: An American dream. *Journal of Country Music* 7:4–61.

Gunter, A. R. 1972. Musical "boundaries" disappearing and country-rock stirs social mix. *Daily Texan* (December 7):14 and (December 8):15.

Hemphill, Paul. 1970. Kris Kristofferson is the new Nashville sound. *New York Times Magazine* (December 6):54–55 et seq.

Herschorn, Connie. 1973. Austin builds country rock base. *Billboard* (September 8):T-13.

Hickey, Dave. 1974. In defense of the Telecaster cowboy outlaws. *Country Music* 2:90–95.

Holden, Stephen. 1973. Review of *Cosmic Cowboy Souvenir*. *Rolling Stone* (August 30):86.

Ivins, Molly. 1974. The university universe. *New York Times Magazine* (November 10):36–58.

Jaxon, Jack. 1976. *Comanche moon*. San Francisco: Rip Off Press/Last Gasp.

Johnson, J. J., and J. E. Lightfoot. 1973. Death and the armadillo: A rediscovery of the Southwestern soul. *Journal of the American Studies Association of Texas* 5:73–78. •

Jordan, Cecil. 1977. Requiem for a scene. Unpublished MS.

King, Ben. 1972. Threadgill unifies cultures with yodels, Rodgers style. *Daily Texan* (September 21):14.

King, Larry L. 1974. Redneck. *Texas Monthly* 2 (August):50–55 et seq.
———. 1976. David Allan Coe's greatest hits. *Esquire* 86 (July):71–73, 142–144.

Lamar, M. B. 1968. *The papers of Mirabeau Buonaparte Lamar*, vol. 6. Austin: Pemberton Press.

Langham, Barbara. 1973. Late train to Nashville. *Texas Parade* 33 (April):42–45.

Latham, Aaron. 1978. The ballad of the urban cowboy. *Esquire* 90 (September 12):21–30.

Lewis, Pat. 1975. Fear and loathing in P. G. County. *Washington Star* (April 25):B1, B3.

Malone, Bill C. 1976. Growing up with Texas country music. In *What's going on? (in modern Texas folklore)*. Francis Abernethy, ed. Austin: Encino Press.

Martin, William C. 1974. Growing old at Willie Nelson's picnic. *Texas Monthly* 2 (October):94–98, 116–124.

Mays, Prissy. 1973. Old is beautiful—in music or on Threadgill. *Alcalde* (May):13–15.

McCoy, Joseph G. 1874. *Historic sketches of the cattle trade of the West and Southwest*. Kansas City, Missouri: Ramsey.

McKenzie, Marty, and Clifford Endres. 1976. Austin city limits. *Austin Sun* (March 25):1, 20.

Middleton, Russell. 1973. Progressive country in Austin. *Advent* 1 (November):20–21, 30.

Miller, Townsend. 1972a. Willie Nelson bringing 'em all together (and ain't it wonderful). *Austin American-Statesman* (August 12):37.
———. 1972b. At 62 Ken Threadgill gets his big break. *Country Music* 1 (October):19–22.
———. 1974. Austin combines traditional and progressive sounds to become Nashville II. *Billboard* (July 9):T-4.
———. 1975. Time for an official song. *Austin American-Statesman* (December 5):55.

Milner, Jay. 1976. Outlaws love Texas. *Texas Music* 1 (May):17–21, 45–47.

Morthland, John. 1975. Country-rockers: Takin' the hard beat down home. In *Sound, the Sony guide to music 1975/1976*. Knoxville: Approach 13-30 Corporation.

Morton, Marian J., and William P. Conway. 1977. Cowboy without a cause: His image in today's popular music. *Antioch Review* 35: 193–204.

Mudon, Bill. 1976. *Cisco Pike, Outlaw Blues*, and *Convoy*. *Picking Up the Tempo* 19:8–10.

Nance, Joseph Milton. 1963. *After San Jacinto*. Austin: University of Texas Press.

Nightbyrd, Jeff. 1975. Cosmo cowboys: Too much cowboy and not enough cosmic. *Austin Sun* (April 3):13, 19.

Northcott, Kaye. 1973. Kinky Friedman's first roundup. *Texas Monthly* 1 (May):95–96.

Oakes, Wayne. 1970. Thousands turn out for Threadgill. *Texas Observer* 62 (August 7):17–19.

Ohrlin, Glenn. 1974. *The hell-bound train.* Urbana: University of Illinois Press.

Olds, Greg. 1970. Threadgill. *Austin American-Statesman, Show World* (July 5):T26–T29.

O'Malley, Suzanne. 1972. Austin—a nice place for music. *Daily Texan, Pearl* (December):11–13.

Patoski, Joe Nick. 1974. Review of *The improbable rise of redneck rock. Daily Texan, Pearl* (November):6.

———. 1976. Guy Clark–Desperado waiting for his fame. *Austin Sun* (January 16):13.

Perry, David. 1979. Cosmic cowboys and cosmetic politics. *JEMF Quarterly,* 15:38–43.

Porterfield, Bill. 1975. In search of the modern cowboy. *Texas Monthly* 3 (October):58–64, 88–96.

Randall, Isabelle. 1887. *A lady's ranche life in Montana.* London: Allen.

Reid, Jan. 1974. *The improbable rise of redneck rock.* Austin: Heidelberg.

———. 1976a. Postscript: The improbable rise of redneck rock. In *What's going on? (in modern Texas folklore).* Francis Abernethy, ed. Austin: Encino Press.

———. 1976b. Who killed redneck rock? *Texas Monthly* 4 (December): 112–113, 209–216.

Reinert, Al. 1973. So long, cosmic cowboys. *Texas Monthly* 1 (March): 38–42.

———. 1978. King of country music. *New York Times Magazine* (March 26):20–28, 50–53.

Rindy, Dean. 1972. Country karma. *Texas Observer* 64 (April 14):17–19.

Roth, Don, and Jan Reid. 1973. The coming of redneck hip. *Texas Monthly* 1 (November):70–76.

St. John, Powell. 1974. Liner notes for Bill Neely's *Blackland farm boy* (Arhoolie 5014).

Savage, William A., Jr. 1979. *The Cowboy Hero: His Image in American History and Culture.* Norman: University of Oklahoma Press.

Smith, Rick. 1979. A musical oasis. *Austin American-Statesman* (February 25):B1, B11.

Spitzer, Nicholas. 1975. "Bob Wills is still the king." *JEMF Quarterly* 11:191–196.

———. 1979. Bill Neely: Life and lyrics of a Texas songster. Unpublished MS.

Staten, Henry. 1971. Armadillo World Headquarters. *Texas Observer* 63 (February 12):18–19.

Tamony, Peter. 1958. Jazz, the word. *Jazz* 1 (October):33–42.

Thorsen, Karen. 1976. Has Austin upstaged Nashville? *Oui* 5 (March): 77–78, 125–126.

Tosches, Nick. 1976. Outlaws as oligarchs. *Village Voice* (May 31):142.

Tucker, Stephen Ray. 1976. The Western image in country music. Unpublished M.A. thesis, Southern Methodist University.

Van Zandt, Townes. 1977. *For the sake of a song.* Houston: Wings Press.

Ventura, Michael. 1977. Queen of the honky-tonks, Marcia Ball. *Texas Sun* (May 27):12–13, 20.

Ward, Ed. 1974. There's a little bit of everything in Texas. *Creem* (April):46–48, 76–77.

———. 1979. '70s the decade/music. *Austin American-Statesman* (December 21):G1, G7.

Ward, Robert. 1976. Redneck rock. *New Times* 6 (June 25):55–62.

West, Richard. 1974. So you want to be a redneck. *Texas Monthly* 2 (August):57–59.

Wiemers, Carl. 1973. Austin next Nashville. *Daily Texan* (July 24):13.

Wilson, Burton. 1971. *Burton's book of the blues.* Austin: Speleo Press.

———. 1977. *Burton's book of the blues*, rev. ed. Austin: Edentata Press.

Worley, Barbara. 1970. How Bastrop '70 got offed. *Texas Observer* 62 (September 18):15–16.

Zibart, Eve. 1978. The cosmic cowboy's new dimension. *Washington Post* (May 3):D15.

Part IV

Expressive Dimensions of Heterogeneity and Change

José E. Limón

The Folk Performance of *"Chicano"* and the Cultural Limits of Political Ideology

When, at the initiative of a minority of the indigenous petite bourgeoisie, allied with the indigenous masses, the pre-independence movement is launched, the masses have no need to assert or reassert their identity, which they have never confused nor would have known how to confuse with that of the colonial power. This need is felt only by the indigenous petite bourgeoisie which finds itself obliged to take up a position in the struggle which opposes the masses to the colonial power (Cabral 1973: 67).

This paper is intended as a contribution to the scholarly study of Mexican culture in the United States, specifically of the cultural process of group naming. It focuses on the problems inherent in the use of the term "Chicano" within the U.S.-Mexican community, especially in Texas, and offers an explanation of these problems in two stages. First, the conversion of this folk name into a public, ideologically expressive symbol in the 1960s did not achieve its intended purpose of political unification. Second, *in part* this failure may be attributed to the unintentional violation of the community's rules about the socially appropriate use of the term—rules keyed on the community's definition of the performance of the term as belonging to the folklore genres of nicknaming and ethnic slurs. As an anthropological folklorist, my primary intention is to clarify the term's folk status; however, I will also consider critically the relationship between mass cultural forms such as folklore and social movements led by political elites.

THE CONTEMPORARY POLITICAL ORIGINS OF "CHICANO"

Scholarly studies of the Mexican people in the United States often take the reader through a preliminary, sometimes lengthy,
historical review—starting at times with the origins of man,
more often with a somewhat later date such as 1848. I shall not
so indulge. I will trust that the readers of these pages possess the
necessary historical knowledge; if they do not, I refer them to the
recent scholarship (Gómez-Q. and Arroyo 1976). Instead, I shall
focus on the significant sociopolitical events which occurred from
1966 to the present, for it is in this contemporary context that
"Chicano" emerged as a politically expressive symbol.

Among such significant events we may count: (1) the continuing socioeconomic subordination of Mexicans in the U.S. into
the 1960s; (2) the responsive resurgence of a limited but influential trade unionism, like that of César Chávez and the United
Farm Workers; (3) the emergence of an activist social movement
among students of Mexican descent, primarily in colleges and
universities; (4) the institutionalization of the latter into off-campus political efforts in a variety of groups and ideologies; and,
finally, (5) the identification of Mexican immigration as the key
issue of the late 1970s and the future. The last three events are of
particular concern for this essay, though they must always be
viewed against the backdrop of the first two.

Certainly the specific contemporary sociopolitical conversion
of "Chicano" lies in the student movement that eventually identified itself with this name and urged its acceptance. While the student movement appeared on college campuses across the country,
including such unlikely places as Harvard and Yale, its greatest
strength and sharpest articulation occurred in the Southwest.
Much of what I have to say applies to this nationwide phenomenon, but the remarks in this section are based principally on my
personal participation in the student movement at the University
of Texas at Austin from 1966 to 1975 and on the ethnographic
observations of this movement and its expressive culture that I
made later in that period (Limón 1978b).

The student movement on the University of Texas campus
was made up largely of lower middle and middle-class students
from the traditionally Mexican areas of southern Texas. They
came to the campus in increasing numbers in the 1960s, largely as a result of an unprecedented availability of financial aid in

the post-Sputnik era and, to some extent, as a result of University publicity efforts in South Texas. Like so many other major campuses in the 1960s, the University of Texas at Austin was the scene of intense ideological debate and political activism, most of it leftist and critical of the United States' international policies, particularly in Southeast Asia, and of its attitudes toward domestic minorities. Together with this activism on the left, the campus also experienced the politically nationalist presence of the black civil-rights student movement. As relatively well-educated members of an exploited proletariat, some of the students of Mexican descent were particularly and intensely stimulated by this developing activist context, even while their historically based sense of strong ethnic boundaries did not permit close participation or cooperation with Anglo American–dominated movements. In the latter category they included the black student movement, although they felt closer ties to this group.

This sense of group identity became even more pronounced in the years 1965 to 1967, with the appearance of the largely Mexican United Farm Workers' labor movement—manifested most concretely in the agricultural strikes in the Lower Rio Grande Valley of Texas. In support of these strikes union organizers led a march to Austin, the state capital, to petition the governor and legislature for redress of their economic grievances. The march of the farm workers to Austin also served to remind Texas-Mexican University students of their social origins and obligations. During the fall of 1966 many such students became actively involved in campus support committees on behalf of their kinsmen in South Texas. This support effort finally produced a formal association in the spring of 1967. Initially known as the Mexican-American Student Organization (MASO), it later changed its name to the Mexican-American Youth Organization (MAYO) in a show of solidarity with other very similar college and secondary-school groups appearing across Texas—most notably at St. Mary's University in San Antonio and at Texas A&I University in Kingsville.

By 1969–1970, MAYO had defined itself as a campus activist group dedicated to political and cultural work on behalf of the Texas-Mexican community across a broad range of issues. Such work included campaigning on behalf of Mexican Democratic candidates for political office in Austin, agitation for ethnic-studies courses in the University curriculum, statewide coordination with other MAYO chapters on school walkouts, and, of course, continuing support of the farm workers. In the 1970s MAYO, in support of a statewide effort, participated in the formation of the off-campus, quasi-separationist, and ostensibly radical group known as La Raza Unida Party. This political party offered itself, primarily to the Texas-Mexican people, as an electoral alternative to the Democratic and Republican parties. In addition to these political efforts, the student movement also promoted an interest in the identification and revival of what was called "Chicano culture," principally through student art, music, literature, drama, and festival.

The students affected their culture also in a less conscious yet ultimately more socially significant manner. While keeping the name "Mexican-American Youth Organization," they nevertheless began increasingly to use the term "Chicano" as a public label and as a political symbol. Certainly, by the early 1970s, the term was widespread within the student sector as a name for their movement and as their name for the larger population of Mexican descent in the United States. Students spoke of "the Chicano movement"; and movement speeches, tracts, and other forms of public discourse often contained statements like "Chicanos are an exploited people. . . ." and "The Chicano community believes that. . . ." Yet even as the term came to be used publicly as an ethnic-group label by the students, it was taking on additional meanings for them. It became an ideological term, designating individuals who were promoting an intense ethnic nationalism that would lead to a (vaguely defined) political and cultural liberation of the "Chicano" community.

Thus, in making a speech or writing a tract, one could use "Chicano" to refer to all persons of Mexican descent in the United States, or one could contextually specify it to identify an ethnic, nationalist individual or position, one opposed to accommodation and assimilation with United States culture and society. However, as activists seeking the political unity of all U.S. Mexicans, the students in the movement hoped for general acceptance of this term and its ideological content. From my Texas experience, I agree with Villanueva's assessment of the larger national ideological significance and the ultimate ideal intention of "Chicano": "As I see it, *chicano*, as it emerged in the 1960s, is an ideological term of solidarity which ideally involves all Northamericans of Mexican descent" (1978 : 390).

But why was this name selected? Why not another from the myriad of possibilities? The choice appears to have been motivated by a number of considerations. The student movement needed a name that would not compromise its strong sense of ethnic nationalism and its strident and anti–Anglo American stance; hence it rejected any use of the word "American," such as "Mexican-American." On the other hand, as ethnic nationalists the students needed a name that would speak directly to the allegedly peculiar sociocultural character of Mexicans north of the Rio Grande—that would not confuse them with Mexicans in Mexico. This particular distinction was especially necessary because, the students claimed, Mexican nationals considered Mexicans on this side of the river cultural traitors—*pochos*. As a result, terms such as "Mexican" or "*mexicano*" were unacceptable. Finally, from the student perspective, the appropriate name should clearly have its origins within the community, especially within its more proletarian elements such as the farm workers. In that way the name could serve as a linking symbol between a socially marginal student sector and the ultimate social beneficiaries of the former's political, educational, and cultural efforts.

While it is not clear when or by whom the term "Chicano" was first suggested, it is clear that by the late 1960s the word had gained widespread popularity among students and other, non-student activists both as a general term and as a political-cultural symbol. However, if the political unity of the Mexican people in Texas and in the rest of the United States was the ultimate ideal of the student movement, it did not aid the cause in selecting this term.

"CHICANO": THE REJECTION OF A SYMBOL

Almost immediately after its public appearance within the student movement, the term set off controversy and debate within the larger U.S.-Mexican community. The general reaction ranged from indifference to outright rejection and hostility. Initially, the student movement treated this negative reaction with disdain, labeling it the reactionary expression of a few members of the middle and upper classes who were assimilationist and politically right of center. And, to be sure, some such individuals did vociferously reject the term precisely because of its association with militant cultural nationalism. Clearly, however, the mass of the Mexican people in Texas are not assimilationist or rightist, and yet there is growing and compelling evidence that this mass pop-

ulation as well as the general U.S.-Mexican community have rejected the label "Chicano."

Perhaps the most telling evidence of this rejection can be
found in a random survey of Spanish-surnamed individuals conducted by Nicholas Valenzuela (1973) in 1972 in cooperation with
the Center for Communications Research at the University of
Texas at Austin. According to this study, only six percent of the
1,500 persons sampled preferred the term "Chicano" as a self-ref-
erent. This evidence is particularly significant as the sample was
taken in Austin and San Antonio, Texas, both sites of important
Chicano student activist movements. One might expect the six
percent total would include some students, and one might also expect the Mexican public's acceptance of the term would be
greater in these areas as a result of constant student propaganda.
Of equal significance is what proved the most popular selection in this sample: some 43 percent of those surveyed chose
"*mexicano*."

Another survey of 158 Spanish-surnamed persons throughout
the Southwest also revealed a generally low preference for "Chicano" and a decided lack of popularity for the term in Texas (Nostrand 1973). Of the sixty-one persons in Texas who were asked to
choose a label of self-reference in English, only four chose "Chicano." To be sure the inclusion of "Chicano" in a choice of terms
in English is puzzling, as is the survey's obvious bias toward the
middle and upper socioeconomic classes and/or toward informants referred to the investigator by managers of Chambers of
Commerce. Like Nostrand, however, Teske and Nelson (1973)
sampled the middle class in several Texas cities (McAllen, Austin, Waco, and Lubbock) and also detected a low preference for
"Chicano."

It might be argued that the rejection of the term comes primarily from the middle class; and at least some of the evidence I
have cited thus far supports that assertion. Yet it is equally clear
that the term is meeting with widespread rejection from the
more working-class sectors of the community. I can report on interview work carried out by my students at the University of
Texas at San Antonio from 1975 to 1978. Some twenty-five under-
graduates of Mexican descent were asked to obtain cultural data
on six informants each from the San Antonio area. They were in-
structed to select informants of Mexican descent whose income
and occupation identified them as members of the working class.
Most of the informants were unskilled or semi-skilled laborers

(janitors, truck drivers, laundry workers, or housewives with spouses in such occupations).

The interviews were carried out in informal conversations and mostly in Spanish. One question is of particular concern here: "*¿Cómo prefiere que le llamen a usted en términos de su cultura?*" [What do you prefer to be called in terms of your culture?]. The choices were: "*latino*," "*méxico-americano*," "*chicano*," "*mexicano*," "*hispano*," "Mexican-American," "Mexican," "Latin-American," "Spanish," and "American of Mexican descent." All of these names were typed on a large index card and handed to each informant for his perusal. Some 65 percent of the informants selected "*mexicano*" and approximately 15 percent opted for "*méxico-americano*." The remaining 20 percent were divided among the rest, with three write-in votes for "American." Only four percent selected "*chicano*" (Limón 1978a). To this evidence might be added the older findings of Grebler et al. (1970), which indicated a high majority preference for "Mexican" and "*mexicano*" among low-income respondents in Los Angeles and San Antonio—although, admittedly, the research team did not include "*chicano*" in their choices. Nevertheless, it is doubtful that its inclusion would have made a substantial difference. More recently, in a survey conducted in a low-income urban *barrio* in Colorado, Rivera et al. (1978) found a 41 percent preference for "Mexican" or "Mexican-American" and a 19 percent rating for "*chicano*."

Recent ethnographic work in the Texas-Mexican community also attests to the relative unpopularity of the term within the working class. In a very recent monograph on Mexican-Americans in Dallas, Shirley Achor (1978:2) reports:

Certain members of the population, particularly those who are actively engaged in movements for sociopolitical change, emphatically and proudly assert "¡Yo soy chicano!" (I am chicano!). However, many barrio residents dislike this word, some saying it applies only to political activists, and others commenting that it doesn't sound "nice." In ordinary conservation, most barrio members speak of themselves as *mejicanos* or use its English equivalent "Mexicans."

We should clearly note that it is *barrio* residents and not middle- and upper-class assimilationists who "dislike this word" and prefer to be called "*mejicanos*" or "Mexicans." Achor's findings support those of Foley et al. in their ethnography of a poor, rural South Texas town: "The term Mexicano was generally used instead of Mexican-American or Chicano because that was how most brown North Towners referred to themselves" (1978:xii). We should note, however, Arthur Rubel's (1966) differing ethnographic report; he found that poor South Texas–Mexicans used "*chicano*" and "*mexicano*" more or less interchangeably. Yet the bulk of the evidence presented thus far brings this assertion into serious question, particularly in light of Américo Paredes' (1977) recent devastating criticism of Rubel's failure fully to understand the expressive dimensions of the Spanish language in South Texas.

To be sure, there is at least some evidence of a relatively greater popularity of "*chicano*" among younger members of the population, although these findings are all questionable, inconclusive, or not particularly overwhelming. Guticrrez and Hirsch's (1973) Crystal City, Texas, teenagers split almost evenly in their choices of either "*chicano*" (49 percent) or "Mexican-American" (47 percent). The unique political climate of this community should be taken into account in interpreting these results; apart from this consideration, one must also question the procedure of limiting the choice of names to only these two. On the other hand Miller (1976), posing the open-ended choice "The name or label you like most for your group?", found a 25 percent preference for "*chicano*" among high-school sophomores in rural southwest Texas—and, strangely enough, an almost nonexistent preference for "*mexicano*" in communities not fifty miles from the Foley field site in South Texas.

In the same vein Metzgar (1974) found younger people in New Mexico preferred "*chicano*" by a percentage as high as 38 percent, although the majority chose "Spanish-American," "Hispano," or "Mexican." These particular data have to be considered in a special light, however, because of New Mexico's peculiar denial of things Mexican and its apparently still-continuing romance with the Spanish past. Further, Metzgar did not offer his respondents the choice "*mexicano*," although I am not sure it would have made a difference in this particular culture area. A more interesting finding with respect to youth is Stoddard's (1970) assessment of an El Paso, Texas, *barrio*. The young people there preferred "*chicano*" by some 19 percent—but only when used within the in-group. The fact that only eight percent preferred that Anglos refer to them in this way demonstrates the relative unpopularity of the term as a form of public address and its even greater unpopularity when used outside of the group—a point that I will emphasize later.[1]

While things may change in the future, at this moment it would appear that "*chicano*" is a relatively unpopular term of self-reference within the larger Mexican community in the United States and, it would seem, especially in Texas. Or, to be more precise, it is a relatively unpopular term of *public* self-reference. That is, the surveys implicitly asked respondents to select a name they would prefer as an official, institutionally transmitted self-reference; the very use of survey techniques sets up this context. Even participant-observation techniques as practiced by some non-native anthropologists may create this kind of context, in which the informants select and perform according to their definition of a situation which includes the presence of an official, non-native investigator. Performing for the interviewer, as Lee Haring (1972) might agree, may also imply non-performance. By now the reader may suspect he or she is being led toward a re-definition of the cultural status of "*chicano*" which allows for a greater community use of the term in a private—that is, an in-group—context. And, of course, such suspicion would be justified.

THE FOLKLORIC STATUS OF "*CHICANO*"

This redefinition views the term "*chicano*" as folklore and finds that it is precisely its status as such that creates part of the problem with the conversion efforts of the Chicano movement. "*Chicano*" functions as folklore in at least two modes of speech play—one negative and one positive. It is negative when used as an ethnic slur or, to be more precise, an ethnic-class slur. Almost without exception, the scholarship on the name defines it as a derogatory term which refers to the poorer, more recent immigrants from Mexico (Gámio 1930). The corollary often implicit in this notion is that the term is used as such by middle- and upper-class U.S.-born Americans of Mexican descent.

Presumably it is the latter who, in their own in-group settings, perform the slur with reference to others; or perhaps they even employ it directly across group boundaries as a taunt. We are not really sure of this kind of performance, because no ethnographic study I know reports such a use of "*chicano*." Nevertheless, I agree to a point, and I can cite at least one working-class informant's report taken from my own fieldwork in San Antonio, Texas:

Si hombre, estos pinches chicanos vienen, no pagan taxas, y se quedan con los trabajos. [Yeah, man, these damn *chicanos* come, they don't pay taxes, and they get the jobs.]

Or we can turn to a historical text which records a similar use of the term in 1911. The report appeared in *La Crónica* (1911a:3), a Spanish-language newspaper published in Laredo, Texas. I translate:

We have received word from Houston that a tamale business established by *chicanos* sells its tamales in the street yelling "Red Hot Tamales! Red, White, and Green, the Mexican flag in!" If this is true, those disgraceful people are an embarrassment to any flag, and the Mexican people in Houston should take steps to protest . . . this low behavior. Because of the ignorance of such men, our people are held in low esteem and not appreciated in Texas.

The quotation is of double interest. First, it clearly associates "*chicano*" with lower-class people—not necessarily people of low economic status but, as we would say in Spanish, "*gente inculta*" (people without manners). Secondly, the passage makes no distinction between Mexicans in Houston and Mexicans everywhere who, presumably, should be equally proud of their flag. It is the ill-mannered, unpatriotic behavior of some that earns them the slur "*chicano*."

Certainly "*chicano*" also has a folkloric use as a negative intra-ethnic class slur, perhaps similar in tone, performance context, and social objective to terms such as "redneck" and "white trash." Yet, if I may continue with comparative Southern examples, it is at least somewhat more similar to the term "nigger"— and in making this comparison I am arguing for the positive mode in which "*chicano*" is used as folklore.

Like "nigger" in all-black in-group settings, "*chicano*" may express closeness and group solidarity when it is performed within the group. Thus "*chicano*" is a kind of group nickname—still another example of a Mexican-Latino tendency toward systematic, extensive nicknaming. Such names can come from animals, individual physical deformities, or special events in a person's life (Foster 1964).

"*Chicano*" can be produced by still another sociolinguistic nicknaming process. In a fine linguistic study, Tino Villanueva (1978) cites a common explanation of the term's origin. According to this interpretation, pre-Conquest Indians in Mexico referred to themselves as "Meshicas." Upon their arrival the Spanish learned this term but would render the *sh* as *X*, according to their own pronunciation and orthographic systems. Nevertheless, the Indians supposedly continued to say "Meshicas," later "Meshicanos," and still later "*shicanos*." The last term then became the modern "*chicano*." As Villanueva notes, this etymology is widely favored within the Chicano movement, especially by those who emphasize the Indian element in their culture.

Nevertheless, while acknowledging its plausibility as a derivation for "*chicano*," he seems to opt for a nonhistorical and much more probable source for the term. Villanueva considers "*chicano*" the product of a phase in child-language development as exploited in an adult expressive naming practice. That is, the Spanish-speaking child will often mispronounce certain consonants such as *g, j, k, s*, and *x* as *č* (*ch*). The result is a child language with words like "*cocha*" for "*cosa*" (thing) or phrases like "*¿qué pachó?*" for "*¿qué pasó?*" (what happened?). The Spanish-speaking child may also drop syllables while making these *ch* sounds—producing, for example, the name "Cheno" for the formal "Eugenio."

While we can be fairly certain that a child did not produce the word "*chicano*," somewhere an adult probably did by using this child language as an expressive folkloric resource—an intensifying practice common among adult Mexicans and other Latin-American populations. If two close friends meet after a long separation one may greet the other with a lilt in the voice and "*¿Qué pachó?*" instead of the formal "*¿Qué paso?*" (What's going on?) Or, in a better-known example, the city of El Paso is often affectionately referred to as "El Pacho" or "El Pachuco." More to the point of this essay, adults themselves may develop or at least maintain personal nicknames derived from this child language. The aforementioned "Cheno" is one example, as are "Cheli" (Araceli), "Wicho" (Mauricio), "Tencha" (Hortensia), and "Choco" (Socorro). In each case, a shortening and a *ch* sound produce a nickname. In actual performance, an adult usually exploits this child-language resource in this expressive way with an attitude of affection and intimacy. The performance affirms and signals close bonds of kinship or friendship.

It is my contention that "*chicano*" is a very similar kind of nickname, albeit a nickname of a group, produced by this two-fold language practice from the formal name "*mexicano*." That is, in addition to its aforementioned use as a class slur, "*chicano*" may also have the affectively positive dimension of a traditional nicknaming practice.

Something of this usage was captured in 1947 in a short literary sketch by a U.S.-Mexican writer. Mario Suarez (1974 : 96) identified the inhabitants of the Mexican section of Tucson, Arizona as:

Chicanos who raise hell on Saturday night. . . . While the term *chicano* is the short way of saying Mexicano, it is the long way of referring to everybody . . . the assortment of harlequins, bandits, oppressors, oppressed, gentlemen and bums who came from Old Mexico to work on the Southern Pacific, pick cotton, clerk, labor, sing, and go on relief.

The quotation also conveys another important characteristic of the term. Suarez uses the nickname to identify, although not derogatorily, all of those "who came from Old Mexico." As a nickname, "*chicano*" seems to emphasize nationality—a use more evident in an anecdote which appeared in an article entitled "Vicios de la Raza" (Vices of the People). Published in *La Crónica* (1911a : 3) in 1911, the article attacks those Texas-Mexicans who dissociated themselves from their native culture and tried to emulate Anglo-American customs and values (Limón 1977). As a satirical introduction to the anecdote, the author tells of one man who canceled his subscription to the newspaper when he left South Texas—he didn't want his Anglo friends to know he subscribed to Mexican publications. We also learn of some Texas-Mexicans who were asked by their Anglo bosses if they were Mexican and replied, "No, mi Spaniard!" Then there was a local Mexican fellow—a "dark man"—who always began to speak English and smoke big cigars whenever he got drunk. Finally, the author narrates the following joking anecdote (my translation):

We know a *tamalera* who got married in the interior of Texas with a *mister* and since she was a bit ignorant she was not received in Anglo society and had to associate with her own people. One day she was invited to a big *tamaluda*—as a birthday party for a *chicano*, and when presented with her plate of *tamales*, she asked, "¿Qué éste?" "Tamales," they answered. Can you imagine their surprise when they saw this Americanized lady eating her *tamales* husks and all! (Motif J1732 Ignorance of certain foods.)

While the entire jest is a folklore item, I am principally concerned with the use of the name "*chicano*" in an anecdotal, conversational context between the writer and his audience. The author develops a character who has betrayed her culture in a number of ways. In addition to leaving the heavily Mexican border area, she married a *mister*—an Anglo-American—and she pretends not to know Spanish when she says, "*¿Qué éste?*" instead of the correct "*¿Qué es?*" or "*¿Qué es ésto?*" (What is this?). Her ultimate betrayal is, of course, her feigned ignorance of a key food item—*tamales*—especially as she was herself a *tamalera*. She appears an absurd, comical figure in her insistence on eating the *tamales* with husks. Dramatically opposed to her is a group that does value these cultural practices, which is coalesced around the birthday honoree who is identified as a *chicano*. The term is closely associated here with cultural conservatism; as far as I know, this is the earliest recorded use of "*chicano.*"

This rhetorical use of the name to emphasize cultural nationality is also evident in the three verbal interactions given below as examples of what I have observed to be a widespread practice. The first was related to me by Professor Américo Paredes and the other two I observed in the field myself. According to Professor Paredes, in 1925 one of his relatives, a culturally very conservative Texas-Mexican, was visiting with his five-year-old niece and her parents. Her Texas cowgirl outfit prompted her uncle to demand "Where did this *gringa* come from?" Probably scared by the loud tone of his voice, the little girl began to cry and, to pacify her and possibly the parents, the uncle quickly said, "No, no, she is not a *gringa*, she is a *chicanita!*" To correct his own inadvertent cultural error in loosely labeling her a "*gringa*" (even if as a joke) the uncle turned to an expressive resource—"*chicano*"—to correct and balance the error by emphasizing the little girl's *mexicanidad*. Apparently it would not have done simply to say "she is a *mexicana!*" In this informal in-group context "*chicanita*" emphasized her cultural identity.

Such folk uses of the name to offset cultural stress are not confined to the past. While doing fieldwork on another project in the Lower Rio Grande Valley of Texas in 1972, I had the following exchange with an elderly, lower-socioeconomic-status Texas-Mexican informant:

LIMÓN: ¿Y cómo se llamaba su amigo? [And what was your friend's name?]
INFORMANT: Roberto . . . Roberto Davis. . . .
LIMÓN: ¿Es mexicano el? [Is he Mexican?]
INFORMANT: ¡Sí hombre! . . . es chicano. [yes, of course! . . . he is *chicano*.]

In the heavily Mexican Lower Rio Grande Valley one often finds descendants of marriages between early Anglo-American settlers and Mexican women. These individuals, such as Roberto Davis, have non-Hispanic surnames yet are thoroughly border-Mexican in their cultural behavior. My question about this name was taken as an expression of doubt about Davis' cultural identity; and my informant's somewhat emotional reaction and his use of "*chicano*" appeared to be a way of affirming his friend's identity and, by implication, his own. His reaction was particularly intriguing considering the negative views he clearly expressed toward the Chicano movement.

Finally, I relate the following interaction collected in a Mexican working-class bar in San Antonio, Texas, in 1977. The bar is atypical in some respects—principally in being located near a very affluent Anglo-American section of the city. While it caters almost exclusively to Mexican working men from a nearby cement plant, occasionally a few Anglo workers also show up. I was questioning one fifty-year-old Mexican man about the presence of the Anglos; he put his hand on my shoulder and said, "*Sí, sí vienen aquí. . . . pero no te preocupes . . . este lugar es chicano.*" [Yes, yes they come in here. . . . but don't worry . . . this place is *chicano.*]

Again, ambivalence in the cultural definition of a scene seemed to bring forth an expressive affirmation using "*chicano*" as a rhetorical resource. Surprised by his use of the term, I questioned him further, producing this crucial exchange:

LIMÓN: Dígame, ¿porqué usó la palabra "chicano" ahorita? [Tell me, why did you use the term "*chicano*" just now?]

INFORMANT: [Surprised and with some hesitation:] Pos . . . no se . . . tu sabes . . . pa' que supieras que este lugar si es mexicano . . . como que "chicano" lo hace más raza. [Well . . . I don't know . . . you know . . . so that you would know that this place is really Mexican . . . like "*chicano*" makes it more *raza*.]

LIMÓN: ¿Quiere decir usted que. . . . [You mean to say. . . .]

INFORMANT: [Interrupts:] Pero no chicano como dicen esos de ese partido de la raza. [But not *chicano* as it is said by those from the party of la raza.]

LIMÓN: ¿Cómo dice? [How do you mean?]

INFORMANT: Tu sabes . . . no es cosa de política y de andar haciendo *speeches* usando la palabra. . . . yo nomás la uso cada cuando como la usé ahorita. [You know . . . it's not a political thing and for going around making "speeches" with the word. . . . I just use it once in a while like I used it just now.]

This interaction has a number of interesting points. It is clear that *"chicano"* is part of the informant's expressive verbal repertoire and that he uses it on certain occasions. As in the printed anecdotes and in the verbal interactions, this bit of folklore seems to emerge during stress-producing situations to affirm cultural identity. Further, this particular interaction involved a cultural and not a manifestly political use of the term, apparently referring to the Raza Unida Party; the informant insisted on the distinction.

THE SOCIOCULTURAL SIGNIFICANCE OF *"CHICANO"*

Whether as slur or nickname, *"chicano"* is folklore with a socio-psychological significance. Duckert (1973:155) notes, with broad insight, that nicknames (and one would think slurs):

cannot exist in or arise from a vacuum. They are by nature social; they must be shared to endure, and their origin is often communal. Sometimes it is a community of enthusiasm . . . some nicknames originate or are widely used in a community of frustration or despair whether real or fancied.

In recent years greater precision has been introduced into the study of folklore as a social phenomenon, as new perspectives have conceptualized folklore as a set of communicative social art forms best understood in the context of their performance in small groups. One theorist of this new orientation has argued for a rhetorical theory of folklore. For Abrahams (1972), folklore permits social groups to deal with the recurrent anxieties raised by internal and external threatening forces. As a set of traditional expressive items, folklore is continually available to the competent folk performer, who utilizes these highly symbolic forms before a group to mirror, objectify, and, in a psychological sense, control the problems which beset the group. Utilizing the formal esthetic and cognitive features of a ballad or a tale, the performer has the power to move and persuade his audience toward a unified perspective on its problems.

Performers also employ minor genres, such as prayer, spells, charms, taunts, nicknames, and slurs, to reflect and comment upon problems in an esthetically engaging manner. Other minor genres seem to work much more literally, although they too can have a rhetorical function (Abrahams 1968). Some curses and taunts, for example, simply apply culturally or socially charged artistic language to a social problem. One possible rhetorical result is a reduction in the social prominence of the problem. Texas-Mexican children use the well-known taunt *"¡Rinche pinche, cara de chinche!"* (Mean ranger, face of a bug!) not against Texas Rangers, but against other children. Through such structured artistic language the folk performer transfers the opprobrium attached to Texas Rangers onto adversary children, thus reducing their status in the eyes of the audience. Very young children may merely respond to the negative connotations of *"-inche"* sounds in Mexican culture. Taunts such as these, as well as curses, bring a negative control to bear on social problems through the power of metaphorical language. One may also deal with problems by evoking positive forces against them. In Mexican culture, as in many others, threats and obstacles to future goals and ambitions are psychologically countered by evoking the support of supernatural beings, as in the common *"Si Dios quiere"* (If God wills it).

In a similar manner nicknames and slurs may direct culturally charged language against social problems, either by objectifying them and thus rendering them psychologically harmless or by countering them directly through the sheer power of culturally valued names (Jackson 1967). At the simplest level, such names may serve to personalize an otherwise impersonal, threatening environment—as when President Ford insisted on being called "Jerry" even after his inauguration. Nicknames have traditionally permitted groups to handle psychologically the anxiety-producing physical characteristics of other human beings. We are all too familiar with "Fats," "Shorty," and "Slim"; and the Mexican community seems to have an even greater propensity to deal with physical deformities by naming them. Thus we find *"el chueco"* (the bent one) for someone with a spinal defect or *"la ardilla"* (the squirrel) for someone with protruding teeth. Social roles and statuses may also be foregrounded and controlled in this manner. Given the high rate of educational failure in the Mexican *barrios* of the Southwest, a particularly scholarly boy will often be tagged *"el profe"* (the professor).

These sorts of nicknames are shared by groups, but are generally applied to individuals. Social groups can also have nicknames for themselves, which may refer to any of several social categories including ethnicity, occupation, religion, or region. Sometimes these group nicknames may originate within the group ("gyrene" for the Marine Corps or "brother" for blacks) and very often such names are really single-word ethnic slurs borrowed from other groups and inverted in their tone, meaning, and contextual use. Names such as "nigger" and "Meskin," when used within the ethnic group in question, serve these groups by foregrounding and psychologically checking the presence of racism in the environment. By using otherwise racist terms in an interpersonal, sympathetic, and somewhat humorous manner, these groups acknowledge and invert the racist thrust of the slurs, converting them into nicknames that augment group solidarity.

"*Chicano*" represents a more interesting and complicated case, for, as I have suggested, it is both an intra-ethnic class-based slur and a nickname. That class is the major determinant of its definition as a slur seems to be without question. Several commentators have noted its application to recent immigrants from Mexico, but it is usually to poor immigrants that it is applied; and, over the years, the term has been used of all poor Mexicans in the U.S., regardless of their date of arrival. I have provided one textual and one contextual example of such a slur usage. When U.S.-Mexican individuals use the term in this manner, they are also managing a problem in their social environment: either competition from cheap labor in a stagnant capitalist economy or resentment at being reminded of their own originally lower socioeconomic status. In any case, it is clear that negative attitudes can be vented through using "*chicano*" as a caustic slur.

Yet, at the same time, the word's very association with the lower socioeconomic classes may be responsible for its potentially positive meaning in other contexts. In a complex society where acculturation is so closely correlated with class mobility, it is the recent immigrant and the still-poor U.S.-born Mexican who are most likely to conserve the values and practices that define *mexicanidad* in the U.S. In the previously described scenes, those who employ "*chicano*" as an affirmative nickname seem to be bringing the rhetorical value of this social resource to bear on culturally ambivalent situations. "*Chicano*" is the agent for the transference of symbolic power.

For the larger folk group, "*chicano*" can be a name for a political movement and ideology, a class slur, or an affirmative nickname. What it is in any one instance depends chiefly on the context of performance. The available evidence indicates that the

Mexican masses in the U.S. do not use it as a political term—
except to discuss it *as* a term and then, more often than not,
with contempt and rejection. The other two uses occur in actual conversation; they are also older and much more widespread
and, as I have been suggesting, they are folklore with a rhetorical
significance.

Yet, if one folk rhetorical use of "*chicano*" is to affirm cultural
identity, why would such usage not be consonant with its use by
the Chicano movement as a symbol of cultural nationalism? Why
would the general populace reject this ostensibly similar usage?
One partial answer may be, quite simply, that the Chicano movement added political meanings to the term which did not meet
with the approval of the larger community. Such a view would
see this community as essentially conservative politically; in rejecting "*chicano*" they were rejecting seemingly "radical" politics. I think not. If anything is being rejected, it may be a 1960s
counter-cultural political *style*, which involved exaggerated rhetoric, dress, and other personal habits; adventurist confrontation
tactics; etc. Mexican society in the U.S. may be essentially conservative, but the history and contemporary life of this community
seem to testify rather to a remarkable willingness to engage in
mass militant struggles on its own behalf when presented with
politically and culturally meaningful alternatives (Limón 1974;
Nelson-Cisneros 1975; Zamora 1975). I would maintain that the
more important source of disharmony lies, not in differing political attitudes, but rather in the disparate ways of performing "*chicano*" in the activist and the non-university sectors of the total
community. I have already spoken of the latter as "folkloric" in
nature; I would now point to the restricted social character of
folklore.

THE FOLK PERFORMANCE OF "*CHICANO*"

Some time ago Alan Dundes (1964) urged folklorists to pay more
attention to the context in which folklore occurs; he pointed out
that a specific social setting may determine both the form and
the function of folklore. The current and more focused concern
with performance-in-context is likely a result of this early advice,
although contemporary theorists would emphasize another aspect of context: the limits a social group imposes on folkloric
performance.

With some exceptions, it would appear that folklore is largely an in-group phenomenon. Whether defined in terms of ethnicity, age, occupation, or other sociological criteria, a group—or more precisely, its specialized performers—perform their myths, songs, speech, and other folklore for those who share their identity. Of course, one evident exception is the "performance" given the out-group folklorist who is eliciting data, usually from a single performer—obviously a very special, limited case. A far more important divergence from this in-group definition of folklore is that elucidated by Richard Bauman (1972). Some kinds of folklore, he argues persuasively, may be performed across group boundaries and, indeed, differential identity may be the necessary precondition for their performance. In stressing this point, Bauman applies a needed correction to the generally dominant definition of folklore as in-group behavior. Nevertheless, in-group performance does appear to be much more characteristic of folklore than those instances when it is shared with out-groups.

Ben-Amos (1972) takes us a step further by defining the in-group sociologically and by pointing to its limiting qualities. He considers folklore truly folklore when it occurs, not only in an in-group situation, but when a relative few of the in-group members are engaged in face-to-face interaction, constituting what he calls the small group. Folkloric performance is limited to such small in-groups. "In other words," Ben-Amos says:

> for a folklore communication to exist as such, the participants in the small group situation have to belong to the same reference group, one composed of people of the same age or of the same professional, local, religious, or ethnic affiliation . . . folklore is true to its own nature when it takes place within the group itself. In sum, folklore is artistic communication in small groups (1972 : 13).

Small groups can affect folkloric form and function and, indeed, their smallness can be a precondition for the very emergence of folklore—but this very characteristic can also take on a normative, limiting aspect. That is, a group norm may emerge that dictates that folkloric actions can authentically happen *only* in such small in-group contexts; such actions in other contexts may be considered unauthorized and perhaps resented.

I am convinced that such a rule of restriction operates within the larger Texas-Mexican community in regard to the use of "*chicano.*" The term should only be used as a slur or as a nickname in certain specified small-group contexts. To repeat the words of my previously cited informant:

no es cosa de política y de andar haciendo *speeches* usando la palabra. . . . yo nomás la uso cada cuando como la usé ahorita. [it's not a political thing and for going around making "speeches" with the word. . . . I just use it once in a while like I used it just now.]

The way he "used it just now" refers, of course, to a small, in-group, somewhat playful, conversation. Or, as another informant in the same bar expressed it:

Cuando se usa, pos, casi todo el tiempo, la gente esta vacilando. [When it is used, almost all the time, people are (speech) playing.]

As a noncasual utterance with symbolic power, "*chicano*" is governed by restrictive cultural rules for performance. I would agree with Voegelin: "It is surely reasonable to say that non-casual utterances are restricted to particular times. . . . these particular utterances would seem inappropriate at other times and in other places" (1960:61). And, he continues:

When a non-casual utterance . . . —as a rollicking ditty—is sung in the wrong place or by the wrong person, persons-in-the-culture find it shocking or humorous, just as they do when some non-verbal behavior is actualized by the wrong person or in the wrong place. . . . There is wide general agreement among persons-in-the-culture in judging appropriateness of non-casual utterances (ibid.).

It is precisely because they carry rhetorical power that non-casual utterances such as "*chicano*" must be socially restricted. The restricted in-group nature of nicknames in particular, and their use as boundary markers, have been well documented for other societies (Pitt-Rivers 1960; Antoun 1968; Dorian 1970; Freeman 1970). And we can adduce evidence from Greater Mexican tradition. What Foster (1964) says about nicknames in a Mexican peasant village may also apply to "*chicano*." Nicknames, he tells us:

constitute a sensitive area of culture. Almost always when I raise the question friends smile guiltily, cover their mouths with their hands, and then, with a little urging, usually launch forth with the pleasure that comes from discussing forbidden subjects. Nicknames are called *apodos* or *mal nombres*, "bad names," potentially damaging, whose danger can be neutralized *only in specific context* (ibid.:119) [emphasis mine].

In such specific contexts:

Nicknames are manipulative, but rather than countering, they accentu-
ate the relationship as it is perceived to be; more intimacy if intimate,
enmity or contempt if distant (ibid.).

The use of nicknames is also limited by sex:

Nicknames, it may be noted, are largely limited to males. . . . Perhaps,
this fact is subconscious recognition of the danger inherent in the use of
nicknames, of the potential enmities that may result from careless use of
aggressive behavior that is seen as appropriate to the male rather than
the female role (ibid.:121).

Like other social groups (see Antoun 1968), the greater Mexican community in the U.S. shares this attitude to some degree—
particularly in the case of "*chicano.*" This might explain why
Mexican women demonstrate a decidedly greater aversion to the
term (Metzgar 1974; Miller 1976; Limón 1978a). If these studies'
findings are accurate, they might suggest a reflective and critical
pause to those who are trying to construct a feminist politics for
the community around the public symbol "*chicana.*"

It is my contention, then, that the folk performance of "*chicano*" is governed by certain cultural rules of restriction. *Ideally*,
an appropriate performance occurs in a small, largely male,
Spanish-language-dominant in-group, with some ludic dimensions. This performance context stands in sharp contrast to the
public, inter-group, English-language, seriously discursive settings in which the term is used ideologically. In part the documented rejection of the term by the larger Texas-Mexican
community may be fundamentally a rejection of a performance
context it judges inappropriate for this essentially folkloric term.

THE CULTURAL LIMITS OF POLITICAL IDEOLOGY

Generally, studies of the relationship of folklore and social movements tend to focus on major genres such as folksong and tale,
and they also tend to emphasize the uses to which the folklore is
put by the movement in question. That is, not much is said about
minor genres or about the attitudes of the folk who are the source
of these materials (Dorson 1966; Kamenetsky 1972, 1977; Oinas
1975). In the present study, I have addressed both of the latter
concerns, giving considerable emphasis to the disharmony created by an appropriation of folk materials. As, again, with folklore study in general, analyses of folklore and social movements

also emphasize the folklore text and its thematic content, noting how these are sometimes distorted for political ends. I have pointed out here how a folklore "text"—a single instance of folk speech—may be perfectly preserved by a movement which at the same time distorts its performance context. In this case, the "incorrect" performance context hindered the conversion of the folklore into a successful political ideology—at least into an ideology that would resonate among the Mexican masses beyond the student sector. However, the conversion was of considerable service to the latter.

When Texas-Mexican students came to the University of Texas at Austin in the 1960s, many experienced a sense of social dislocation which stemmed from two related sources. First, from their predominantly working-class origins in Mexican South Texas, they entered a middle- and upper-class, Anglo-dominated academic ambience. Second, as they entered this very different scene, they witnessed a leftist and ethnic-nationalist criticism of the Anglo-American authority many of them had secretly resented but had never thought to criticize openly. The arrival of the farm workers in Austin dramatized all of these concerns even while the sight reminded the students of their own sociocultural origins.

All of these forces set the student movement in motion and initiated a search for a new ideology. In its search the movement could have turned to its own native political tradition—to the Mexican social organizations already working on behalf of the community such as the League of United Latin-American Citizens (LULAC) or the American G.I. Forum. However, these were contemptuously rejected for their accommodationist attitude toward U.S. politics and culture. A new cultural politics was needed, and this was quickly born and expressed in the rhetorical symbol appropriated from folk tradition—"Chicano."

"It is a loss of orientation," Clifford Geertz tells us, "that most directly gives rise to ideological activity, an inability, for lack of usable models, to comprehend the universe of civic rights and responsibilities in which one finds oneself located" (1973:219). It is at such times, "when neither a society's most general cultural orientations nor its most down to earth 'pragmatic' ones suffice any longer to provide an adequate image of political processes that ideologies begin to become crucial as sources of sociopolitical meanings and attitudes" (ibid.).

Such ideologies, however are rarely set forth in bloodless, discursive modes:

> it is, in turn, the attempt of ideologies to render otherwise incomprehensible social situations meaningful, to so construe them as to make it possible to act purposefully within them, that accounts both for the ideologies' highly figurative nature and for the intensity with which, once accepted, they are held (ibid.: 220).

Ultimately, "the function of ideology is to make an autonomous politics possible by providing the authoritative concepts that render it meaningful, the suasive images by means of which it can be sensibly grasped" (ibid.: 218).

In the 1960s and into the 1970s, "Chicano" was the organizing principle behind a number of ways of talking, acting, and performing. It became a suasive image and authoritative ideological concept which did enjoy some large measure of success. It generated solidarity and a new vision of political autonomy *on behalf of* the Mexican people, but it did both these things largely *for* student and student-related activists. Its persuasive impact beyond the university student community has been limited to the youthful sectors of the population, and even here the results are quite mixed and not overwhelming. Ironically, the other large receptive audience for the term has been the Anglo-American world—its government, educational circles, and mass media. All of them make free use of this important bit of folk culture transmitted to them by an insistent, and, perhaps at times insensitive, student movement. But the final irony is that which I have elaborated in this paper. As an ideological symbol, "Chicano" does not appear to have exerted much suasive power over the larger community for, as Geertz (1973) has also noted, cultural ideologies formulated by nationalist intellectuals sometimes misfire and fail to take hold among those whose unity and support is sought. In his essay he discusses one such failure in Indonesia and, in the present study, I have analyzed the causes of another within an ethnic group in the United States.

If I am correct in this analysis, then perhaps the time has come for a critical assessment of the Chicano movement's appropriation of this folk name and, by implication, of its free use of other folk names—"*raza*," "*barrio*"—and other folkloric genres such as food, music, and festival. The folk may not always be happy with what youthful, student, political people do with their expressive culture; and those who would use folklore and other aspects of culture should pay attention not only to textual accuracy but to such things as context, performance rules, and the folk's attitudes toward its own folklore.

Indeed, and ironically enough, it is quite possible that *because* of the Chicano movement's public appropriation of the term, the larger community may use "*chicano*" less and less in the expressive interactions of everyday group life. I have already detected such a reluctance as well as an as yet unfocused tendency to generate expressive alternatives such as "*chicas-patas*" (those with small feet) that have the same folkloric definition and intent as "*chicano*." The process is reminiscent of Halliday's (1976:582) anti-languages, which are:

used for contest and display, with consequent foregrounding of interpersonal elements of all kinds. At the same time, the speakers of an antilanguage are constantly striving to maintain a counter-reality that is under pressure from the established world. This is why the language is constantly renewing itself—to sustain the vitality that it needs if it is to function at all.

If this new usage takes hold, it would be an interesting double inversion for, as Américo Paredes (1961) tells us, "*chicas-patas*" originally and ironically referred to the allegedly big-footed (*patón*) Anglo-American. Over time "*chicas-patas*" has been redefined in jocular interactions as another nickname for *mexicanos* (Paredes 1978:84–85). It is possible that with the institutionalization of "Chicano," the larger community may be intensifying "*chicas-patas*" as an alternative, affectionate, folkloric way to refer to themselves. In the sometimes tense relationship between political elites and the larger community, the latter may yet have the last folkloric word.

CULTURE, NEW POLITICS, AND OLD NAMES

It has become both an anthropological and popular commonplace of our time to say that cultures are not static, that they change. Yes, of course. Yet, on the other hand, some parts of them remain stable, constant, and persistent even while there is change. The question of maintenance and change in ethnic cultures embedded within complex societies is of importance to all, but perhaps personally more so to the politically engaged intelligentsia from these ethnic societies. There are more than enough forces inducing, indeed forcing, culture change in the world today; the participation of an ethnic intelligentsia in these processes should be an object of particular moral scrutiny. To the extent that this group has anything to say, should a culture change? What should change? Is change of political or moral importance? These are thorny matters and one hopes for at least deliberate and critical reflection. Writing about his own passage from his native ethnic society through a university Ph.D., Richard Rodríguez concludes:

But perhaps now the time has come when questions about the cultural costs of education ought to be delayed no longer. Those of us who have been scholarship boys know in our bones that our education has exacted a large price in exchange for the large benefits it has conferred upon us. And what is sadder to consider, after we have paid that price, we go home and casually change the cultures that nourished us. My parents today understand how they are "Chicanos" in a large and impersonal sense. The gains from such knowledge are clear. But so, too, are the reasons for regret (1974–1975:28).

While Rodríguez's parents may "understand" they are "Chicano" in some large and impersonal sense, I am not persuaded that they, their generation, and others of Mexican descent beyond the universities accept the term in the way that it has been put to them contextually by those within academe, or that their "gains" are so clear. Rodríguez's parents and others—the *mexicano* janitors who smile in quiet wonder, pride, and amusement at the *Chicano* students in the halls at the University of Texas—these ordinary individuals have their own view of culture and their own uses for "*chicano.*" To build a politics mindful of and in sensitive and critical dialogue with that society and culture is the task that faces those who would labor actively on behalf of the community.

Some members of the native intelligentsia have made a decision on this question of names, opting to follow the community's apparent preference. Some older leadership elements of the student movement are returning to the terms "*mexicano*" or "Mexican" as names for use in public discourse, even while reserving "Chicano" for in-group use (Gómez-Q. 1978). From an anthropological point of view one can only note that such a selection is consonant with wider community practice. In Texas, as well as in other areas such as Los Angeles and Colorado, men and women of

222 / José E. Limón

Mexican descent prefer to identify themselves publicly as "*mex-icanos*," "Mexican-Americans," or, finally, "Mexicans."

A politics constructed around a common public name might enjoy greater success with those members of the community who are now citizens of the United States. It also has additional importance viewed against the background of the current massive immigration from Mexico—workers who also call themselves "*mexicanos*" and "*mexicanas*." A thoughtful former Chicano student leader, now an activist intellectual and Raza Unida Party worker in Texas, has noted the dual thrust of this new cultural politics. I conclude with a quote from him. "The term Chicano," Tatcho Mindiola tells us:

has proven to be exclusive rather than inclusive since by definition it excludes *mexicanos* who were born in Mexico. Thus it is argued that *chicano* is a word which works against solidarity among all Mexicans. The use of the word Mexican or *mexicano* has only recently begun but a debate is sure to follow if its usage continues to gain acceptance. . . . Why continue to emphasize differences if solidarity with all Mexicans is one of the goals? It seems that we have indeed gone the full circle. Going through Latin American, Spanish American, Mexican American, and *chicano* phases we wind up where we started—*mexicanos*. Proclaim it (1977:10).

NOTE

This study was written during my tenure as an Institute of American Cultures postdoctoral fellow with the Department of Anthropology and the Chicano Studies Center at U.C.L.A., 1978–1979. My special thanks to Juan Gómez-Q., director of the Center. This essay is dedicated to my mentor, Don Américo Paredes.

1. While Texans of Mexican descent have used the name "*tejano*" as a public referent, I have not taken it into account here for three reasons: (1) it appears to be a largely historical usage; (2) it has been used primarily in limited conversational situations, i.e., to distinguish between a *mexicano* from Mexico and one from Texas; and (3) it was not offered as a choice in the various surveys cited in this study.

BIBLIOGRAPHY

Abrahams, Roger D. 1968. A rhetoric of everyday life: Traditional conversational genres. *Southern Folklore Quarterly* 32:44–59.

————. 1972. Personal power and social restraint in the definition of folklore. In *Toward new perspectives in folklore*. Américo Paredes and Richard Bauman, eds. Austin: University of Texas Press.

Achor, Shirley. 1978. *Mexican Americans in a Dallas barrio*. Tucson: University of Arizona Press.

Antoun, R. T. 1968. On the significance of names in an Arab village. *Ethnology* 7 : 158–170.

Bauman, Richard. 1972. Differential identity and the social base of folklore. In *Toward new perspectives in folklore*. Américo Paredes and Richard Bauman, eds. Austin: University of Texas Press.

Ben-Amos, Dan. 1972. Toward a definition of folklore in context. In *Toward new perspectives in folklore*. Américo Paredes and Richard Bauman, eds. Austin: University of Texas Press.

Cabral, Amilcar. 1973. Identity and dignity. In *Return to the source: Selected speeches of Amilcar Cabral*. Africa Information Service, ed. New York: Monthly Review Press.

La Crónica. 1911a. Vicios de la raza. Anonymous. July 27, p. 3.

————. 1911b. Hot tamales! Anonymous. December 14, p. 1.

Dorian, Nancy C. 1970. A substitute name system in the Scottish Highlands. *American Anthropologist* 72 : 303–319.

Dorson, Richard M. 1966. The question of folklore in a new nation. *Journal of the Folklore Institute* 3 : 277–298.

Duckert, Audrey. 1973. Place nicknames. *Names* 21 : 153–160.

Dundes, Alan. 1964. Texture, text, and context. *Southern Folklore Quarterly* 28 : 251–265.

Foley, Douglas, Clarice Mota, Donald Post, and Ignacio Lozano. 1978. *From peones to políticos: Ethnic relations in a South Texas town, 1900–1977*. Monograph no. 3. Austin: University of Texas Center for Mexican-American Studies.

Foster, George. 1964. Speech forms and perception of social distance in a Spanish-speaking Mexican village. *Southwestern Journal of Anthropology* 20 : 107–122.

Freeman, S. T. 1970. *Neighbors: The social contract in a Castilian hamlet*. Chicago: University of Chicago Press.

Gámio, Manuel. 1930. *Mexican immigration to the United States*. Chicago: University of Chicago Press.

Geertz, Clifford. 1973. Ideology as a cultural system. In *The interpretation of cultures: Selected essays*. New York: Basic Books.

Gómez-Q., Juan, and Luis L. Arroyo. 1976. On the state of Chicano history: Observations on its development, interpretation, and theory, 1970–1974. *Western Historical Quarterly* 7 : 156–185.

————. 1978. *On culture*. Los Angeles: Aztlán Publications.

Grebler, Leo, Joan Moore, and Ralph Guzman. 1970. *The Mexican American people: The nation's second largest minority*. New York: The Free Press.

Gutierrez, Armando, and Herbert Hirsch. 1973. The militant challenge to the American ethos: "Chicanos" and "Mexican Americans." *Social Science Quarterly* 53:830–845.

Halliday, M. A. K. 1976. Anti-languages. *American Anthropologist* 78: 570–584.

Haring, Lee. 1972. Performing for the interviewer: A study of the structure of context. *Southern Folklore Quarterly* 36:383–398.

Jackson, Bruce. 1967. Prison nicknames. *Western Folklore* 26:48–54.

Kamenetsky, Christa. 1972. Folklore as a political tool in Nazi Germany. *Journal of American Folklore* 85:221–235.

———. 1977. Folktale and ideology in the Third Reich. *Journal of American Folklore* 90:168–178.

Limón, José E. 1974. El Primer Congreso Mexicanista de 1911: A precursor to contemporary Chicanismo. *Aztlán* 5:85–117.

———. 1977. *Agringado* joking in Texas-Mexican society: Folklore and differential identity. *New Scholar* 6:33–50.

———. 1978a. Interview reports by students in "Bicultural-Bilingual Studies 3023 and 5023," 1975–1978.

———. 1978b. The expressive culture of a Chicano student group at the University of Texas at Austin, 1967–1975. Ph.D. dissertation, University of Texas at Austin.

Metzgar, Joseph V. 1974. Ethnic sensitivity of Spanish New Mexicans. *New Mexico Historical Review* 49:49–73.

Miller, Michael V. 1976. Mexican Americans, Chicanos, and others: Ethnic identification and selected social attributes of rural Texas youth. *Rural Sociology* 41:234–247.

Mindiola, Tatcho, Jr. 1977. Mexicanos: To be or not to be. *El Mirlo canta de Noticatlan: Carta sobre estudios chicanos de UCLA* 7/8:1 ff.

Nelson-Cisneros, Victor B. 1975. La Clase trabajadora en Tejas 1920–1940. *Aztlán* 5:239–266.

Nostrand, Richard L. 1973. "Mexican American" and "Chicano": Emerging terms for a people coming of age. *Pacific Historical Review* 42:389–406.

Oinas, Felix, ed. 1975. Special issue on folklore, politics, and nationalism. *Journal of the Folklore Institute* 12:2 & 3.

Paredes, Américo. 1961. On "Gringo," "Greaser," and other neighborly names. In *Singers and storytellers*. Mody Boatright, Wilson Hudson, and Allen Maxwell, eds. Dallas: SMU Press.

———. 1977. On ethnographic work among minority groups: A folklorist's perspective. *New Scholar* 6:1–32.

———. 1978. The problem of identity in a changing culture: Popular expressions of culture conflict along the Lower Rio Grande border. In *Views across the border: The United States and Mexico*. Stanley Ross, ed. Albuquerque: University of New Mexico Press.

Pitt-Rivers, J. 1960. *The people of the Sierra*. Chicago: University of Chicago Press.

Rivera, George, Jr., Aileen Lucero, and Edward Salazar. 1978. Curanderismo in a Chicano barrio: A study of *envidia* and *susto*. *The Eastern Anthropologist* 31 : 333–339,

Rodríguez, Richard. 1974–1975. The new American scholarship boy. *The American Scholar* 44 : 15–28.

Rubel, Arthur. 1966. *Across the tracks: Mexican Americans in a Texas city*. Austin: University of Texas Press.

Stoddard, Ellwyn R. 1970. Ethnic identity of urban Mexican American youth. Paper presented at the Southwestern Sociological Association meetings. Dallas, Texas.

Suarez, Mario. 1974. El hoyo. In *Mexican American authors*. Américo Paredes and Raymund Paredes, eds. New York: Houghton Mifflin.

Teske, Raymond, and Bardin Nelson. 1973. Response to terminology among middle class Mexican Americans. Unpublished MS.

Valenzuela, Nicholas. 1973. Media habits and attitudes of Mexican Americans. *Report from the Center for Communication Research*. Austin: The University of Texas at Austin.

Villanueva, Tino. 1978. Sobre el termino "Chicano." *Cuadernos Hispanoamericanos* 336 : 387–410.

Voegelin, C. F. 1960. Casual and non-casual utterances within unified structures. In *Style in language*. Thomas Sebeok, ed. Cambridge: MIT Press.

Zamora, Emilio. 1975. Chicano socialist labor activity in Texas, 1900–1920. *Aztlán* 5 : 221–238.

Thomas A. Green

Folklore and Ethnic Identity in Tigua Nativism

The proposition that folklore educates as well as entertains, embodies wisdom along with wit, has become axiomatic in the discipline of folkloristics. Many scholars have explored the polyvocal character of traditional art. As Américo Paredes writes, for example, concerning the use of humor to articulate strife between the Mexican-American and the Anglo, "jests are not after all intrusions into a session of stories expressing intercultural conflict; they also are expressions of the same kind of conflict" (1968:113).

This variety of conflict and these strategies for its resolution are common where cultures collide. This essay examines the similar techniques for coping with intercultural dissension employed in one such context: the Tigua nativistic movement. The study attempts to integrate, in a single case study, the phenomena of folklore, ethnic identity, and nativism—all widely studied in their own terms or in terms of limited interrelationships, but seldom viewed as aspects of a unified whole.[1]

CULTURAL CONTINUITY

The modern Tigua of Ysleta del Sur are the descendants of a party of Tiwa, Piro, Manso, and Towa Indians who accompanied Spanish refugees fleeing the Pueblo Revolt of 1680 (Hackett and Shelby 1942:200–202). Since the majority of this transplanted group were from the Tiwa Pueblo of Isleta they adopted the designation "Tigua" (from the Spanish spelling of their name). They

further distinguished their settlement a few miles east of contemporary El Paso, Texas, from their ancestral home far to the
north near Albuquerque, New Mexico, by christening the village
Ysleta del Sur (Isleta of the South). Records from the Spanish
and Mexican periods attest to the stability of this settlement and
to the group's adherence to an indigenous lifestyle. A land grant
awarded to the group by Charles V of Spain further confirmed
their status. This "four league grant" encompassed thirty-six
square miles around their mission (the Misión de Corpus Christi
de los Tihuas de Ysleta).

In 1864 Abraham Lincoln, in accordance with the Treaty of
Guadalupe Hidalgo (which established that land grants awarded
to the Pueblos by the Spanish crown entitled them to retain possession of their land), assigned reservations to the other Pueblos.
But, due to their residence in the Confederate state of Texas, the
Tigua of Ysleta did not receive protected status at that time. In
fact, they remained in what may be termed a legalistic limbo until well into the twentieth century—despite the fact that "in 1849,
while situated in the disputed area [encompassed by the terms of
the Treaty of Guadalupe Hidalgo] the Ysleta Pueblo in Texas was
inventoried as one of the Pueblo Tribes under Federal control and
jurisdiction" (Minter 1969 : 38–39). This historical accident, as we
shall presently see, proved a turning point in Tigua history and
provided impetus for the group's nativistic revival and the rejuv-
enation of Tigua folklore.

From this point forward, in spite of occasional notice taken of
the Tigua (usually tinged with obituary-mongering) by anthropologists (e.g., Fewkes 1902), it was presumed that they had simply
ceased to exist, or had been "lost," in the words of Steiner (1972).
Fortunately, the Pueblos of Ysleta del Sur did not read the anthropological literature. Despite increasing pressures from the
non-Indian cultures which hemmed them in, they refused to re-
linquish their traditions.

Although my discussion of the use of folklore in the service of
ethnicity and nativism must necessarily be selective, a brief survey of the social and cultural indices of Tigua allegiance to their
traditional lifestyle is needed to provide a context for analysis

Items of material culture represent perhaps the most tangi-
ble evidence of the persistence of the Pueblo heritage. Well into
the 1970s many of the conservative Tiguas resided in characteristic Southwestern adobe dwellings. To observers familiar with

both villages, the modest single-storied houses (many of them containing no more than two or three rooms) seen at Ysleta del Sur are not unlike those at Isleta, New Mexico. The typical *horno*, a beehive-shaped adobe oven borrowed from the Spanish by the Pueblos, continues to be employed for baking by many Tiguas. Most traditional material-art forms, however, did not survive into the twentieth century.

Most of the past survived in political structure. The Tigua preserved essentially the same form of native government that they brought with them in the 1680s—generally the system instituted under Spanish control in the seventeenth century. Tribal officials include: a governor, the liaison between the people of the pueblo and the civil government; a lieutenant governor, the official who assumes the governor's duties in his absence; an *algua-cil*, who enforces the pueblo's legal codes; and *mayor domos*, men who originally served as irrigation-ditch superintendents, but who are now responsible for the organization of Ysleta del Sur's central religious event, the Fiesta de San Antonio. The modifications the Tiguas made in the system imposed by the Spanish demonstrate a resolute Pueblo character, gravitating ever further away from Catholicism and Euro-American governmental systems. For example, the two Spanish-created offices most intimately associated with the Church, the *sacristan* (priest's assistant) and the *fiscales* (supervisors of mission discipline), had disappeared by at least 1895 (Fewkes 1902:62–64). Moreover, these two officials, unlike other native officers, are never mentioned in the group's folk history. The remaining members of Tigua village government are the *cacique* and the war captain. The *cacique* fills an indigenous office; he acts in Ysleta as tribal patriarch and supreme religious authority. The war captain and his assistants were originally designated by the Spanish to lead the Pueblo militia, but are now ceremonial authorities second only to the *cacique*, entrusted with guarding the village's ritual paraphernalia.

OFFICIAL RECOGNITION

This study focuses most intently on Tigua history from the mid-1950s to 1975, a period which saw a cultural revival among the people of Ysleta del Sur and the granting of "legitimacy," as defined by various governmental agencies, to the Tiguas. Until the

Tigua began this concerted effort for cultural revival and moved for legal recognition as a tribal entity, thus inviting the interest of the Texas Commission for Indian Affairs (the agency invested with the supervision of the state's Native-American population), they could have been described as marginal citizens of El Paso. Although they had the option of joining that city's labor force while still maintaining their ties to their traditional ceremonial life and native political systems, that continued allegiance frequently prevented them from establishing viable relationships with "acceptable" (i.e., mainstream) religious or governmental systems. Euro-American religious systems characteristically demanded the Tigua give up his traditional beliefs and ceremonies in order to gain full status. Similarly, the external government required that native customs and government be subjugated to its authority. The obvious course for a Tigua who wished to retain his sense of ethnic identity was to enter into the non-Indian sphere on an attenuated, primarily economic, basis. This strategy necessarily prevented the full participation in civil government and in social and religious life which is essential to produce a sense of citizenship and all that notion entails. Many of Tigua ancestry chose the alternative of severing all but the most intimate kinship ties to lead a mainstream existence.

Just as the Pueblo residents of Ysleta del Sur had often been deprived of the social involvement and sense of identity enjoyed by full-fledged citizens, they were also deprived of their territorial rights. Oral tradition among the modern Tiguas maintains that they lost their lands to the city.

This tradition among the Indians appears to derive from the fact [that] the Texas State Legislature in 1871 enacted a law incorporating the Pueblo area into the city of Ysleta and giving such corporation the authority to dispose of the land to actual or intended settlers. Two years later this law appears to have been recognized [as] unconstitutional under the Texas Constitution, as it was repealed, however, in the meantime the Indian natives had been dispossessed of their Pueblo lands [granted by Spain.] (Texas Commission for Indian Affairs 1970: 2–3).

Almost a century later, during the 1950s and early 1960s the Tigua were subjected to increasing external pressure by the civil government of El Paso.

On March 15, 1955, [Ysleta del Sur] was annexed by the City of El Paso. These people [the Tiguas] suddenly became subjected to property taxes which amounted to over $100 a year per family, yet their average income per family unit was under $400. They soon faced institution of foreclosure proceedings on their property by the local taxing authorities (Minter 1969:30).

In response to this overt threat to their remaining land rights, the Tigua began a legal battle which culminated in their official recognition as a legitimate Native-American tribe entitled to protection by the federal government and by the state of Texas. While the case itself drew on traditional materials as evidence, and to a certain extent created a sense of unity among the Indian residents of Ysleta del Sur, the reemphasis on Pueblo traditions that followed is of more central concern to the present discussion. Folklore was revitalized and reevaluated at this time due to the fact that the Tigua perceived the annexation as a threat to their cultural integrity and to their right to pursue a traditional and satisfying way of life.

NATIVISTIC MOVEMENTS

A nativistic movement, as Ralph Linton first defined this method of cultural reorganization, is "any conscious, organized attempt on the part of a society's members to revive or perpetuate selected aspects of its culture" (1943:230). Functionally, nativism is a complex of emergency strategies which operate to preserve cultural integrity in the face of an external threat. It emphasizes, in common with other movements of social reorganization, renewal through rejection of social, political, economic, and religious systems that have not worked or that have proved inaccessible to the movement's members.

Such evidence for the inefficacy of established systems comes from rethinking the relationship between the supposedly superior outsiders and the nativistic group. That is, the group must recognize the presence of dominant others capable of undermining its continued integrity, and it must self-consciously redefine its traditional lifestyle as being superior to that of its cultural enemy. Although the complex of reformative strategies we categorize as nativism is not the only means to cope with this subordinated sociocultural situation, only when such a perspective takes hold can nativistic strategies be formulated.

The actuation of nativistic strategies, then, requires identification of one's community as an esoteric group. This demands the inculcation of a concept of its own cultural superiority within the threatened group, which becomes the rationale for building a new vision of itself and society based on traditional native terms. Although students of such phenomena have argued that nativism is directed toward salvaging only selected aspects of culture (cf. Linton 1943), the leaders of these movements tend to argue for their group's monolithic superiority, if only to strengthen their rhetorical stances. If this rhetoric fails, any attempt at social reorganization based on traditional models will also fail.

Arguments for the superiority of a traditional lifestyle to assimilation are usually couched in traditional forms—in those expressions which Burridge calls the "cultural idiom" (1969:30–32). The traditional verbal arts, as Roger Abrahams notes, may be "often primary channels for the expression and enactment of values (especially the ideals) which a group seeks to claim for itself" (forthcoming: 2) under optimal circumstances—i.e., when the life of the group maintains the order and predictability necessary for the normal range of social variation. When the group perceives a massive threat to its integrity, however, its lore may become a means not only of articulating "selfness" but of preserving life itself—at least cultural life. Abrahams goes to the heart of the matter when he writes: "When confusions become . . . profound, such as when a culture is politically and economically dominated by another and their entire world order thus placed in jeopardy, it should come as little surprise that again the group will go to their performers, to their reembodiers of experience, demanding that they search their repertoire for a means to reorganize and revitalize" (n.d.:23–24).

The group uses folklore to deal with domination as well. As a preliminary step to resisting subjugation it employs exoteric strategies. It can invoke its traditions to establish the existence of social and philosophical boundaries between itself and the dominant group and, additionally, to limit its membership so that it can reorganize itself in what it considers traditionally relevant terms.

Thus, in the service of nativism, Tigua folklore embodies notions of "what we are" and "what they are," of "how they see us" and "how we should be seen." It can accomplish these ends, and even fling insults in the teeth of the dominators, by exploiting that quality of folklore that allows it to be both entertaining play and deadly serious work, often in the same performance.

FOLK HISTORY AMONG THE TIGUA

The customary account of the Tigua's arrival in Ysleta associates them with the Spaniards who fled to Texas after the Pueblo Revolt of 1680. In a period when the group is articulating its superiority to and its separateness from Euro-American society, however, such an explanation is inconsistent with the Tigua's favored self-image. The Tigua have an alternative legend that nativists draw upon, one which both refutes the customary account of their migration and turns stigma into triumph.

Such utilization of folk history is far from uncommon during periods of nativistic activity. A society which turns to traditional models to reorganize must necessarily coordinate its beliefs about its history with its contemporary situation. For such movements to come into existence the people must believe in their superior cultural flexibility or strength, relative deprivation, and limited access to a desired lifestyle. And they need a special perception of history because, as Charles Hudson (1966:54) points out, a "society's belief system articulates not only with the present of a society . . . but also . . . with the society's folk history. One could even go a step further and say that a people's belief system also articulates with their perception of the future, and 'nativistic' movements should perhaps be understood in this light." Therefore, any movement for social reorganization must incorporate a strong, purposive sense of history into its ideology. A view of present conditions motivates reorganization; a view of the past provides traditional explanations for the present circumstances as well as traditional patterns for reorganization. A view of the future as bringing either a new order (a return to the "Golden Age") or the continued destruction of the group's social and cultural integrity is equally necessary for the formulation of nativistic strategies.

In pluralistic societies, where needs and the ability to satisfy them differ greatly, the "same" historical events may be explained in significantly different ways. The hypothesis that "folk history is refracted into opposed versions in ways that are governed by critical features of social structure" (Hudson 1966:61) is borne out in Tigua legends, for the areas of Tigua life that produce the most intense social conflict are those that provide the themes for their historical narratives.

Among the Tigua, as among many groups, folk history is exegetical; it attempts to explain ongoing circumstances in terms of past occurrences and, thus, affects present behavior (cf. Hudson 1966:54; Sturtevant 1966:22). Nativism demands a firm delineation of the boundaries between groups in confrontation and of their relationships to each other—and folk history has been described as an instrument that "sets down and defines relationships between groups" (Cunnison 1951:25). Consequently, folk history can explain the existence of social boundaries as well as provide a device for creating them.

Folk history, due to its explanatory and rhetorical capacities, is especially suited to the articulation of social relationships. Exoterically, it explains the motivations of contemporary social systems (especially of those which threaten the nativistic group) and, esoterically, it provides the foundations for creating an ethnic group—which, as Barth (1969:10) notes, is simply a category of "ascription and identification by the actors themselves"—by embodying the positive self-image necessary for the pursuit of nativistic goals. I will illustrate these arguments with some examples of contemporary Tigua legend.

At one point during my fieldwork among the Tigua I witnessed a heated discussion between one of my informants from Ysleta del Sur and a resident of Isleta del Norte. The latter taunted my informant with a reference to the Tiguas' alleged loyalty to the Spanish during the Pueblo Revolt. My informant retorted:

> People say that the Tigua ran away with the Spanish after the fight over there in New Mexico [Pueblo Revolt of 1680], but, you see, that is not true. They [the Tigua] got here long time before. There, uh, was Indians here already. There are old pueblos in the sandhills and level places where they would plant at Hueco [area near modern Ysleta]. That's why the Spanish people don't stop here. That's why they move down to Juarez to stay. They are afraid to [of] the Tigua.
>
> The first people came a long time ago. They followed Coronado. They follow Coronado to kill him.
>
> Coronado came to New Mexico to take the things the Indians had, to kill the people, even the womens and the little babies, but he wore that armor, and the people couldn't kill him with their arrows, you see. He wore the gold he took from the Indians here on his arms and around his neck, you see, and he wore a crown made out of gold on his head, *una corona*, and that is how he got his name of Coronado ["the crowned one"], from that *corona*, you see.
>
> So, these Tigua people got the idea to kill him, and they followed him. They were like servants and pretend to be afraid of him, and waited all the time to catch him without that armor on. So one day Coronado

decided he would not need to worry about these people any more, and took off this thing he wore over his chest. *Como se dice* [How do you say it?], Green?

Green: His breastplate?

Sí. He leave it off, and when they see him, *chinga el cabrón* [fuck the bastard], they shoot him with a poison arrow. ·

Then when those people kill Coronado, they don't go back to New Mexico. Maybe they are mad with those people at [Isleta] del Norte because they will not help to kill Coronado, who can say? But that is how the oldest people say we got here.

Clearly this legend expresses the feelings of the Tigua about themselves and others. This account of the Tiguas' migration to Ysleta del Sur depicts them as warriors rather than pacifists, as enemies of the Spanish rather than accomplices. It is told (to both Tiguas and outsiders) as a reason for pride and as an example to the Tiguas of how they may overcome superior forces by relying on wit, patience, and courage, a strategy that remains viable in their contemporary struggles against assimilation.

Of special interest here are the divergent views of the Tigua migration taken by the two related Native-American groups: Isleta del Norte and Ysleta del Sur. The residents of Isleta del Norte regard the departure and subsequent settlement in Ysleta del Sur as evidence of the Tigua's low regard for their people and for the sanctity of home—which to the Isletans can only be New Mexico.

An analysis of Tigua folk history in general and the Coronado legend in particular reveals a radically different attitude. The Tigua say they left New Mexico to take revenge against the Spanish, whom they portray as thieves and murderers. Instead of traitors, then, the Tigua argue, through their legends, that they are the descendants of the only Pueblos willing to bring Coronado to justice. This narrative reveals not only a hostility toward the first European oppressors, but also a sense of superiority to the people of Isleta del Norte. The Tigua did not return to New Mexico because they resented their fellows' demonstration of weakness: "They don't go back to New Mexico. Maybe they are mad with those people at del Norte because they will not help to kill Coronado." This resentment, rather than fear of Spanish retaliation, is the reason presented in oral tradition for the Tigua failure to return "home." We have in Tigua oral narrative, then, a positive interpretation of what might otherwise appear an act of capitulation.

At the time of my investigation the Tigua were uniformly reluctant to discuss the migration accounts of Isleta del Norte. On
the other hand, their own positive interpretation of the emigra-
tion was one of the first oral traditions informants would volun-
teer. There were other reasons besides maintenance of a positive
self-image for this tendency. For almost two decades the Tigua
were engaged in a struggle with the civil authorities to gain property rights and official recognition. Since the Pueblo of Ysleta del
Sur had not been enfranchised with the rest of the Pueblos—as
one informant succinctly stated, "We ain't got the paper"—the Tigua used folk history to validate their claims. For them, at least,
such accounts provided suitable verification. The story, moreover,
is a full and a consistent one, including the means by which their
rights to the land they inhabit might be established:

So when they kill Coronado they went over to the sandhills [east of
El Paso], and they make this pueblo—somewhere over there. And so,
they, they plant over there, you know, like corn, beans, and things like
that, and they hunt to wild animals, for meat, like deer and things like
that and rabbits, jackrabbits and whatever they found.

So then they move over, they move over to Hueco [an area near El
Paso, sacred to the modern Tiguas]. They stay over to Hueco for, I don't
know, for several years I guess or for maybe—yeah, because they plant,
too. Because we found some level places over there on Hueco, you see,
and when you found those places level, it means that they plant over
there, you see, so then they move over to the old pueblo over there. . . .
And, uh, they stay there for a while I guess.

The way they used to tell me, you see—the oldest people, that they
was over there somewhere [gesturing to the northeast], you see. I think it
was on the old pueblo and they said that they, some of the people, not
all . . . they came over this way, you see, just to found out what they can
found around here.

So they came over this way, and they found the river. On that time
the river is not like now, you see. The river was, sometimes the river was
over there close to the sandhills, because it is still over there, the river
[bed?]. I can go and show it to you one of these days. I show you the river
where they come. And they found the river over there, you see, and then
they went back, you see. And then they tell to the other peoples over
there, "Well, we found the water," or "We come over through there," you
see.

Then they make this reservation [settlement] . . . over there by
where they kill that Comanche [Loma del Apache]. . . . And then, they
came over to Juarez, and they found the Spanish people again over
there.

So, uh, I don't know what they [the Spanish] think over there, so then the Spanish people, they was afraid to the Tiguas, you see, because they killed Coronado over there. That's the way I know.

And then when, uh, they [the Spanish] was afraid to them [the Tiguas], and then they, the way I know is they told them to come here, you see, they going to give them this land here to the Tiguas, so they can, and they are going to send a padre with them, you see, to come and, you know, to give them religion, or whatever they want and build a church up here. . . .

Yeah, so uh, that's the way they told me, you see. . . . You see, they [the Spanish] came and put a post over there by the Palo Clavado [a wooden cross] and then they go straight ahead and put another post over there close to Zaragosa, and then they come over that way through La Loma del Negro, they used to call him [it], you see, and then they go straight up to the sandhills up here, you see and then they [the Spanish] tell him [the Tigua], "All this belongs to you." Because I think they don't want them to bother the Spanish people. They was afraid to them, you see? And they [the Tigua] stay here you see, and the Tigua that stay over there [Isleta del Norte] one part and one part here.

Thus, the Tigua can base their claims to their territory on the right of conquest. Other legends in this oral corpus detail the Tigua's subsequent defense of the land granted to them by the Spanish against a wide variety of marauders and exploiters: Comanches, Apaches, and Mexicans. In the narratives of these battles the Tigua assume almost epic proportions. The message transmitted is that the people of Ysleta have survived only by virtue of their constant vigilance and their determination to fight for their existence regardless of the odds. The relevance of these narratives in the present context is apparent.

More contemporary legends also serve the goals of nativism. These narratives deal with individuals who, within the memory of older residents of Ysleta, have confronted the representatives of civil government to defend Tigua rights against unwarranted incursions and who, as a consequence, have been elevated to the status of folk heroes. The protagonist of the following legend, Mariano Colmenero, exemplifies these heroes.

So they [the Tigua] went to hunt . . . over on the mountains. All the time they killed deer over there, because he [Mariano Colmenero] was an Indian, and he know the land belongs to them, you see. That's why they got the land over there. That's why they fight for it, you see. . . .

So they want to hunt over there. All the time we used to hunt that way, you see. So they bring, I mean, they dry 'em over there, on the rocks, you see. They cut 'em in little pieces and dry 'em over there, the meat, and put 'em in sacks, you see. They bring it through here, and they had meat all the time, you see.

So that day he [Mariano] came back from the mountains. He was hunting with his people, some other Indians, and uh, he came over to his house.

He was over there, he was, all the time had a chair, old, old chair, and he put it over there in front of the house where, uh, close to the door. All the time, he got his rifle, all the time he got his rifle, all the time. So, uh, they came over there.

That time they start to sell those hunting license, you see. Ah, and they came over there [to Mariano's house] and old Jess Wallbridge was one. . . . He was the game warden at that time, the first one. He was a big man, and, uh, he came over to him [Mariano] and he says, "Mariano."

Say, "Yes."

"I heard that you want to hunt."

He says, "Yes, I want to hunt. Why? There is lotta meat. Go ahead and eat some. Eat until you get full."

Said, "No, I don't came to eat."

"Well, what you came here for?"

Says, "I came here because you know that you cannot hunt any more like you used to hunt."

He says, "Who say that?"

"Well, that's the law."

He says, he says, uh, "No, I don't care about the law. I am the law here. I am an Indian, and I hunt any time I want. I am, uh, an Indian, and I am the chief, and I, we gonna do here this way, because we supposed to hunt. This land is our land. So how come you want us to go and buy a hunting license? We don't gonna buy, and they gonna hunt any time. You know where I go, they [the Tiguas] gonna go hunt with me."

Says, "Well, that's okay. I don't want to talk too much with you. I came to take you over to the courthouse."

He said, "Nobody going to take me over to the courthouse."

"Well, they need you over there."

"They need me over there, tell him I be over there tomorrow."

"They need you over there today."

"I say, no! I say tomorrow, and that's all and get outta here. Go and tell him." You know, he got his rifle and nobody say nothing to him. He was like a Texas Ranger [apparently a reference to his toughness and fearlessness]. Something like that, you see. He got the law anyway, you see.

So then they [Wallbridge] say [informant assumes a whining tone], "Well, that's what they send me here for."

"Well, okay. I don't, I don't care who send you here. Just get out of my land, and tell him I'll be there tomorrow."

So Jess says, "Well, okay," so he went out. He went over to El Paso.

So early the next morning he [Mariano] told to Cleofas and my brother, to put his, uh, horse on the little buggy and, uh, so, uh, he's going, we're going to El Paso.

So he [Cleofas] says, "Okay." So he went over there, you see, and put and fix his horse and put him on the buggy, and says "*Tio*, the horse is ready. Your buggy's ready."

"Okay," so all the time he got a bunch of shells, you see. He got a handkerchief like the one I use. Right over there. Got his shells all the time in that handkerchief, you see. So they pick up the handkerchief and his rifle. I got the rifle. We got the rifle. My sister got him at the house.

So he get on the buggy and they go over to, over to the courthouse. . . . So he went over there and they was smoking over there in the court, and, uh, so the trial comes.

They say, "Well, Mariano Colmenero, we send Mr. Wallbridge over there to take it [you] out, to bring you here, to tell you that you cannot hunt any more like you used to hunt."

Then he [Mariano] says, "Who gonna do that?"

"The law, that's the law."

Says, "No, I am the law here. I am an Indian, and I am supposed to hunt any time I want, and nobody gonna stop me, and nobody gonna stop my people either. Because this land is our land, and we gonna hunt. Whenever we want to go to hunt, we gonna hunt, and nobody, we not gonna pay any license, nothing for to go hunting over there. If you want, I gonna be there for some of these days, whenever I, I'm run out of meat, I'll be over there, hunting some more meat. So nobody gonna stop me go hunting over there."

They says, "Well, you got to do it."

He says, "No sir! Somebody want to try it, go over there where I am. I got my camp over there." They used a camp on a place. They used to camp all the time, you see. They used to have a little, uh, *tinajas*, those water holes. Over there was it, and over there, out this way to the, uh, west there was a big *tinaja*. They call him *tinaja*, a waterhole. They call him La Tinaja. No, they call him La Agua de Picota. They call him, that water there. There was a great big *tinaja* over there, and, uh, there was some more over there, you know. They used to water his horses. Uh, so I know the place where he hunt all the time, you see. So no, nobody stop him until he die.

In a period when the Tiguas were desperately trying to hold on to their cultural and territorial rights the relevance of such hero legends is obvious. Confronted by a display of strength, Tigua folk history teaches, the enemy has always backed down.

Therefore, the legends of Ysleta del Sur educate as well as entertain. They articulate relationships between the Tigua and competitive groups. Others deserve little trust because, as outsiders from Coronado to Jess Wallbridge have demonstrated, "they are out to take what we got." That phrase occurs in so many narratives that it is virtually a convention in contemporary Tigua legends. These oral traditions also contain models for meeting such threats. Modern Tiguas must, like Mariano, "know the land belongs to them"—and not only the land but other unique rights as well: the rights to hunt, to govern themselves, to practice their traditional forms of religion, and to adhere to all other elements of their traditional lifestyle. The strategies dictated by this self-assurance are clear. They must be steadfast, or even "mean" (as some of the heroes are described), but they must be just in exercising their rights.

The legends, then, carry both esoteric and exoteric import. The pride in past accomplishments and the ancestors is clear; the narratives effectively argue for Tigua superiority. In this perspective, the "others" are merely a background against which the successful collective "self" struggles and is illuminated and even ennobled. Simultaneously, the stories effectively and economically exhibit the negative aspects of the other, competitive groups.

TIGUA RELIGION AND THE FIESTA DE SAN ANTONIO

It is in festival that one can see most fully the group acting as a unit to dramatize its sense of community. Whether a particular festival focuses on moments of transition in the yearly or individual life cycle, commemorates a mythical figure or historical personage, or celebrates "communitas" itself—in it we can witness a playing-out of the central motives around which the group organizes its sense of distinctiveness. Foregrounded in festivals, moreover, are those symbols which have traditionally encapsulated the community's attitudes toward itself and others. Where there is both a growing ethnic awareness and a desire to manifest this ethnicity to outsiders, the festival may serve both to focus group efforts to establish cultural integrity and to express publicly the sense of separation that is vital to the pursuit of nativistic ideals (cf. Abrahams forthcoming).

The Fiesta de San Antonio, a saint's-day festival held on June 13, is the principal religious event in the lives of the contemporary Tigua of Ysleta del Sur. It is important to the present discussion because the Tigua use it: (1) to focus their hopes for community development; (2) to foster unity and identity; and, by extension, (3) to display the boundaries between themselves and the non-Tigua even while momentarily breaking such boundaries down (by opening them up).

Although San Antonio is a Roman Catholic saint and his festival as celebrated by the Tigua contains Catholic elements, there is here, as in other such "Catholic" observances throughout the New World, much more to the community's faith in him than simple acceptance of the Euro-American religious complex. This ambiguity comes through clearly in a curious statement made by one of my informants: "We don't like the priests too much. It's my religion, okay, but I'm an Indian and *that's* how *I* got to believe."

The Tiguas, like many similar groups, feel no difficulty in rejecting orthodox Catholicism while practicing a sort of folk Catholicism combined with indigenous elements. Many of the more conservative members of the community accept this belief system and discuss it often, especially in the context of the festival:

We don't believe too much on the padres. We believe on God and our *Gran* Spirit and things like that, but we don't believe on the padres. Because the padres, or whatever they was on that time, you know, they kill a lot of our people when they came through to stole our gold, or whatever we got. That's what they came here for. Religion's okay. Their religion is pretty good, because we got to believe in something, but these padres, that's why they, uh, nobody believes too much on them. Well, lot of people believe too much on the padres . . . because they talk pretty good, but no, some things is not true, you see. . . .

Gran Espíritu. Yeah, that's what we believe. We believe on, uh, on the moon, on the sun, on the land, on the water, on all those, because the sun they give us light to walk on the daytime, to work, to make our living, to plant; and the water give us the life because we can plant, we can drink it, we can cook, we can do everything with it; and we believe on the moon, because the moon give us light, everything. We got to believe on that, and, uh, we believe on God all right, because we know that we got a God, one God that help us. We got our *santos* like they got 'em on the church. Okay, we believe on San Antonio. He is our, he's our *santito* that we believe a *lot* on. We ask him something and pray for him and he *do* it. When we ask for something he do it pretty good. We know, because, well, I think it because we believe. That's why, that's why we make promise to him, and we'll do it. We'll do our promise when we made a promise to San Antonio. That'll [he will] help us a lot. And, uh, that's what we believe on.

But Gran Espíritu is our god we got. We got another god, the Indian's god. We got a god. We believe on him, and his is alive. And, uh, we used to see him, too. Whenever we don't do something right on our tribe, they have [he has] come. He came many, many years ago. They

[he] came through here when they make things they ain't supposed to do, and maybe the way we go here with these people [reference to a non-conservative faction of Ysleta] that they are jealous and things like that, maybe someday he come and put us straight like the way we got to be. You know, maybe someday he will be here with us, because he is alive. They [he] never die.

When I was working on Hueco, we'll, we'll see some things like that [manifestations of the supernatural]. We believe and *I* believe . . . and my family believe on him. . . . Don't care they are Catholics, or whatever religion we are, we got to believe on our things we got. And the way I believe too . . . we are Indians, and we are born Indians, and we gonna die Indians and we gonna be buried over there and we gonna be Indians.

The foundation of contemporary Tigua religious life is visible in such discussions: the importance of the natural order; tenuous adherence to Catholicism; the guardianship of the Gran Espíritu; and reverence for life, especially for the living process. The ways of man are integrated with the ways of nature—the natural order. Hence, disorderliness in the affairs of man creates imbalance in the natural order. The social disorder represented by the Euro-American threat to Tigua cultural integrity and the factionalism alluded to by the informant may provoke direct intervention by the Gran Espíritu.

Perhaps this is the guiding spirit behind the belief in a "new world," for many conservative Tiguas make such millennial references, especially at present. One of these centered on the passing of the comet Kohoutek which, I was assured, would bring an end to this world dominated by whites. But one informant stated, on seeing an artist's representation of the comet with its long, flowing tail: "I don't worry. He has long hair and an Indian name."

Moreover, it is certainly no accident that unity in tribal affairs and "being good with everybody" were repeatedly advanced as fundamental precepts of Tigua religious doctrine. In such declarations one may detect the use of religion to promote the intra-group cohesion necessary for social reorganization based on a traditional model.

Another transcendent aspect of Tigua religion is the belief in Abuelo or Abuelito (Grandfather). This grandfather entity (or, more properly, complex, since ultimately it involves Abuelito, Gran Espíritu, and San Antonio), is not uncommon among Native Americans, who conceive of him as a paternalistic protector of life.

On one hand, "Abuelo" refers to a persona in a dance the Tiguas define as their kachina dance. Abuelo's contemporary importance is not as a character in a dance, however, but as a supernatural figure. He is a guiding spirit who periodically makes himself visible to the Tigua, especially during times of great stress. In fact, during the period of my residence in Ysleta, Abuelo was expected to appear to rectify the current state of affairs. The millenarian argument that many informants pursued emphasized that the pollution, war, and violence of the non-Indian world demonstrated that the white man would soon destroy himself. But Abuelito or Gran Espíritu (terms often used interchangeably) would save the Indians and make the earth new again.

Many of my informants had seen Abuelito, often at Hueco Tanks or, especially, Cerro Alto, the highest mountain in the area. One informant reported he looked like a hermit. He added: "He is just like a man, like you and me. Only too [very] old, with a big beard." This description sounds more Christian than Pueblo. Not all descriptions, however, are anthropomorphic:

> My grandmother say . . . how we call Abuelito, that's our god . . . she said there was days when they used to have *juntas* [tribal meetings], and she told me one year that they were having a *junta*, and they used to make them in closed houses, you know, real closed, and then they heard a whole bunch of noise, and, uh, they all went out, and they saw this bright thing, you know. They came out and everybody look around, and they start to look around. It was some kind of, uh, tracks that, you know, they start realizing who it was [Abuelito]. So I believe on it.

Abuelito acts for the Tiguas' benefit and often appears at times of tribal stress, which reflects the fact that his name is a term of endearment ("dear little grandfather"). Of course, identifying supernaturals with oneself or one's group, especially by use of kinship terms among groups in which kinship demands reciprocal obligations, is a powerful mechanism for approaching and controlling a frightening situation (cf. Parsons 1939, vol. 1:208).

Whether as Abuelito or the more formal and cosmic Gran Espíritu, he is, as one of the preceding informants stated, a "second god," a specifically Indian god concerned with the welfare of the Tiguas and willing and able to intercede on their behalf. Unlike the God of orthodox Roman Catholicism, he is not accessible only through the Church or through priestly intercession. He is also traditionally associated with San Antonio:

GREEN: Who are your dances [those performed during the festival] for? Are they for San Antonio? Are they for the Gran Espíritu?

JS: It's, well, uh, it's on that day [i.e., they are performed on the day of the festival]. I think, so, it's for both St. Anthony and the Great Spirit, because we think *Gran* Spirit and St. Anthony is one.

As stated above, the Tiguas make promises to San Antonio in return for special favors. These promises are characteristically associated with his fiesta itself: to collect money or food for the fiesta by walking barefoot from house to house, to dance for him during the fiesta, or, in one case, to buy a new image of him for the tribe's use. Significantly, this figure is kept in the *tusla*, the Tigua ceremonial house, rather than in the church.

While all three god-figures appear to be aspects of a single persona (taking "persona" in its broadest sense), each seems to have a discrete function and is approached differently. Gran Espíritu may be conceptualized as a pervasive force, more impersonal than the other two figures. While he is in many ways identical to Abuelito, he is referred to in more abstract terms. A manifestation such as a bright light, a noise, or the bearded old man is generally designated an appearance of Abuelito. He is thus a more personal and accessible form of Gran Espíritu. Both of these aspects of the cosmic personage are non-Christian. They are related to Roman Catholicism only through the idea that "*Gran* Spirit and St. Anthony is one." This relationship is significant, however, since San Antonio is only tenuously related to the Church in the collective Tigua consciousness.

San Antonio represents a syncretism of Pueblo beliefs and orthodox Catholicism, an overlap between the two systems on several levels. The Fiesta de San Antonio offers dances to both the saint and the indigenous supernaturals. Only San Antonio, however, is courted in the Catholic manner, with personal penance and promises. The other two personae of this complex are involved only indirectly, as when an individual dances at the fiesta in fulfillment of a promise. Gran Espíritu is appeased by adherence to Tigua traditions and morality. In other words, life runs smoothly when lived in harmony with the cosmic order, and becomes the "good life." Abuelito intervenes unbidden (unlike San Antonio) to put tribal affairs back in order during times of social disturbance.

San Antonio, however, answers prayers, requires "payment,"

and performs very much like the traditional Catholic saint. But, as noted above, he is not necessarily bound to the Church. His image resides in the *tusla*, and it could be placed there only after a purification ritual conducted by the *cacique*. San Antonio as venerated by the Tigua, therefore, is not a purely Catholic figure, although he, unlike the other supernaturals, combines both Tigua and Catholic elements. Like Gran Espíritu and Abuelito, however, he is supposed to take a special interest in the Tigua and functions as both a source of power and a focus for group identification for nativists.

Moreover, while the promises to San Antonio are executed by individuals, most of them benefit the community because, as noted, they add to the festivities on his feast day. Thus the practice is in keeping with the general Pueblo rule that individuals gain virtue by serving their village. In addition to being the major religious occasion for Ysleta, then, the festival functions as a primary means of unifying the people of the Native-American community. As one informant observed:

They [the Tiguas] all seem to be like one big family, and times, there was times there was arguing or something. You know, the way the tribe was running, the pueblo, then, they, uh, but still keeping together. It was arguing, but when it comes to the fiesta . . . they all be there.

The fiesta, it seems, by cutting across factionalism, serves as a major cohesive force within the pueblo. It provides at least one opportunity during the year for members of the community to come together in an atmosphere of mutual acceptance and to communicate, to both the world and each other, their ethnic allegiance and the bonds that persist between them. Working together to stage the festival (preparing food and ceremonial apparatus, rehearsing the dances, etc.), Tiguas may put aside their petty disputes for the sake of the common good. Thus, not only the fiesta proper—a day marked by processions, traditional dances, feasting, and, least importantly, an almost perfunctory mass—but the periods preceding and following it are times when factionalism gives way to harmony.

With the rise of nativism, the fiesta provided a cultural resource, a model of action, not available otherwise in the cultural repertoire. As the activity least subject to external influence it allows for unlimited expression of tribal fealty. In addition to promoting unity from within, it provides a means for creating boundaries between the conservative Tiguas and those parties whom they believe threaten the integrity of their traditional way of life. These boundaries proved necessary when federal recognition added a new peril to the obvious threats posed by non-Indian society to Tigua self-determination.

It was necessary, in order to gain aid from the civil government, to resolve the question of tribal membership according to uniform criteria. Therefore, the records of the Texas Commission for Indian Affairs state:

> using the guidelines established by the Bureau of Indian Affairs for the Pueblo Indians and the traditional custom of the Tigua Pueblo, which are the same, this agency has been conducting a genological [*sic*] census of the Tigua Indians to determine who are tribal members (1969:1).

As a result, all families whose male heads had at least one-eighth Tigua ancestry became eligible for membership and its concomitant benefits. Most informants, however, view this method as inequitable and not at all in keeping with their established criteria for tribal membership. Their most important standard for inclusion, they argue, has been participation in the affairs of the community—especially in the Fiesta de San Antonio. This violation of Tigua criteria developed into a genuine source of friction.

A major irritant has been the inclusion of what conservatives have termed "new Indians" on the tribal roll without review by the officials of the native government. The "new Indians" are those persons of Tigua ancestry who, before governmental recognition, had resigned from participation in community affairs and, in some cases, disclaimed their heritage; they preferred to assimilate into Anglo-American and Mexican-American society. According to conservative informants, these people became reinvolved in the community only to get the benefits which resulted from governmental recognition (e.g., employment and college scholarships). An employee of the Commission explained the problem this has engendered and the motivations of the "new Indians" to me in the following manner:

> The only people *barrio* people [conservative Tiguas] recognize as being Indians are those that have participated in their activities, like in dances, fiestas. They sort of have resentment against what they call the new Indians that have come about since the Commission was formed and we've set up programs, and they look down on these people as claiming to be Indians just to get something for free. . . .
> The economic motive seems to be very strong. It's brought in a lot of new people.

Ethnicity among the Tigua is determined by active display—they have a performance orientation, if you will. The reasons are clear. Indianness cannot be determined strictly by residence in a particular locale, because at the time of the inception of nativism in Ysleta del Sur even the so-called *barrio indio*, the Indian section of the community, was 80 percent Mexican-American. Nor can ethnicity, in the present context, be defined strictly by kinship, if we are to follow Barth's criteria, mentioned above. Far too many persons of Tigua ancestry simply have no sense of their indigenous culture, due to their voluntary withdrawal from the traditional acculturative procedures. Ethnicity to the Tigua, then, must necessarily be a matter of "Indian is as Indian does." The conservatives thus consider only those who have consistently identified themselves as Indian by participation in tribal affairs (in 1974, only about half of those listed on the tribal roll) as truly Indian, real Tiguas.

The Tigua conservatives could enforce their definition to a degree, during the period under consideration, in spite of the compromise forced upon them, because they controlled access to the display of ethnic identity. That is, in order to be integrated into the ethnic group one had to display his or her ethnicity by active participation in the Fiesta de San Antonio. And the only way one could actively participate was to be invited by the *cacique* or war captain, or at least to receive their permission to participate. Any attempt to circumvent these authorities would fail because these officials control both the teaching of the ritual knowledge and the apparatus (e.g., drum, bows, and rattles carried while dancing) necessary for participation. Although my informants stated that the tribal elders would generally not turn away a Tigua who wants to participate actively in the festival, the applicant would have to subject himself to tribal authority in order to acquire the requisite knowledge. By doing so, he would be forced to recognize the primacy of traditional authority and to assume the responsibility which participation carries with it. His reward, however, would be ethnic identity.

Roger Abrahams has noted that "the same performances may on one occasion (or in one historical situation) be employed as a private means of exclusion and on another may publicly proclaim the community open to view" (forthcoming: 3). The Tigua Fiesta de San Antonio, I believe, allows for the simultaneous expression of both motives. To the conservatives the festival is, of course, their most important religious commitment of the year.

For nativists, however, social and cultural motivations exist as well. In this situation participation serves as a means of exclusion, a means of marking the boundary between "real" Tiguas and the resented parvenus. In addition, this act publicly proclaims to all who observe the performance the ethnic identity of the active participants.

THE USE OF HUMOR

During New York's highly publicized financial difficulties of the mid-1970s the following UPI release appeared in the nation's newspapers:

> ST. LOUIS (UPI)—The Tigua Indian tribal council at El Paso recently voted to buy financially-pressed Manhattan for the same price—$24— the white man originally paid the Mohicans. Thursday a St. Louis bank offered to lend the tribe the $24, even to the point of not requiring security other than the island itself.

Although the Tigua have used folk history and their saint's-day festival as the primary means of promoting nativism and ethnic identity through folk tradition, the struggle has not ignored the power of humor.

While humorous narratives have not constituted a major device for articulating inter-group strife, I did, during the course of my fieldwork, collect a small body of jokes from a single informant. These narratives would not have seemed significant except for the context in which they were performed. My informant told these jokes about a parrot and his owner in rapid succession immediately following a serious discussion of bureaucratic ineptness at Ysleta del Sur. In order to check my conclusion that these jokes were symbolic vehicles for articulating the relationship between Indians and whites, I stated "That parrot sounds like you, always raising hell." His answer—"We both got plenty to raise hell about"—served to convince me that, at least at some level, my assumptions were plausible. The jokes follow in the order performed.

> This man had brought his girlfriend to his house, and they were sitting on the couch eating crackers. He had a pet parrot, and he wanted to make it talk for his girlfriend. He kept holding out crackers to the parrot and saying, "Polly want a cracker? Polly want a cracker?"
>
> But the parrot wouldn't talk. The man wouldn't let the parrot alone,

though. He just kept on holding out crackers and saying, "Polly want a cracker?"

So the parrot finally turned around to him and said, "*You* crack her. You brought her."

There was a man who had a parrot, and one morning he was in the bathroom shaving, and the parrot was in there with him. The parrot was watching him shave, and he kept saying, "You better be careful. You're going to cut yourself. You're going to cut yourself."

After a while, the man told the parrot, "If you say that one more time, I'm going to flush you [down the toilet]."

But in a little while the parrot said, "You're going to cut yourself." So the man took the parrot and threw him in and flushed it and closed the lid.

Later his wife came in, and was on her *comadre* [menstruating]. She opened the lid and sat down. Then the parrot looked up and said, "See, I told you that you were going to cut yourself."

There was a priest who had a parrot that he taught to help him in the church. Every Sunday morning when the people came, he would tell them, "Sir, you sit over there. Ma'am, there's a seat for you over here."

But this parrot just wouldn't leave the hens alone. Every time the padre wasn't watching him, he would go to the chicken coop and try to screw the hens. And the padre kept telling him, "You chicken-fucker, if you don't stop that I'm going to shave your head!" But the parrot would just go back out and fuck the hens whenever the priest wasn't around, so he finally shaved his head.

The next Sunday morning after the parrot got his head shaved, the priest came in the back of the church and he saw a whole row full of bald men and they were mad. So he walked up to the front and there was this bald man and his wife standing there and the parrot was saying, "You can sit right here ma'am, but you get back there with the rest of those chicken-fuckers."

Clearly these comic tales are not unique to the Tigua. They have, in fact, been widely collected among other folk groups (see Rosenberg 1964). It is the immediate context of the activity which make them significant. As portrayed in these narratives, the parrot's situation shares important features with the Native American in conflict with non-Indian society. The parrot, like the stereotypical Indian, is regarded as childlike and ignorant, impulsive and ruled by his appetites. He is prejudged as linguistically incompetent and as unable to adopt what is considered proper behavior. But inevitably he gets the last word, even if it is only a jest.

As previously noted, nativism perceives the native group as a superior community unjustly dominated by outsiders. Since stereotyping is a primary means of maintaining and justifying the subordination of any dominated group, the nativistic group must come to terms with such negative categorization to achieve any measure of success. My informant did not direct his jokes, however, to those who cling to the stereotype most fiercely, but to those who see its inaccuracies and seek to counteract it. The stereotype, in this case, is attacked within the group itself. Inversion of a stereotype (i.e., the conversion of negative attributes into aggressive strategies) in folk narrative is a viable means for articulating social and cultural differences and for questioning the alleged superiority of dominant groups.

These narratives, while not traditional in and of themselves, follow the traditional Pueblo strategy of using humor to subject power structures, economic relations, and other elements of the social system to reversal, inversion, and transposition for normative purposes (Hieb 1972 : 185). As Ortiz notes, the Pueblo burlesque and caricature what they "find serious or absurd, baffling or wrong, fearful or comical about life and about other people" (1972 : 147). In at least one performance, then, jokes seem to have functioned as a device for coping with the negative aspects of an ethnic identity. My informant apparently articulated the stereotype used to subordinate not only the Tiguas and the Native-American population in general, but other relatively powerless groups as well. The jokes' punchlines, however, force us to reassess the stereotype and to reevaluate not only these preconceptions, but the authority figures in the narratives who misled themselves by basing their responses on such inflexible prejudices.

Our exploration of Tigua folk tradition and its relationship to nativism has indicated that these traditional items can speak with many voices and yield multiple levels of meaning. Not only do these forms educate as well as entertain, or display a sense of self while serving as an act of religious devotion, but they attack simultaneously the twin problems that face any nativistic group: to oppose domination and to engender a sense of pride in a lifestyle imminently threatened with destruction. By casting these arguments in traditional forms the task of persuasion and the task of perpetuation that constitute the core of nativism become a single effort.

NOTE

1. A comprehensive review of the vast literature on ethnic identity and nativism is beyond the scope of this paper. For conceptually and bibliographically useful surveys of ethnicity, see Bennett 1975 and Cohen 1978. On folklore and identity see Orso 1974 and Abrahams and Kalčik 1978. On nativism and related types of social movements see Kopytoff 1964, and the preface and appendix to Worsley 1968.

For previous studies of Tigua nativism and folklore, see Green 1976a, 1976b, and 1978. The field research on which that and the present work are based was conducted at the pueblo of Ysleta del Sur, Texas, east of El Paso, from 1972 to 1974 and during the summer months of 1975 and 1976. The 1972–1974 fieldwork was supported by PHS grant no. 17216 from the Center for Urban Ethnography of the University of Pennsylvania.

BIBLIOGRAPHY

Abrahams, Roger D. Forthcoming. Verbal arts. In *The Harvard encyclopedia of ethnic Americans*. Cambridge: Harvard University Press.
———. N.d. A poetics of everyday life. Unpublished MS.
———, and Susan Kalčik. 1978. Folklore and cultural pluralism. In *Folklore in the modern world*. Richard Dorson, ed. The Hague: Mouton.
Barth, Fredrik. 1969. *Ethnic groups and boundaries*. Boston: Little, Brown.
Bennett, John W., ed. 1975. *The new ethnicity: Perspectives from ethnology*. St. Paul: West.
Burridge, Kenelm. 1969. *New heaven, new earth*. New York: Schocken.
Cohen, Ronald. 1978. Ethnicity: Problem and focus in anthropology. In *Annual review of anthropology*, vol. 7. Bernard Siegel, ed. Palo Alto: Annual Reviews.
Cunnison, Ian. 1951. *History on the Luapula*. London: Oxford University Press.
Fewkes, J. Walter. 1902. The Pueblo settlements near El Paso, Texas. *American Anthropologist* 4:57–75.
Green, Thomas A. 1976a. Folk history and cultural reorganization. *Journal of American Folklore* 89:310–318.
———. 1976b. El Nativismo, la autodeterminación y el mantenimiento de límites entre los Tigua de Ysleta del Sur. *América Indígena* 36:847–862.
———. 1978. Stereotype manipulation in contemporary Native American humor. *Midwestern Journal of Language and Folklore* 4:18–26.
Hackett, C. W., and C. C. Shelby. 1942. *Revolt of the Pueblo Indians of New*

Mexico and Otermin's attempted reconquest, 1680–1682, vol. 2. Albuquerque: University of New Mexico Press.

Hieb, Louis A. 1972. Meaning and mismeaning: Toward an understanding of the ritual clown. In *New perspectives on the Pueblos*. Alfonso Ortiz, ed. Albuquerque: University of New Mexico Press.

Hudson, Charles. 1966. Folk history and ethnohistory. *Ethnohistory* 13:52–70.

Kopytoff, Igor. 1964. Classifications of religious movements: Analytical and synthetic. In *Symposium on new approaches to the study of religion*. June Helm, ed. Seattle: University of Washington Press.

Linton, Ralph. 1943. Nativistic movements. *American Anthropologist* 45:230–240.

Minter, Alan H. 1969. The Tigua Indians of the Pueblo de Ysleta del Sur, El Paso County, Texas. *West Texas Historical Association Year Book* 45:30–44.

Orso, Ethelyn. 1974. Folklore and identity. In *Social and cultural identity*. Thomas Fitzgerald, ed. Athens, Ga.: University of Georgia Press.

Ortiz, Alfonso. 1972. Ritual drama and the Pueblo world view. In *New perspectives on the Pueblos*. Alfonso Ortiz, ed. Albuquerque: University of New Mexico Press.

Paredes, Américo. 1968. Folk medicine and the intercultural jest. In *Spanish-speaking people in the United States*. June Helm, ed. Seattle: University of Washington Press.

Parsons, Elsie Clews. 1939. *Pueblo Indian religion*, 2 vols. Chicago: University of Chicago Press.

Rosenberg, Neil V. 1964. An annotated collection of parrot jokes. M.A. thesis, Indiana University.

Steiner, Sam. 1972. *The Tiguas: The lost tribe of City Indians*. New York: Crowell-Collier.

Sturtevant, William C. 1966. Anthropology, history and ethnohistory. *Ethnohistory* 13:1–51.

Texas Commission for Indian Affairs. 1969. *Budget estimate: Fiscal years 1970 and 1971*. Ysleta del Sur Pueblo: Texas Commission for Indian Affairs.

———. 1970. *Brief history of the Tigua Indians*. Ysleta del Sur Pueblo: Texas Commission for Indian Affairs.

Worsley, Peter. 1968. *The trumpet shall sound: A study of "cargo" cults in Melanesia*, 2nd ed. New York: Schocken.

Rosan A. Jordan

Tension and Speech Play
in Mexican-American Folklore

In her study of traditional storytelling in the Toronto Jewish community, Barbara Kirshenblatt-Gimblett (1972) defines the "immigrant period" in a group's history as a time of large-scale permanent immigration which produces a substantial immigrant community with a thriving, ethnic social and cultural life. She characterizes this period as one of vigorous biculturalism and bilingualism, marked by a clash of cultures, world views, and language which gives rise to a rich body of special narrative lore.

But what happens when immigration is not restricted to a well-defined phase of development in the history of the community? For Mexican-Americans in the Southwestern United States, new immigrants from Mexico (along with rural Mexican-American migrants into urban centers) constitute an ever-present, problematic sector of the community's population. As time passes, the new arrivals evolve both cultural and individual mechanisms for dealing with their new environment, and are absorbed into the ethnic community. But there are always new arrivals in the community who still have ahead of them the ordeal of learning to cope with the new culture. The plight of the newcomers who must struggle to survive in a foreign culture is one which elicits the sympathy of even highly acculturated Mexican-Americans. Yet, at the same time, these new arrivals remind the already acculturated and the native-born of aspects of their cultural heritage they regard ambiguously or which they have rejected in the process of acculturation. Furthermore, since racial discrimination encumbers the assimilation of Mexican-Americans into the majority culture, the continuous flow of new arrivals constitutes an ongoing problem for the community as a whole—which must both support the in-migrants and deal with the fact that the behavior of these newly-arrived individuals highlights some of the very cultural features self-consciously rejected by the assimilated.

In a sense, then, the clash of world views, cultures, and languages which accompanies immigration is never resolved for even relatively acculturated Mexican-Americans, as long as they continue to draw on their ethnic heritage as a source of both individual and group identity. Urban Mexican-Americans, particularly, cannot avoid dealing with cultural diversity. It is not surprising, then, that much of the expressive culture of Mexican-Americans grows out of situations which emphasize their bilingual/bicultural competencies in some manner. Their access to two languages and two cultures both provides Mexican-Americans with widened cultural resources and, in some settings, stimulates creative expression—even though the two cultures often do clash. In fact, much Mexican-American folklore may be seen as a creative response to the problems and tensions engendered by their conflicting cultural loyalties.

Much in-group Mexican-American humor, for example, is based on a stereotype of the unacculturated Mexican, the immigrant, the bracero farm laborer. Scholars have especially noted the humor which deals with the newly arrived Mexican's absurd misunderstandings of the foreign language and culture (Paredes 1966, 1968; Jordan 1972; Dorson 1964:450–454; Rael n.d.). Maria Herrera Sobek (1978) has reported that jokes about the misadventures of this comic figure circulate among the immigrants themselves in California. The stories emphasize the need to learn English in order to avoid trouble, and provide catharsis by enabling the newcomer to objectivize and share his anxieties.

For acculturated Mexican-Americans who still identify themselves with the group, the comic figure of the unacculturated Mexican has ambivalent associations. Given the low esteem which the members of minority groups receive in this country in general, and the individual Mexican-American's lack of options about remaining in the ethnic category, ambivalence seems a reasonable reaction to a figure whose presence reinforces the ethnic stereotype. Such ambivalence may simply reflect a rejection of the low status and poverty which are all too often the lot of Mexican-Americans. For example, Américo Paredes (1968:112–113) notes, in his analysis of a series of jests told by highly accultur- ated but socially conscious members of the middle class in the strongly Mexican-American region of South Texas, that the jests reflect the impatience of his informants with "the slow accultura- tion of the average Mexican-American and his low economic and social status." At the same time, the jokes also demonstrate these people's strong sense of identification with the unacculturated Mexican and even with certain remnants of folk belief, as part of their own heritage.

The jests Paredes cites ridicule ingenuous or outlandish folk medical practices; but they also protest the coldness and lack of compassion lower-class Mexican-Americans often encounter in Anglo doctors, hospitals, clinics, etc. The jests, then, represent a creative and tension-reducing response to a situation in which the "clash of cultures" is encountered repeatedly by those in the process of acculturation. The esoteric nature of the jests Paredes cites, moreover, affirms the in-group solidarity of the participants in the jesting—for to enjoy the humor of the jests requires close familiarity with serious narratives about *curanderos* and their healing methods and, at the same time, enough sophistication to view such medical practices and practitioners with a critical, even cynical eye. It is, in fact, the difficulties inherent in recon- ciling these conflicting cultural systems which such humor emphasizes.

A spontaneous joke which I observed in the field dramatizes those same difficulties. A native-born Mexican-American friend and I, while driving through a mixed ethnic neighborhood in Fort Worth, Texas, passed a crudely lettered sign. The top word of the sign was "liberation" but the final letter was out of place, so that my friend read it aloud as "liberatio." Then she saw the *n* and gave the word a Spanish pronunciation: "*liberación*." Then she noticed that the word was spelled with a *t* rather than a *c*, as- sumed it was misspelled Spanish and mispronounced it accord- ingly. Finally, as it dawned on her that the word (and also the rest of the sign) was in English, she laughed and said, "Why are we speaking Spanish?" She added, "That just looked like the kind of stupid sign a Mexican would make."

My friend's question referred to a familiar joke about two *mexicanos* who converse in English-accented Spanish—until they discover that they are both *mexicanos*. One of them then asks, in Spanish, "Then why are we speaking English?" I give this joke as

I collected it from another informant. All of the Spanish phrases except the last (*"Pos ¿qué.* . . .) are rendered in an English accent; the last line is spoken with Spanish phonology:

Este otro *joke*, de unos mexicanos que andaban cazando. You know, they were out in the field. Iba andando uno, y se encontró con otro que venía. Dice, " ¡Ah! Ese parece mexicano. ¿Será mexicano o no?" Y el otro tambien decía, " ¿Será mexicano?" So they met, you know. Y le dice, " ¿Como está Vd.?" "Oh, bien ¿y Vd.? ¿Qué está haciendo por acá?" "Oh, pues, yo ando cazando venado. ¿Y Vd.?" "Oh, yo ando cazando liebres." " ¡Ajá! Está bueno. ¿Como le ha ido?" "Muy bien. Muy bien." [Pause.] " ¿Vd., es de México?" "Sí. ¿Y Vd.?" "Yo también. Yo soy de México." "Oh, ¿entonces Vd. habla español?" "Sí." "Pos ¿qué estamos haciendo hablando inglés?" dice. [Laughter.] They thought they were talking English.

This other joke, about some Mexicans who were out hunting. (You know, they were out in the field.) One of them was walking, and met the other coming his way. He says, "Ah! This fellow looks Mexican. Is he Mexican or not?" And the other one also said, "Is he Mexican?" (So they met, you know.) And he says to the other, "How are you?" "Oh, fine, and you? What are you doing out here?" "Oh, well, I'm hunting deer. And you?" "Oh, I'm hunting rabbits." "Aha! That's good. How's it going?" "Very well. Very well." [Pause.] "You, are you from Mexico?" "Yes, and you?" "Me too. I'm from Mexico." "Oh, then you speak Spanish?" "Yes." "Well, then, what are we doing speaking English?" [Laughter.] (They thought they were talking English.)

The spontaneous joke my friend created about the sign clearly indicates her consciousness of the message of this traditional joke and of the cultural reality which underlies it: the need to be able to alternate cultural frames of reference with ease. The joke also underscores, in humorous, expressive terms, the complex dimensions of bilingualism—what linguistic features constitute speaking "another" language?—and multiple cultural identities.

Much of the expressive culture of urban Mexican-Americans exhibits an evident delight in playing with language. Among other things, this play displays the expressive alternatives and the ambiguous places between the two tongues. Indeed, studies of the social and psychological implications of bilingualism in the Southwest (and elsewhere) would be considerably enhanced by the study of speech play and verbal art, which such efforts have so far almost universally neglected.[1]

Mexican-American conversation is replete with colloquial expressions, and with creative variations of colloquial expressions, in Spanish alone. For example, the word *"madera"* (wood) has come to mean, in a number of expressions, "flattery."[2] Thus the expression *"¡No me estéis madereano!"* means "Don't flatter me!" or, translated literally, "Don't be wooding me!" As one informant told me, it is used "when someone compliments you and you don't think they are entirely sincere." Alternate responses are: *"Ya tiene suficiente madera"* [You already have enough wood]; *"Con más madera, más pronto hago mi casa"* [With more wood, I will make my house sooner]; and *"¡Pura madera!"* [Pure wood!]. The proliferation of phrases seems endless, and this kind of playing with language is typical.

Bilingualism only serves to widen the scope of this creativity. For example, translating Spanish idioms or colloquial expressions literally is a favorite source of humor. The intransitive verb *"chiflar"* means "to whistle." As an active verb it also means "to joke" or "to cut up"—I often heard women scolding children by calling them *"chiflados"* (the past participial form of *"chiflar"*).[3] The reflexive expression *"¡No me chiflas!"* [Don't kid me!] would probably be rendered in idiomatic English as an incredulous "You don't say!" or "No kidding!" In a bilingual, bicultural conversation, however, I once heard a Mexican-American quip, "Don't whistle me!" To understand this bit of repartee one needed to be familiar with Texas-Spanish colloquialisms as well as with English. Translating such an idiom literally gives it more force than it would have in the customary code.

The knock-knock jokes collected in the University of Texas Folklore Archives offer another example of the way in which bilingualism can amplify the resources available for word play.[4] Knock-knock jokes, familiar to most American children, begin formally when the joke teller approaches his audience with the phrase "Knock, knock!" When the person addressed asks "Who's there?" the teller replies with a word or phrase which purports to be a name (for example, "Madame"). The second person asks for the full name of the "knocker" ("Madame who?"), and the joke teller then repeats the first word or phrase as part of a longer phrase which involves a play on words ("Madame foot is caught in the door"). In the context of the longer phrase, "Madame" is understood to be "My damn." In this particular example, the word play also involves (for children) the pleasure of using a taboo word with impunity. Usually the word play distorts the word or phrase played upon—as when, in another knock-knock joke, "orange" is used in the phrase "Orange you glad. . . ." The additional discontinuity caused by the lack of exact fit between the pronunciations of the two words contributes to the comic effect.

The eight Mexican-American knock-knock jokes in the Texas collection utilize bilingualism in various ways. Two use the "Knock, knock! Who's there?" framework in English but switch to Spanish for the first and second answers (or "names"):

A: Knock, knock!
B: Who's there?
A: Cinco. [Five.]
B: Cinco who?
A: Cincomida [sin comida] me muero de hambre. [Without food I'll die of hunger.]

A: Knock, knock!
B: Who's there?
A: Elsa.
B: Elsa who?
A: Elsapato [el zapato] me aprieta. [My shoe pinches.]

Although these texts use both Spanish and English, the word play itself does not involve bilingualism (although one could argue that "Elsa" is an English word, since it is also a name in English). The other six texts do utilize bilingual word play; that is, an alternate meaning for the first name offered emerges when it is used in the context of a longer phrase in a different language. In three of these texts what appears to be a Spanish word turns, when heard in context, into an English phrase (although again, the "fit" is not perfect—which heightens the effect):

A: Knock, knock!
B: Who's there?
A: Hueso. [Bone.]
B: Hueso who?
A: Hueso [What's the] matter, honey?

A: Knock, knock!
B: Who's there?
A: Güera. [Blondie.]
B: Güera who?
A: Güera [Where are] you hiding the cookies?

A: Knock, knock!
B: Who's there?
A: Apio. [Celery.]
B: Apio who?
A: Apio verde [Happy Birthday] to you.

The remaining two texts appear to be totally in English until in the final phrase, the English "name" is transformed by context into Spanish:

A: Knock, knock!
B: Who's there?
A: Jam.
B: Jam who?
A: Jam me [Ya me] voy a acostar. [Now I'm going to bed.]

A: Knock, knock!
B: Who's there?
A: Kelly.
B: Kelly who?
A: Kelly [¿Que le] importa? [What does it matter to you?]

These jokes represent the bicultural child's preoccupation with the demands not just of mastering the two languages themselves but of keeping them separate, using each one appropriately and switching codes with ease. For example, Annie Loredo, when recording these jokes, explained that a Spanish-speaking child hearing the song "Happy Birthday" might misunderstand the first line as "*Apio verde* [green celery] to you." In the joke this mistake becomes the source of humor; those who share the joke demonstrate that they do not mistake English for Spanish and that they recognize the incongruity of "*apio verde*" as a corruption of "happy birthday."

This delight in playing with language no doubt stems in part from the atmosphere of "vigorous bilingualism and biculturalism." The very availability of two languages and the creative ferment of a bicultural environment heighten Mexican-Americans' sensitivity to language and to language play in general. However, I would also suggest that the tensions created by the biculturalism—the "clash," the being caught between—increase the need for certain kinds of control. The circumstances of real life, of the bicultural situation, are fraught with anxiety, hence the greater desire to control language within certain recurrent problem situations.

During a year of fieldwork among Mexican-Americans in Texas, I found that a number of expressions the adults used were remnants of certain adolescent routines which employ rhyme and, frequently, dialogue. In one such routine, for example, the insult "*Estás loco*" [You are crazy] calls for the rhyming response, "*Te patina el coco*" [Your brain is skidding].[5] (My informant's translation was: "Your brain can't get going; its wheels are spinning.") The routine could continue with the counter-response, "*Y a ti te pajuelea el callo*" [And your corn is wobbling]. This expression, my informant noted, "means you're odd, not all there." I observed however, that adults used the last phrase by itself, without the rhyme preceding it, and not to counter or to return an insult as in the adolescent routine but, at least ostensibly, to express admiration. For example, an informant used the expression jokingly to make a great show of being impressed when he saw me recording a joke he was telling me in Spanish. He explained: "It means like, 'You're good'—or, no, it's just an expression like 'Gee whiz?'" As synonym she listed "*te arrastras*," (lit., "you drag yourself along"), "*te avientas*" (lit., "you're fanning yourself"), and, in English, "you throw yourself."

These phrases are among a large body of expressions which are used in local slang to mean "you are excelling."[6] The words all denote making a *physical* effort to push oneself forward but in context indicate a push toward *success* (social, economic, intellectual, etc.) thus poking fun at the impulse to push oneself ahead of one's peers. The English expression referred to, "you throw yourself," is simply another variant in the routine, translated literally from Spanish into English. The effect of using these expressions in a strange frame of reference is very comical, incidentally. It seems likely that the humorous activity of proliferating the expressions based on this model, each one more ridiculous than the last, functions to relieve the tension created by conflicts about upward mobility. These conflicts affect primarily those Mexican-Americans who are moving into the middle class and often, concomitantly, undergoing the process of acculturation.

Writing about the function of what he terms the play genres,[7] Roger Abrahams (1969:115) has said:

Play, by definition, arises in an atmosphere which produces the illusion of free and undirected expression while remaining under control. By effecting a removal from the real world into the stylized one, a tension is established through the involvement power of sympathetic identification with the enactment at the same time as a psychic distance is established through the creation of the stylized world and the mannered presentation.

Abrahams is discussing here the more formal genres of folklore, rather than the more spontaneous speech play considered above. Yet this sort of "free" speech play also seems very much like an attempt to exert a subconscious control over language which consciously, is free and undirected. Just as adolescents seek control in a time of growing anxieties and insecurities by returning to familiar childhood speech forms (as Abrahams has maintained elsewhere [1964:44–45]), so may adults facing adult anxieties seek control through use of a variety and even a set of fixed forms which refer back to childhood or adolescent speech play.

This demonstration of control may be especially important to persons to whom language itself seems to be at the source of or at least symbolic of their anxieties—as is precisely the case with persons who are daily faced with the need to reconcile the demands of two cultures and two languages. Especially significant in this regard would be the gratification gained from *bilingual* word play; the power to play with both languages suggests the power to control both cultures and hence to deal effectively with one's biculturalism. I have noted above several examples of the tendency to play with both languages. I would like to conclude with a discussion of two jokes which reveal the same fascination for bilingual word play. They provide support for the thesis that the attempt to control language, and especially two languages simultaneously, is an important reaction to social anxiety.

A Mexican-American male informant, in recounting to his wife and me the jokes he had heard the day before from two friends, told several jokes which revolved around language or word play. One was the joke discussed above about the two *mexicanos* who think they are speaking English when they deliver their Spanish with an Anglo accent (see above). Another involved a pun in English:

> *No has oido el* joke *de* [you haven't heard the *joke* about] ten toes in Tennessee? These people were hunting a record, "Ten Toes in Tennessee." They were trying to get hold of it and they couldn't, so they started calling different record shops. "You got 'Ten Toes in Tennessee'?" "No." They said, "It's an old record, you know." So finally they called . . . they called the wrong number. They called this colored fellow. "Hello?" "You got 'Ten

Toes in Tennessee'?" [Laughs.] He says, "No, I got ten kids in Alabama."
The guy said, "Is that a record?" Says, "No. It's not a record. It's about
average."

And, finally, a third joke involved literal translations into English
of Spanish names. This joke is incomplete because the informant
at first insisted that I turn the tape recorder off. Once he got
started, however, he allowed me to turn it back on. The beginning
of the joke explained that a *mexicano* had been called to court to
interpret for two defendants who knew no English.

> . . . que fuera si pudían ir a ser su interprete, y luego fueron a corte y [el
> juez dijo], "What's your name?" Dice el *guy*, "Quiere saber cómo te lla-
> mas." "Pos, me llamo Casimiro Guerras." Pues el *guy* le dijo, "He says his
> name is Almost See Wars." [Laughs.] Ya me anaba de risa. And the other
> guy's name was—I'm trying to think what that other guy's name was—
> *algo*, something Palomares. [Pause.] Creo que—I don't know his first
> name, but anyway his last name *era* Palomares. Y le dijo, "He says his
> name is John Pigeonhouses." [Laughs.]

> . . . that it were if they could go to be his interpreter, and they went to
> court and [the judge said], ("What's your name?") The (guy) says, "he
> wants to know your name." "Well, my name is Casimiro Guerras." Then
> the (guy) tells him, ("He says his name is Almost See Wars.") [Laughs.] I
> was already about to laugh. (And the other guy's name was—I'm trying
> to think what the other guy's name was—something, (something) Palo-
> mares. [Pause.] I think—(I don't know his first name, but anyway his last
> name) was Palomares. And he told him, ("He says his name is John Pi-
> geonhouses.") [Laughs.]

This joke was clearly my informant's favorite, as he continued to
chuckle over the punchline for hours afterward.

The joke is particularly interesting in that one must understand both Spanish and English to appreciate the humor. It also calls on the "deep" cultural knowledge that the acculturating
immigrant tends to translate everything. However, my informant's appreciation of the joke seemed to lie not so much in ridi-
culing the foolishness of the literal-minded translator as in the
word play for its own sake. The double meaning of, for example,
"Palomares" the surname and *palomares* the things emerges not
through context of situation as in most puns, but through translation into a language (English) which uses the word in only one
meaning: "Pigeonhouses" is not an English surname. But, in the
context of the joke—"Palomares" the Spanish surname *can* be
transformed into an English surname—suggesting, at least in

fantasy, that linguistic and cultural differences can be reconciled, that one can "have it both ways," be simultaneously Mexican and American without having to compromise. In fact, it seems likely that one important function of much bilingual word play among Mexican-Americans (and, probably, among the members of any group who feel caught between two cultures) is to reconcile in ludic speech what cannot easily by reconciled outside it. My informant's pleasure in the joke lay in how it manipulated the code switching to make congruous cultural realities which are incongruous outside this special, temporary context of speech play. This feat is made possible by possession of bilingual skills.

The knock-knock jokes discussed earlier demonstrate this same preoccupation with code switching on a juvenile level. Knock-knock jokes in general are concerned with names and naming. The joke teller pretends to introduce and name himself, but the humor resides in the fact that the "name" turns out to be not a name at all. Perhaps children enjoy these jokes because they negate social practices which adults take seriously (introductions, correct identification of each other) and because they make light of a situation which troubles any child: the question of his growing self-identity, especially in relation to other people's identities. The bicultural, bilingual child may experience particularly strong identity conflicts. His or her use of bilingual knock-knock jokes makes light of growing problems of identity (as he or she moves toward the adult world) through specifically bicultural language play. That is, the jokes are a way of dealing not only with the questions of identity all children face, but also with the particular problems of cultural identity. The need to assert an identity, expressed by giving a "name" in one language (which is associated with one culture), is negated and mocked when the second language is used to show that the name is no name at all. The implication is that the existence of the second culture makes the "need" for a monocultural identity foolish.

The joke about Casimiro Guerras and Juan Palomares is especially revealing because it involves an exaggeration of a phenomenon common among Mexican-Americans: anglicizing the pronunciation of Spanish names. The trend may represent an acknowledgement of the inevitable fact that Anglos mispronounce Spanish surnames. Anglicization, then, recognizes that, unlike the blithe play between cultures in the joke cited above, actual acculturation involves the deeper and often more painful process of non-reciprocal accommodation. The Mexican-American who fits into American culture gives up something of his Mexicanness. Ambivalence about such shifts in cultural loyalty is reflected in jokes such as the quip I once heard from an educated and ambitious young man named Márquez. He announced that some day he would be known as Mr. Marquee. Whether he meant "marquee," which brings to mind the image of his name "up in lights," or "marquis," the French title of nobility, I am not sure. Either way, however, the young man was projecting for himself a successful future which involved transforming his ethnic identity, as expressed in his name, into something more grandiose and non-ethnic.

Yet at the same time he was mocking his own ambition. In fact, both the Márquez joke and the one about the literal-minded translator poke fun at pretentiousness and call attention to the folly of rejecting or disguising one's own ethnic identity, while recognizing the pressures which induce one to do just that. Both jokes, on one level, state the problem: group members who feel the tension between cultures are perhaps tempted to abandon one for the other, but cannot and, indeed, should not do so. However, on another level, the jokes provide a solution; in the fantasy of the word play which requires mastery of the language of each culture there is a subliminal merging of the conflicting cultures, and hence a psychological reconciliation of opposites.

In summary, then, we might say that long-term and continued immigration has helped to sustain bilingualism and biculturalism as both a resource and a "problem" among Mexican-Americans, even among those who are acculturated or American-born. The humor discussed in this essay deals with the tensions which arise from the conflicting demands of cultures in contact. It also suggests the possibility of resolution (albeit temporary), by easing tensions through the catharsis of laughter and giving the participants the feeling of control gained through manipulating language.

NOTES

1. Orenstein (1973) mentions the study of verbal art among the interdisciplinary tasks he urges for inclusion in research efforts on Southwestern U.S. bilingualism (biculturalism). Two excellent analyses of code switching in the narratives of bilingual storytellers are Hasselmo (1970) and Kirshenblatt-Gimblett (n.d.).

2. Cerda, Cabaza, and Farias (1970:144) list a transitive verb, "*madrear*," for which they give the meaning "*halagar*" (flatter, praise). They define the phrase "*dar madera*" (lit., give wood) as "*Adular, ensalzar de una manera no muy sincera*" (Flatter, extol in an insincere manner) (ibid.:293).

3. Cerda et al., writing about Texas Spanish, define "*chiflado/a*" as a person who has a high self-concept (1970:75). For the reflexive verb "*chiflarse*" they give the meaning "*vanagloriarse*" (be vain, glorify oneself) (ibid.:76).

4. I would like to thank Richard Bauman for sending me these texts. They were contributed to the University of Texas Folklore Archive by Annie Loredo, who remembered them from her childhood in San José, California.

5. The expression "*te* (or *le*) *patino el coco*" is listed in two lexicons of phrases peculiar to Texas-Mexican Spanish. An article in a Chicano publication, "La Perika Tejana" (Anonymous 1973:65), translates it as: "You're crazy; you're way off." Similarly, Cerda et al. interpret it to mean: "*A veces, parece que pierde el juicio*" [At times, it seems that one loses one's good judgment] (1970:266).

6. Cerda et al. list "*arrastrarle a alguien*" and the verbs "*chicotearle*," "*pajuelearle*," "*papalotearle*," "*rezumbarle*," "*zumbarle*," and "*arrastrarle*" as meaning "*Da a entender que alguien tiene mucha habilidad para hacer algo*" (Give to understand that someone has a great ability to do something) (1970:252). The article "La Perika Tejana" (Anonymous 1973:65) defines the phrase "*se avento*" as "really well done." The phrases I heard used this way most frequently were "*te avientas*," "*te tiras*," "*te sales*," and "*te arrastras*."

7. Various other ends served by speech play—"comic . . , religious, artistic, mnemonic, competitive, rehearsal and practice . . . sheer play with verbal resources for its own sake"—have been discussed more recently in Kirshenblatt-Gimblett and Sherzer (1976:1).

BIBLIOGRAPHY

Abrahams, Roger D. 1964. *Deep down in the jungle*. Hatboro, Pa.: Folklore Associates.
———. 1969. The complex relations of simple forms. *Genre* 2:104–128.
Anonymous. 1973. La Perika tejana: A study of the Texas Chicano dialect. *Magazin* 1:60–66.
Cerda, Gilberto, Berta Cabaza, and Julieta Farias. 1970. *Vocabulario español de Texas*. Austin: University of Texas Press.
Dorson, Richard M., ed. 1964. *Buying the wind*. Chicago: University of Chicago Press.

Hasselmo, Nils. 1970. Code-switching and modes of speaking. In *Texas studies in bilingualism*. Glenn Gilbert, ed. Berlin: de Gruyter.

Jordan, Rosan A. 1972. Language loyalty and folklore studies: The Mexican-American. *Western Folklore* 31:77–86.

Kirshenblatt-Gimblett, Barbara. 1972. Traditional storytelling in the Toronto Jewish Community: A study in performance and creativity in an immigrant culture. Ph.D. dissertation, Indiana University.

———. N.d. Multilingualism and immigrant narrative: Code-switching as a communicative strategy in artistic verbal performance. Unpublished MS.

———, and Joel Sherzer. 1976. Introduction. In *Speech play*. Barbara Kirshenblatt-Gimblett, ed. Philadelphia: University of Pennsylvania Press.

Orenstein, Jacob. 1973. Toward an inventory of interdisciplinary tasks in research on U.S. Southwest bilingualism/biculturalism. In *Bilingualism in the Southwest*. Paul Turner, ed. Tucson: University of Arizona Press.

Paredes, Américo. 1966. The Anglo-American in Mexican folklore. In *New voices in American studies*. Ray Browne, Donald Winkelman, and Allan Hayman, eds. Lafayette, Ind.: Purdue University Studies.

———. 1968. Folk medicine and the intercultural jest. In *Spanish-speaking people in the United States*. June Helm, ed. Seattle: University of Washington Press.

Rael, Juan B. N.d. *Cuentos españoles de Colorado y Nuevo Méjico*. 2 vols. Stanford: Stanford University Press.

Sobek, Maria Herrera. 1978. Verbal play and Mexican immigrant jokes. Paper delivered at the annual meeting of the American Folklore Society, Salt Lake City, Utah, 1978.

A Traditional Storyteller in Changing Contexts

Ed Bell is a masterful storyteller who in recent years has extended his audience from a group of sport fishermen and local residents around the Gulf Coast town of Indianola, Texas, to people attending national folk festivals and members of women's clubs and other civic organizations. These shifts in context have caused him to expand his repertoire of stories and made him increasingly aware of the importance of selecting stories adapted to the setting in which he will be telling them.

I first encountered Ed Bell during a field trip along the Gulf Coast of Texas in the summer of 1967. In interviewing Ed I acquired extensive descriptions of the usual storytelling situations at his bait camp on Matagorda Bay. I collected from him again in 1971 while he was still operating the bait camp. The next time I talked to him was in 1975 at his family ranch near Luling, Texas, where he had retired. I was working for the Smithsonian Institution's American Folklife Festival at the time and recommended Ed as a participant for the 1976 Festival. He was invited and spent a week in Washington telling stories on one of the outdoor stages at the vast Bicentennial Festival. I worked at the Festival introducing Ed and another storyteller, and used the opportunity to interview him again at length.

The next year Ed was invited to tell stories at the National Storytelling Festival in Jonesboro, Tennessee, and he has returned to this same event. This event resembles the Smithsonian Festival except that it confines itself to storytelling whereas the American Folklife Festival also features music, dance, and crafts. This national exposure brought Ed more fame at home, and he was invited to tell stories over the radio and as guest speaker at civic luncheons and women's club meetings. He has also continued to tell stories when he returns to the bait camp and at the local feed store in Harwood near his ranch. Thus, the situations in which he performs and the nature and size of his audience have changed radically since the first time I recorded him, and he has adjusted his storytelling accordingly.

The changing circumstances of Ed Bell's storytelling suggest four topics for analytic focus: (1) the general effect of place on storytelling; (2) the effect of large-scale festival exposure on traditional performers; (3) the effect of change of context on repertoire; and (4) the performer's own sense of his art. The effect of place on storytelling can be most clearly discerned by comparing the performance of one storyteller in several different situations. Ed Bell has told stories in four distinctly different settings: the bait camp, the feed store near his ranch, folk festivals, and civic club meetings. The greatest adjustment he faced was to perform before large audiences of strangers at festivals when he had been used to telling stories to small groups of friends and customers. He has adapted his repertoire to fit each situation, basing his choice of tales on several principles. Finally, as Ed Bell has gone through each stage of change, he has become more aware of his role as a performer and amazingly articulate about his art.

One effect of place on storytelling is to provide the storyteller an appropriate setting for projecting his social identity. Richard Bauman (1972) sees this process as central to verbal art at the LaHave Island general store where men used to gather to swap stories. The sessions at the store "afforded the participants a continuous opportunity to engage in personal and social identity-building by presenting the self in personal narrative and receiving like accounts about others in the same form" (ibid.: 336). The manipulation of social identity is a factor in all of the places Ed Bell performs, but it is most important in his own community, in the bait camp and the feed store. There are distinct differences in the images he projects even in these similar settings. I have described the bait camp elsewhere (Mullen 1978: 130–136); its salient features were that Ed as proprietor was the center of attention as a known raconteur and that he had an ever-changing audience of customers, sport fishermen visiting from nearby cities for a day or a week. In this setting Ed projected his own identity through personal-experience narratives, tall tales, anecdotes, jokes, and legends, but he did not usually receive "like accounts about others in the same form." One of the sport fishermen might interject a story every so often, but it was clear that Ed was the star performer. In this he differed considerably from the men at the LaHave store where "although telling yarns was an important component of the process of establishing a social identity, being a good storyteller was not itself a significant identity feature" (Bauman 1972:337). For Ed Bell, being a good storyteller is *the* significant identity feature.

The feed store provides a situation more akin to the LaHave general store because there Ed is only one of many local talkers. My observations at the feed store were that the regulars share in the talking; no one person seems to stand out. Interviewing Ed at his ranch in 1977, I asked him about the circumstances at the feed store:

MULLEN: Well, around here locally in everyday situations, do you tell many stories, like down at the feed store sitting around with the. . . ?

BELL: You know I tell little things there, but I don't tell things like I do off over there [at festivals] hardly. I don't hardly tell those stable jokes that I carry out to those places like that folklore meetings and such as that. Why, I don't, I don't hardly tell them around; I'll tell them [the men at the feed store] something funny that happened out there about I started off carrying a watermelon, and I, it fell and I busted it, and when I started to eat I found it full of sand, or something. That's about all I'd tell.

Ed's social identity at the feed store is that of any other local rancher. Short, current, personal-experience narratives reflecting everyday incidents of ranch life are the appropriate verbal forms for projecting a social image of equality. In this setting, Ed's tall tales are not appropriate since they project a larger-than-life social identity.

I seldom ever tell stories like I told out there [at the festivals] because, huh, I don't know, it just doesn't seem like they enjoy it. They want something that just happened, and they know that I'm not, that if I tell one of those windy drawn-out things, that it's just a big lie. Probably they might have heard it before so that I don't like to tell it.

At the folk festivals, Ed has an entirely new audience, who has never heard him before; he can thus select freely from his available stories. But the festival setting has an even more profound influence on his social identity. Ed becomes a celebrity at the festivals, one of the star performers, telling stories to large audiences. This new self-image is a key factor in his growing awareness of his art. He first became aware of the significance of the change of place on storytelling at the 1976 American Folklife Festival. I interviewed him on this topic after several days at the festival:

BELL: I don't know why I wanted to get, learn so much about telling these jokes; I never did intend to do anything like this. Had no idea even when I was talking to you. I thought, "Well, he sure is taking his ducks to a poor market." [Laughs.] I don't know whether you know what that means or not. Do you know what that means?

MULLEN: I think I know. Taking your ducks. . . .

BELL: Well, it's not doing the very thing that would help you very much. For instance, if a girl married an old never-do-good boy that's not ever going to turn out worth a darn, she's taking her ducks to a poor market. And then if you, huh, if you go set a hen on rotten eggs, you're taking your ducks to a poor market.

MULLEN: Yeah, I see.

BELL: The results won't be worth it.

MULLEN: Yeah. So I was doing that?

BELL: I thought that you were when you had, took that tape record-ing of what I was talking about. I thought that you was taking your ducks to a poor market. Well, I never realized, really didn't although I just dearly love to sit down and listen to somebody tell an exceedingly good joke or a good story, but I never realized that other people might want to hear that too. It doesn't seem possible that anything like that could interest people to the degree that it does.

The proverbial saying is an apt metaphor for Ed's realization of his change of identity as a storyteller; from his former humility he came to realize that he could entertain an entirely new and larger audience than he had ever encountered before. The Fes-tival made him in one sense a "professional" storyteller (although he was only paid a small honorarium); he was responsible for attracting and entertaining a diverse audience. The audience at the 1976 American Folklife Festival numbered in the millions; however, there were five or six stages operating simultaneously, offering music and dance and scores of craft and cooking demon-strations. The storytelling stage was in a grove of trees on the edge of the Festival area. Many people passed through on their way to other parts of the Festival, so that the audience was constantly changing. Ed took note of this turnover from the very first day he performed.

BELL: And I'll tell you, there's another thing that I noticed that I was way shy on up there [on the stage]. I had never had to pay any attention to public reaction before. An old fisherman, he'll laugh at anything anyway, you know. And you don't know really whether you've told a good joke or not. Those people up there were deadly serious. They's looking for something there that's interesting. Well, they didn't care, they didn't know who I was. They didn't give a darn what I was doing there. They wanted to see, and if there was anything that'd interest them, then they perked up and took notice.

MULLEN: Yeah.

BELL: Got to please those kind of people.

MULLEN: Right. You didn't have. . . .

BELL: Makes a whole lot of difference telling a joke to a fisherman out there at the fish camp.

MULLEN: Didn't have to do that, didn't have to be worried about that?

BELL: With them out there, it didn't make much difference whether it was funny or not. They were going to laugh; all I wanted to do anyway was to keep their attention until they decided to go fishing instead of going back to town.

Change of storytelling place also means change in the characteristics of the audience. The most recent setting for Ed's storytelling has presented him with audiences segregated by sex, so that he needed to make another conscious manipulation of social identity. He appears in one guise before men's civic groups and in another before women's clubs.

And then another thing, I was asked to talk ten minutes over the ladies' hour on the radio at Seguin, and I couldn't understand why the ladies wanted me to talk over the ladies' hour because I lack a whole lot being a lady. I'm a pretty rough old man. And that girl over there, they said that they was very, very pleased to have me, that I was one of the, that the ladies was more my fans than the men was. And then I was asked to appear before the ladies' home demonstration club in Luling, and to tell them a few jokes and kind of freshen up the atmosphere. And I got it freshened up a little bit for them all right. I had them laughing pretty good over some of those jokes.

Ed plays up his identity as "a pretty rough old man" before women's groups by telling stories about masculine pursuits like hunting and fishing; these tales fulfill the women's expectations of the male role he should play and probably provide a welcome change from their usual talks. His stories give them a glimpse into a world ordinarily hidden from their view.

A different factor influences Ed's performance at men's clubs. He has carefully evaluated them as an audience and adjusted his storytelling accordingly.

Well, I'll tell you. I like to tell something funny especially to businessmen that might be kind of tired. You know if a person's out there working, he's kind of, he's kind of out of sorts with the world anyway part of the time because he's over his head in work, and if he can just sit back and laugh at some funny story for even thirty minutes, he can go back to work with a whole lot better feeling, and he'll clap louder at something funny like that than he will at a real outlandish big lying tale. So I figure that a businessman likes something funny to laugh at at noontime.

Here Ed becomes like "one of the boys" who might usually exchange jokes with each other—except that in this situation he is a star performer who entertains the rest of the group. The men's and women's club settings resemble the festivals in spotlighting Ed as the star.

All of these settings have had a profound influence on Ed's repertoire. He has followed certain clear patterns in adjusting it. Kenneth Goldstein (1972:63) formulates some factors which account for changes in a traditional performer's repertoire. Although Goldstein applies these patterns to traditional singers and their songs, they also can apply to storytellers and their narratives. Especially relevant to the study of Ed Bell's repertoire are Goldstein's points about topicality, taste and esthetics, social roles and identity, and change or loss of audience.

Ed's retirement from the bait camp to his ranch brought his first change of audience.

MULLEN: Since you're no longer staying at the bait camp, has that changed the amount of stories that you tell?

BELL: Yes, it has in effect because I'm not there much of the time, and when I'm out at the ranch, there's no one there to listen to them but my wife, and there's very little use in telling them to her. Once in a while I'll try to repeat one because she knows them all. . . . I lost my audience for part of the time. Still when I go down there to the bait camp as soon as they find out about it, why they go drifting around and get me started. They go to feeling, you know, jabbing me with little things here and there to try and get me started. And if I don't tell them something, they

[say], "Bell, you kind of sick or something? You lost your stuff? What's the matter, you letting that garden up there get under your hide?" Some crazy question like that, you know.

Because of the situation at the ranch, many of Ed's stories became inactive; only when he made trips back to the bait camp did the context demand their reactivation. This state might have continued had Ed not been invited to appear at folk festivals.

Goldstein (1972:65) notes that "new audiences are occasionally created for a singer" by coffee houses, concerts, and folk festivals. In Ed Bell's case this new opportunity made topicality an important factor in his repertoire. For folk festival audiences, Ed reactivated and updated one old story that had been dormant. He calls the story "The Pet Fish":

In the year 2000 pollution had already gotten so far out of control that all the, practically all the fish in the world had already died, most of the birds in the air were gone, they were dead, all killed by pollution. Man had managed to survive because man was the strongest thing in the world, and these fish were so far gone that I caught one; it was a real oddity. It was a small fish, and so seemed so cute, and he'd say "Yok, yok" to me. So, you know, I can't eat that fish. I'm not fish-hungry anyway, not really. And then pollution too, you know, you might be a little afraid to eat. I says, "You know, I believe I'll keep that for a pet."

Well, we had a real deep water well there, that the water still wasn't badly polluted in. So I used that water to keep this fish in for a while, and then I got the idea that that water, the trough that I was keeping him in was getting pollution because he acted like it was bothering him a little. So I take him out of this water, and leave him out for a few seconds at a time to start with. And day by day I increased his time out of the water until he didn't need the water any more at all. And he followed me around all over the place. The only thing I'd do is just wet his skin down to keep it from drying up and crumbling. I'd wet his skin three or four times a day, and he was just as happy as he could be. He'd get to following me around a good deal. And I got to where I'd just take special walks to give him exercise. He'd flop, flop, flop along behind me, and it looked like he was trying to grow some legs. I just knew he was even going to grow legs and I was so proud of that fish because by this time all the fish in the world were gone, they were done; they'd started dying in the seventies when the pollution got so terrible bad in the nineteen-seventies, and by the year 2000 they were all gone. This was the last fish in the world, and he wouldn't, I don't know whether you'd call him a fish or not; he wasn't in the water any more.

Well, anyway I was so fond of that fish, and I decided to take him for a walk down across the creek one day and let him see, see if he knew

what water was, what he'd do about it. And the bridge had real wide
cracks in it, just an old wood bridge. And I started across it, and I's kind
of watching him; he was flopping along like that, flop, flop, flop. Well, he
got right over that creek, and he fell through one of those wider cracks,
and he fell in the water and drowned.

Ed does not tell this story at the bait camp—the Festival provided him with the opportunity to use it. He invented the tale
although it uses a traditional motif (X1306, Lie: tamed fish lives
on dry land).[1] I asked Ed where he got the idea for the story. "Oh,
I don't know. Somebody said one time that their poor little old
fish fell overboard and drowned." He also explained that he had
added to the story down through the years:

I made that story up about twenty, twenty-five years ago, and I never
used it very much. And the huh, I have grown on that story on the pollution part. That's only come in lately. Used to we didn't know anything
about pollution; shoot, if water wasn't good, or it was bad, or something
you know, it was awful good drinking water. But now it's pollution. So I
brought that in on that.

The expanded audience calls for more up-to-date stories, and Ed
now incorporates current events into his narratives.

Esthetics and social identity both influence Ed's repertoire in
the settings of the men's and women's civic organizations. The
masculine role which Ed seeks to project at the women's clubs
determines his choice of stories on those occasions. He has fig-
ured out their taste in stories and how to play on it.

BELL: And the ladies, I like to tell them just as far out of reach as I
          possibly can because I like to watch their eyes get big and then
          kind of pop in their faces, you know. [Laughs.]
MULLEN: So you tell them the tall tales?
BELL: I tell them the tallest ones that I can get. I really do.

A typical tall tale Ed would relate to these women involves
hunting and fishing:

I like dogs. I like all animals really, but especially dogs. And I've always
had more or less of a hunting dog or some kind of a dog around. And this
dog was one of the smartest dogs I ever saw in my life. He was just as
smart as he could be; in fact, I thought sometimes he's might near smarter than a human. So I got to noticing that dog that everytime I'd picked
up my shotgun to go hunting he'd go to pointing quail. And I, he knew I
was a good quail, a big quail hunter. And I thought, well now I wonder if

that's a coincidence. So one day I wanted to go get some squirrels, so I picked up the .22, and I walked out, and he went and treed a squirrel. He wouldn't fool with nothing but squirrel that day. So I tried him two or three more times, back and forth, and every time when I got the shotgun, he'd point quail, and when I got the .22, he'd hunt squirrels. Said, "I'm going to fool that durn dog. That dog ain't as smart as somebody. I'm going to fool that dog."

So next day I went over there and picked up my rod and reel, started out of the house, trying to whistle, just kind of through my teeth. This dog run along by me, trotted along by me, and whining and cutting up. Every once in a while he'd bark, kind of a questioning bark. I says, "Well, come on boy, let's go get 'em." He run plumb around me, about twice. "Arf, arf, arf." I [said], "Well, what in the world's the matter with that crazy dog now?" And he just turned and tore back to the house as hard as he could go, about a half a mile. I's laughing about it, started to go on fishing, and I happened to think I better go on back and see what's wrong with that dog. He's acting kind of crazy. So I went on back to the house, and I asked Mama, she was at the front door. I said, "Did you see old Willie come in?" "Oh yeah, he come in about ten, five or ten minutes ago." I said, "Where'd he go?" "Oh," says, "he's just going around the house scratching dirt as he went, right around the back somewhere." Said, "Maybe he's got a bone buried there." "I don't know. There's something wrong with that dog." I went back there, and there was that dog around behind the house, had a tin can, and he was digging worms. (Motif X1215.8, Lie: intelligent dog)

Tall tales had been a staple of Ed's repertoire at the bait camp, but when he retired to the ranch he had ceased telling them. Then his new audiences became available. The tastes of sport fishermen and women's club members are similar enough that he can again tell tall tales. His social identity as a traditional liar and larger-than-life character at the bait camp is close to the identity he projects at women's meetings; the tall tales are an appropriate means of expressing this image in either context.

Ed also bases his social identity before the men's civic organizations on the esthetics of the audience, and adjusts his repertoire accordingly. He chooses to play a comic role before these groups in order to entertain them and, since he is dealing with an all-male audience, the comic stories can be slightly obscene. He would never tell a dirty joke to a group of women, but he often tells the following risqué narrative to men:

But this old boy was driving freight across the country, and he got in front of this big old two-story farmhouse. I guess it was a farmhouse, an old two-story house. And a big mudhole in the road right there, and he got stuck, and it was late in the evening. Well, he badgered his team and hollered and whooped around a while. Old farmer came out on the porch and finally he walked out there to him and said, "Young man," says, "you're not going to get out of that mudhole." Says, "You ain't got much time before dark." Says, "Why not unhitch your team, turn them loose there in the lot, come on in, we'll have supper, and give you a place to sleep; next morning you'll get a fresh start and feel more like it." He says, "Old-timer, I hate to impose on you, but I don't mind if I do." Says, "I am getting tired." Says, "Come on, unhitch your team and bring them in."

So he unhitched them, left the wagon out there in that mudhole, put his team in the pen, went in there and washed up for supper. And all that they had for supper was turnip greens; they had that old salt pork just in there real nice like, you know, and they's just about right to suit him, and he just ate and ate and ate. He did eat away a lot of those turnip greens. This old man looked at him, shook his head a minute, and he says, "Say, young fella," he says, "that's all we're going to have for breakfast. If you eat all of them up tonight, we won't have none for breakfast." Well, that sure embarrassed that old boy; he just pushed back right quick, and he just quit eating those turnip greens.

So that night the old man says, "Well, we got a great big bed," and says, "All four of us will have to sleep in the same bed." Says, "My daughter," says, "she's eighteen years old. Me and Ma, we'll all have to sleep in the same bed." Says, "We got lots of rooms, but there ain't no other beds." So they all went to bed in this big old, great big old wide bed, about as, maybe a little wider than a king-size like they got nowadays. During the night, why the team got to cutting up, and you could hear the barb wire screeching in the stables, you know. And the old lady punched her old man, says, "Old man, old man, wake up quick." Says, "That team's fighting out there. Sounds like some of them are hung up in that fence." Old man says, "You know I can't see very good. You're going to have to come along and help me." The old lady says, "Well, I might of known that'd be coming up." So she got up, and they staggered off downstairs and out to the lot. This girl reached over and punched this old boy and says, "Hey, now's your chance. Now's your chance." So he jumped up and run down there and eat up the rest of them turnip greens.[2]

With new opportunities to tell stories, Ed has started to look for new jokes to expand his repertoire. Most of his stories are from oral tradition, but he gets a few from printed sources. He has used the humor publication *Texas Brags* as a source for at least one new story. The festivals have also added to his repertoire; the National Storytelling Festival was especially fruitful in this way. He tells one of these new stories by first placing it in the context of the Festival, in order to give credit to his source:

There's a lady getting ready to go over and tell some stories at Washington, D.C., at huh Tennessee, and this O'Connell fella was going to introduce her, and then he got to telling about what she had done before she came to work that morning. Said, "I'll tell you," says, "that woman got into a mess. She went out into the yard, and there was all this lawn mowing needing to be done, she just knew it had to be done right away, so she grabbed up her lawn mower and started mowing." Said, "She come up there about middle ways, and there's a great big old toad frog, biggest one she'd ever seen, mean looking toad frog too. Well, she nudged him a little, and he wouldn't move, so she just went to going around him. Finally she'd mowed all the yard except right up here where this big old toad was sitting. Well, she says, I, I'll get you some way or another, and she nudged him here and nudged him there. Finally she got mad and just raised the lawn mower up a little bit and dropped it right on top of him. Here come grass and dirt just a-flying out from under that mower all around, and she says, Well, how come that dirt? That grass looks like it's got roots on it. Said, Man, that's awful. So she got down right quick and looked under that mower, and there that old frog was trying to jump those blades, and that's what was kicking up all that dust and grass." (Motif X1342, Lies about frogs).

Ed admired O'Connell as a storyteller, and the toad story was his favorite O'Connell tale. Ed especially appreciated how O'Connell could adapt a story to a particular person he was introducing, as he did with the toad story; fitting a tale to a particular situation is part of Ed's esthetic of storytelling. In this he resembles the Nova Scotian storyteller whose esthetics Richard Tallman (1974:127–128) has described.

Ed Bell has a highly developed sense of his own esthetic, which he freely articulates, unlike other traditional storytellers folklorists have studied. Tallman's Nova Scotian storyteller was reluctant to talk about esthetics, and George Carey found his Maryland Eastern Shore raconteur similarly inhibited (Carey 1976:87). Ed Bell's experience with festivals has increased his concern with esthetics, but since Alex Kellam in Carey's study has appeared at the Smithsonian Festival more than once, festival appearances are not the sole factor that determines a storyteller's willingness to discuss esthetics. The fact that Ed Bell has been writing fiction over the last several years may have added to his sensitivity toward esthetics. He has also read an article I wrote on his storytelling style (Mullen 1976), which must have increased his self-awareness. He will no doubt read this paper as well, so that there is an on-going dialogue between folklorist and storyteller about style and esthetics.

Ed's sense of esthetics has been sharpened by the changing contexts of his storytelling. Part of this growth was a response to the demands of the American Folklife Festival audiences. He had to hold his listeners' attention to keep them from drifting off to other attractions.

Well, at Washington, D.C., I found out that it was awful nice to tell one or two long tales, and it didn't matter if it was just old-timey happenings, but don't let it ride out too long to where you reach in and pull out a real funny one to get them to look back again and sit back down a little bit harder on the stool again because most of them are getting loosened up on that stool to leave when you tell something long. And huh if, it don't make no difference how long it is if you can bring something funny in once in a while. If you've got nothing funny to bring in there, well don't make it too long, cut it off a little short so you can bring out something funny because people that are out just for the fun of things and for an outing, they're not going to just sit there and listen to something that they don't like. They're not going to do it.

In Ed's previous storytelling experiences audience desertion had not been a concern; now he had to invent new timing techniques. Large audiences presented problems that small-audience techniques could not solve.

However, Ed has carried over some of the storytelling techniques of a small-group context into large-group situations. For instance, he observed individuals in the audience at Jonesboro in order to help his timing:

At Jonesboro I didn't have a chance to find out anything about that [the audience leaving during a performance]. They put me in the back end of a church there that [had] a capacity crowd was probably three hundred people. And they had about fifty people in there more than a capacity crowd, and I was very thrilled to find out that when I got outside, they had a loudspeaker out there, and people were stacked as much as a hundred yards away trying to listen to that loudspeaker. And I was inside there telling these jokes. I would love to have been looking at some of those people. About the only person that I could see in there, four or five that I knew, and one good-looking girl that sat right out in front about as far, I guess about fifteen feet out in front of them, maybe only ten. And her eyes and her whole face would change every time I'd change the expression of my voice telling about these crazy happenings, you know. Whenever I'd get to something pretty big, I'd make it a little bit more expression on that, and drag it out a little bit deeper, you know. And her eyes'd get a little bigger around or something, look like she was kind of going to blow up, and she's almost laughing all the time, and I couldn't help but look at her, and I'd make things a little bit rougher. You know, louder or something while I was looking at her. And I believe that that really did help me a lot to see somebody that seemed to be appreciating that so much that they was letting expression of all this stuff appear on their face. I think that helped me a whole lot.

The face-to-face interaction of a small-group situation is still possible, in a limited way, in a large group.

Ed Bell's ability as a storyteller developed over the forty years he ran his bait camp. When the opportunity arose to tell stories in new contexts he was able to use the same narrative skills and awareness of his audience as a basis for expanding and adjusting his repertoire to fit the new situations. He already had a conception of himself as a performer which he was able to use in relating to larger, unknown audiences. His perceptiveness enabled him to adjust rather quickly to the demands of these new listeners. He is still a traditional performer, but the shifts in context have definitely altered his performance. Changes continue to take place; as of this writing there is a possibility that Ed will be videotaped telling stories. Certainly this new context will produce even further alteration in the telling of his stories; but at the core Ed Bell remains true to his tradition.

NOTES

I am indebted to Richard Bauman and Roger Abrahams for valuable suggestions, which helped shape the final form of this paper.
1. This and all subsequent motif numbers refer to Thompson (1955–1958).
2. Legman (1971 : 121) gives a variant of this story.

BIBLIOGRAPHY

Bauman, Richard. 1972. The LaHave Island general store: Sociability and verbal art in a Nova Scotia community. *Journal of American Folklore* 85 : 330–343.
Carey, George. 1976. The storyteller's art and the collector's intrusion. In *Folklore today, a festschrift for Richard M. Dorson.* L. Dégh, H. Glassie, and F. Oinas, eds. Bloomington: Indiana University Press.
Goldstein, Kenneth. 1972. On the application of the concepts of active and inactive traditions to the study of repertory. In *Toward new perspectives in folklore.* Américo Paredes and Richard Bauman, eds. Austin: University of Texas Press.

Legman, G. 1971. *Rationale of the dirty joke: An analysis of sexual humor.* New York: Grove Press.

Mullen, Patrick B. 1976. The tall tale style of a Texas raconteur. In *Folk narrative research.* Juha Pentikäinen and Tuula Juurikka, eds. Helsinki: Finnish Literature Society.

———. 1978. *I heard the old fishermen say: Folklore of the Texas Gulf Coast.* Austin: University of Texas Press.

Tallman, Richard. 1974. You can almost picture it: The aesthetics of a Nova Scotia storyteller. *Folklore Forum* 7 : 121–130.

Thompson, Stith. 1955–1958. *Motif-index of folk literature.* Bloomington: Indiana University Press.

Manuel H. Peña

The Emergence of Conjunto Music, 1935–1955

The emergence, in the years between 1935 and 1955, of a highly popular style of Texas-Mexican music known as "conjunto" poses interesting questions for ethnomusicologists. These questions hold significance for other social scientists as well, because, as the ethnomusicologist John Blacking (1974) has suggested, the interpretation of musical activity can serve as a key to understanding other aspects of social organization. Thus, in tracing the development of modern conjunto music from its embryonic appearance in Narciso Martínez's first commercial recording in 1935 to its full-blown stylization by such artists as Paulino Bernal in the mid-1950s, we might well ask two questions. The first is musicological: How can we describe the style of conjunto music? The second question is ethnomusicological: given that the accordion and the other instruments used in conjunto music have been extant along both sides of the border for at least a hundred years, why did a distinctive, durable, and highly identifiable style of music not reach fruition until after World War II?

It is my purpose in this paper to attempt preliminary answers to these questions. I have worked out the ideas presented here on the basis of about a year of ethnomusicological research into this music, as well as some twenty years of performing and hearing it. I should note that the style is sometimes identified with *norteño* music (a form common throughout northern Mexico). However, most Texanos prefer the label "conjunto." What differences do exist between northern Mexican and *texano* accordion music are quite subtle. For example, until recently the saxophone was more commonly identified with Mexican *norteño* groups. I feel, however, that the changes in conjunto music I will be describing (including the first use of the saxophone in a conjunto group) were generally wrought by *texano* musicians and only then emulated by their Mexican counterparts. In any case, the distinction blurs considerably when we learn that some important Mexican groups, such as Los Alegres de Téran, have set up permanent residence in the United States.

I would also note that the research on which this essay is based has actually focused on a comparative analysis of conjunto music and what is commonly known among Chicanos[1] as "*orquesta texana*" music (or simply "*orquesta*"), another popular style. Together the two forms comprise "*música texana*." I will restrict my comments here to conjunto music, although some references to *orquesta* will be necessary.

THE EVOLUTION OF CONJUNTO STYLE

There are two explanations of how the accordion, the instrument fundamental to conjunto style, was first introduced to the border area. The first posits that European settlers, especially Germans, first brought it to the attention of Chicanos, who quickly adopted it for their use; the other, held by some of the older accordionists such as Pedro Ayala, that it came from Mexico, specifically Monterrey. Neither theory has been conclusively proven, to my knowledge.

In either case, we know that the accordion as a solo instrument was popular by at least the 1890s, particularly among the predominantly poor, rural Mexicans on both sides of the Texas border. An article in the *San Antonio Express* of 1897 mentions an "accordion artist who wends his way through the chaparral."[2] And my own father, who was born in 1895 in the border village of Salineño, Texas, has described for me some of the *bailes de jacal* (usually patio weddings) of the turn of the century, which featured accordion soloists accompanied by what was known as "*tambora de rancho*" ("ranch drum").[3] Narciso Martínez and Pedro Ayala,[4] two popular accordionists who started their musical careers in the 1920s, corroborate this information. According to them, the one-row button accordion was commonly used in those days at dances, either as a solo instrument or in combination with the *tambora de rancho*. This latter instrument, incidentally, was evidently fashioned out of native (i.e., not store-bought) materials—including its skin of *cuero de chivo* (goat skin), the wooden mallets used to play it, and even the body of the drum itself. Only occasionally were the guitar, *bajo sexto*, or a violin used to accompany the accordion. Thus it is clear that, by the 1890s at least, the accordion had become so popular among the working classes that it had begun to replace other types of music (such as *orquesta típica*[5]) as the *marco musical* (musical frame) for weddings, *bailes de regalos*,[6] and other domestic celebrations.

Certainly, as a solo instrument much in demand from those early days up until the 1920s, the accordion must have undergone some common stylization by musicians of the same sociocultural background. Narciso Martínez, Pedro Ayala, Santiago Jiménez, and other accordionists of the 1930s were undoubtedly heirs to this stylization. But the variability of the early accordion ensemble, such as it was, would probably insure not only that this earlier music differed from modern conjunto, but that a well-defined style, using certain instruments in certain prescribed combinations, was unlikely to develop. We may thus posit, as the date of the emergence of a definable conjunto style of music, the year 1935—when Narciso Martínez recorded his first polka, "La Chicharronera," for commercial distribution. This is however a more or less arbitrary date; Chris Strachwitz (1974a) claims Martínez had commercial precursors, notably Bruno Villarreal and Lolo Cavazos, either or both of whom recorded as early as 1931.

To be sure, Martínez was not the sole exponent of the music in its early days. Less popular musicians, such as San Antonio's Santiago Jiménez, contributed their talents as well. A recording by Lolo Cavazos from 1939 comes remarkably close, in its articulation, to the style of the next generation of musicians, who launched the mature phase of the music. I will have more to say about the musicians who were important in shaping conjunto style later. For now I merely wish to emphasize that it was in the 1930s that this incipient style, featuring at first only the two-row accordion and *bajo sexto*[7] (and occasionally the guitar), began to take hold in the area from the Rio Grande to San Antonio. And it was with Narciso Martínez, whose popularity exceeded that of all other conjunto musicians in the 1930s and 1940s, that the style took off.

Since the 1930s, and especially since the early 1950s, when musicians like Martínez began to tour as far away as California and Chicago, conjunto music has gained currency over wide areas of the United States (and Mexico). The diffusion of the style seems to have coincided with the migration patterns of Texan and *norteño* Mexican workers, who, quite naturally, took their music with them wherever they traveled. Many such individuals, as we know, have migrated, particularly to California and the Midwest, and their cultural impact on the Chicanos of these regions has undoubtedly been significant. However, studies of such intra-cultural assimilation are almost nonexistent. I can only cite, from personal experience, the fact that by the 1960s both *orquesta* and conjunto music were firmly established in the music-and-dance tradition of central California.[8]

Chris Strachwitz (1974b) has called Narciso Martínez the "father" of conjunto music. The label is apt, I believe. He was the most popular musician of the 1930s and of the better part of the 1940s. He was an innovator; according to Pedro Ayala, who started his career at the same time, Martínez strongly influenced those who followed him. Martínez, like most conjunto musicians before and after him, came from a rural working-class background.[12] Now in his sixties, he was born in Reynosa, Tamaulipas, Mexico, across the river from the Rio Grande Valley, and was brought over to the United States as a small child. Having received almost no formal education, Martínez started his professional career in 1927. By 1935 he had graduated from the antiquated one-row button accordion to the newer two-row model. His professional opportunity came when Bluebird, a recording subsidiary of RCA that was developing regional talent in Texas, brought him to San Antonio, liked his music, and put him on commercial recordings.

Martínez's first record, "La Chicharronera" (flip-side: "El Troncanal"), was released in 1935. An instant success, "La Chicharronera" set the stage for the emergence of a definable and enduring conjunto musical style. The recording itself shows that style in its embryonic form. It paired up Martínez on accordion with Santiago Almeida on *bajo sexto*; the two instruments have since become staples in the conjunto. Martínez's technique is especially noteworthy with respect to the style's subsequent development. Like the accordionists who followed him until the late 1940s, Martínez played with a fluid legato which connected all the notes within a phrase. The polka, which became by far the most popular dancing tune, was played at a brisk 120–130 beats per minute. The sixteenth-note patterns common in the polkas of Martínez and his contemporaries made the phrases seem to run into each other in rapid succession. The overall articulation

sounded rushed, as Martínez himself pointed out to me in a recent interview. The phrases run into and trip over each other. The
bajo sexto, serving as both harmony and bass line, tended to emphasize the bass notes over the upbeat strum.

Santiago Jiménez was only slightly less popular than Martínez in the 1930s and 1940s. A native of San Antonio, Jiménez
started his career in the early 1930s. Like Martínez, he grew up in
the relative poverty of the proletarian Mexican worker. Despite
their popularity, neither of these two early musicians was ever
able to rely exclusively on his music for economic support. Both
had to turn to other occupations traditionally available at that
time to Mexicans in the United States. Jiménez spent a good part
of his working life as a public-school janitor, while Martínez alternated between truck driving and working in the fields. Pedro
Ayala and other early conjunto musicians faced the same hard-
ships. Professionalism, in the sense of sole economic reliance on
music, was not to become a reality until the next generation of
musicians arrived on the scene.

Jiménez recorded his first selections in 1936: two polkas, "Di-
ces Pescao" [sic] and "La Luisita," with the Decca label. The fluid-
ity of his articulation probably indicates Martínez's influence,
although it also reflects the prevailing conception of what the accordion should sound like. Jiménez did make one important contribution to the then-emerging conjunto style: he was the first to
incorporate the contrabass, generally known as a "*tololoche.*" No
one else did so until after 1948.

The commercial distribution of the music of Santiago Jiménez, Narciso Martínez, and other popular conjunto musicians
of the 1930s undoubtedly had much to do with the course of the
music's stylization. Many other conjunto musicians (such as Lolo
Cavazos) also recorded for major labels, whose financial backing
added impetus to the music's popularity.

One may argue, as some have with respect to the mass distribution of American pop music and other commodities, that
such commercial dissemination of conjunto music "froze" conjunto style into a more or less common form. Particularly after
World War II when, as one informant told Limón (1977a), the popularity of public ballroom dancing increased dramatically, competition among conjunto musicians was keen. Each group strove to
please not only its audiences but the local recording companies
which had replaced the large labels after the war. This competi-

tion probably tended to restrict the range of stylistic innovation, although we must keep in mind that the style had been changing gradually since the 1930s—and changed dramatically after 1948. However, I do not feel that commercialization can adequately account for either conjunto music's strong stylization or its overwhelming appeal to Texas-Mexican proletarian workers. On the contrary (and major-label support notwithstanding), conjunto music came of age at precisely the time that conditions seemed least favorable for its development, as I will explain below. Moreover, other types of musical groups, such as *orquestas típicas* and singing duets with assorted accompaniments, recorded both in Texas and California, and Greater Mexican music in a wide variety of styles, were as popular then as now among Mexicans in the United States. Yet, of all these possible musical influences, only the accordion style introduced by Martínez and Jiménez was incorporated into the fully evolved and eminently popular conjunto style of music, whose mature expression began to take form in the late 1940s.

In the meantime the popularity of Narciso Martínez, in particular, soared. He earned the epithet "El Huracán del Valle," as a sort of recognition (or advertisement) that he was a trailblazer. Santiago Jiménez was never quite as influential as Martínez, perhaps because, unlike Martínez, who toured extensively throughout the Southwest, he rarely ventured outside San Antonio. Both Martínez and Jiménez recorded prolifically, usually dance music—the ubiquitous polka as well as such universal favorites as redowas and schottisches. They and other conjunto musicians also recorded the *norteño* variety of the Mexican *huapango* and a brisker version of the redowa called the "*vals alto*." Then, as now, when we speak of *texano* music we must include the dance. The two elements, music and dance, form one symbolic structure.

Elements of the redowa (which Texas-Mexicans also called "*vals bajito*") and *vals alto* were incorporated into the modern conjunto (and *orquesta*) version of the *vals*, or *canción, ranchero(a)*.[10] The *canción ranchera* first appeared as such in recordings of the late 1940s. Played in the ¾ time of the *vals*, in a slow ⅝ time, or in the ¾ polka meter, these songs (often the lament of an abandoned lover) enjoy wide popularity today through their performance by both conjuntos and *orquestas texanas*. No other genre, however, brought Martínez, Jiménez, and their colleagues of the 1930s and 1940s more acclaim than the polka, whose distinctive performance in even the early recordings adumbrated the fully "Chicanoized" (if I may use the term) polka.

Consequently, and not surprisingly, the polka and its variations (such as the later addition of *ranchera* song lyrics) emerged by the early 1950s as the quintessential expression of Chicano music and dance.[11] As I mentioned, of the other genres prevalent in the conjunto's early days only the adaptation of the redowa and *vals alto* to the *canción ranchera* has remained popular. The durability of the polka and *ranchera* is, I feel, related to the whole push of conjunto music, during its twenty years or so of development, toward a common stylistic denominator. And this push, as I will propose below, was in turn linked to the high levels of social interaction and integration among a class of people, the proletarian workers. To this group conjunto musicians were intimately tied, both socioculturally and economically.

Pedro Ayala, a contemporary of Martínez and Jiménez and also from the Rio Grande Valley, started his musical career at the same time as Martínez. He made his recording debut rather late, however—in 1948, only shortly before a number of younger musicians such as Valerio Longoria, Tony de la Rosa, and Daniel Garcez propelled conjunto music into the next level of development. Yet Ayala's style in 1948 clearly presaged the changes which were about to transform the conjunto sound into its modern expression. Whereas the accordion technique of Martínez and Jiménez tended to be fluid and the phrasing and articulation blurred by their extreme legato, Ayala's first recordings evince a marcato quality carried further in the deliberate staccato of de la Rosa and those who followed him. In addition Ayala, together with bandleader and saxophonist Eugenio Gutierrez, was probably the first to attempt the important union between the conjunto and *orquesta* styles.[12] The two recorded the polka "El Naranjal" in 1948—quite possibly this was one of the first times the alto saxophone was incorporated into the conjunto style of music. Shortly thereafter, however, Martínez and the "father" of the modern *orquesta texana* style, Beto Villa, went a step further. They incorporated the accordion into the *orquesta*, recording, among other selections, "Rosita Vals" and (surprisingly) the American tune, "San Antonio Rose."

After 1948 the final, mature phase of conjunto music took shape rather rapidly, as a younger generation of musicians emerged. Among the most influential of these was Tony de la Rosa, from Corpus Christi. He was possibly the first (although this honor might belong to Valerio Longoria) to record with the instrumental ensemble that has since become thoroughly traditional—the three-row accordion, the *bajo sexto* (amplified by an electric pickup), the electric bass guitar, and the standard dance-band drum set. De la Rosa and Longoria, who performed in the Corpus Christi–San Antonio area, were caught up in what in retrospect were significant changes that were taking place not only in the music but in the whole music-and-dance tradition. These changes seem minor, yet they were important to the style's direction and for its relationship to the contemporary social scene. What de la Rosa and others did was to slow down the tempo of the polka from the earlier accordionists' brisk 120–130 beats per minute to 100–110 beats—or less.

These slower speeds made it easier to play the accordion with a more deliberate, choppy, staccato technique (or else the adoption of the staccato technique forced the tempo to slow down). Additionally—as can be heard, for instance, in a de la Rosa recording of the "Flamingo Polka" from the early 1950s—a wholly novel but soon characteristic prominence was given to the drums. Lastly, as the electric bass took over the bass line, the *bajo sexto* developed a characteristic emphasis on the upbeat accompaniment strum of the polka that has endured to this day:

(from: etc.   to: etc.)

The overall effect of these changes, particularly of the slowed-down, staccato style of articulation on the accordion, was to set off rather sharply the new, revised conjunto style of de la Rosa and others from the older style of Martínez and his contemporaries. The links were there, of course (Tony de la Rosa always declared his teachers were Martínez and the other early players), but with the new additions and changes conjunto music could finally be said to have come of age. By the early 1950s the new style had completely caught on, and thereafter it became a kind of ideal, almost normative, conjunto sound. The final change was the deliberate grafting of the new style to a new dance style that, according to Narciso Martínez, had made its appearance in San Antonio in the late 1940s.

This new dance, "*el tacuachito*" ("the possum"), quickly became popular all over Texas among working-class people, whose support had been vital to the development of conjunto music. The name of this dance identified it metaphorically as uniquely native by associating its gliding movements with another popular native inhabitant—the opossum. By the early 1950s the new dance had become a standard feature of the traditional Saturday-night Chicano dance. Young working-class Chicanos, many of whom had also adopted the characteristic style of the *pachuco* (vaseline-groomed ducktails, baggy slacks with ankle-tight cuffs, shellacked double-soled shoes, etc.), added their own peculiar movements to the basic dance form. As a member of a migrant farm-working family who "tagged along" as my two older brothers regularly attended Saturday night dances, I witnessed many of these dances during the 1950s in cities and towns from McAllen in the Rio Grande Valley to Lubbock in the Texas Panhandle.

Within this special Saturday-night dance setting, young men and women came to meet each other, to break the monotony of the hard labor in the cotton fields, and to celebrate their youth in their own way. In dancing *el tacuachito* they stamped their own interpretation on a durable Chicano esthetic reality. Older people did not usually attend these dances—not because they did not like the music but because it was understood that young people went there to meet potential mates. (Many young women were escorted by watchful mothers.) At other types of dances, such as at the frequent weddings, young and old participated alike. And, whether one attended dances or not, conjunto music was always available over the air waves; Spanish-language radio stations were common enough even then. In this way, then, conjunto music proliferated and came to pervade the daily life of the Chicano working class.

One last exponent of conjunto music deserves mention. Paulino Bernal is recognized as one of the best accordion players of all time. His group took conjunto as far as it was to go until recently, when younger musicians such as Oscar Hernandez and Esteban Jordán began to revitalize the style. Besides refining the style by perfecting the staccato and exploiting the high register (indeed, the whole range) of the accordion, Bernal's group generally raised the conjunto sound to a new level of sophistication. He achieved this step by adopting (possibly the first conjunto musician to do so) the vastly more flexible *acordeón cromática*. This chromatic four- or five-row button accordion obviously facilitated key changes and more complex harmonization. Bernal also had much to do with integrating *ranchero* song texts into the conjunto style (not previously a common practice—although in the late

1940s Narciso Martínez provided instrumental backing for various groups, and Los Alegres de Terán, a Mexican conjunto which featured a vocal duet, had begun its rise to fame). The Bernal group's renditions of *canciones rancheras*, both in polka and *vals* meters, are, by common consensus among Chicano musicians, some of the best in the conjunto repertoire. The group's phenomenal success since the mid-1950s (which Bernal later parlayed into his own recording company) clearly supports this peer appraisal.

Organized in Kingsville, Texas, in 1952, El Conjunto Bernal began introducing its own material shortly after de la Rosa had broken new ground with his innovations. The polka "La Capirucha," which features a marvellously fast sixteenth-note staccato effect, and the *vals ranchero* "Mi Unico Camino," which incorporated three-part sung harmonies into conjunto for possibly the first time, are some of Bernal's earliest performances and reflect the changes he wrought. These changes included the rapid staccato patterns and the three-part harmony, as well as a similarly staccato style of singing, more complex chord progressions, crisp drumming (with well-placed double rolls for more effective breaks), and a heavily emphasized upbeat strum on the *bajo sexto*. Immensely popular and highly influential, Bernal's style could easily be said to represent the apex of the Chicanoized, pachucoized *tacuachito* polka.

By the mid-1950s, then, conjunto music had evolved into a highly identifiable musical structure—particularly with respect to the polka, which was by far the most prevalent genre. It is worth noting that after World War II the primary occupation of the best professional and semi-professional conjunto musicians was to play for dances of all kinds—weddings, *cumpleaños*, anniversaries, *jamaicas*, and so forth. After 1948, a rapidly increasing public-ballroom commercialization of the music allowed the most popular musicians to turn fully professional. Many were busy the year round touring all over the Southwest and beyond, parlaying the popularity of their records into dollars by their appearances at large public dances throughout the Southwest. (By the early 1950s Narciso Martínez, Tony de la Rosa, and others had made touring a common practice for conjunto musicians.) Given the music's immense popularity in this commercial context and the economic livelihood it now afforded, it is not surprising that it, and especially the polka, its quintessential genre, should have been subjected to such elaboration and stylization. Conjunto musicians strove both to bring fresh variety to their music and to maintain a valued tradition.

Since the mid-1950s, however, and until recently, only minor changes were made in conjunto style. An alto saxophone often alternated with the accordion between the melody line and the so-called "*segunda*" (a line usually parallel to and a third below the melody)—but usually in Mexican *norteño* music rather than in conjuntos. Moreover, this combination was not really new, since Pedro Ayala and Narciso Martínez had combined their talents with saxophonists Eugenio Gutierrez and Beto Villa, respectively, in the 1940s. In the 1960s and 1970s, as conjunto and *orquesta* converged with each other (for reasons which I can only touch upon briefly in this paper), the former did develop a more complex system of chordal progressions. Particularly as the Mexican bolero, with its more demanding harmonies, gained increasing popularity, modernized conjuntos like that of Bernal began to substitute the more harmonically flexible guitar for the *bajo sexto*. By this time also, in recognition of the electronic age and the requirements of large ballrooms, amplification systems had been added. One consequence had been the permanent substitution of the electric bass for the old *tololoche* (contrabass). Additionally, after the mid-1950s the instrumental polka gradually gave way to the sung *ranchera*, which was superimposed over the polka rhythm. The accordion thus functioned less as a solo instrument and more as a counterpart to the singing. But by and large the general style had evolved by the mid-1950s and remained rather static thereafter, while its sister style, *orquesta texana*, oscillated between it and other domains of music.

Since the mid-1970s, however, conjunto groups such as those of Esteban Jordán, Oscar Hernandez, and Roberto Pulido have begun to revitalize the style. Pulido has achieved a remarkable synthesis between conjunto and *orquesta*, successfully integrating two alto saxophones into the ensemble to create a blended sound. Jordán's innovations have been wide-ranging; he has incorporated elements from such disparate styles as hard rock, blues, and jazz into the more traditional conjunto sound. Oscar Hernandez, who once played with Bernal, has probably replaced him as the best technical virtuoso; his style evinces clean, rhythmically (and harmonically) complex lines. El Conjunto Bernal, which Paulino has quit because of religious convictions, has achieved modest innovations. However, it is too early to assess the impact these explorations will have on the direction of conjunto music, other than to note the style's revitalization and its definite convergence with *la orquesta texana.*

AN ETHNOMUSICOLOGICAL INTERPRETATION

Now that I have described in a summary fashion the historical development of conjunto style, I would like to address myself briefly to the question of the style's timely appearance. Because conjunto music and *orquesta texana* have evolved in a dialectic with each other, and because the limitations of this essay do not allow for a full explication, I must necessarily abbreviate my comments on this question. Briefly, then, I propose that conjunto music has historically represented the response of the Texas-Mexican proletarian worker to the antagonism, not only of an America which threatened from outside an ethnic boundary (cf. Barth 1969), but of the emerging Chicano middle class. This latter group, whose growth was spurred by the Second World War, openly considered the poor and/or unacculturated Mexican an impediment to Mexican-Americans' upward mobility in American society. They felt the proletarian workers clung unreasonably to Mexican values, weighing themselves down with what Murguia has called "excessive cultural baggage" (1975:3), and thus hindering all Chicanos' chances for acceptance in American life.[13]

The Second World War—and even the decades before, for there had always been an incipient, if small, middle class—had ushered in an era of increased opportunities, as well as of increased socio-political awareness on the part of Chicanos, that saw the number of middle-class Chicanos gradually rise (Grebler et al. 1970:302 ff.). These Chicanos, a number of whom had been involved in the war, developed egalitarian ideals and a desire to be like other Americans—in short, to assimilate into American society and gain a share of the affluence that surrounded them. These were the Chicanos who formed the backbone of a new and increasingly Americanized, or Anglicized, group which began to aspire for new cultural symbols to express its new-found identity (cf. Gomez-Q. 1979:63). It was at this point, in the late 1940s, that modern *orquesta* music emerged among and for the middle class, partly as a result of that search for new cultural symbols. Not surprisingly, to these people conjunto music, like so many other aspects of Texas-Mexican culture, smacked of *lo ranchero,* i.e., the rustic and backward, or *lo arrabalero* ("from the out-skirts"—low class)—in short, of the lower-class proletarian society from which they were trying to dissociate.

Dismay and antagonism can be discerned in some of the language then (and I suspect even now) in use among upwardly mobile, assimilative Chicanos: "they" (that is, the lower, less acculturated class) were *el peladaje, la plebe, la gente corriente, gente ranchera, animal de uña, gente arrabalera*, and any number of more or less pejorative terms. "We," on the other hand, were *gente de razón, gente de roce social, gente decente*, and other genteel expressions. Not surprisingly, the differences ascribed in language carried over into the realm of music evaluation. While both groups of Chicanos inherited a culturally deep tradition of music and dance the two musics, conjunto and *orquesta*, seemed to articulate the divergence in values and ideologies that the linguistic terms indicated. The musics were, to borrow Bauman's (1972) terminology, expressions of differential identities. Narciso Martínez stated his understanding of this differential identity very succinctly: "*la orquesta es pa'* 'high society'" [*orquesta* is for high society]; "*el conjunto era pa' la gente ranchera, era musica ranchera*" [conjunto was for rural folk, it was rural music]. (However, I would add that conjunto music appealed just as much to the poor urban worker.)

Let me cite a case of differential identity expressed in music. In Weslaco, Texas, in the mid- and late-1950s, Saturday-night dances were commonly held in the town plaza. They featured conjunto musicians, such as Ruben Vela and others, who were then popular among the laboring class. These open-air dances naturally attracted large crowds of *pachuquillos* and other lower-class types, so that the dances evinced a distinctive working-class ethos. On more than one occasion I recall hearing Chicanos whom everyone would consider "*de buenas familias*," i.e., of middle-class orientation, make disapproving remarks such as "*Que indecente se ven*" [how vulgar they look] about the *tacuachito* dancers they observed. This association of conjunto music with the supposedly coarse lower class is not an isolated case. While I was playing one time in an *orquesta* for a predominantly middle-class audience in Fresno, California, an annoyed woman complained to me that the band was becoming too *ranchera*, and thus sounding too much like the conjuntos which played in the "low-class cantinas" in West Fresno. She had made the association because she felt we were playing too much *música corrida* (i.e., songs in polka tempo conjunto-style). And recently an informant in Corpus Christi, the wife of a deceased *orquesta* leader who had been prominent in the 1940s and 1950s, told me about the kinds of people who had gone to her husband's dances. "A los bailes de mi esposo iba pura gente buena" [Only "high-quality" people attended my husband's dances, she said]—as opposed to the vulgar types who supported conjunto music.

Narciso Martínez clearly understood the split musical consciousness of Chicano society. He deprecates his music, recalling how ashamed he was to play in front of the great Luis Arcaraz from Mexico. "Esas eran orquestas," he says, "no mugrero" [Those were *real* bands]. It was his own music that was *mugrero* compared to the power and brilliance of such a band. And, as he said, he wouldn't dare venture into the big cities of Texas and California for head-to-head confrontations with *orquestas* without reinforcing his *débil* (weak) accordion with a pair of saxophones. "Iba bien peltrechado con dos saxofones" [I was well reinforced with two saxophones], he said, to give his music a little class. In a mood of self-abasement he added, "La [*sic*] acordeón siempre disminuye para la orquesta" [It's true that the accordion doesn't measure up to the *orquesta*]. Why is this so? Because the accordion is *ranchera* music, for the common people, and no match for the *orquesta*, which is the music of the high-powered, "high society" people of the city. Still, on another occasion Martínez talked proudly of the power of his own music. He recalled an instance when *la gente* spurned a "high society," tuxedo-clad band playing across the street to flock into the place where he was playing. And another time some people in Fort Worth had complained to Luis Arcaraz, "No toque usted, no toque usted; que toque Chicho [Narciso]" [Don't you play, don't you play; let Chicho play]. "Don't blame me," Martínez said in his broken English, implying that his own music, after all, had more appeal.

The two musics, then, communicated different class ideologies (and values). Class consciousness was the crucial differentiating factor. *Orquesta* music catered to the middle class; the lower class favored conjunto music overwhelmingly. The exclusivity was mutual (though not total—recall that accordionists Ayala and Martinez recorded with *orquesta* leaders Gutierrez and Villa).

In sum, the accelerating changes that occurred in the postwar years split the different segments of Chicano society—or, more likely, intensified nascent differences which had merely been arrested by the Mexicans' confrontation with the dominant

Anglo-American society.[14] And the challenge of the Americanized
Chicano middle class to the fundamental values of the relatively
unacculturated working class I believe, spurred on the rapid evolution of conjunto music.

Viewed in this light, the changes that Tony de la Rosa and
others introduced in the late 1940s and early 1950s take on added
significance. These shifts in tempo, articulation, and so on sym-
bolized the reactions that were taking place socially. In other
words, the musical developments transcended the universe of
musical discourse and interacted with developments occurring at
the level of social discourse. Or, like language and social life (see
Hymes [1972]), music and social life relate on many levels. The
changes de la Rosa, Bernal, and others wrought in conjunto style
reflected the maturation of a musical esthetic which objectified
the traditional proletarian ideals being challenged at that time
by the Americanized Chicano middle class. This esthetic culminated in the emergence, simultaneously with the musical
changes, of the new dance style *el tacuachito*. Clearly, changes in
the social structure were being transformed into changes in the
musical (and dance) structures. The move toward assimilation by
some segments of Chicano society was countered by a corresponding move by the proletariat to strengthen its cultural position. And the music-and-dance innovations symbolically articulated this move.

CONCLUDING REMARKS

The cleavage between the Chicano working class and the more
assimilated middle class has never been as sharp as my analysis
might at first seem to indicate. The potent American hegemony
has kept the differentiation of Chicano society from becoming absolute. Indeed, a synchronic ethnography of Chicano music (even
of a narrowly defined Texas-Mexican music) reveals multilayered
structures of signification (to borrow from Geertz [1973]) which
transcend class differences. For one thing, *orquesta* music has,
since the 1960s, been increasingly appropriated by the less assimilated, proletarian workers. Or, to put it in the vernacular, *orquesta* has had to go *ranchero* to survive. Thus, in many ways *orquesta* and conjunto are what we might call paired styles, which
have interacted and influenced each other from the beginning.
The musicians, at least, have always been aware of the prove-

nience of the two musics and of the intricate relationships, both musical and social, which exist between them. Narciso Martínez, again, phrased it very well when he said, "*La orquesta es pa' 'high society'; pero ya horita 'ta muy concentrada en la polka, porque es lo que les deja . . . es lo que les acarrea la gente—la polka, el movimiento, la cumbia—todo eso*" [The *orquesta* is for "high society"; but these days it concentrates on the polka, because that is what lets . . . that is what draws the people—the polka, the rhythm, the *cumbia*—all of those]. That is, *orquesta* and conjunto both tend toward the same musical denominator, and consequently come close to being a common musical expression.

On another front, both American and Mexican musics have exerted powerful influences on conjunto. This influence, however, has been felt more strongly by the *orquestas*, which have tended to reflect Mexican, American, and the more conservative conjunto styles in turn. *Orquesta* expresses the cultural duality (cf. Marks 1974) of Chicano society, it functions as a kind of symbolic style-switching, somewhat analogous to Blom and Gumperz's concept of metaphorical switching (1972), allowing Chicanos access to both Mexican and American socio-musical systems. The outspoken *orquesta* leader Little Joe has perceptively interpreted this dual access as demonstrating the "flexibility" of Chicanos.

In sum, then, the symbolic structure(s) of conjunto and *orquesta* reflect the state of flux in which Chicano society is maintained, owing to the push and pull across the ethnic boundary (Barth 1969) or the play of what Jansen (1965) calls the esoteric-exoteric factor. This factor may be described as the element which maintains the differences in the sense of ethnicity and of class that the various segments of Chicano society ascribe to themselves and others. And that esoteric-exoteric factor itself operates on the principles of cultural confrontation and accommodation (cf. Barth 1969; Bateson 1972), or what Paredes (1976) has described more specifically as the intercultural conflict between Chicanos and Anglos. It is against this backdrop that conjunto and *orquesta* have played out their dialectic.

Finally, I would repeat that the surprising fact is not so much that conjunto music became popular so rapidly as that it did so under conditions which seemingly should have militated against its progression. These conditions include the American tendency to pressure "outsiders" into some sort of public conformity and the desire of self-described "middle-class" Chicanos to identify themselves with the public American culture from which that conformity emanates. I mentioned earlier that commercialization could not adequately, let alone totally, explain conjunto music's phenomenal success—especially as the major recording labels withdrew their support after World War II. One might ask how commercialization could succeed in face of a hostile Chicano middle class and a dominant American culture—which, in the words of Luis Valdez (1972), threatened to overwhelm us with its discarded *chingaderas*: its used cars, plastic flowers, and TV sets. Yet the music has endured and continues to thrive, even as it is undergoing revitalization.

Perhaps as Pedro Ayala once told me, "*El dia que a la gente le toquen otra música no se les paran ni las moscas*" [The day they play a different music for the people, not even the flies will stop in].

NOTES

1. Throughout this paper the term "Chicanos" is freely interchangeable with the phrase "Mexicans in the United States"; no further connotations are intended.
2. This article was pointed out to me by Dan Dickey.
3. Personal communication. For a recorded example of this combination see *Texas Mexican Border Music*, vol. 4, edited by Chris Strachwitz. For discographic details on this and other recordings mentioned in this paper see the discography.
4. Interviews with Pedro Ayala, Narciso Martínez, and Santiago Jiménez provided much of my information for this article—hence the frequent appearance of their names.
5. For some recorded examples of *orquesta típica* music (not to be confused with its modern counterpart, *orquesta texana*), see *Texas Mexican Border Music*, vol. 5.
6. These dances date back to at least 1850 in Texas (Dinger 1972). According to Dinger, "For the privilege of dancing with a chosen partner, each youth must bring an offering of candy, cake, cookies or some other delicacy" (ibid.: 37). The youths bought these *regalos* from crude stalls set up by vendors for the occasion. According to Pedro Ayala, the *baile de regalos* disappeared in the 1920s.
7. The *bajo sexto* is a modified, double-coursed, twelve-string guitar. The name literally means "sixth bass," although the instrument is not tuned in sixths.
8. As a member of a band that played *orquesta texana* at dances in Fresno, California, I had the opportunity to witness that community's growing acceptance of the style during the 1960s and 1970s.

9. See *Texas Mexican Border Music*, vol. 10, for additional biographical information.
10. A *ranchera* song (from "*rancho*," ranch) is a lyric composition which, to Mexicans everywhere, evokes rural, pastoral settings. In contrast to the sophisticated music played by complex groups such as orchestras (including symphonic orchestras), *rancheras* recall the simple, unencumbered life of the common folk. But there is some ambivalence here, because the term "*ranchero/a*" also connotes "rustic," "backward," and sometimes even "coarse."
11. José Limón (1977a) has recently drawn attention to the symbolic import of the polka's counter-clockwise movement within the whole music-and-dance tradition.
12. This union became especially important in the 1970s. The cultural nationalism of the Chicano movement accelerated the convergence between conjunto and *orquesta* to such a degree that the renowned *orquesta* Little Joe y la Familia could join forces with the famed conjunto musician Esteban Jordán to produce an appropriately titled album, *La Voz de Aztlán*.
13. For some accounts of the social, economic, and political development of Mexicans in the United States, see Meier and Rivera (1972, esp. chs. 13 and 14); Acuña (1972); and Grebler et al. (1970). For a bibliographic history see Gomez-Q. and Arroyo (1976), and for some account of intra-cultural conflict see Limón (1977b) and Paredes (1968).
14. The literature on this confrontation is voluminous. Some of it is vicious, some polemical; it is rarely objective. For a critical bibliographic treatment, see Gomez-Q. and Arroyo (1976).

DISCOGRAPHY

This selective discography lists recordings representative of the styles and artists discussed in this paper.

Texas Mexican Border Music Series. Chris Strachwitz, ed. Folklyric Records.

Vol. 4 (9006): *Norteño accordion—Part 1: The first recordings* (includes Narciso Martínez, Lolo Cavazos, Bruno Villarreal, and others).

Vol. 5 (9007): *The string bands—end of a tradition.*

Vol. 10 (9017): *Narciso Martínez, El Huracán del Valle: His first recordings, 1936–1937.*

Vol. 12 (9019): *Norteño accordion—Part 2: San Antonio, Texas, the 1940s and 1950s* (includes Santiago Jiménez and others).

Vol. 13 (9020): *Norteño accordion—Part 3: South Texas and Monterrey, N.L., the 1940s and 1950s* (includes Pedro Ayala, Narciso Martínez, Los Alegres de Terán, Tony de la Rosa, Paulino Bernal, and Ruben Vela).

Bernal, Paulino. *El Baile grande* (LP). Bego, BG 1006.

—————. "Quiero mas"/"Te voy a olvidar" (45 rpm). Freddie, FR-289-1.

De la Rosa, Tony. "Flamingo"/"Tome y olvide" (78 rpm). Nopal, NOP-711-A.

Martínez, Narciso, and Beto Villa. "Rosita"/"Madre mia" (78 rpm). Ideal R-149.

Little Joe y la Familia, and Steve Jordan. *La Voz de Aztlán* (LP). Leona, LRC-007.

Pulido, Roberto, y Los Clasicos. *On tour* (LP). ARV-1045.

BIBLIOGRAPHY

Acuña, Rodolfo. 1972. *Occupied America*. New York: Canfield Press.

Barth, Fredrik. 1969. *Ethnic groups and boundaries*. Boston: Little, Brown.

Bateson, Gregory. 1972. Culture contact and schismogenesis. In *Steps to an ecology of mind*. San Francisco: Chandler.

Bauman, Richard. 1972. Differential identity and the social base of folklore. In *Toward new perspectives in folklore*. Américo Paredes and Richard Bauman, eds. Austin: University of Texas Press.

Blacking, John. 1974. Ethnomusicology as a key subject in the social sciences. In *In memoriam Antonio Jorge Gias*. Lisbon: Instituto de Alta Cultura.

Blom, Jan-Petter, and John J. Gumperz. 1972. Social meaning in linguistic code-switching in Norway. In *Directions in sociolinguistics*. John Gumperz and Dell Hymes, eds. New York: Holt, Rinehart, and Winston.

Dinger, Adeline. 1972. *Folklife and folklore of the Mexican border*. Edinburg, Texas: Hidalgo County Historical Museum.

Geertz, Clifford. 1973. *The interpretation of cultures*. New York: Basic Books.

Gomez-Q., Juan. 1979. Toward a concept of culture. In *Modern Chicano writers*. Joseph Sommers and Tomas Ybarra-Frausto, eds. Englewood Cliffs, N.J.: Prentice-Hall.

—————, and Luis L. Arroyo. 1976. On the state of Chicano history: Observations on its development, interpretations, and theory, 1970–1974. *Western Historical Quarterly* 7 : 155–185.

Grebler, Leo, Joan Moore, and Ralph Guzman. 1970. *The Mexican-American people*. New York: Free Press.

Hymes, Dell. 1972. Editorial introduction to *Language in Society*. *Language in Society* 1 : 1–14.

Jansen, William H. 1965. The esoteric-exoteric factor in folklore. In *The study of folklore*. Alan Dundes, ed. Englewood Cliffs, N.J.: Prentice-Hall.

Limón, José. 1977a. Texas-Mexican popular music and dancing: A symbological interpretation. Unpublished MS.

———. 1977b. *Agringado* joking in Texas-Mexican society: Folklore and differential identity. *New Scholar* 6:33–50.

Marks, Morton. 1974. Uncovering ritual structures in Afro-American music. In *Religious movements in contemporary America*. Irving Zaretsky and Mark Leone, eds. Princeton: Princeton University Press.

Meier, Matt S., and Feliciano Rivera. 1972. *The Chicanos: A history of Mexican-Americans*. New York: Hill and Wang.

Murguia, Edward. 1975. *Assimilation, colonialism and the Mexican-American people*. Austin: Center for Mexican-American Studies, University of Texas.

Paredes, Américo. 1968. Folk medicine and the intercultural jest. In *Spanish-speaking people in the United States*. June Helm, ed. Seattle. University of Washington Press.

———. 1976. *A Texas-Mexican* cancionero. Urbana: University of Illinois Press.

Strachwitz, Chris. 1974a. Jacket notes. *Texas Mexican border music series*, vol. 4. Folklyric Records no. 9006.

———. 1974b. Jacket notes. *Texas Mexican border music series*, vol. 10. Folklyric Records no. 9017.

Valdez, Luis. 1972. Introduction: La Plebe. *Aztlán: An anthology of Mexican American literature*. Luis Valdez and Stan Steiner, eds. New York: Vintage Books.

Part V

Conclusion: A Look toward Future Concerns

Roger D. Abrahams

Shouting Match at the Border:
The Folklore of Display Events

When such neighborly names as "gringo" and "greaser" erupt
in public they are commonly mouthed by hotheads daring each
other to step across the lines. Private antipathies explode into
open antagonism and threaten to become public events as the onlookers and overhearers gather to find out what is happening. Everybody loves, and fears, a good fight, even when it generates
spontaneously out of a sit-in, a strike, or a demonstration. But
numerous planned-for events also capitalize on such antagonisms
and energies, constraining them and using them as fit materials
for a show, a spectacle, a festival, or a fair. These are times when
"anything goes"—at least in principle—times when people give
themselves the license to play, to drink and eat and shout and
dance too much. Or they willingly enter into inchoate worlds
where they may be taken in, or do some taking-in on their own;
they may fool others or be made the fool.

It seems high time that trained observers of culture entered
this twilight zone, this no man's land, since it is often at these
very points of confrontation that the most creative responses to
social tension and intercultural strains are found.[1] In the neutral ground of the stadium or the arena, or in the highly charged
symbolic movements of the dance, the parade, the pageant, or
the ball game, accumulated feelings may be channeled into contest, drama, or some other form of display. Here I will outline
a morphology of such planned-for public occasions—"display
events"—in which actions and objects are invested with meaning
and values are put "on display." These events are as disparate as

expositions and meets, games and carnivals and auctions. In the main, my focus here will be on the festive motives, on the times and places of perilous play.

If the boundaries of folklore study are to be constantly renegotiated, as the essays here indicate, the renegotiation should be carried out on the basis of an evolving theory of folklore. Yet folklorists, especially of the Texas persuasion, have been slow to build such a disciplinary superstructure precisely because of the factors which my colleague and I discussed in the introduction—the strong identification of the Texas folklorist with both the folk and the lore. Strangely enough, in spite of the great number of very public, traditional, celebratory events which form a major strand in the fabric of the cultural lives of the many different groups in Texas, there have been few descriptions and analyses of such events in the scholarship. Rather, both in our theorizing and in our fieldwork, we have intensified our interest in the more homely, private segments of life (the area characteristically studied in American folklore in general). Under the influence of sociolinguistics, the ethnography of communication, and symbolic-interactionist sociology, we have primarily concerned ourselves with the relationship between the structure and texture of conversation and of storytelling events. This is precisely the theoretical concern most of the articles here illustrate. Yet the essays by Mullen and Bauman are notable for taking this concern a step further—the storytelling interactions of their main informants occur in public events (a festival and a trade fair).

In the public anonymity of display events like fairs and festivals masks are worn and dramatic roles played out; the stereotypical neighborly names can be employed to exorcize, at least for the moment, unneighborly feelings. For, in the public events with which I am concerned here, there is a place and time for everyone, even the stranger, the freak, and the derelict. If these events in part dramatize and reinforce the existing social structure, they also insist often enough that such structure be ignored, or inverted, or flatly denied. Display events, then, often sanction the calling-out of neighborly names, as a means of simultaneously projecting and breaking up social differentiations. If one wishes to find a successful model for cultural pluralism in operation, let him or her look to these fairs and festivals—as the folk have for millennia.

THE OPERATIONS OF CULTURAL DIFFERENCE

In the introduction to this book we argued the uniqueness of doing folklore in Texas, a uniqueness which arises out of the close cultural identification of the Texas folklorist with traditional materials and practices as well as with the "folk" themselves. That most of those practicing folklore in Texas came from the kind of community about which they write is certainly the major reason why their writing describes how and where and by whom the lore was used. It gives their work, too, a strong sense of topicality, of the social and economic situation of the folklore audience. Especially important, then, are the political questions which arise about ethnic pluralism. The work of the Texas folklorists, especially that of Américo Paredes, may be characterized as "engaged," because it brings to the fore the antagonisms and inequities of everyday life as perceived by the performance community and as played out within the larger society.

To analyze lore in terms of how the group projects and plays upon its own image, in relation to stereotypes of other groups within a complex society and a pluralistic cultural situation, is to alter significantly the very study of folklore. Under such circumstances, lore can be used to gauge the intensity of the feeling of separateness between different segments in the larger polity (Jansen 1965; Bauman 1972). This also means that lore of an in-group (or esoteric) sort—lore which is commonly performed within the confines of a group socially (usually ethnically) set apart from others, and which comments in some way on this separation—becomes a matter of public record. The lore of communities which have experienced social exclusion and economic and political exploitation reflects these experiences. To bring such "protest" material into the open is, in a real sense, to make public what has to this point been a private, in-group technique of bonding and boundary-making.

An important part of the celebration of ethnic difference has often, in fact, been precisely this move: going public with materials and practices long confined to the privacy of the family or close groups of friends. The study of folklore in Texas began with discussions of the lore itself and its uses in earlier times. Soon it came to include analyses of the ways in which the folk employ the lore. And from this altered perspective folkloristics, as the discipline has come to be called, began to describe the role of traditional performances and practices in dealing with other cultures, in negotiating with them—especially with what is perceived as mainstream American society. Thus, one could trace a development from: (1) studying lore in stable, isolated community situations; to (2) regarding lore as emerging from the social and cultural changes engendered by encounters among different cultures and communities; and, finally, to (3) studying the dynamics of lore as it is performed and practiced at the boundaries, even across the borders, between and among people of varying languages, classes, and cultures.

This third phase seems to posit the ideal that understanding should arise through the celebration of status and ethnic differences. Such celebrations, however, involve an extremely complicated, self-conscious process of analysis and presentation. By emphasizing the centrality of context, of occasions for interaction, the recent development in folkloristics tends to focus increasingly on private and domestic revelations, on the one hand, and on relating these forms to larger and more public events and attitudes, on the other. The essays presented in this book employ three approaches: (1) relating performance forms and performances to more casual or conversational interactional styles (the Graham and Jordan essays, which look at the ways in which specific, previously unexamined, traditional forms of expression are employed in household or neighborhood interactions); (2) studying those practices susceptible of becoming part of larger public events which involve both insiders and observers, often from other cultures (the essays by Thomas Green, McDowell, Bauman, Stoeltje, and Peña); and (3) focusing on performance forms which can bring together, in a community of spirit, numbers of ethnically related peoples—by "popularizing" local forms and styles (the studies of McDowell and Peña), or by constructing public stereotypical roles that members of various groups can play out and/or interpret for themselves (the cowboy image discussed by Archie Green as well as by Stoeltje, and the term "Chicano" analyzed by Limón).

Such scholarship aims to underscore the cultural realities of a multicultural social system, realities in which intercultural understandings and misunderstandings arise all of the time. Those public activities which bring such different cultures together to celebrate eliminate (at least for the time of the event) such class and cultural disparities, and substitute for them the festive world, in which celebration provides most of the mood and the structure of relationships.

Ethnic groups in Texas display an unusual pattern and complexity of interrelationship. One cannot underscore too heavily the importance of Afro-American and Mexican-American lore in the configuration of Texas traditions—for both groups have neglected, even rejected, the usual model of cultural change toward mainstream American norms. The assimilation-oriented way of analyzing lore has emphasized the strong incentives of the folk to acculturate, both in their language and traditional practices. European immigrant communities seem to obey a three-generation rule of thumb. In the first generation the immigrants themselves discourage the public display of old-fashioned (usually Old World) behaviors, only the most home- or church-based private practices endure. In time a new lore and language arise, through the interactions of members of the first generation among themselves and with the second generation, which specifically reflect the changes being lived through and the recurrent problems encountered by group members, individually and together. This lore tends to become the object of nostalgia, especially when learned by the third and other following generations; often it develops into self-conscious commemorative events such as "Pioneer Days."

The Euro-American agrarian communities of the eastern half of Texas took more than three generations to assimilate—the generation model is more characteristic of urban ethnic communities. But assimilation of Mexican- and Afro-American communities in Texas differs qualitatively from this model—in both manner and intensity. Indeed, assimilation is often denied such ethnic groups because of continuing exclusion, marginalization, and exploitation. Furthermore, certain historical aspects of the traditions of these ethnic groups have disappeared altogether: the African heritage of the blacks and the Native-American heritage of Chicanos. Thus, the process of bringing private lore to public notice through ethnic-pride festivals has taken significantly different directions with African- and Mexican-Americans. Often their celebrations have commemorated politically significant events like "Juneteenth" and "Cinco de Mayo." In a real sense, until recently the non-European dimensions of Afro- and Mexican-American lore have been disregarded by both scholars and members of those very communities. Rather than celebrating the cultural traditions of their ethnic heritage, their commemorative events have focused on history, on their long struggles with adversity.

THE RATIONALE OF THE FOLK FESTIVAL

Local pride movements throughout the world, even those with separatist political intentions, highlight language and cultural differences not in order to close off the community's borders but to give the community a more powerful position in the national polity or the world of nations. It becomes a matter more of attempting to attain political, social, and economic equity than of asserting cultural integrity or separation. The intimacies of the group are thus opened up rather than closed off, as one would suppose would happen if we judged only from the rhetoric of separatist discussions.

Perhaps the most characteristic development of these trends has been the folk festival. These planned-for gatherings are put together for the explicit purpose of celebrating cultural differences, with the further objective of displaying man's range of creativity even within the confines of traditional expression. These displays aim toward the most "authentic" presentation of the life of the ethnically distinct family and community. Thus, they are judged by how well they maintain the everyday character, the spontaneity and integrity of the home or community event. Accordingly, the festival producers try to translate family or community celebrations into a setting in which the performances can stay as close as possible to their original form. But the event is framed and introduced so that non-members of the group may understand and appreciate what is going on.

In such folk festivals the effort is made, then, to open the domestic setting up to public view. This attempt to translate essentially private or at least in-group occurrences into public presentational events seems to be an aberration unique to these festivals put on by folklorists and their fellow-travelers. In part—perhaps even in great part—this pattern arises because folklorists in the United States have been so little interested in studying public celebrations—real festivals, fairs, commemorative events, and expositions. But, if the papers collected here are an indication, we shall soon have a great number of studies which look closely at much larger community events.

THE UNIQUENESS OF THE FESTIVAL SETTING

Many of the articles in this collection reflect the realization that inevitably follows once lore is studied within actual cultural situations, as part of the process of give and take which makes up the life of individuals in groups. That step is the recognition that lore arises and persists not only within groups but between them; that the lore of "betweenness" may be as important as the lore used among community members; and that it is in the larger public events that such interchange between groups occurs.

The idea of the "folk community" has been a useful fiction; it has enabled us to talk about the sense of shared values, the practices, and the social boundaries that can be set up and maintained by a group which has lived and worked together over a period of time. This fiction has provided folklorists the focus and energy for the collecting of traditional performances and practices. Drawing on the corollary fiction employed by functionalists, we folklorists have assumed that such lore somehow contributes to the maintenance of the community and of its sense of boundedness. Yet, when the assumptions on which these fictions rest are spelled out the circularity of the argument becomes evident: we know that these communities exist and have boundaries primarily from observing the lore being put into practice. Moreover, close scrutiny reveals that the lore itself is often found in a wide range of social situations—not all of which, by any means, we would associate with folk groups. The songs, stories, and handmade objects to which we assign value as folklore because they are made by group members for others within the community can also be found, and in greater abundance, in simple large-scale events—at fairs, swaps, festivals, and sporting events, on occasions and in places in which congregate people from contiguous and often antagonistic communities and classes, perhaps even people who speak different languages.

It has become increasingly evident that we can have access to the texts and objects which we folklorists most like to study more easily and in greater abundance at the places where there is none of the usual sense of community that arises from shared lives and values. In fact, if any feeling characterizes such public gatherings it is one of license; they provide built-in and prepared-for excuses to enter into contest with each other, to perform to or even outwit each other.

The pattern of observing and analyzing the small homogene-

ous community has apparently held for so many years in folkloristics for two related reasons: (1) our basic yearnings to maintain
the viability of the extended family and to see any inheritance
from the past as contributing to that sense of community; and (2)
because in taking the text as the essence of folklore we differentiate firmly between the oral and written worlds, projecting many
of our feelings of loss (of wholeness and innocence) onto the oral
world of the past. The notions of literacy and family have a very
strong historical connection. For so long the single most important object bringing the family together was the Bible, which encouraged private discussion and contemplation and which also
was interpreted to discourage all play activities, especially performances and large-scale games. The lore most often collected
and highlighted has come from the household or fireside, or from
places of assembly like the church which serve as an extension of
family manners, values, and practices. This kind of lore can also
be recorded in units of expression that are whole, that have an
integrity of construction and a moral purpose which are easily
and quickly comprehended. In their monologic (single-voiced)
character, they are easily separated from all other types of communicative experience—even from other kinds of display behaviors. But the great majority of articles in this volume attests to an
unwillingness to live within the limitations of this monologic
model any longer.

In some part, this felt need to change has arisen because of
the folk festival movement itself. It has forced those many folklorists who have become involved in such productions to think
about the questions involved when private work and play behaviors become public displays. More than this, however, folklorists
as observers of creativity in culture, have come to recognize that
much household-based lore must be regarded as relics, as objects
of memory-culture. On the other hand, traditional festive behaviors and events have maintained their vitality and even grown in
importance. This seems especially true in Texas, where almost
every marked occasion has turned into a fiesta, feast, fair, frolic,
fête, or, to put it into the terminology of different locales—into a
Watermelon Thump, an Old-Timers' Day, a Chilimpiad, a Wurst-
fest, or a humongous Fourth of July picnic.

These display activities take place on public grounds larger
than the household. In fairs or festivals people gather in neutral
and licensed space for larger and less familiar give-and-take en-
gagements, ones in which all the participants are *not* known.

Everyone, under such conditions, is fair game to be contended with, conned, lied to, dazzled, entertained, exploited. This way of looking at life is, to be sure, much less settled, much more open-ended, more subject to constant reinterpretation because participants are in constant negotiation for something—even if that something is only to entertain and be entertained.

Rather than employing the family or household gathering as the model of folkloric interactions, this extension of the performance-centered approach considers the fair and the festival more reflective of the range of materials that seem significant to an understanding of how traditions emerge and operate. Fairs and festivals are, of course, deeply related in that both occur at the major places of coming together. Both bring people together for the purpose of licensed negotiation. They differ primarily in the focus of the occasion, in what is being negotiated.

Festive entertainments are as different from the usual performances studied by folklorists as one can imagine. They involve an absence of any single focus—in fact, a wandering-around within an almost-anything-goes universe. Indeed, as many ethnographic observers of festivals have noted, each person involved is able to write his or her own script of what is going on, what is taken in (Vogt 1955; Smith 1975; Grimes 1976). But, most important for the present argument, this very diversity brings all segments of a plural or stratified community together (at least ideally) within this playfully licensed context. Thus a festival not only includes performances from the many segments within the larger community, and engineers playful contests among them, but it also encourages these various segments to have what amounts to their own festivals going on side-by-side.

This multiplicity produces a practical acting-out of ethnic or some other social identification, as both a contrast and a complement to the self-presentations of others. Games, performances, and other activities may operate simultaneously as ethnic displays and as part of a larger statement of multi-ethnic cooperation. Whether or not this pluralism works in actual practice, in specific, recurrent events, the pluralistic sentiment is certainly an important aspect of the *ideal* of such large-scale cultural events. In this sense the interest in festivals, sporting events, and community commemorative activities is an organic extension of the previous concerns of Texas folklorists. Festivals and other such licentious events, by placing "strangers," "animals," "clowns," and "freaks" at the center of the engagement, and by holding the events in betwixt-and-between times and places, make it possible to exhibit the most revolutionary type of confrontation behavior in a context in which these antagonisms may be usefully given voice without being regarded as politically motivated. The multi-leveled structure of such public events, then, make them fit candidates for analysis by the next generation of Texas folklorists, those who seek to understand the cultural dynamic in its most active sense and most acted-out forms.

More than this, however, the new way of looking at lore through such large-scale public events must be sufficiently flexible to include all those events which, in fact, bring the various segments of the community together into some kind of negotiation. On the purely native (or "emic") level, the words "event" or "show" or "spectacle" apply as commonly to fairs as to festivals, to flea markets and bazaars as to carnivals.

THE VARIETIES OF FESTIVE EVENTS

For a number of reasons, a strong tendency exists in contemporary America to turn public assemblies into spectacular events, planned-for occasions in which a range of activities are carried out, all of which depart in significant ways from the constraints of the familiar and the everyday. Because a number of the activities which have come to be attached to such shows and displays are intended to make money and draw on the various mass media to publicize them—thereby making them into events simply because they are "newsworthy," notable for their "drawing powers"—such festivities are often regarded as products of popular or mass culture, and therefore as beyond the ken of folkloristic analysis. But the Tigua celebration in El Paso, the Texas Cowboy Reunion in Stamford, First Monday in Canton, and other such activities developed upon traditional patterns and practices often, like the folk festivals described above, try specifically to counteract the effects of mass production with moves toward the self-consciously amateur, the involvement-centered, the authentic. These events selectively upend the everyday criteria of judgment, to the point where the participants invite disequilibrium on every front—from the dizziness of the carnival, circus, or drunken bash to those trade events (not only dog trading but also auctions and flea markets) where participants are encouraged to break all of the usual rules of retail commerce.

One feature of Texas life has become ever more apparent: not only are events being promoted constantly, but every community is attempting to develop a calendar event that will become that community's signature. Moreover, various interest groups, especially hobbyists and recreationists, form organizations with their fellow "freaks" on a subject (from birding and caving to owning different kinds of gear—vehicles, communication equipment, hunting and fishing devices, and so on). Like local and ethnic pride groups, such organizations attempt to publicize their existence by staging festive events or fairs of some sort. In this, Texas is probably no different than any other state or region. But the number of and interest in these events does seem to be remarkable here. Further, and most important, the ways in which they are planned and prepared for, framed and mounted, pose a range of extraordinarily interesting questions for students of culture, especially folklorists. Not least of these concerns is how the relationship between the celebrations of the old agrarian calendar—feasts, fairs, and festivals—have been maintained and elaborated under the altered conditions of a technological and post-technological society. The production and consumption patterns of everyday life continue to be dramatized and subverted in our yearly round of celebrations.

A wide range of event-types in our culture can be included in the overall concept "festivities." The term signifies all those goings-on in which people come together of their own free will to *play* in some manner. Play events which are tied to the family and friendship networks are called "parties." Different types of parties are held at different places, times, and occasions. They are mainly house-based activities. When they are held outside the house, in fact, they tend to have another name attached to them: "picnic," "barbecue," "reception," "dinner." The farther away from the house setting, of course, the more public the event can become. At the farthest extreme are those festive events held in the open, in some public space in which those in attendance are excused to some degree from everyday norms and manners: at carnivals, circuses, and other special performances; at sporting events; and at parades and festivals.

From an experiential or phenomenological perspective, participants in these shows, displays, and performance events seldom have any problem in recognizing and interpreting that something beyond the everyday is taking place. That is, the participants, the spectators, are obviously expecting something different. As opposed to everyday happenings, where a good deal of activity is going on, at a show one seldom has to ask "What's going on?"—unless the show itself is engineering such bewilderment to induce focus-in-common and participation. Moreover, a sense of possibility arises because the events take place in already valorized public spaces like theaters, arenas, or showgrounds. Finally, they are events that we are able to prepare for and look forward to. They are special in that each type of festival exists within its own space and time frame—it is a festive world which invites all into the experience equally. Inasmuch as each carries this invitation, and calls for a suspension of the usual constraints on behavior, each is to be enjoyed to the extent that we are prepared for what is going on and can appreciate the experience for itself. Our concerns are not for what we can carry away from the experience—except perhaps as trophies or mementos of the good time.

Festivities may occur on only a limited number of occasions. The nature of the occasion provides the focus for the event, and the primary means by which expectations and actual behavior are intensified. These occasions, in general, fit into the following categories: a performance or set of performances; a game, contest, or sporting event; a calendric festive gathering, celebrating a time of year (harvest, midsummer) or a personal milestone (a birthday, a wedding); or a commemoration of an historical event. Performances mark the occasion by a mimetic, playful activity which calls attention to itself, and which distinguishes participants as performers or audience. With games and sports, the focus is agonistic; conflict produces winners and losers. This kind of activity insists on distinguishing players from spectators. Festivities seek to bombard the senses with too much drinking and eating and dazzling costumes, lights, floats, and display, all leading to surfeit and dizziness; ideally, all participants are coequals in such encounters, an experience designated by Victor Turner (1974) as "liminoid."

Commemorative events, on the other hand, tend to intensify status distinctions by displaying high-status ways of talking and acting. Speech-making and other ceremonial activities provide the core of such intensive experiences. Of all large-scale festive events, commemorations are most like ritual; rites also often have a strongly ceremonial component. The difference, of course, is that rituals are both obligatory and bring about (or potentiate) social transformation, while commemorative displays are optational and confirm rather than transform the statuses of the participants and onlookers.

Such distinctions between types of events are common-sensical; we make them as a matter of course so that we may prepare to enjoy ourselves properly. The one overriding feature of all of these events is their licensed and celebratory character. But while we recognize the nature of the event and carry into it a certain set of appropriate expectations, we also know that such festivities can stretch whatever boundaries and rules are involved. For one thing, any one type of playful gathering tends to attract acts and activities from all of the others. A performance, for instance, such as a concert or circus will also involve festive-style eating and drinking, may use a festival parade to advertise the event, and will often be accompanied by speeches of welcome from leaders of sponsoring organizations. Similarly, games or sporting events will call forth parades, special foods and beverages, a range of performances (like half-time shows, cheerleading and band playing during the game, etc.), and will often be marked by opening speeches and the giving of an invocation. Finally, a commemorative event like July the Fourth or Juneteenth centers on the speeches which spell out the meaning of the day, but attracts to it all of the paraphernalia of the picnic or barbecue, a wide variety of musical and comical performances, and the choosing-up of sides for and playing of games. There is, then, a limited vocabulary that all playfully intensive events draw upon to make the experience varied and pleasurable, even exciting. The major differences among the events lie in the occasion and the focus of activity, not in the range or even arrangement of what goes on.

I have described the variety of activities associated with these public events in order to dramatize the difference between household traditions and the experiences and relationships in these larger and more public events. For once one walks through the licensed play-spaces of an arena, a theater, a stadium, or a festival-grounds, it becomes evident that the experience differs both qualitatively and quantitatively from the domestic scenes which have enthralled folklorists. In a public event it is difficult and often impossible to "be yourself" without losing yourself in some way. One commonly goes into such events, in fact, to be swept away by the experience, to take on new and often totally different roles. And nowhere is this difference so fully spelled out as in pure festival. For in such an event, when successful, there is a kind of perfect balance of excitement among the senses, and

between hilarious or ludicrous behavior and the highest seriousness. Though we have few adequate studies of community festivals, those we have suggest that they are capable of epitomizing
the most cherished ideals of the community along with the most
highly valued symbolic movements by which the community as a
whole describes and celebrates itself. Surely, investigating the
displays in other cultures would reveal patterns of spatial and
temporal organization and movement which epitomize the ways
in which the group gives value to itself and to life, even while the
event also summons forth the most derelict characters and even
diabolic motives.

PROFIT AND PLAY

The anthropological scholarship has paid particular attention to
how intensive events equalize material resources in subsistence
economies. Usually the wealthier members of the community act
as patrons of the saint's-day celebration or whatever other commemorative event is regarded as an authentic community celebration. Though resources are organized very differently in the
more complex cultures and in capitalist, surplus economies, the
role of patron has been maintained, along with the principle of
sponsorship as a means of providing general community access to
celebration. Indeed, patronage is, in a real sense, expanded upon
in those situations, where local businessmen's groups, clubs, and
especially elite social organizations provide the time, energy, and
resources for putting on the event. Moreover, the principle of de-
voting any profits to charitable causes (another version of resource redistribution) holds firmly for most festive events, except
for those *produced* by showmen-entrepreneurs, people who are in
the business of putting together "good times." The banishment of
the profit motive from the ideal of festive play through an insistence on the primacy of enjoyment is a major criterion of the authenticity and success of the event.

This does not mean that commerce is forbidden in these pleasurable celebrations; rather, the motive of profit must be masked
in some way, and any selling itself must either be made a part of
the show (as in the auctions which are important features of a
number of festivals and fairs) or placed at the periphery of the
major play activities. The ticket-sellers and vendors are relegated

to the margins of "where the action is," and even then often have to wear an appropriate costume and develop a selling "pitch" or "line" in harmony with the occasion.

The relationship between the show activities and the place of products and services for sale is precisely where fairs differ from festivities. Both types of occasion intensify experience, by creating quality times and spaces to carry out extraordinary activities and by staging a large number of acts simultaneously; all of this contributes to the overall—and overwhelming—experience. But the focus of festivities is on the exchange of energies among participants in the many play activities, while that of fairs is primarily on the exchange of goods or services. Though fairs may have a strong playful component, they are primarily concerned with displaying work techniques and work products. If buying and selling are not the major features of a fair or exposition, the event is best regarded as an extension of marketplace business. Whereas merchandising is relegated to the periphery of festive events—things are sold "at the door"—such activity is at the center of the fair. Moreover, when play arises at such trade and trading events it is relegated to the margins, and even then placed at the service of the flow of the merchandise, as in "raffling."

This subordination of play to the exchange of goods is nowhere more evident than in that most performance-like trade event: the auction. There is little doubt that a great many people attend auctions because they are such a good show. The great auctioneers know that they must perform to draw a crowd of potential bidders. But it is equally clear that the business at hand is the selling of things, at the highest price possible. Auctioneers, like carnie pitchmen, develop their routines much as bards do. They stitch together set units of expressions, or formulas, with fluency and even eloquence. Their "routines" force the audience of potential buyers to pay them the kind of constant attention accorded a virtuoso performer. Their performance consists of cadenced calls for bids interrupted by jokes about the goods on sale or someone in the audience. Much of the effect of their sales technique is predicated on building up a wall of sound, in fact, in order to stun the prospective purchasers into silence and immobility.

This intimidation, moreover, is intensified by the feeling common among the audience that any movement may be interpreted as a bid—a belief which, in fact, is a misapprehension. Indeed, one of the major problems for someone wishing to buy is learning how to establish oneself as a bona-fide bidder, and how to sign one's bid correctly. A successful auctioneer, moreover, will increase the distance between himself and the audience by placing a crew in front of him. These intermediaries hold up the object for sale, "pick up" bids from the audience and relay them to the auctioneer with a yell, make jokes, coax specific prospective buyers, and in general contribute to the noise and bustle among the sellers which contrast so dramatically with the fixity and silence of the buyers. If ever there was an unequal shouting match over a dividing line, it is at such barn and open-air auctions.

The tremendous and growing popularity of auctions is paralleled in other merchandising events, such as bazaars, flea markets, and sidewalk and garage sales. All of these are somewhat less boisterous but they are held for the same reason: to attract a buying public with the possibility of getting something for (practically) nothing. The objective is to get a "buy" through being able to bargain well or at least to find a bargain.

Both types of display events, festivals and fairs, involve scenes of intense exchange, the passing of significant objects and actions across a high-energy field in which the participant is involved, knowingly and willingly, in a negotiation. While play is taking place, the negotiation is usually for intangibles. But how different are a trophy and a bargain, really? Ultimately it is the display and the potential intensity of the experience that count, not what is taken away from the event.

The effect of festive play and celebration, as of games and performances, is made possible by the license the occasion affords—the rules of everyday life are suspended and given over. License is only sometimes, in deep play, licentiousness. It really means the ways in which alternative rules of behavior and judgment are made to govern an intense and focused exchange. There is little question what kind of license prevails at a ball game, a concert, a circus, or a picnic. Each frame produces its own way of looking at the goings-on, its own way of anticipating what is to come, of enjoying the activity, and of judging whether it is successful. The license which, in fact, governs all play is the license to engage in actions for their own sake without the need to produce anything.

On first blush, this set of criteria would not seem to be applicable to trade events. Yet the two extraordinary worlds comment on each other in some interesting ways. For just as, say, a circus demands the license to suspend the law of gravity and the distinctions between man and animal, an auction calls for the abrogation of the buyer-seller code of decorum which characterizes everyday commerce.

Indeed, it could usefully be argued that the trade equivalent of the license to play might be the license to coerce, exploit, lie, connive, to con or be conned. In a trade event that announces itself as such, the principle of *caveat emptor* is highlighted, but is used to titillate more than warn. For those who go into such events realize that one of the things under negotiation is truthfulness. As Bauman explores in his article, the dog trader and his customer do not take veracity for granted in a trade encounter. Both participants are looking to outsmart the other dramatically, no matter how much each avows that he is only looking for a fair deal. If there is license, it is to pursue a sales pitch or line which will be judged *and* interpreted on both its veracity and the skill of its delivery. There is a performance dimension to all face-to-face business exchanges. We look for good service as well as for goods. And sometimes—at auctions as well as many other kinds of markets—that service we look for is a good shouting match, one which quickens our sense of life and makes us forget about the rest—at least for the moment of truth-and-consequences.

CONCLUSION

If we have traveled some distance from the socially engaged approaches to folklore it has been in search of some larger insight which might come from looking at the entire range of expressive events in our lives-in-common. A folkloristics of the future simply cannot address contemporary questions unless it takes traditional expressivity where it is to be found.

My feeling is that these display events have maintained a counter-culture of far more revolutionary potential than the radical tactics that brought life to a halt and the authorities to their knees in the sixties. Far more subversive are these events that maintain the momentum and flow of life, which bring us together in celebration but let each of us "do our own thing," write our own scripts of progress within the event. These mad moments in the margins of time continue to provide us with models of revolution, as many commentators have pointed out. But more than this the trade fair, in league with the festival, maintains our sense of alternatives to what Marx called the fetishism of commodities. For, in these extraordinary road marches and parades, these shouting matches and shooting matches, the possibility of hanging on to the *use* and value of things and acts is defended, in the face of those who would turn all of life into acts of consumption. Such occasions openly draw upon and subvert the machine-made, die-stamped elements of our material lives. We tend to remake, to customize ourselves under such circumstances.

But such activity calls on us to reconceive our notions of reality and authenticity. As long as we folklorists were primarily concerned with domestic products and practices, the question of traditionality could be determined by how handmade or personally supervised was the object and activity. But in festivities personal engagement is as much a matter of subversion and masking and jocularity with neighbors and strangers. The shouting match, in such events, is raised for the sake of the larger entertainment. To be sure, these speculations bring us to the border between folklore and popular culture—but that problem has become constant and, moreover, has posed some of the most interesting questions for performance-oriented folklorists. Furthermore, from the point of view expressed by the events themselves, the ultimate subversion (a folklike activity) is to use the devices of popular culture as throwaways or mementos. It is not products that are important, these events avow, but the relationships we creatively assert in moments of negotiation. Both festivals and fairs can be profitably considered events of exchange, but exchanges which take place in the neutral territory along the borders and boundaries, in carefully constructed in-between spaces where everyone involved can at least try to get the better of the deal.[2]

NOTES

1. Such structural explanations are legion in the ethnographic literature on the festive component of ritual, but such studies rarely explore the creative dimensions of the occasion. See, for instance, Bateson 1958; Firth 1940.
2. My thanks to Dick Bauman, Archie Green, and especially Janet Sue for discussing these ideas and for help in revising out some of the infelicities.

BIBLIOGRAPHY

Bateson, Gregory. 1958. *Naven*, 2nd ed. Stanford: Stanford University Press.
Bauman, Richard. 1972. Differential identity and the social base of folklore. In *Toward new perspectives in folklore*. Américo Paredes and Richard Bauman, eds. Austin: University of Texas Press.
Firth, Raymond. 1940. *The work of the gods in Tikopia*. London: Percy Lund, Humphrys.
Grimes, Ronald L. 1976. *Symbol and conquest*. Ithaca: Cornell University Press.
Jansen, William H. 1965. The esoteric-exoteric factor in folklore. In *The study of folklore*. Alan Dundes, ed. Englewood Cliffs, N.J.: Prentice-Hall.
Smith, Robert J. 1975. *The art of the festival*. Lawrence: University of Kansas Publications in Anthropology, no. 6.
Turner, Victor. 1974. Liminal to liminoid, in play, flow, and ritual. *Rice University Studies* 60:53–92.
Vogt, Evon Z. 1955. A study of the Southwestern fiesta system as exemplified in the Laguna Fiesta. *American Anthropologist* 57:820–839.

Contributors

Roger D. Abrahams, Alexander H. Kenan Professor for the Humanities and Anthropology, Scripps and Pitzer Colleges, Claremont, California.

Richard Bauman, Department of Anthropology and Center for Intercultural Studies in Folklore and Ethnomusicology, University of Texas, Austin, Texas.

Alicia María González, Department of Anthropology, University of Southern California, Los Angeles, California.

Joe Graham, Department of English, Texas A&M University, College Station, Texas.

Archie Green, Department of English, University of Texas, Austin, Texas.

Thomas A. Green, Department of English, Texas A&M University, College Station, Texas.

Rosan A. Jordan, Department of English, Louisiana State University, Baton Rouge, Louisiana.

José E. Limón, Department of Anthropology and Center for Mexican-American Studies, University of Texas, Austin, Texas.

John Holmes McDowell, Department of Folklore, Indiana University, Bloomington, Indiana.

Patrick B. Mullen, Department of English, Ohio State University, Columbus, Ohio.

Manuel H. Peña, Department of Chicano Studies, University of California, Berkeley, California.

Beverly J. Stoeltje, Department of Anthropology and English, University of Texas, Austin, Texas.